THE LIFE AND TIMES OF JOHN STEELE

THE LIFE AND TIMES OF JOHN STEELE

Mormon Kingdom Builder

KERRY WILLIAM BATE

THE UNIVERSITY OF UTAH PRESS
Salt Lake City

LIBRARY OF CONGRESS CATALOGING-IN-PUBLICATION DATA
Names: Bate, Kerry William, 1950- author.
Title: The Life and Times of John Steele: Mormon Kingdom Builder / Kerry William Bate.
Description: Salt Lake City : The University of Utah Press, [2025] |
Identifiers: LCCN 2024047436 | ISBN 9781647692186 (cloth) | ISBN 9781647692193 (paperback) | ISBN 9781647692209 (ebook)
Classification: LCC BX8695.S776 B38 2025
LC record available at https://lccn.loc.gov/2024047436

For EU safety / GPSR concerns:
Email: gpsr@mare-nostrum.co.uk
Physical address:
Mare Nostrum Group B.V.
Mauritskade 21D
1091 GC Amsterdam
The Netherlands

Frontispiece: John Steele, Isle of Man, 1877, BYU Harold B. Lee Library.

Errata and further information on this and other titles available at UofUpress.com

This book is dedicated to Gary Hall Callister and Genevieve Sooy Jensen, the conscientious keepers of the John Steele family papers, and to my late friend Lloyd Sharp Pendleton, an inspirational and storied Mormon warrior against homelessness.

Marilyn Eileen Turner Bate
22 October 1945–13 February 2025

CONTENTS

ACKNOWLEDGMENTS

As a high schooler I became interested in the history of my nineteenth-century Mormon forbears and found myself at what is now the LDS Church History Library trying to make sense of a microfilmed copy of the "Journal History of the Church of Jesus Christ of Latter-day Saints." An index took me through a tedious film to a specific date, which seemed like a laborious effort, and then to my disappointment the "source" was just a page cut out from B. H. Roberts's *Comprehensive History of the Church of Jesus Christ of Latter-day Saints*, a book I'd already read. Without context, I didn't understand this source or its importance, and gave up. Soon I was an eighteen-year-old freshman at Weber State College and I signed up for a Utah history class taught by Donald Moorman, who liked to joke he was a Moorman but not a Mormon. The class text was Leonard J. Arrington's *Great Basin Kingdom: An Economic History of the Latter-day Saints, 1830–1900*, a fat paperback, and I inscribed on the front endpaper "Kerry Bate | 31 Mar. 1969 | Moorman | 11:00 MTW LB38."

I was startled, amazed, and delighted to find out from Arrington that the Mormon Kingdom was built under a sophisticated master plan, something I missed in my four years of Mormon seminary classes. Ironically, Arrington's main source was the "Journal History" that so puzzled me. I remember later, breathlessly and nervously, giving a "street speech" to a group of pacifists in Eureka about the unheralded radicalism of the Mormon past. Eventually, after working with the late Lloyd S. Pendleton and other LDS members to end homelessness, I realized that admirable parts of that past are also very contemporary. First and foremost, then, I want to acknowledge Leonard J. Arrington and Donald R. Moorman for taking me on that exciting tour of former years. This biography represents the life of one man dedicated to building the Kingdom that Arrington describes.

I am indebted to numerous other individuals. The late Dr. Wesley P. Larsen, once owner of the John Steele home in Toquerville, shared information, reintroduced me firsthand to the flora and fauna of my Washington County boyhood, and took me down a red gravel road amid stately pecan trees to Gary Hall Callister's under-construction Hurricane home. Gary owned John Steele's trunk of family papers and, with Wes vouching for me, for the first time allowed someone to take the papers out of his house. There were so many it took me several trips to copy all of them at the Hurricane Library, the Ben Franklin store, and the Aztec Copy Center in St. George. I thank my friend Kathleen Cooper, mayor of Myton, for helping me with that. I made two sets, one for myself and one for the Utah Historical Society. On July 23, 1987, Gary said I should write a biography of Steele, but I was working on a biography of the women in Steele's family and was so put off by some of Steele's brutal letters to his wife Catherine that I recoiled. By the time I wrote a sketch of him for the *Utah Historical Quarterly*, I'd warmed to the project. My intention here is to go beyond my earlier article and give a chronological story of Steele's life, yet straying sometimes to develop themes, such as his role with Native Americans in the 1860s.

Genevieve Sooy Jensen and Jennifer Jensen Stephens owned more papers that had come from the trunk and sent me transcripts made by Iona Jeanne Poling. Poling was excellent at deciphering nineteenth-century handwriting, and over and over I've thanked her accuracy as I've systematically double-checked her work.

Both the Callister and Jensen papers were acquired by the L. Tom Perry Special Collections, Harold B. Lee Library, Brigham Young University, and can be consulted there.

Hilga Judd Frier generously shared records and enthusiasm, while her scholarly sister, Ileen Judd Johnson, recovered and shared copies of some of John Steele's correspondence with his Australian relatives. The late Wanda Steele Cox gave me photocopies of the letters John Steele received from his sister in Australia, Elizabeth Steele Connelly. Australian cousins—Janet O'Hara Ellis, Edith Meredith, and Jean Aileen McMurtrie Curry—provided letters that Steele sent his Australian niece, Letisha Connelly Todd. My friend the late Will Bagley shared information, most importantly a copy of Frank A. Beckwith's manuscript "Shameful Friday: A Critical Study of the Mountain Meadows Massacre." Beckwith's early interest in John Steele resulted in the publication of Steele's now-missing memoir in the *Utah Historical Quarterly* in 1933, and some invaluable articles about him in the *Millard County (UT) Chronicle* based on original documents Beckwith had access to but are now missing.

Drafting a book is challenging, uplifting, and depressing. Jana Riess gave my manuscript a critical reading after I'd put it aside; her sharp observations, enthusiasm, and recommendations gave me new energy that led to Jedediah Rogers of the University of Utah Press. His response invigorated me, especially his question about John Steele: "Is he the Forrest Gump of Mormonism?"

Todd Compton and Sondra G. Jones were my manuscript readers, and their encouragement, insights, and challenges bolstered me to complete a better book. Compton is a hero historian to me; Jones had new information and gentle suggestions about tone that I hope I've addressed. My kinswoman Anadel Smith Law has become my pen pal, and we've exchanged tips, documents, photos, insights and encouragement. Her excellent ancestral multi-biography is nearing completion and will be celebrated for careful workmanship. Anadel's and her sister Shirley Smith Larson's beautiful biography, *A Man Undaunted: J. Fish Smith: His Life and Times,* has just been published.

The talented mapmaker Chelsea McRaven Feeney drew five superb maps to illustrate the text and help ground the reader in the geography and communities of Steele's times. She has made the first map of what I believe was the earliest recorded circumnavigation (1852) of what is now Zion National Park. She has been accommodating, quick, and sensitive to the needs of the project.

I have especially appreciated the L. Tom Perry Special Collections at Brigham Young University, particularly the vigilant archivist Cindy Brightenburg. I've enjoyed working with Ryan Lee, then the accessioning archivist and associate librarian, as I've been able to supplement the Steele collection with minor donations.

I also thank the Special Collections at Southern Utah University (Cedar City), where I first found out about Frank A. Beckwith's interest in John Steele through the William R. Palmer Papers. Other useful archives are at Utah Tech University (St. George) and the Church History Library of the Church of Jesus Christ of Latter-day Saints in Salt Lake City, which has put an enormous number of critical documents online. After the Steele Collection at BYU, this has been my most valuable source. I also thank the Family History Library, Salt Lake City; Utah Historical Society and Utah State Archives, Salt Lake City; Washington County, Utah, Library; Special Collections at the J. Willard Marriott Library at the University of

Utah; and many online newspaper collections. I tape-recorded interviews with Reba Roundy LeFevre, Charles Andrew Olds, and Plorn J. Williams, all helpful in this project. Olds remembered getting a broken arm splinted by Steele. Reba, my great-aunt, told family stories and also shared many mementos and photos. Thanks, too, for the expert and sensible help from copy editor Alexis Mills; I have learned much from her. And I'm awed by Jessica A. Booth's subtle and effective design work for *The Women: A Family Story* and also for this book.

I've benefited from a surprising number of historians who have led me through all kinds of historical highways and side trails. An alphabetical list isn't enticing, but reading the works of the following will be: Will Bagley, Juanita Brooks, Barbara Jones Brown, Howard A. Christy, Todd Compton, Dan Erickson, Joseph Fish, Sherman L. Fleek, Richard Francaviglia, Sarah Barringer Gordon, John S. Haller Jr., Andrew Jenson, Janiece Johnson, Sondra Jones, Martha Knack, Andrew Karl Larson, Gustive O. Larson, Anadel Smith Law, John Doyle Lee (diarist and memoirist), Glen M. Leonard, Edward Leo Lyman, James Henry Martineau (also a diarist), Patrick Q. Mason, John Gary Maxwell, William R. Palmer, Ardis E. Parshall, Charles S. "Chas" Peterson, Paul Dean Proctor, D. Michael Quinn, Josiah Rogerson, Kathryn H. Shirts, Morris A. Shirts, Gary Topping, Richard E. Turley Jr., Ronald W. Walker, and John Frank George Yurtinus. I apologize to anyone I've missed; I feel kindly bonded with all of these.

INTRODUCTION

Radicalized by the starving poverty of industrial Glasgow during the "Hungry Forties," Irish-born John Steele embraced a teetotaler brotherhood and radical political reformation, and listened sympathetically to utopian socialists on Glasgow Green. This was background for his 1843 conversion to Mormonism, driven by utopian fervor to build an egalitarian Kingdom where Christ would rule in the last days.

In 1986, on the underside of the lid to Steele's honey-colored pioneer trunk, circled by six heavy rivets, was a 1903 laminated diploma from Professor Harraden's correspondence course at the College of Hypnotism, earned by Steele when he was eighty years old. The Kingdom needed every kind of talent, and he contributed both the conventional and unorthodox.

A local United Order minute book in the trunk hadn't been his, but Steele belonged to the Toquerville United Order, where Latter-day Saints sought to counteract Eastern capital and exploitation through communal economic arrangements. Steele would have agreed with the Church's *Deseret News*: "Generally the laborer, out of whose toil and sweat come the dollars to make dividends, is squeezed a little harder that he may receive less while Money-bags obtains more."[1]

Steele's loyalty to Mormonism has caused some to valorize him as a pioneer, but his legacy is more complex than that. He described himself as a "thrasher" of the Lord's people and had been an enforcer who had threatened dissidents and jeered them into exile. He was enthusiastic about using coercion to build Utopia but oblivious that there can only be persuasion in paradise.

Steele was a founding father of Salt Lake City, and his wife Catherine Campbell Steele was a founding mother. Only her face was carved into the Salt Lake City-County Building because she had the first Mormon child born in the Valley.[2] I've written *The Women: A Family Story* about Catherine and other females in her family. Catherine and John were both founders of Parowan, and John was one of the founders of Las Vegas, with a pivotal role in establishing the town of Hurricane.

His trunk contained his handsewn 1851 Paiute dictionary, written on blue paper supplemented with white, a reminder that Native people are pivotal actors in Mormon millennialism. Some believe that redeemed Indigenous people and Mormon faithful will unite in the last days to destroy unbelievers; thus, the first Americans would—drawing on Jeremiah 51:20–26—cooperate as the "battle axe" of the Lord. John Steele was involved when in 1857 local church leaders in southwest Utah reached for the "axe" at Mountain Meadows, slaughtering more than a hundred California-bound emigrants. It was militia members who directed, led, and perpetrated that September 11th slaughter, but they framed Native peoples who were there as Mormon pawns and an alibi.

Steele's Native missions included exploring and mapmaking. He got lost circling what is now Zion National Park, but local Paiutes directed him to safety. He was the first to record a circumnavigation of the Grand Canyon—on a mission to the Hopi—and knew what it was like to have an empty flour sack, grit in his teeth, and be so hungry and angry that he dropped the frills of faith and had to be restrained from having a shoot-out with a name-calling comrade who stood a foot taller and weighed twice as much as he did.

Though he remembered his interactions with Natives affectionately—"I have found many good traits of charracter among them; one is, true to their friends"[3]—it wasn't all fondness: his upbringing and 1846–47 service in the Mormon Battalion prepared him for military service. His trunk had bundles of partly dated or undated penciled military telegrams sent to "Major Steele" during the Black Hawk War as he organized logistics for southwestern Utah and misdiagnosed the enemy. He played an outsized role in displacing Natives, with war, starvation, and European diseases doing their part.

Steele's collection of papers, books, magazines, correspondence—including copies of letters he wrote that he thought important—illustrate frontier life. A brief journal of his visit to Utah's 1897 Pioneer Day celebration chronicled how, at seventy-six, he walked hand in hand in the parade with his thirty-six-year-old ex-wife, Tamar. (His first wife, Catherine Campbell, had died, and his brief polygamist marriage to Mary Jane Harmon quickly ended in divorce.) Tamar was diagnosed later with "Manic Depressive Psychoses,"[4] but for the moment their notorious public battles were forgotten and her fate in the state insane asylum a conjecture.

About a third of the trunk held books, magazines, and pamphlets addressing Steele's wide-ranging interests. He subscribed to *Scientific American* and *Raphael's Prophetic Almanac.* In the waning days of 1851, he joined a circle of aspiring astrology enthusiasts studying in an isolated, newly built fort shaped like a Greek cross, the wood so green it still smelled of old-growth forest. Steele was so inexpert then that rather than centering his first horoscope on a date in a square surrounded by astrological squiggles, he wrote it in a vertical column. The trunk also had dozens and dozens of conventional horoscopes as well as his *Grammar of Astrology.* That, combined with *Solar Biology,* was useful to the self-taught doctor because he combined astrology and medicine with magic, charms, uroscopy, and crystal reading to treat the sick.

When Steele died in 1903, newspapers across Utah described him as "A pioneer well known in Salt Lake," despite his not having lived there for over fifty years. Christian romance novelist Diane Noble borrowed his name for a fanatical, ahistorical Danite character who orchestrated and led the Mountain Meadows Massacre;[5] contemporary obituaries ennobled him. His trunk shows he was more than a saint or villain, and his unparalleled story is an enlivening view of his life and times, as well as a wondrous array of half-forgotten mystical, magical, and folk customs. A study of John Steele illuminates the construction of the Mormon Kingdom.

I

IRELAND

"My Sown John was Born the 21st March in The year of our Lord 1821 at 4 in ^the^[1] Morn[ing]," thirty-one-year-old Nancy Kennedy Steele wrote in her Bible. The "4 in ^the^ Morn[ing]" suggests an interest in astrology, and the hour was important to this future astrologer.[2] It also hints that this shoemaker's daughter expected important things of her only son.

He was born in Holywood, County Down, near Belfast, where only a few houses were elegant enough to boast slate roofs. His forty-seven-year-old father, John Steele Sr., had just failed to win an appointment as a Belfast police officer, though he had a recommendation from his former Downshire Militia commanding officer. Maybe the elder Steele found the birth of a son and namesake some comfort.[3]

Young John arrived to the embrace of his parents, older sisters Elizabeth and Jane, and his grandfather Arthur Steele. (His older half-brother, William Steele, was a soldier for the Empire who died in Maulmain, now in Myanmar, when John was only six.[4]) Grandfather Steele had passed away by the time John Jr. was three. Arthur's first wife (and cousin), Elizabeth Greenfield, was part of the prosperous Greenfield network, so clannish they married their cousins to keep the property in the family, giving young John a potentially important kin network. There were plenty of uncles, aunts, and cousins, most in trades, and some quite successful.[5]

John Sr.'s brother, hazel-eyed Jackson Steele, was praised for his professionalism during the Napoleonic Wars ("a most excellent Man & a good Soldier") but was pensioned in 1814 because of testicle problems "occasioned by a Fall he received upon the Retreat from Madrid in the Autumn of 1812 while labouring under some Venereal Complaints which had been contracted in that Capital."[6]

The formative influence on young John was his father, who arrived at manhood during French Revolutionary turbulence, when soldiers were demanded. John Sr. joined the Downshire Militia in mid-September 1795, around the time Protestant "Peep O'Day Boys," some from County Down, slaughtered two dozen Catholics at the Battle of the Diamond.[7] He was a twenty-one-year-old linen weaver with brown hair, gray eyes, and a "fresh complexion."[8]

The royal cause wasn't especially popular. When British misrule united Protestants and Catholics and led to the Irish Rebellion of 1798, twenty-seven Presbyterian ministers were implicated, including Holywood's Rev. Arthur M'Mahon, who escaped to France before he could be hung.[9]

John Sr. enjoyed soldiering enough to leave the militia for the Royal Scots and become a professional soldier, rising to the rank of noncommissioned officer. He was stationed over eleven years in the West Indies in racially integrated units, then transferred to Portugal to serve in the Peninsular War. In his last great fight he was with the Third Battalion, Royal Scots, at Waterloo. The sword the old soldier is supposed to have used in the East Indies is now in the State House Museum in Fillmore, Utah.[10] Meanwhile he'd had time to marry, father a son, and become widowed.

John Sr. mustered out as a private on March 26, 1816—"woarn out"—and was designated a Chelsea Hospital out-pensioner.[11] "It is considered a great matter to be in the pay of the Government," wrote an Ulsterman of a later generation[12]—such a great matter that government pensions were most often the province of the ruling class and their dependents.

John Sr. leased a house and field in Holywood and married Nancy (Ann) Kennedy, daughter of shoemaker William Kennedy by his wife Jane McIlvene; when Nancy's son was writing his memoirs during the late Victorian era, women were mostly ignored because they were believed to be part of private life and, in any case, not significant to history. We have only a few references to her. Many years after Nancy's death, Rachel Connelly wrote of "Your mother's friend, Miss [Jane] Greenfield [who] died about six weeks ago in Holywood."[13]

A surviving letter of Nancy's dated August 1, 1844, reports "I ReCeived your letter and i am very glad to no you are oll well as this leaves mee well at present think god for it," and after providing some family information she signed off, "i remane your afectinot mother Mrs Steele."[14] (John Sr.'s literacy is uncertain; he signed his discharge in a clear, firm hand but spelled his surname "Steel." His brother Jackson signed his discharge papers with an *X*.)[15]

John Sr. was "a British officer And had a Salary from Government, he also had a Small farm that Supported the Family very Comfortably, Kept our own Cows Hogs and poultry,"[16] John Jr. remembered. The foundation of the family's relative prosperity was the pension, Steele's son recalling, "Brittins money raised me and I honor the Flage."[17]

The seemingly eternal chaos of Ireland hardened people to cruelty, and their aspirations were for liberty to manage their own affairs—"natural liberty."[18] John Steele Jr.'s passion for radical individualism was checkmated by a trait he inherited from his father, a simultaneous belief in radical authoritarianism. He never resolved those contradictions.

The *Belfast News-Letter* published a story in 1835, "Military Punishment of the Old School," about a "Lt. John Steele" who may have been John Steele Sr. (Steele was a member of the Royal Scots and had a brother in Ayr.) This John, in County Ayr, Scotland, around 1807, was ordered to parade his men, likely because many of them had missed the previous day's muster. Steele, who was among those who had "defaulted," took the squad to the seaside, where he marched them into the sea up to their necks before dismissing them. Dripping with saltwater, they had atoned for their default, and the commander was satisfied.[19] If this man wasn't John Steele Sr., he represented that man's rigid integrity.

Young John was taught how to muster, recalling that the old soldier "used to train me with his walking kane when I was a child."[20] It may have passed the time for his nostalgic father but it was definitive for the boy. Years later his great-granddaughter, who knew and heard stories from John Jr.'s daughter, recalled this childhood training: he was "brought up as a military man. You was strict with what you done. You done exactly what they said," summing up this authoritarian philosophy as "You do as they say!"[21]

One suspects God, as understood by the younger Steele, had an uncanny resemblance to Steele's father. "The Lord has his own way of punishing his Children he uses the Rod to make them learn whare they Stand and to whip them into Subjection as we would do a fractious Horse,"[22] he wrote.

Belfast Lough (bay) was also an influence. I "was always stout & hearty and fond of a sea life of Which I have had a large share," he recalled. When asked "Where early boyhood was passed, with interesting incidents thereof," he again referred to the sea: "Early Boyhood was passed mostly on the Shores of the Belfast laugh on the Atlantic Ocean followed Sailing

^&^ Fishing When not at School." When asked "Where was your early manhood passed?," he expanded: "Sometimes at Sea, and Sometimes on the Farm, Sometimes in the Carpenters Shop, Sometimes upon the Shoe bench, Just as fancy took me." "I comensed the Study of navigation intending to follow the Sea," he explained.[23]

T. H. Kennedy, of the main Holywood gentry family (unrelated to Nancy Kennedy Steele), with the help of young, powerful seamen—including John Jr.'s uncle James Davison—accomplished the nearly impossible, rescuing two men from the rigging of the *Marcella*, which had run aground during a violent storm. Davison, whose talents eventually brought him to the rank of captain, may have been a mentor to his nephew.[24]

"I grew up healthy & Strong," Steele summarized. "Fishing and Boating was my Chief amusement working on the farm with My father & Going to school was all that Caracterised the Early part of My life."[25]

John got "A liberal Common School Education"[26] when it was only available from church schools. He was a "Nonsubscribing Presbyterian," attending Holywood's First Presbyterian Church. For most of John's boyhood his ministers were Rev. James Alexander Johnston and then Rev. Charles J. M'Alester, successors to the rebel Arthur M'Mahon.

The *Belfast News-Letter*'s report of the Holywood free school examination in 1826 was probably typical of John's education. Under the leadership of the parish clergyman, students demonstrated what they'd learned in reading, spelling, and writing; Bibles and arithmetic books were awarded for progress, attendance, good conduct, and worthiness.[27]

Young John might have earned a math book, but a report that he "walloped his school master and then walloped the bully who hit the master"[28] implies good conduct may have been out of his reach. Probably he attended a Lancasterian school, where advanced children taught younger classmates, so it was a fellow student he bragged about taking down.[29]

Steele was considered educated by his contemporaries and also spent a lifetime in self-education.[30] The range of his library is astonishing: architecture, astrology, art, beekeeping, chemistry, education, engineering/surveying, farming, forestry, gardening, geography and maps, grammar and languages (English, French, German, and Spanish), history, hypnotism, irrigation, medicine, the occult, the military, phrenology, political tracts, religious dogma, and self-improvement.[31] Nor were these all casual interests: he practiced many crafts, including astrology, law, and surveying.

As John grew, his interests branched into radical reform, the United States having set the example some in Ireland wished to follow. County Down people had enough sympathy with the American Revolution that a Holywood landowner named his estate Bunker's Hill, and more than one local boy was called George Washington.[32] Evangelicalism also played an outsized role in the argument for change, providing leading voices in the Anti-Slavery Society as well as groups attacking drink and promoting education and sanitation.

The Parliamentary Reform Act extended the franchise and eliminated many rotten boroughs, but this didn't reach John's social class. About 1832, John Steele Sr.'s house was valued at "£4 4s. 0d.,"[33] not enough to meet the £10 voter threshold.

John was about fifteen when he started thinking about a trade.[34] His mother's cousins, the Belfast bakers John and Robert Crawford, were advertising for apprentices with "respectable connexions," but apparently that didn't interest him.[35] Nor was he lured into the woolen and clothing business of his father's Greenfield cousins, so prosperous in Belfast that Greenfield's-court was named for them (while Elbow-lane and Squeeze-gut Entry apparently honored more physical features).[36] But John never showed an inclination toward the trade which made one of the Greenfields rich enough to marry into a knighted family.[37]

*

Belfast was a bigger lure. It boasted it was the "Athens of Ireland,"[38] and even a bad road and sometimes nearly impassable footpath from Holywood over the crumbling Long Bridge to the larger town didn't lessen the village's dependency.[39] Many from Holywood found a livelihood and even prosperity there, so much so that at the annual meetings of the Holywood Agricultural Society there was always a toast to the "Town and Trade of Belfast" or even "'The Town and Trade of Belfast, to which Holywood is indebted for so much of its prosperity.' (Nine times nine.)"[40]

"I was Very Independant in my Character," John recalled, "and followed different Callings [and] was bound five years to Cabinet Makeng [and] Served Some time at Boot Making."[41] He might have been bound—apprenticed—for five years to cabinetry, but the indentures were broken before they expired; either he bought out his time or was relieved of his obligations. There were

Belfast, Ireland – 1840

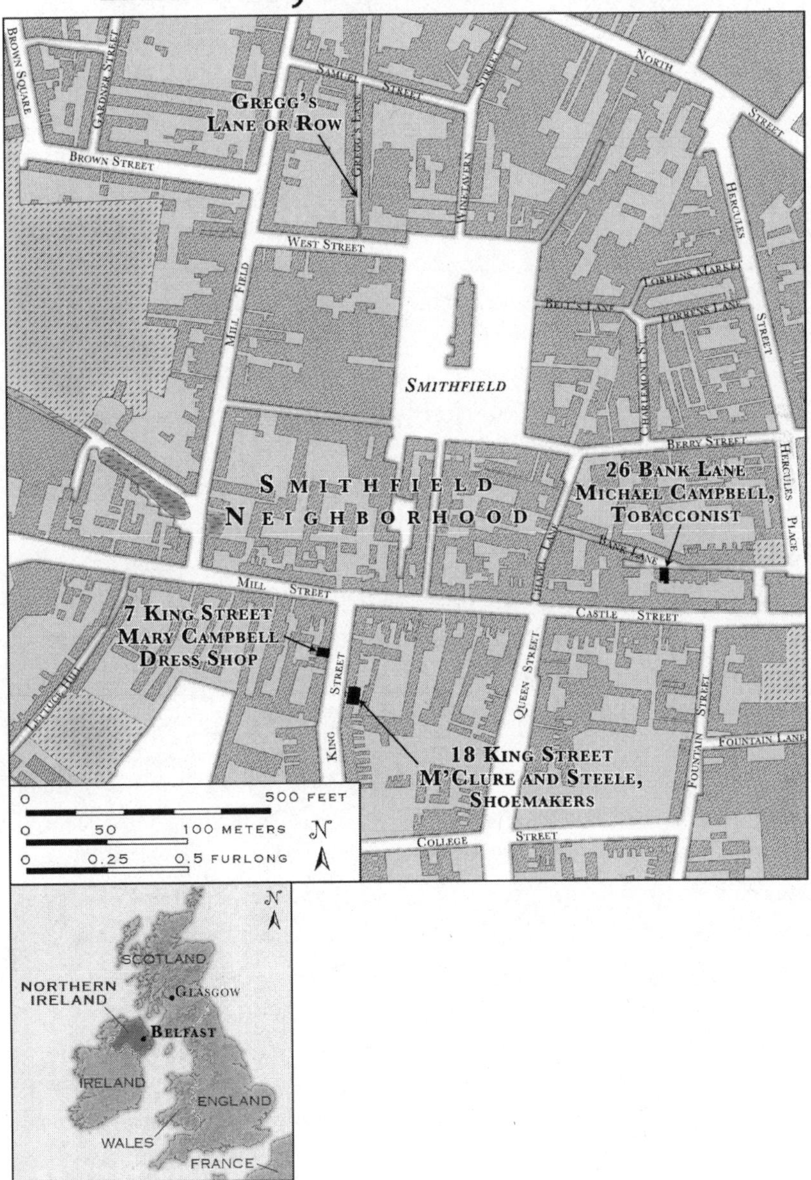

Belfast, Ireland, 1840. *Map created by Chelsea McRaven Feeney.*

several Belfast cabinetmakers named Kennedy; possibly he was apprenticed to a relative. He did become a skilled cabinetmaker.[42]

After cabinetry John went into boot- and shoemaking for a year, left it, and then returned.[43] His maternal grandfather, William Kennedy, had been a shoemaker, as was his uncle Michael Steele (alias Greenfield), his uncle Robert M'Clure (husband of his aunt Elizabeth Kennedy), and his cousin William M'Clure. Young Steele's shoemaking career began around the time Belfast shoe manufacturers put down a workman's "Trade Combination" (union); maybe he skipped the usual apprenticeship because he was a strikebreaker.[44]

Because of his incomplete apprenticeship, I looked for a shoemaker relative who was a master and found one in William M'Clure, who by 1832 had a boot and shoe business on Belfast's prestigious King Street.[45] We know John Steele Jr. worked with M'Clure because *Martin's Belfast Directory, for 1840–41* lists both of them as shoemakers at 18 "King-street," and M'Clure had been there some years.[46]

"I went to Belfast and Commensed buisnes for myself and Kept a Boot & Shoe shop in my 18th year," John wrote.[47] That he didn't mention M'Clure isn't entirely surprising since he had a tendency not to credit others. In a penciled diary entry dated July 23, 1847, he wrote, "last night E D Mecham and I discovered a cave to the right of our road some 300 feet high." When he rewrote his journal, this became "last might [night] I went and discovered a cave about 300 feet high."[48]

With a respectable trade and respectable kin, John was also full-blooded and lusty. Born before Victoria ascended the throne, he had a pre-Victorian attitude toward sex and understood lust, as shown by a poem called "Forbidden Fruit" written in his later years. He accepted moral conventions, arguing, "If once you've tasted of that fruit / You'r[e] Sure to taste again," and asserted children should be married at fourteen. That, he claimed, would lead to the closure of "the assignation House" and "There'd be no wild begotten Child / To Spread evil Seeds abroad."[49]

Belfast did have "assignation houses," an 1839 report explaining with surprising detail "we have only 59 brothels, containing 236 abandoned female inmates," and that "all the prostitutes of Belfast, except twelve, are of the very lowest description."[50] (One of those houses was kept by Nell "Steel," a name we don't find in the admittedly incomplete records of John's family.[51])

John Jr.'s King-street opened into Smithfield, the greatest slum in Belfast. Life there was spelled out by the stories of thieves like Martha Madden, five feet, two inches, with a ruddy complexion, a "Scar on the right side of forehead, two on centre on upper part of same, scar under right ear, lost nail of forefinger of right hand, two scars on back of lower left arm, scar on little finger of left hand"—all advertising her traumatized life.[52]

Her ostensible trade was laundress but she was an old hand at shoplifting, stealing clothes, fencing, and trying to pass forged notes. Martha first came to public notice in 1816, at age eleven, when she along with Eliza and Henry Madden—the latter her father—were involved in counterfeiting British shillings and tenpenny pieces.[53]

Martha was devoting herself to the family profession when she made a brief appearance in the *Belfast News-Letter* in 1839: "Committed to Carrickfergus Jail, for trial at next Quarter Sessions . . . May 2: Martha Madden, for stealing an egg-stand, the property of Catherine Campbell, Smithfield, Belfast."[54] Besides the egg-stand she was accused of stealing "a jug and three cups."[55]

When Madden was prosecuted, the name of the victim was changed from Catherine Campbell to Alexander Spiers—a publican on Shankhill Road.[56] Campbell may have had temporary custody of the goods when the robbery took place; Madden was found guilty.[57] Within a year of her run-in with Campbell, Madden capped her career by being transported to Australia, where she served her time, married, and presumably lived happily ever after.[58]

A few months later another malefactor announced himself at the Belfast Petty Sessions: "Committed to Jail, for trial at the January Sessions . . . William M'Larnon, for stealing a silk handkerchief, the property of Mary Ann Campbell, Gregg's-row."[59] M'Larnon, known familiarly as "Billy Plug," was described as "An unfortunate idiotic creature" who was also alcoholic; there is no record of his prosecution for this crime, but a few years later he drank himself to death when a cruel benefactor gave him all the liquor he wanted.[60]

Our interest is in the victims. Mary Ann Campbell's neighborhood, Gregg's-row (also known as Gregg's-entry or Gregg's Lane), near where robbery victim Catherine Campbell also lived, was in the northwest corner of Smithfield and was described in 1853 as "the common surface sewer of the whole region."[61]

There were two Campbell sisters in Belfast named Catherine and Mary Ann, but whether either or both were the victims in the crimes outlined above is uncertain. John wrote about one of Belfast's Catherine Campbells: "In my 19th year I got acqua[i]nted with Miss Catherne Campbell daughter of Michael & Mary Campbell," placing his courtship after March 1839.[62]

John met seamstress Catherine in her father's home, and a Mrs. Mary Campbell was a dressmaker at 7, King-street, across from the M'Clure Boot and Shoe shop.[63] The dressmaker may have been Catherine's mother, Mary Knox Campbell, which would explain why Catherine and several of her sisters excelled as seamstresses. However, when Catherine's father, tobacconist Michael, appears in the Belfast directories, he's at 26, Bank-lane, while dressmaker Mary Campbell is still at 7, King-street. (After Catherine's mother died, "Mrs. Campbell," the King-street dressmaker, disappeared from the directories.)[64]

Textiles were one of the great drivers of Belfast's prosperity, which included spinning cotton and linen, tailoring, and dressmaking.[65] Making clothing was time consuming, giving opportunities to many women and men. In 1831 it was calculated that "the number of stitches in a shirt as is usually made at present: Body 9506; sleeves, 10,160; breast 9042; collar 2712; total, 31,421; exceeding the total number of stitches in a coat by 6178."[66]

Clothing was so valuable it was common for Belfast children to be lured into alleys by plausible looking women and stripped so their clothes could be sold; then the naked children were abandoned.[67]

Catherine's profession may be why she had a lifelong taste for fine clothes and a love of Irish lace. Besides her needlework abilities, one family story suggests she had a man in her life when she met John. Supposedly she "was engaged to a Kings guard[sman]."[68] Ireland was an occupied country, and soldiers weren't always respectable—some got drunk and brawled, some engaged in "Affairs of Honor," a few turned to crime[69]—and some eventually revealed themselves as women.[70] But most were as respectable as John's father, and apparently none could overpower John Jr.'s persistence.

At eighteen he was young for a serious courtship, and Catherine was twenty-three. John was the more assertive and had some attractions, including, maybe, their very different personalities. At his full growth he claimed to stand five feet, six inches, near Catherine's height; she may have been slightly taller.

John Jr. later said he weighed 150 pounds in his prime, though he was always a lean man and in later years topped the scales at 133. It is doubtful Catherine weighed even 130 pounds; in middle age she had only a twenty-seven-inch waist. He had almost-sunken hazel eyes, a dark complexion, and apparently brown hair;[71] Catherine, in contrast, had a fair complexion and likely sandy or red hair.

John "had a firey temper, and keen sense of right and wrong, and the man never lived that he feared," recalled a grandson. "All in all he was one of the most remarkable men I ever knew, and I fondly cherish his memory."[72] Catherine, according to the same authority, "was very proud, refined and well educated. She carried herself like a queen and seemed more or less out of place in the hardships of pioneer life. . . . She always seemed to be a balance wheel to the exuberant spirit of her husband."[73]

Maybe she was regal because her family had a vague claim to "royal blood," the head of Clan Campbell confident of his descent from King Arthur. But her known relatives were tradespeople; her uncles Robert and Ephraim Campbell were tobacconists, like her father, Michael. Her mother was born Mary Knox and came from a talented Strabane family; her uncle William Knox had been a staymaker and was one of two attorneys in the Strabane Provost's Court. Later, an emigrant Knox first cousin married a grandniece of President James Madison and became a Virginia blueblood.[74]

As her grandson remembered, Catherine was well educated, writing with a clearer hand and better spelling than John did. In a newspaper advertisement that could have been about Catherine, we learn of "A YOUNG WOMAN who has served her Apprenticeship to one of the first Dress-making Establishments in Belfast, and also perfectly understands making Linen Shirts—is an excellent Plain Scholar, and can give unquestionable security for her general good conduct."[75]

John probably found her intelligence, poise, and apparent passivity appealing—passivity considered especially feminine in the nineteenth century.[76] She found in John a short man with impatient, grand ambitions, related to some of the established merchants and tradespeople in Belfast but with no pretensions of high status. If she had the better education, he had a more inquisitive, impulsive, and curious mind; he also had wit. When he and a group of his friends in an isolated community were left out of a public festival, he wrote, "I sopose we live so near Heaven that we could not be Reached without a ladder."[77]

Years later John told of visiting his sick daughter, who responded to his wit with "Oh Father don't Joke any more as I Cannot laugh it hurts me So."[78] Tired and with eyesight problems, John joked with a friend, "I am Writing this Letter I am like the Irishman when he was drunk I can see double."[79]

Catherine had a more subtle sense of humor, appealingly free of ego. "I have written Several letters to day and my hand hurts and I have got a very poor pen," she writes, "but that is the way with all poor work men they always get bad tools."[80]

They chose to be married in the new Presbyterian meeting house, Fisherwick Place Church; the portico, with columns twenty-seven feet high, was meant to look like an Ionic temple but would pass for an American post office.[81] They were married at 10 a.m. on January 1, 1840, by Rev. James Morgan.[82]

John's poetry presented marriage as a passionate time: "How beautifull! Yea & how char[m]ing to thee / Senses and fielings of man, is the lovely young & / Beautifull Bride when Standing by his side / Dressed in her bridal robes."[83]

But "things did not prosp[e]r with Me at this time Many trials we ware Caused to pass through which Caused us to think the wourld was an enomay to its own," John remembered.[84]

In early 1839 Ulster was battered by a hurricane; two people died in Holywood and two in Belfast, many houses lost shingles, some were unroofed, trees were blown down, and damage surrounded John on Kingstreet. The storms aggravated a food shortage, which led to riots, and the Belfast winter of 1839–40 was marked by a number of child abductions.[85]

John's cousin and mentor, William M'Clure, decided to join his parents and siblings in America, a place seized by Europeans who thought of themselves as civilized and Christian, but got much of their wealth through conquest, land theft, and slavery. It also offered unparalleled political rights to white men, even promising, as one historian wrote, a "swarm" of imagined Utopias to be choked with virtue and free of vice.[86] John Steele Jr. was to dedicate his life to this utopian dream.

Poverty was not something John knew personally. Holywood was so prosperous that in 1839 "there were only 50 paupers in a population of 8,000."[87] The most immediate problem was John Steele Sr.'s dropsy, or retention of water. His daughter Elizabeth recalled him staking his legs with a big needle to let the water out.[88] The weakening of a revered, if feared, authoritarian parent may have had a depressing and disorienting effect on his son.

Maybe the only welcome news was that "on the 23rd of Decemb^r ^8 Am^[89] 1840 I had a daughter born to Me ^Mary Campbell^."[90] The joy of this early Christmas present on a warmer than usual day for late December[91]—a girl named for Catherine's mother, Mary Knox Campbell—must have hardly been exhausted when John Steele Sr. died. John Jr. finished the sentence above with "And on the 12 day of Janÿ 1841 My Fath[e]r died and on the ^Feby^ 8th I started for the City of Glasgow in Scotland."[92]

Holywooders grew up speaking "mongrel Scotch"[93] and were so close to Scotland that when Presbyterianism was outlawed in Ireland, they rowed to Scotland to hold services, then rowed back the same evening.[94] Glasgow was also a cheap escape from a country soon to be cursed with a great famine.

It isn't surprising that within four weeks of his father's death John was packing for a Glasgow exploratory trip. A few years after he was born, the *Glasgow Chronicle* complained that low steamboat fares were flooding the country with Irish beggars, and by the 1840s thousands of Irish a year were migrating to Glasgow.[95] The Irish were accused of illiteracy, contributing to the slum problem, and driving down wages.[96] Luckily for John, Glaswegians preferred Protestant Ulstermen who had a trade, though they were often anti-Reformers disliked by the radical middle classes.[97] But John was practically a Scotsman anyway, and wherever he lived, he socialized with them as ethnic brethren.

He applied to George M'Tear of 33, Donegall-quay for a ticket on the Belfast and Glasgow Steam Shipping Company's *Aurora* under the command of Captain Anderson. He sailed Monday, February 8, 1841, at 10 p.m., in steerage for 2s. 6d; despite freezing weather, he benefited from a nearly full moon on his night voyage.[98]

2

SCOTLAND

John Steele was crammed in steerage with his ragged countrymen, the acrid smells and clacking, grunts, and bellows of poultry, turkeys, pigs, and oxen besieging them as the *Aurora* sailed up the beautiful Clyde River. The first whiffs of Glasgow were of poisonous chemicals that had driven out the city's botanic gardens, and the first sight was a 435-foot tapering chimney, a belching, stinking black reminder of rancid laissez-faire economics unwillingly fathered by Glasgow University's late Adam Smith.[1]

The British Empire was living through the "Hungry Forties";[2] by 1842 at least twelve thousand men were out of work in Glasgow and Paisley, and there were "whole families of beggars."[3] Shoemakers were the worst-paid craftsmen; tailors, dyers, bakers, and smiths earned more. Maybe consequently, shoemakers, along with sometimes starving and riotous handloom weavers, were the most radical.[4]

"I readily obtained work at a first-rate shop at boot and shoemaking,"[5] John wrote, but he doesn't mention where he worked. Maybe his shoemaker-uncle Michael Steele (alias Greenfield), his aunt Peggy Steele McDade, or his multiple Scottish cousins helped steer him.[6]

He soon sent for his family, and the night of June 6, 1841, the census taker found John, "Katherin," and Mary at 19 Great Dovehill (or Dove Hill). He was a bootmaker, Catherine was a dressmaker, and Mary was five months old.[7]

Great Dove Hill paralleled Little Dove Hill in one of the despairing wynds (slums) of Glasgow, afflicted with what a parliamentary reporter called "filth, crime, misery and disease." Another wrote, "In the courts off Argyle Street [near Great Dove Hill] there were no privies or drains, and the dung heaps received all the filth which the swarms of wretched inhabitants could give."[8] Five spirit dealers lived on the little street to tranquilize those suffering from pervasive poverty.[9] Catherine's brother Robert

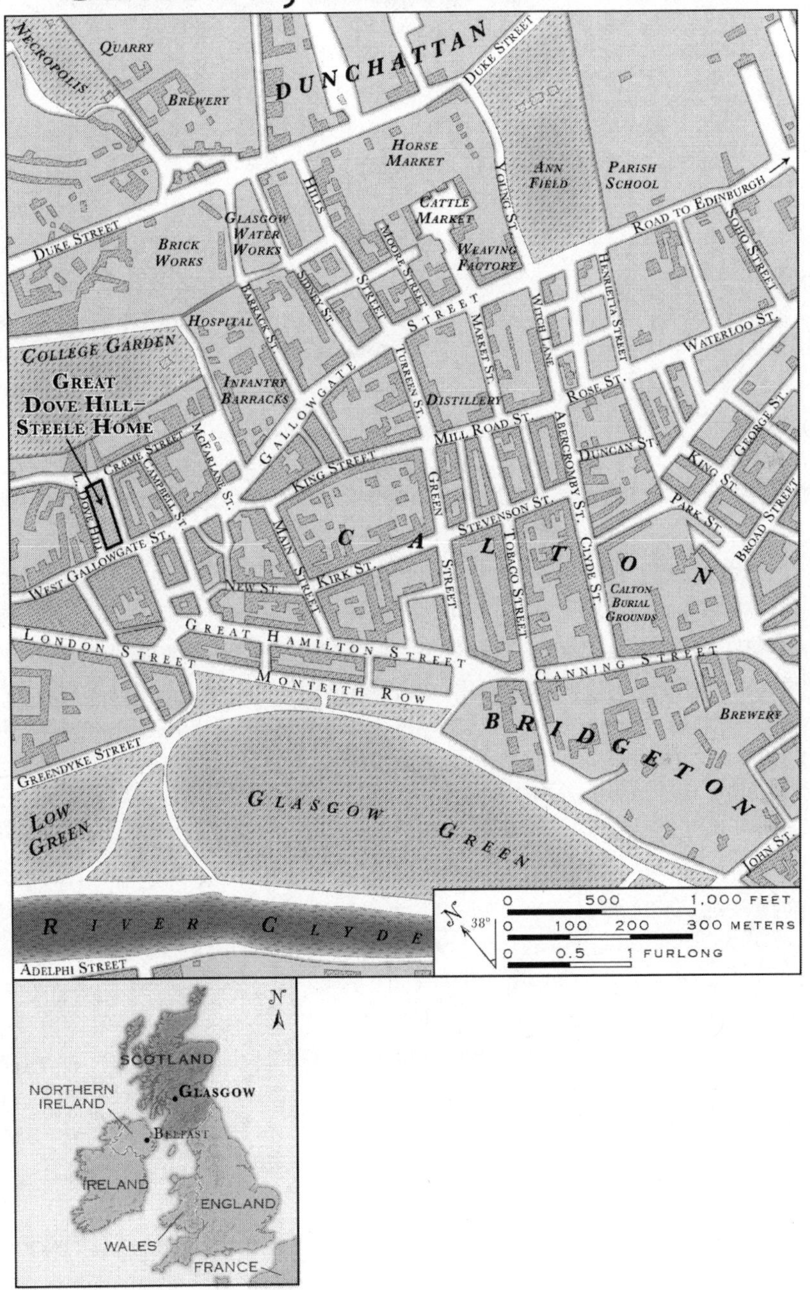

Glasgow, Scotland, 1840s. *Map created by Chelsea McRaven Feeney.*

Campbell visited and was not impressed; he wrote years later about their life "since you left Great Doo Hill in overcrowded Glasgow with all its pinching poverty."[10]

But the two Dove Hills were within feet of 410-year-old Glasgow University, and not much farther from College Garden, the Hunterian Museum, and MacFarlane Observatory. Holywood's rebel Presbyterian minister, Arthur M'Mahon, was a Glasgow graduate, and Belfast's Rev. James Morgan, who performed John and Catherine's marriage, attended a session.[11]

A thousand feet south was Glasgow Green, a public park abutting the Clyde River where John spent his spare time reading and studying, if not also watching the penny shows, the circus, lolling, and maybe occasionally watching the resuscitation of the apparently drowned at the Humane Society building. Catherine undoubtedly joined other women doing laundry.[12] Social missionaries representing all kinds of causes joined religious proselytizers here to promise Utopias now or in the hereafter.

A few weeks after the census was taken, the teetotaling Rechabite Club led a temperance rally on the Green, practically on Steele's doorstep.[13] The *Glasgow Courier* described it as "the most imposing demonstration that has ever been made by the disciples of teetotalism in the West of Scotland" and reported there were 5,120 marchers accompanied by bands, bagpipes, flags, and insignia.[14]

John was impressed. "I joined the Raccabite [Rechabite] Clubb," he wrote.[15] The Rechabites—not to be confused with the rioting, mostly Welsh, anti-toll movement, the Rebeccaites—grew out of the temperance movement, friendly societies, and the Oddfellows. Convivial singing and drinking led members to "pass the hat" when someone was in need; these groups turned into friendly societies to assess dues and provide financial relief in sickness and death. They did for working people what 1840s piratical capitalism wouldn't: provide some security against catastrophe.[16] John elaborated: "About this time there was a society purporting to be very old and also for the benefit of mankind formed called the Rachobites wherein those who belonged to the society could have money to help support them when sick and means to pay funeral expenses when dead."[17]

John also admired their rejection of intoxicating drinks. He quickly found himself "in a conspicuous position among them,"[18] prompt promotion being the norm of this group.

"Prosperity soon began to dawn upon us," he recalled,[19] but it was unsatisfactory, especially in the summer of 1842, when there were strikes and riots across both England and Scotland. August 1842 headlines in the *Glasgow Herald* include "Colliers' and Miners' Strike," "Strike, Mobbing and Assault at Mile-End," "Fearful Riots in the Potteries," "Disturbances in the Mining Districts," "The Rioters at Dunfermline," and "Weavers' Strike," and in September readers were greeted with "Strike of Dandy-Loom Weavers."[20] "I soon found myself on one of the trade committees of one thousand who were on strike for wages," John wrote.[21]

"Soon after [joining the Rechabites] I became a Chartist and was ve[r]y fond of hearing the Socielists and thought very strong of joining them,"[22] John wrote. When the Socialists were expelled from their "Hall of Science"—where they'd scandalously played the fiddle on Sunday—they took over the old St. Ann's, which had belonged to the Chartists. Socialists debated on the Green but were considered disreputable.[23] The local newspaper, describing a public confrontation between "a lean-looking lad, whose impudence appeared equal to his ignorance," represented the "vileness of socialism," while the defender of the status quo was "a little lame Irish cobbler."[24] This would have entertained John, but the socialism he was attracted to was the Owenite variety—"a blend of communitarian theory, anti-capitalist economics and a science of society."[25] Karl Marx came later.

The Chartists called for male suffrage for those twenty-one or older, of sound mind and not being punished for crimes; the secret ballot; abolishing property requirements for members of Parliament (MPs); payment of MPs so working- and middle-class people could represent themselves; equal electoral districts; and annual elections.[26] Their rallies on the Green were great events, too, and one drew between 2,500 and 3,000 people, but the reporter for the *Glasgow Herald* wrote disdainfully, "The speakers were of the usual class, and all obscure persons, whom it is needless to dignify by putting their names in print."[27]

The mildly reformist *Belfast News-Letter*, when John was still in that town, wrote that most of these issues were "fair subjects for discussion." But universal suffrage? "To suppose that every ragamuffin who walks the streets is to have a voice in the election of Members of Parliament," when thousands didn't have enough property to "purchase the fee simple of a decent grog-shop," was "so glaringly absurd, that it were utter waste of time to bestow upon it a single word of refutation."[28]

Ignoring Britian's notorious favoritism to class and wealth, the *Glasgow Herald* quoted the *New Monthly Magazine* to explain to Glaswegians that opulence was generally the result of industry and poverty of idleness.[29]

Chartists had less than a half-dozen parliamentary favorites, but among them was William Sharman Crawford, a handsome, dark-haired man with a Wellington nose whose mother was a Kennedy from Cultra in Holywood Parish.[30] Crawford was beloved by the Holywood farmers; the town gave a great dinner for him where two of John's Greenfield cousins were among the three vice presidents of the managing committee. John's minister, Rev. Charles J. M'Alester, blessed the event by saying grace. Crawford's radicalism was such that he presciently pointed out before the great potato famine that "Ireland was the only place where people were permitted to starve."[31]

Maybe Crawford's enthusiasm for John's causes comforted him as he moved in a direction far from his father's support of rulers and repression.

"About this time," John wrote, "I began to think seriously about religeon it occupied my time day & night I did not think that any of the professing Christians ware right."[32] This was of a piece with his work to reform himself through Rechabite principles and reform the state by embracing Chartism.

Evangelicals like Belfast's Reverend Morgan forced an end to slavery in the British Empire and prioritized amelioration of poverty through education, temperance, and charity, but only marginal religions were sympathetic to economic radicalism. John's ancestral Presbyterianism was the established church in Scotland, so little political agitation for working people was coming from them. But in response to the spiritual longings of Chartists—who argued, "The man who is not a Chartist is not a Christian, otherwise than in name"—a number of Christian Chartist Churches sprang up to fill a void.[33]

As John was studying religion, Presbyterianism was on the edge of another internal schism, the "Great Disruption of 1843."[34] In contrast, radical Primitive Christianity promised a restoration of the excitement, brotherhood, faithfulness, and sacrifice of the mythical early times.[35] That meant spiritual gifts like prophecies, healings, revelations, and communitarianism. These appealed to John. As Emerson wrote, "Why should not we have . . . a religion by revelation? . . . The sun shines to-day also."[36]

"Shortly after this [around mid-March 1843]," John wrote, "I heard of the Book of Mormon by seeing a hand bill posted up purporting to be an ancient writing by an ancient people who lived in America and that an angel of God had appeared by whose ministrations the records of ancient America had been discovered."[37]

Mormons had first come to the notice of *Belfast News-Letter* readers in late 1838 under the headline "Extraordinary Sect of Fanatics in America." The article told how the new religion was generating violent conflicts in Missouri. It had been founded by a young Yankee named Joseph Smith who said he was guided by God to dig up "golden tablets" from which he translated the Book of Mormon, claimed to be the Christian prehistory of America, and Smith assumed the role of prophet.[38]

After recounting a good deal of qualified misinformation and hearsay about this new sect, the reporter added, "I am given to understand, that the Mormons are by no means immoral, and that their domestic laws are good. They build Churches, have schools, a Bank, and coin paper money, among themselves." One reporter speculated that the real cause of the conflict was "a silly fanaticism."[39]

John Steele was intrigued by their story and borrowed a Book of Mormon from power loom weaver Graham Douglass, maybe a compatriot in strikes for reform.[40]

Mark Twain called the Book of Mormon "chloroform in print,"[41] which shows Twain didn't grow up on the Presbyterian heresy-hunting controversies that Steele was exposed to. He remembered he "would repair to the banks of the Clyde on Glasgow Green and read it through in two weeks."[42]

Mosiah 4:16–21 in the Book of Mormon demanded: "succor those that stand in need of your succor" and denounced those who would say, "The man has brought upon himself his own misery," arguing, "For behold, are we not all beggars?"[43] The text was described as "a document of profound social protest," and historian Leonard Arrington wrote that Mormon economic plans were "collectivism not tarred by the Marxist brush!"[44]

"I read P. P. Pratt's Voice of Warning and attended all their meetings," Steele wrote. The *Voice of Warning* argued for biblical literalism. When "men are left at liberty to transform, spiritualize, or give any uncertain private interpretation to the word of God, all is uncertainty,"[45] Pratt wrote, rejecting allegorical and metaphorical explanations that theologians had used for centuries to explain textual difficulties. Steele found Pratt's fundamentalism convincing and echoed it: "dont Spirritualize but let the Scriptures tell their own tale as though written to you personally."[46]

He also wrote that anyone can see "the Judgments of the Lord being poured out on all nations as predicted in the 24 Chapter of Mathew," and cited "the distress of nations, the Sea & the Rivers overflow, Fires, Explosions, Earthquakes, Collisions, both on Sea, and on Rail roads, Capital against Labor and the poor against the Rich, and the vice vercy." Even astrologers warned that great changes were coming.[47]

For biblical literalists it's always the End of Times; wars and rumors of wars, dissensions, and strife never end. Mormonism embraced this millennialism as well as the concept of the Kingdom of God—a perennial dream with a partial lineage to the beliefs of Joseph Smith's New England ancestors, when John Winthrop described the New World experiment as creating "a city on a hill"[48]—and even further, to Augustine of Hippo. Smith interpreted this to be a literal kingdom ruled by the Mormon priesthood preparing a place for Christ's earthly return. This required that converts "gather" to avoid the destruction of "Babylon."[49] There was little contingency in this Kingdom for dissidents, unbelievers, and doubters. Since Satan was fighting the great work, troublesome persons out of harmony were at least implicitly the devil's allies.

John Steele, satisfied with the new revelation, the proofs he saw for it, and kingdom-building, was baptized the evening of April 10, 1843.[50] The ordinance was performed by another enthusiastic County Down convert, plump-cheeked nineteen-year-old John McEwan.[51] Steele was converted, he proudly reported, "in four weeks from the first sermon I heard"[52]—a brag that he caught on quickly to the new truth. "My Wife [Catherine] did not Believe untill I preach[e]d[53] the Gospel to her and in a few weeks she was Baptised also ^May 3, 1843 9:30 pm^."[54] Catherine and John brought an expanding family to the congregation for his son John had been born in 1842, and his daughter Margaret would be born in 1844.

British missionary leader Thomas Ward estimated that by the fall of 1843 there were eight thousand or nine thousand Mormons in Great Britain,[55] and the rapid growth cried for experienced leaders. The British movement was led by a tall, sallow-faced American missionary in Liverpool named Reuben Hedlock, who bustled to keep up.[56] Dissensions in Scotland sent him to Glasgow, where among other things he and Elder John Munro ordained John Steele as a priest on November 5, 1843.[57]

John began missionary work first at Rutherglen, three miles southeast of Glasgow's city center. It's possible this was to take advantage of the turnout at the town's November fairs. Rutherglen had heavy industry and coal mining, the kinds of industrial conditions that were fertile fields for converts.[58] Continuing in a southeast arc from Glasgow along the Clyde River, John preached at Tollcross (Fullarton Steel Works), where coal miners had recently met to debate striking;[59] the village of Uddingston, like Tollcross on the north side of the Clyde; and Blantyre (coal mining) and Hamilton, both on the south bank of the Clyde. He traveled northeast to Falkirk (iron and steel works) and Airdrie, site of the "Radical War" of 1820, when weavers and others tried to organize a strike, and now angry miners were demanding better conditions.[60] His success made him more zealous, but emigration depleted the congregations. John McEwan, who baptized Steele, left in the summer of 1843 for America and service as a clerk to Joseph Smith. Many others preceded or followed, for as the *Latter-day Saints' Millennial Star* reminded converts, leaving "Babylon" was the key to their temporal and spiritual salvation—only then could they build God's Kingdom.[61]

In 1844 the Nauvoo Kingdom in Illinois was fighting for its life. Scottish newspapers in the summer carried headlines like this one in *The Dundee Warder and Arbroath and Forfar Journal*: "War Against the Mormons." The paper reported that Joseph Smith was alleged to have destroyed a Nauvoo newspaper unfavorable to him, whereupon the anti-Mormon *Warsaw (IL) Signal* predicted "war and extermination" and demanded "every man to make his comment 'with powder and ball.'" "There is no disguising the fact, that the news of a bloody battle, or peradventure of a massacre, as in Missouri, is feared," the *Warder* said.[62]

The reporter's conclusion was aimed at British readers: "Sincerely do I hope that the ominous circumstances I have described, even if the fearful excitement should pass harmlessly away, will deter any more emigrants from England from coming out and enrolling themselves among the miserable dupes of that would-be modern Mahomet, Joe Smith."[63]

The next piece of news changed things for John. On August 2, 1844, the *Glasgow Herald* reported, "The Mormons have lost their leader and prophet, Joe Smith, who was murdered in cold blood by a gang of ruffians, who attacked the gaol in which the prophet and his brother had been placed for security."[64]

But as another newspaperman, Frank A. Beckwith, wrote of John, "This irascible old pepper box this Irish midge no bigger than a pint o soap

The *Palmyra and Camilla* at sea. *Alamy stock photo.*

after a hard day's wash took no sass from anybody big or little, just itched for a fight and when he saw a scrap begged for permission to get into it!"[65]

John was going to get to Nauvoo. "[A]ll who will take hold and help build up the Kingdom of God on the Earth shall live and reign in it on the Earth When Christ shal come for his coming is near at hand," he wrote.[66] He asked his mother, Nancy, for details of his half-brother William's military service because he might be able to claim money to emigrate.

She answered on August 1, reporting that William Steele had enlisted in Dublin, and she sent him the prize ticket an officer had sent John Steele Sr.[67] Among John Sr.'s effects was an 1830 note from the War Office explaining money due for William and an (inaccurate) note in a later hand says, "The money received was used to Emmigrate to Utah";[68] maybe it was used to emigrate to New Orleans.

John and his family left Glasgow on January 14, 1845, and got to Liverpool the next day. His sister Jane and her family were there, having emigrated to Lancashire (his sister Elizabeth went to Australia later), and John met her before boarding the *Palmyra*—with a fare for adults of £4. 4s.[69]

The ship made good speed. Passenger Ann Pitchforth, an inexperienced seafarer, found parts of the trip terrible and wrote of their "perilous condition." In an autobiographical fragment written on the back of a blank subscription list for *The Scientific American* of 1875—possibly a part of John's missing autobiography—he gives a vivid description of an episode on the voyage. On February 24th they spied something that "roled heavily Which puzzled our officers to make out what She was when She . . . was rolling in the sea."[70]

Despite a heavy swell the *Palmyra* sent a weather-beaten and unreliable boat to the *Camilla* which managed to rescue the crew. The ship was in bad shape but insured, so, as John reported, "it was thought best to Scuttle her and Sink her out of the way," and they set the ship afire. He wrote, "Every thin[g] above water being So dry She Burned Awfully Grand and if there is one thing more awfully Grand than another it is to See a Ship on fire at Sea[.]" They sailed away but could still see the flames as "Darkness of Evening Closed down upon us."[71]

Thereafter, John wrote, "The weather being fine and a light breeze Soon brought us to the Bahama Islands and Sailing in between the Island of Cuba and Cape Sable the extreme north point of Florida we So[o]n Entered the Gulf of Mexico." Here they had "a touch of Cyclone but the Greatest force of it was about three miles to the West of us." "Such a Storm of rain I never Saw our lee scuppers had a perfect rever of Water running in them, if it did Some harm it did Some Good for we Got our Casks filled with fresh water Which was Much needed as our, water was beginning to taste bad."[72]

A partial-sentence reminiscence in his later journal didn't mention any problems, instead abbreviating the trip to "a plesant Voige of six week[s] & thre[e] days."[73] "We Soon signaled for a pilot and Soon a long lanky [*missing*]."[74] We "arived at new orleans on 7th of March ^1845.^"[75]

3

NAUVOO

The United States was celebrating the rainy inauguration of a new president, James K. Polk, when the Steeles reached New Orleans. Maybe John celebrated this promotion of a fellow Ulsterman but neighboring Mexico didn't.[1] In the dying days of the Tyler administration, a Louisiana newspaper reported, "On the strength of the passage of the Texas [annexation] resolutions, Gen. [Juan] Almonte, the Mexican minister, has started for home."[2] His departure signaled the threat of war.

On March 11, 1845, five days after reaching New Orleans, the Steeles were bound for St. Louis aboard the *Alex Scott*, a floating horizontal hotdog with two incongruous chimneys sticking up at one end.[3] They stayed in St. Louis to earn enough money to get to Nauvoo. "I went to work for Mr. Bates on 3rd street at boot making," John summarized. "Made money. My wife would do the fine stitching and I would side them up and bottom them."[4]

Delaying the trip to Nauvoo to earn money was necessary. Steele wrote that when Erastus Snow came to St. Louis to collect tithes for the Nauvoo Temple on May 12, 1845, "I Consecrated My first offering of a tenth of all I posessed in the wourld," which by his calculation was three dollars.[5] Snow was to be an important figure in John's life.

"After working there three months I started for Nauvoo, July 8th 1845," Steele recalled. He believed the city, "As near as could be made out," had 20,000 people. It also had "many fine buildings, costly mansions, many fine farms cultivated round the city, plenty of woodland close by and a beautiful situation, a large Masonic hall, of which I had the honor to be a member."[6]

The Steeles spent their first night in Nauvoo in a tent but soon moved into Philo Dibble's frame house on Hyrum Smith's farm. John wrote that he "Joined the Tanners & Shoemaking associati[o]n." He found work at Nauvoo's boot and shoe factory, organized as a community effort.[7] The Nauvoo Tanners and Shoemakers may be the same as the earlier Nauvoo

Leather, Harness, Boot, and Shoe Manufactory, and a successor to the Nauvoo Boot and Shoe Establishment, organized in late 1844 on Mulholland Street, a place that meant enough to John that a later nineteenth-century picture of it was among his effects.[8]

His new home was mostly devoid of the stereotypical exploiting capitalists and grasping landlords, while working men had power and were respected. His church organized and directed capital for community purposes, encouraging agriculture in the farmlands and organizing trades in Nauvoo.

Steele advanced as rapidly among the Mormons as he had with the Rechabites. He joined the 29th Quorum of Seventies on July 27, 1845.[9] "Seventies," Joseph Smith's contested successor, Brigham Young, explained, "are ordained Apostles, and when they go forth into the ministry, they are sent with power to build up the Kingdom in all the world, and consequently they have power to ordain High Priests, and also to ordain and organize a High Council."[10]

"On the 15th day of August," John wrote, "I joined the Masonic Fraternity, and soon became well acquainted with the old brethren."[11] The Nauvoo Lodge had been disaffiliated from other masonic lodges in 1843 for irregularities, including advancing members too quickly.[12] The Lodge records show that John's proposed membership was backdated to June 5, 1845, when he was still in St. Louis, and misreported that on June 19th the Lodge balloted for John Steele and others and in each case found them "duly received."[13]

Steele was initiated in Nauvoo to the first and second degrees of masonry on August 8th. On August 18th, he and others received the sublime degree of master masons, the highest degree in the brotherhood.[14]

The Rechabite-type rituals included the "Ancient Mysteries," secret passwords, and blood oaths. "The first lesson of Masonry is the virtue of secrecy," wrote a historian, something especially important in Nauvoo, where there were other rites and rituals known only to the select.[15]

Seemingly snugly ensconced in the Kingdom, working his craft, practicing his religion, and enjoying Masonic fellowship, Steele had a life that was deceptively calm. But Illinois governor Thomas Ford wrote of claims of Mormon "kidnapping, land speculation, abuse of the Nauvoo municipal court's powers of habeas corpus, counterfeiting and treason," and felt that because of the city's unique charter, the Mormons were independent of state laws. That was the general view of their enraged neighbors, and their charter was repealed.[16]

Summer 1845 headlines in the anti-Mormon *Warsaw (IL) Signal* were building from hysteria to reports of mobbing: "Another Outrage at Nauvoo" (June 4, 1845), "Trouble in the Holy City" (June 11, 1845), "Mormon Gull-Traps" (June 18, 1845), "Farce in Nauvoo" and "Murder in Nauvoo" (June 25, 1845), and on and on.

The murderers of the Smith brothers went unpunished, as did Orrin Porter Rockwell, who killed Franklin Worrell, a Carthage anti-Mormon merchant—and this, as Governor Ford recognized, advanced the death of constitutional government.[17] The Mormons still had some political power, dominating the August polls in Hancock County and electing as sheriff J. B. Backenstos, whose brother was married to Joseph Smith's niece.[18]

According to Ford, anti-Mormons arranged for a few harmless shots to be fired at a house where they met as an excuse to rouse the countryside for vigilante action.[19] Nauvoo being currently impregnable, they attacked outlying Mormon farms and villages.

Ramus, which was too far from Nauvoo and too close to the anti-Mormon town of Carthage, had an unsavory reputation after a group of Mormon thieves were exposed and expelled, having claimed church leaders approved as long as they only stole from "Gentiles" (non-Mormons). Nauvoo authorities dissolved the Ramus High Council, renamed the town Macedonia, and appointed reputable leaders, but it was still a canker to its neighbors.[20]

Macedonian and Manxman (Isle of Man) convert Thomas Callister, acting as a spy, said townspeople were advised by Nauvoo leaders "to be ready at A moments warning to take up Arms And defend ourselves And to organize the Componys belonging to the [Nauvoo] Legion."[21] When anti-Mormons began drilling in nearby Fountain Green, Macedonia's leaders sent anxious letters to Brigham Young: "Many are Sick & some without Arms."[22] They requested fifty to a hundred troops immediately. The letter was forwarded to Sheriff Backenstos with a note from Brigham Young saying Gen. Charles C. Rich could send twenty-five or thirty men without delay.[23]

On September 12th John joined the Nauvoo Legion because mobs were "burning the houses Barns & Stacks of Grain."[24] He was unarmed, unless he had his father's Napoleonic War sword.[25] He had a strategy, though, telling his older shop-mate, Hartley Mercer, "If you will shoot down one of the mob, I will go into their ranks and get his gun."[26]

"Great Cry of they Mob's Coming to destr[o]y the City they Said they would destr[o]y it if Jesus Christ should Stand at their head," John wrote. "I and a number of the others were detailed to bring up the guns," getting forty stands of muskets from Captain Augustus Farnham.[27]

Now he was armed.

John was to start for Macedonia on September 20th to guard the carding machines, but he and his fellow soldiers didn't leave Nauvoo until September 22nd, probably because the officers had a challenge raising and equipping the men. They marched out at sundown. "When we got to the corner of Joseph's farm, the Captain ordered us to load our guns. I did load mine and never tasted anything so sweet in my life as did the powder."[28]

Being a soldier brought back childhood memories of when he was twelve and his father drilled him in Holywood. "At night we arrived at Macedonia, were paraded before Uncle Billy [William G.] Perkins' house as he was called. Volunteers were called for. I volunteered to stand guard on the carding machine as that was the night set to burn it."

"As we drove into town," Steele recalled, "the mobocrats heard us come but all hostile intentions were stopped for the time being. As the men did not dare show their faces they sent their women to visit sister [Dicy] Perkins as we were all staying at Uncle Billy Perkins place and our guns were standing in the corner of the parlor."

"Those women all declared There were 500 stands of arms there and 500 of us and 200 Indians they knew!" John wrote. "As a matter of fact there were forty one Mormons and TWO Indians! So you can see how the wicked are afraid and flee when no man pursueth and the imagination of their own wicked deeds makes good men multiply in their sight."[29]

Steele and Mercer were standing guard at an old bridge "over an hour when we heard the rattle of a wagon in the distance," he remembered. "We thought that it was them and we prepared, unbuttoned our cartridge boxes, saw to our priming, found all ready."

"Brother Mercer," Steele said, looking at the small moon, "you stand in the shade of the crooked fence. I will stand in the shade of the porch and I will bring them to a halt and you grab the horses as they come over."

When the suspects came up "we both sprang out at once. I brought my gun up within six feet of them as they sat in the wagon, and demanded,

'Halt!' Brother Mercer at the same time caught the horses. It was quite a surprise to the midnight travelers as they returned from a long ride to find themselves prisoners in their own town." They didn't know one another "but after much questioning I found it was Utica [Ute] Perkins and long Andy [Perkins] as he was called, both brethren. So we let them go," an anticlimactic ending to Steele's Nauvoo soldiering. He returned to Nauvoo on September 30, when "some change had taken place in affairs."[30]

The change was Brigham Young negotiating a voluntary exodus for the following spring, 1846.[31] Young, who was accepted as the leader by most of Nauvoo after Joseph Smith's death, led the retreat from Missouri, organizing the community with a deep commitment to the needs of the poor. "The Mormons attempted to make up through superior organization what they lacked in economic assets," wrote historian Leonard Arrington.[32]

As the *Nauvoo Neighbor* published a "Bill of Particulars" on October 29th, listing down to the last nutmeg the supplies needed for the trek, the night riding and terror slowed.[33] But Steele found himself sick in Nauvoo's unhealthy season, and "my wife sick of the fever and ague,"[34] a disease now known as malaria.

"Only Mary was able to hand us a drink of water and she only four years old! She would set a little pot on the fire and carry the water by less than a cup full until she would have enough to cover the potatoes that she would wash one by one and put into the pot." Mary couldn't pour the water off, so Steele "would crawl out of bed" to do so. "We all suffered much."[35]

Officious "Mother Bullock"—Henrietta, wife of Thomas Bullock—had suffered through the fall with malaria, too, treating it with quinine, blisters, and putting her feet in peppers.[36] Eventually she was well enough that "in the m[i]dst of our trials" Bullock "Came in to My house and said to me Broth[e]r Steele you'r[e] going to die and you'r Wife's going to die and you Must give Me Mary." Mary was "the only one who Could hand us a drink Whare upon I raised and told her I would not die nor my Wife should not die and I would Not Give her Mary and I Commensed to ament [mend]."[37]

But "For want of the proper care my son John died on the 10th day of December A. D. 1845," a day Nauvoo diarist William Clayton called "very fine and pleasant but cold." The bereaved Steele wrote, "I hired Br. Samuel Burgess to dig the grave. He got a team, we took him to the graveyard on Friday the 12th and on the next Thursday [December 18th] Margaret died and was buried Fri. Dec. 19, 1845. Thus drew near a close that memorable year 1845 to me."[38] It wasn't until after John and Catherine left Nauvoo that the church Trustee in Trust booked his last donation: "1 Pr. of small shoes John Steele .50"[39]

The deaths were devastating to John and Catherine, and he bitterly attributed them to persecution by anti-Mormon mobocrats.[40]

Once Steele had been challenged back to life by Mrs. Bullock, he recovered enough "to wo[r]k as a Carpenter on the Temple untill I was Called elswhare."[41]

The first half of 1846 was a terrible time for the Steeles; making donations must have been a sacrifice. As late as July, John wrote that he and Catherine "were both sick of ague and fever, I have two shakes a day, and I had been in that situation many months."[42]

"On the 28th day of January [1846], I and my wife were called upon to go into the House of the Lord and get our endowments," wrote Steele.[43] Maybe most significantly for John's future, the ceremonies included an oath "to avenge the blood of the prophets upon this nation, and that you will teach the same to your children and your children's children unto the third and fourth generation."[44] Persecution is the father of vengeance.

Brigham Young explained the significance of the temple ritual, which was to give signs and tokens "pertaining to the Holy Priesthood, and gain your eternal exaltation in spite of earth and hell."[45] These rituals also served as a communal bond.

The decision "to leave and go into the Western Wilds," John remembered, meant he "set to work parching Corn Meal to live upon[,] a thing I Could not Eat at best of times."[46] But flour was hard to find and corn was cheap—30,000 bushels had been harvested the previous fall.[47] "[T]he faithful saints began to make wagons" and "in various ways prepare for a long journey not knowing to where or how long it would take to perform it, but trusting in the Lord, through our leaders, Brigham Young and the rest of the Twelve [apostles]."[48]

Poor, sick, and in a city where everyone was trying to get a "Good strong wagon" and their nutmegs—to say nothing of teams and other stock—the Steeles were late in leaving Nauvoo in the most existential crisis of their new faith.

"I got ready and started from Nauvoo on the 4th day of May, A. D. 1846," Steele remembered. "[I] hired my passage in Brother Samuel Burgess' wagon, not having team and wagon of my own. I made him and his family

Nauvoo Temple baptismal font. *Alamy stock photo.*

boots and shoes to haul me and my folks I knew not where." Burgess, one remembers, was there when John and Catherine needed him at the burial of their children.

"[A]s there was his folks and my family and our effects to go into one wagon and only one yoke of cattle and a pair of 2 yearling calves to haul it you may suppose we could not bring much but our provisions which consisted of parched corn meal."

But, he wrote, "leave we had to and go we must, so I got up and left all of my furniture standing as we were wont to use it. The clock hung on the mantle piece, and everything as though we were just gone out on a visit, only the beds were gone but not the bedsteads." Afterward he realized he needed a hammer so he went back to his house and found three looters "quarreling [over] who should have the clock. I opened my toolchest, took out my hammer, closed the lid and sat down upon it, and heard them awhile, then started on my journey."[49]

He could eventually see the humor in that, but he was furious about events. In a retained fragment of a letter Steele wrote years later he shared his bitterness from this time: "Sir we ware H^o^useless Homeless in our own land driven by Mobs Rob[b]ed plundered and great Hopes Entertained that we would be driven into the Pasific ocean."[50] And when years later his wife Catherine died, he mourned for her whose children "Sleep in that Fare City Nauvoo where by wicked mobbs they ware consigned to an Early Grave and in the midst of poverty Sickness and Distress."[51]

Yet the Steeles and their coreligionists had a powerful resource: before leaving Nauvoo, the Mormon people covenanted "to use ourselves & our means to the uttermost for removing this people from that region."[52] However bumpily and sometimes angrily the future played out, the promise of communal responsibility was Mormon bedrock.

4
MORMON BATTALION

The Steeles slip-slopped through the Iowa mud with Samuel I. Burgess, Steele working as a teamster without his own team. Burgess was contracted to take them to Council Bluffs, but his team failed at Grand River, ninety miles short. Steele paid Lewis Zabriskie to "hall us on." Zabriskie, a veteran of Joseph Smith's ill-conceived "Zion's Camp" march to reclaim Missouri, was chosen as one of the bishops at Council Bluffs. A few weeks later Steele left his affairs in the bishop's hands.[1]

Belfast newspapers of John's boyhood often featured stories about Native Americans, their housing, "naughty" dress or undress ("as naked as their father Adam"), food, music, and dance.[2] Indigenous Americans were important to Mormon cosmology for they were considered Hebrews, and when converted, they were to be a pillar of the Kingdom of God. Steele's own interest is shown by his detailed report of a Meskwaki (Fox) council.[3]

On July 10, 1846, camping on the Nodaway River, about a hundred Mormons held a meeting with the "Big Chief" Poweshiek and fifty or sixty of his entourage. Poweshiek *was* big, about 250 pounds, and his tribe was in a situation like the Mormons'.[4]

Brigham Young identified himself and, through an interpreter, Poweshiek got confirmation the Mormons would be friendly. Then the chief, as Steele wrote, "asked if the Grait spirrit would always suffer the Indian's to be driven about as the had been."[5] (Steele often wrote "the" for "they.") Young assured him they would not, but Poweshiek went on to "state how that the states had used them and that the had drove them and now said he the have proposed to us to leave this land within two years or if we dont our money and yearly payments for our other lands will be stoped so you se[e] we have to go." Realizing only firepower could protect them from encroachments, Poweshiek asked if the Mormons "would learn us to Make Gun's Powder & Lead & to Live like White Man and when the saints would be ready to receive them and the would go and live with us." Young promised that in two years he would send a guide to bring the Meskwaki west. (Young did send emissaries two years later, but the Meskwaki didn't move to the Rocky Mountains.) Meanwhile they asked for "a beef" and two were given them, Steele recorded, and they "praised God by lying with their heads round the root of a tree and their Bells Ringing."

Steele, signifying his great interest in Indigenous Americans, took pains to describe the Meskwakis. They were "decorated in native costume with about 2 or 3 pound's of Beads round their neck and their Ears all round linked in with jewels and fine Brass wrist Bands on their wrists."[6]

*

President James K. Polk, having barely averted one war with Great Britain over Oregon, stumbled unprepared into another war with Mexico over the annexation of Texas. Brigham Young's nephew was lobbying for the Mormons in Washington, while Missouri's governor, John C. Edwards, wrote that his state needed soldiers "to keep the Indians and Mormons in check."[7] The Mormons insinuated that without government help they would collude with the British while also claiming their American loyalty. Polk ordered five hundred Mormons be enlisted when they reached California. He didn't need them—the Army had more volunteers than it could use—but it was politic and humane.[8]

John and his family were suffering from ague at Mount Pisgah when Col. James Allen arrived and claimed authority to raise a five-hundred-man battalion, Polk's orders to enroll them after they got to California having mercifully been missed by governmental bureaucracy.[9]

"You can better imagine my feelings than I can describe them," Steele recalled. "I must ask pardon for thinking or saying they may all go to hell together." He blamed "the whole United States" for "those who have mobbed, robbed, plundered and destroyed us all the day long and now seek to enslave us to fight for them."[10]

Yet the military offered seven dollars a month, a clothing allowance, and rations, and at discharge they could keep their military equipment. Brigham Young didn't miss Allen's pledge to give "an opportunity of sending a portion of their young and intelligent men to the ultimate destination of their whole people, and entirely at the expense of the United States."[11] The canny Young turned himself into a recruiting officer after he also wrested permission from Allen for the remaining Mormons to spend the winter, illegally, on Native lands.

John enlisted on July 18, 1846, and probably he and Catherine joined the camp in celebration. Captain Pitt's Brass Band played and they danced into the night to the sounds of "violins, horns, sleigh bells, and tambourines."[12]

Why did Steele change his mind? "President Brigham Young, [and Apostles] Richards, Kimball, [Ezra Taft] Benson and others . . . preached faith into us for we were all mad," Steele wrote, noting that "it was preached from the stand that this was the Command of the Lord then the Breathern began to take Courage." The leaders "said it would all be overruled for the best, and the only thing left for was us to furnish 500 men and march against the Mexicans, and they would try what could be done to have us get the country of California for fighting for it, and also get us discharged with our guns and accoutrements."[13]

Allen, anxious to fill the Battalion—it meant a promotion for him—allowed men to bring not just their wives as laundresses (Jefferson Hunt brought two wives) but also children and hangers-on, presenting problems others would have to solve.[14]

Upon enlistment, Steele wrote, "the captain told me to go and bring My family down so that I gladly Consented."[15] Catherine became one of the Company D laundresses; the others included Ruth Markham Abbott, who would be midwife for Catherine's next baby. Five-year-old Mary Steele was one of forty-four children.[16]

Steele's company commander was Capt. Nelson Higgins, "a fine sort of a man,"[17] Steele wrote. He knew George P. Dykes, for Dykes had been captain of his third ten traveling group.[18] Dykes became company adjutant ("responsible for all correspondence, muster rolls, official orders, and returns; and also special assistant to the commander"[19]).

Probably John's enlistment jogged him to start a journal. He used a small, leather-covered blank book and wrote his name and something now illegible on the cover. Inside and upside down in blue ink he announced, "Care of Thomas Bullock Austin P Office | Huntsuchars Ferry Atchison Co Missouri | Via Boston & Halifax | Royal Mail."[20] Presumably he wrote Bullock's contact information so if his journal were lost, there would be a reliable place to send it; Bullock was later John's financial agent.[21]

After twelve pages of autobiography Steele began daily entries in blue ink on July 10, 1846, but may have back-filled these earliest entries. Like many diarists, he seemed to run down after two very full postings,[22] but when things became interesting, his record could get lively and is still treasured by historians for its candor and quotability.

The day after enlistment Colonel Allen marched his new battalion to Peter A. Sarpy's trading post to get supplies, much of it on credit: "blankets, provisions, kettles, knives, forks, plates, spoons, and other standard army equipment," though no weapons or tents.[23] Steele found himself lying "down on the cold ground one blanket under and one over us, and then I felt as though it was hard fare." This was tough for "those that was used to ly on good Beads."[24]

According to his cousin and fellow apostle Willard Richards, after the fifth and last company was filled, Brigham Young "prophesied that every man will return alive if they will go in the name of the Lord & pray every morning & evening in every tent." Young revealed that the Mormon destination was the Great Basin, then considered "Upper California."[25] (He had previously given general or misleading statements to prevent preemption.)

On their march to Fort Leavenworth, Kansas—or "Fort Elevenworth" to Sgt. Elijah Elmer[26]—they stopped to get liquor. Steele was censorious—"Some of the men were so bad for it that the pulled it out of the hands of the owner and drank."[27] But he and his "mess" shared a pint "that refreshed us after." He blamed his subsequent cramps on cold water.[28]

John was impressed with the country, finding "beautifull lands well adepted for Cultivation" (July 25, 1846), where "the potatoes oats Hemp & Tobacco Growes a plenty" (July 26), and "the Country is w[e]ll cultivated in some places and Green corn a plenty" (July 27).[29]

Despite Young's command to conduct themselves well, the rich farms were enticing.[30] "The farmers along the rout[e] thought we were a rough sett," Abner Blackburn recalled. "Chickens, ducks, pigs, and all kinds of vegetables suffered without price. Some of those fellows would steal anny thing. One set of thieves carried [off] several bee hives while the o[w]ners were at dinner."[31]

They were in Fort Leavenworth only briefly, practicing maneuvers and getting supplies. "When I drew our tent and camp equipage for the mess I got another tent which I used for my family," John wrote.[32] The white A-frame (or wedge) tents could house six; in comparison to their messmates, John, Catherine, and Mary must have luxuriated in such ample quarters. (Two young men at Fort Leavenworth, spying the Mormons with their handsome canvas shelters, enlisted because of "a desire to live in one of the little white tents."[33])

Hot weather, maybe combined with swimming in the Missouri River on August 3rd, brought back "the Chills & Fever very bad" on August 4th, which continued to afflict John. When Apostles Hyde and Taylor arrived to haul back whatever money they could get from Battalion members to help their stranded Iowa comrades, Steele drew his $42 clothing allowance, sent $6 to Lewis Zabriskie, who was caring for his affairs, $4 to the poor, and loaned his captain, Nelson Higgins, $10.[34] He was paid $10.60 in October and again contributed to the Kingdom, sending $8 to Heber C. Kimball.[35]

The next important destination was Santa Fe, and Steele traveled like an intelligent and curious tourist, recording weather and other natural as well as manmade details of interest. A great storm found him standing inside his tent to prevent its collapse while the rain "filled My Boots and the Hail Stones Come so hard that I was almost ready to give it up." When it was safe to go outside, the soldiers found all but five of the tents flat and many wagon covers blown off. "[T]hey began to Chear"—maybe relieved that no one was hurt, though Melissa Coray was in a wagon "Blown into a revene [ravine]."[36] The storm was taken as a divine rebuke; the next day was something of a religious revival.[37]

Several times John found ancient Indigenous sites, which he explored with fascination—he went two miles out of his way to visit one—and he identified them as "Antiquities of [the Book of Mormon] Nephites." He attributed walls, fortifications, and even a stone axe to the same origin: they "Most Certainly had been Used by the old [Nephite] settlars."[38]

When they ran out of wood, Steele recalled, "our cooking must be done with buffalo chips, and it would do a person good to see the men when they began to draw close to camp, draw their ramrods, not to ram home cartridges but to stick it through the largest chip they could find and string them on as long as one could be put on there like as many pancakes." Despite European mores, "many times the cakes were laid on the burning chips to finish baking."[39]

After Captain Allen began ailing, he was left behind, and when he died, the more inflexible Lt. A. J. Smith replaced him. Smith, slowed down by the sick, directed Capt. Nelson Higgins (head of Steele's company) and

Quartermaster Sebert Shelton to take the sick and some families to winter at Pueblo, Colorado.[40]

When Lieutenant Smith split the Battalion again on October 3rd so he could get the majority to Santa Fe by his October 10th deadline, the remaining "sick, weak, and disabled were left also the gave out stock" to catch up as they could. Steele was angry that he was one of those left behind: "I say we, for as I had my wife and little girl along, I was to stay behind. We had the beef stock that never had looked through a bow, and I concluded I would drive the team the women rode in."[41]

The first Mexican town they reached fascinated him: he called it "Beigus" but it was Las Vegas, in present-day New Mexico. He was struck by the mud houses and flocks of sheep and goats. Eventually living in a mud house himself, he wrote, "[T]hey were made of what is called adobe or sundried brick which answer very well for a dry country. They are one story high with flat roofs mostly covered with poles and earth to a great thickness, and they go up there to sleep. At a distance it looked to us like a great brick yard ready to be burned."[42]

Here they saw Mexican women sitting atop the houses who, spying women with the Mormon Battalion, sent a man down to "invite us and our Ladies to Com[e] to se[e] them." Steele and Catherine did so and were treated kindly, he wrote. "As soon as I saw it I made the sign of the cross on my breast. Then the old Spaniard took me by the hand as if I had been his long lost brother."[43]

After sharing whiskey, the visitors resumed their march. On October 12th Steele recorded: "at last came to the far Famed City of St Afee about 5 PM."[44] News that the city had been conquered and surrendered had reached the Battalion September 10th, and Steele happily found "The American flag was flying and all went merry as a marriage bell."[45] Gigantic red-haired Col. Alexander Doniphan—respected by the Mormons for refusing an order in Missouri to execute Joseph Smith—greeted the Mormons with a one-hundred-gun salute.[46]

Capt. Philip St. George Cooke took command in Santa Fe and was promoted to lieutenant colonel. He had orders to march the Battalion eleven hundred miles more to California, "for the much greater part," he remembered, "through an unknown wilderness without road or trail, and with a wagon train." He evaluated his prospective troops: "It was enlisted too much by families; some were too old,—some feeble, and some too young; it was embarrassed by many women; it was undisciplined; it was much worn by travelling on foot, and marching from Nauvoo, Illinois." Nor, did it appear, had they wasted their clothing allowance on clothes, for they were very ragged.[47] Steele added another concern of Cooke's: "He thought the Mormons were an ugly set as he had taken a bout with Thomas S. Williams, 'who was notoriously aggressive,' just the day before, and the impression made on him was that the Mormons were all fighters."[48]

Eighty-six men were deemed "inefficient" because of sickness and were ordered, with nearly all the women, to join the sick detachment at Pueblo.[49] Sending the women to Pueblo without their husbands didn't sit well. "There was a plan Got up to send all the Sick to ^Bents Fort^," Steele wrote (though Pueblo is seventy-four miles northeast of Bent's Fort). "But to this the Husbands ware not willing to agree and every plan was wrought by G P Dikes & others to get them to Go"[50]—George P. Dykes having earned himself a role as a self-important martinet.[51]

When Steele told Adjutant Dykes he wanted to go to Pueblo with his wife, Dykes sent him to Dr. Sanderson. Sanderson asked him if he was sick. When he said no, the doctor said he couldn't put his name down, to go see Adjutant Dykes.

"I saw there was something wrong," Steele wrote, "and so I went to all the men who had wives, and asked them to go along with me and see Col. Cooke, but I could not find a man who would go." He eventually found one: Private John Hess, but he said Hess was timid. "[W]hen we got opposite where they sold whiskey," Steele recalled, Hess "said, 'lets go in and get a glass we can face the Colonel better.'"[52] (Maybe Hess was a lover, not a fighter; he eventually fathered sixty-two children by seven wives.[53])

"You can go in and take one but I must be only sober," Steele answered, apparently well acquainted with his own temper.[54] (Historian Hamilton Gardner described Steele as being "unctuous" when he claimed the need for sobriety.[55])

Steele reported, "John Hess & I went to Lieutenant Colnol Cook ^who asumed the Command of-the Battalion^." He said he got three denials before making headway; in his autobiography he gave more details, or embellishments, making himself the hero. (Hess's autobiographical account naturally revealed that he played the central role.)[56]

"We went and found him in a long low cellar in company of about 30 officers," Steele remembered. "I asked which of the gentleman there

John W. Hess. *Findagrave.com.*

is Col. Cooke. Then there arose a man from the further side of the table, measuring about 6 ft. and 4 inches," which, given Steele was at most five feet, six inches, meant he was looking at a giant. "I told him I had understood he had issued orders for all the sick men and all the women to go back to Bents Fort." Cooke said he had. "I told him I had my wife there and would like the privilege of either having my wife go on to California with me or going back to Bents Fort with her."

When Cooke said he would have liked to have his wife along too, Steele thought, "He spoke very saucy." Steele claimed to have responded in like. "I told him very likely his wife was in Washington or some other good seaport among her friends, while mine was in Santa Fe among her enemies, and to have her left there with only a guard of sick men, I would not stand it, and the more I talked the more angry I got until at last I could have thrashed the ground with him."[57]

Both Hess and Steele agree that the reference to Cooke's wife—Steele didn't think he really had one—seemed a turning point. There may have been a reason: in 1838, while stationed at Fort Gibson on the Iowa frontier, Cooke accidently shot his wife Rachel in the jaw. The bullet passed through her lower lip, taking out half her teeth.[58]

"Colonel Cooke, seeing that things were becoming serious, said he would go and see General Doniphan," Steele recalled, but maybe Cooke was more touched by references to unprotected wives than Steele's self-professed tantrum. The two men were still huffing at each other like roosters with their feathers fluffed. Steele said he'd go too, and Steele remembered that Cooke "walked as fast as his long legs could carry him, but I kept alongside of him and the faster he walked the faster I walked. It made him very angry because I wouldn't fall behind so I stopped outside when he got to General Doniphan's door."

Cooke and Doniphan "had a small consultation," Steele remembered, "and in a few minutes Col. Cooke came out, looking altogether another man, and asked me very politely to call his orderly, who was Mr. [William] Muir," and, Steele added, because it mattered to him, "a Scotchman." He continued, "I did so and the Colonel told him to go tell the adjutant to stop making out the returns, and come down to him immediately. Then I knew I had gained my point."

The men reconciled, according to Steele, who wrote "the Colonel was very anxious that I should go with him into California."

"I then returned to John Hess and told him I would now take a drink with him, and so we came back to camp, and orders were issued that every man who had a wife there had the privilege to go to Bents Fort," Steele recalled. "Thus I fought the battle alone and gained the victory for twenty men and their wives who otherwise would have been separated, perhaps for years, perhaps for life."[59]

Military historian Hamilton Gardner discredited Steele's story because Cooke's "entire military record of fifty years shows no instance of his indulging in an unseemly quarrel with one of his enlisted men, no matter how rude or undisciplined the latter proved."[60] Historian Sherman Fleek, who has written an invaluable, foundational book about the Mormon Battalion, concluded, "Cooke would never have allowed such a scene to occur" and adds, "Doniphan was reasonable when it came to such situations; Cooke was not and most likely would have arrested both Steele and Hess."[61]

Given the contemporaneity of Steele's initial record, the consistencies of two other versions he wrote, and the vivid details in his autobiography,

Steele was likely correct in his general account but heroized his role and, as Gardner and Fleek hint, may have exaggerated his pugnaciousness. Interestingly, though not dispositive, Philip St. George Cooke's biographer Otis E. Young studied both the Hess and Steele accounts and generally accepted Steele's version, but "There is some question as to how the interview terminated."[62]

Cooke's report explained his rationale was to send "a sufficient number of able-bodied men (husbands of the women) to take care" of the laundresses he was exiling to Pueblo.[63] That is consistent with Steele's and Hess's concerns.

Cooke also managed to rid himself of another troublesome Mormon captain when he assigned James Brown of Company G to lead this group. Steele remembered, "Captain Brown selected me and sergeant David Wilkin (although I was only a private) to go and select cattle from the herd to draw our baggage wagons." Steele had been a teamster since shortly after leaving Nauvoo, and "being well acquainted with the stock, soon selected out 7 yoke for each wagon and seven yoke of beauties for the team I was to drive, as I was to take as many of the sisters as could be stowed in one wagon. There were several changes made here."[64]

He may have indeed taken the best stock to Pueblo, for Cooke complained that half the mules he had left "were utterly unfit to commence an ordinary march," and the oxen not much better; "I was obliged to exchange them two for one."[65] But even Steele, in his ballad "Trip to Pueblo," described the Pueblo-bound teams as "brok[e] down."[66]

Two of Steele's oxen were stolen on the Pecos River, and when the group began running out of supplies and were down to a quarter pound of flour a day, they killed some of the animals. "I had a poor old ox that laid in a mud hole all night and in the morning was not fit to travel, so I held him up while one of the boys shot him, and he was tough. I had the toothache all the way for a month," Steele recalled.[67]

On Friday, November 6th, they found fourteen yoke of cattle and one mule at Willow Springs that had been left behind by some men taking supplies to the army in Santa Fe. When the owners of these animals came back, Captain Brown let them take some but requisitioned the rest for Pueblo. There, Steele complained, Brown "took 4 Yoke of them and the rest ware devided among the Favourits of the captain and Many other Kettle & mules ware picket up & Kept [by] Alexander Brown the Capta[i]n son."

Young Brown "picked up one that Had U. S on it He swaped it off for a spanish poney and many other such tricks ware played."[68]

*

"Puebelo is situated on the Arkansass River 75 miles up the River from Bent's Fort, and 20 miles from the mountains, six days ride to Touse [Taos] over the mountains and in a Cotton Wood Grove," wrote James Glines, John Steele, and William Walker to Heber C. Kimball after they got there. It didn't rain and there was little snow, yet "The grass is from 4 to 8 inches long & has the substance of Grain[.] Cattle & Horses get fat here through the winter season." They also noted, "This is a good Game country Deer and Antelope are pleanty. Ther[e] are a few Spanyards here & also deleware Indians there is also a trading house kept by an American there are also a few other Americans here."[69]

Historian Francis Parkman, in Pueblo weeks before Steele, described "the little valley" where "Tall woods lined the river."[70] One of the first things John's detachment did was take axes to those tall woods.[71] By "Friday 20 [November 1846] got our Houses Built and by Thursday[72] the ^24^ we ware all into our Houses and felt some what comfortable."[73]

Steele's journal is somewhat sketchy after that, with no entries after November 24th until "nothing of any Consequience took place to Monday 21" of December.[74] But "nothing of any Consequience" isn't what he told federal pension authorities later. He may have neglected his journal because, as Lyman Stevens and Orson B. Adams attested, on November 24th, "While assisting in the erection of Barracks at Pueblo a large [house] log was let go upon him while standing in a strain or twist," causing an injury to his lower back, loins, and kidneys. Dr. James Affleck later testified four ribs on Steele's right side were dislocated.[75] Dr. William McIntyre treated him, but as Dr. Frederick Clift later reported, "For some 6 weeks after the accident at Pueblo he says that he passed great quantities of blood with real pain—That condition ^gradually^ improved, but he has never been able to pass water freely since."[76]

It seems certain Steele exaggerated his disabilities when he applied for a federal pension many years later. He recollected, "I was confined in bed about six (6) months," but Higgins remembered the injury "Prevented him from doing duty for several months."[77] The only physical activity Steele

James Brown. *Utah Historical Society.*

mentions in his erratically kept journal from November 24th through May 24th is parading a few times, so his claim of having been bedridden for six months is obviously overstated.

Meanwhile, Catherine was pregnant again, and the first few months must have been trying for her because it appears that not only was her husband laid up for a time, but Pueblo leaders were particularly demoralizing and sometimes contemptuous of women.

Captain Brown, an intelligent man who could dance around a campfire singing the old ballad "Pretty Betty Martin" and then skillfully kick in the fire at the denouement, was not remembered in Pueblo as an entertainer.[78] Colonel Cooke's ridding himself of Brown made that man front and center of Steele's life all winter, spring, and summer of 1847. Steele felt so aggrieved about Brown that he wrote to Heber C. Kimball complaining that "the captain has lost all reason and sence if a man contrad[i]cts what he says he calls him a ^God^ damned Liar and threatings to put Him under Guard and what he says is Law whether Justice or not." Brown forbade James Glines from teaching dancing and manners, and outlawed playing cards. "Here on Earth our soul is Vexed dayly becaus[e] our officers the are worse than any Gentiles."[79]

For the next five months this group of around 275, sharing a religious bond but afflicted with tactless officers and endless boredom, and trapped in a Colorado winter, did all they could to annoy and depress each other. Military leaders like Brown wanted soldierly obedience; religion-drenched soldiers like Steele wanted moral inspiration that Brown couldn't provide; and there was continual bickering if not outright mutiny.

On Christmas Eve, 1846, the camp was joined by Thomas Woolsey and John H. Tippets with dispatches for Council Bluffs. When they asked Brown if two of his men could go with them, he refused. Steele was privy to the consequent desertion of William Casto and Jackson Shupe to accompany Woolsey and Tippets. Steele blamed "Tale tellers and tattlers Back Biters"[80] for alerting Brown about the missing men, and Brown paraded and browbeat the soldiers about the deserters and threatened to have Casto and Shupe shot. Steele and Glines quoted Brown as saying, "I know there is men Here that Knows the have diserted and If the do not come out and confess they shall share the same fate If they are Found out."[81] (Steele was one of those men.) The deserters were tracked down, but instead of being shot, each one had to haul five loads of wood as punishment. Brown wanted to complete a meeting house, but Steele said that when "the boys" found out he intended to also use it as a guardhouse, "there was only 3 or 4 turned out and so it was never built."[82]

Brown's speeches didn't help: they were full of hectoring ("Captain Brown is something above all the men that is Here in priestly authority & he has told us often that we do not Know who he is he is so High"), placating ("He soft soaped as Much as he was able"), and laying down unenforceable rules (forbidding cardplaying and dancing).[83] It didn't help when Brown verbally attacked the women, and since Steele wrote about this, one suspects his wife Catherine was among those insulted.

Steele wrote, "[A]ny Soldier or Landress that Should be found Speaking against an ^o^ffiser should be put under guard & if a woman she should be dis Charged." He recalled that Brown set a curfew and threatened violators with the guardhouse and an immediate court martial.[84]

Another touchy issue with the women was the open practice of "Spiritual wifery," or polygamy.[85] Steele and many others had taken oaths of secrecy, and he was appalled at the indiscretions in Pueblo: "the whole

Scistom of the Spirritual Wife Doctrine is unfolded it is now no longer a secret and Six or Eight jentiles there from Missoury the know all about it now and for oughts I Know all other Mistreys are revealed." He also reported the rumor that recently widowed Martha Jane Sargent Sharp had married Captain Brown, and the officers sermonized that only "Men that stands high in athority Can Save them= This for fear the Soldiers would try to practise on the example Set by their Commander."[86]

Some of the privates turned to writing poetry. John's friend George Deliverance Wilson, having arrived in Pueblo on January 15, 1847, with a big enough grudge against his captain to build a bridge back to Santa Fe, made his poetry personal. That drew more ire, and Captain Higgins's response lost him Steele's earlier regard: "Captain higgans oponed the Me[e]ting by speaking about some poetry that has been soposed to be written by one of Liewtennant W Willis'es Company Containing some slurrs as they say[.] I did not se[e] the Writing My self But as W W Willis says it was a perfect Master piece But Captain Higgans says it was not." After haranguing the men and calling Wilson, the supposed writer of the anonymous verses, "a ^DmD^ rascal," the men were dismissed.[87] (Someone had made sure to drop copies of the offending verses near the officers' quarters.[88]) Wilson's verses included one apparently aimed at Captain Brown: "Old Blaso he would quickly be / Ass wiper in eternity."[89]

John's surviving verses were sometimes witty, but too often unreadable doggerel and feeble compared to Wilson's bite.[90]

The colony celebrated marriages and births, and mourned a few more deaths but was generally healthy. When mountain man John Albert rode into Pueblo on January 25th with news of American deaths during the Taos revolt, the men had something to think about besides their squabbling.[91] Steele had neglected his journal for a few days, but this news brought him back to it. Word of a battle and exaggerated accounts of casualties got everyone's attention.[92]

Brown prepared for an attack, putting out pickets while families prepared to flee, but the result was anticlimactic. A large "force" supposedly approaching the Pueblo camp turned out to be only a herd of elk. People especially laughed at Captain Higgins's trembling voice at the height of the scare; he "furnished fun for days to come," wrote William Kartchner.[93] Steele celebrated in poetry, hitting the mark a little better than usual with "That night we all paraded ware, / to hear the dismal news, / and Captain B-n himself was ther[e] / and to us he gave his views." Brown, assuring the men the "Spaniards will be here," got all in readiness while everyone was "throw^n^ in to a fright," but when the foe turned out to be elk, "an other with my self that night / went to Know how the [pickets] Felt / prepareing the ware with all their might / to Meet that herd of Elk."[94]

When Brown and Higgins tried to make amends to the soldiers, the reception, according to Steele, was tepid: "Captain Higgans purraded the men and mad[e] a bungland [bungling] speach saying that we ought to be kind and have a forgiving spirrit and wanted us to pray for them and out of a Hundred & thirty Men six or Eight seid the would." Brown claimed that "he would Confess his Sins before the Boys and partly Confessed & tryied to smo[o]th it over and asked the Boys if the would for give him if he had done them any harm and promised to do better for th[e] time to Come." This was short-lived: "next morning the Tromendious Oaths that came from his mouth was Horible & his Common word is God dam their Souls to Hell = But I will have their God damned Throats Cut Just as if we ware as many Megars [*sic*, Negroes] in the south."[95] (Steele would have been aware of the horrors of slavery from his time in St. Louis.)

On his birthday Steele's journal entry was succinct: "This day Twenty Six years ago at four oclock on a Wednesday morning I was Ushered into this wourld And Since that time I have passed through Many Trials both by Sea & Land."[96]

It must have been a great relief to Brown and Higgins when they all decamped, though unsure if they were going to Council Bluffs or Great Salt Lake Valley. One imagines Catherine was hoping they would reach their destination by her August due date.

*

While the Pueblo evacuees were heading through what is now Colorado, Brigham Young and his vanguard reached Fort Laramie and ran into a party of the "Mississippi Saints" who had also wintered in Pueblo. One of them told Young of the dissensions in the Pueblo ranks and quarreling over where they were to go. Young sent Apostle Amasa M. Lyman with a letter and instructions to correct things. Steele recorded that Friday, June 11th, "there was a cry made that Wolsy & Tippets was come with

Amas A Lymon I went with all Speed & found it so."[97] John Hess was so happy to see Lyman, he "kissed him for joy."[98]

The following Sunday, Lyman, a gifted preacher, lectured and Steele seemed satisfied with the results, including the mild chastisements: "said to leave off our Card playing & profain Swearing and return to God and a grait many other things he Said we ware not as bad as he expected to find us." Then Brown "got up and made an axknowledge ment & said he had just played one guame and how he had kept up publick Worsh[i]p & Preaching twice a week."[99]

Similar remarks were given by Lyman and Brown the next Sunday, June 20th, but this time Lyman didn't spare Brown: Steele recorded in his penciled diary, "Captain Brown [got?] [up?] said he was Bit pretty hard and he acknowledged his faults and determined to do better for the time to come and then went on to run down his Boys."[100] Steele found Brown's remarks personally offensive: "Said one man had the Ausemption to Contradict him in pl[a]ceing out a picket guard and Said it is not worth while to plant them on the top of an high hill after dark for the cant see and said he was not going to be counceled by any private Soldier his Councellars was offisers[.] I am the man and I tried it and could Neither heare nor se[e]."[101]

Lyman wrote Brigham Young and the council saying that "all is well with us," and "the instructions from the council which had the effect to quell the spirit of mutiny" had worked. He claimed that good spirits were restored.[102]

All now seemed bearable; a few weeks later, on July 16th, Steele and the other soldiers celebrated the "morn that freid us from U: Sam." In his penciled journal he wrote guns were fired "to celebrate the day of our mansopation."[103]

In his memoirs, Steele wrote that when they got to Fort Bridger, "We found the old mountaineer [Jim Bridger] and in conversation he told us we could not live in Salt Lake valley for it froze every month of the year and would give us a thousand dollars for the first ear of corn raised there, but if we would give him $1000 he would take us to the best G-d-d valley ever was." Steele wasn't impressed with Bridger's language: "I spoke to Captain Brown if it was a G-d-d valley we did not want to go there. We bought buckskins and horses and traded considerable with him."[104]

Nearing the Salt Lake Valley, Lyman gave another speech to remind his followers that living without "Gentile" interference was not going to mean heaven on earth just yet. "Told us we had got out from jentile persecution and now we would be troubled with Devils in our own midst And Said that there was Some of the darkest caractures he[r]e that could be & the offisers were run upon and their orders disobeyed." Captain Brown felt compelled to speak, asking "if he had not acted as a father to us and tell how good he had been not a man spoke becaus[e] we ware told when we would get to head Quarters all would be Right He is such a Father as the Devil would be to us."[105]

And finally, "Wednes 28 [July 1847] Came 18 miles all the ^18^ Way through brush & Firs came to the Top of the Hill from whence could be seen the [Salt Lake] valey where our breathren are planting."[106] The Kingdom was already being built in their New Zion. But rather than proceed on Thursday, they "lay too all day" because some of the brethren's wagons had broken down.

5

GREAT SALT LAKE CITY

"Our men that looked natural enough when they left Council Bluffs, now looked like mountaineers, sunburned and weather beaten, mostly dressed in buckskin with fringes and porcupine quills, moccasins, Spanish saddles and spurs, Spanish bridles and jinglers at them, and long beards," John Steele recalled as he looked down at the Salt Lake Valley. "If I looked in the glass for the young man who left the Bluffs a year ago, I would not have known myself. Went away afoot, came home riding a fine horse and receiving a hearty welcome and a 'God bless you' from the Lord's ministers: was worth all we suffered."[1]

"One of the most uncommon rains fell" the day they entered the Valley, Steele wrote. "Thomas Richardson was crossing Red Butte creek and the flood came down as big as a wagon box and carried him several rods down the stream, horse and all." Because of the flash floods, "Captain Brown sent me ahead with 12 men to make good the crossings in Canyon Creek by cutting birch and tying them in bundles and laying them in the creek. I took sergeant Thomas S. Williams as one which was rather turning the tables,"[2] since Williams had been a noncommissioned officer lording it over Steele and others (although Steele had some affection for him, despite calling him "Almighty Thomas Williams").[3]

Steele rode into the Salt Lake Valley on July 30, 1847. "The President and the Twelve came out to meet us," Steele remembered. The "Boys" got a hearty welcome.[4] One of the Twelve, Apostle Wilford Woodruff, estimated the Mormon Battalion group at about 240 people with a hundred horses and mules and three hundred cattle and was grateful for the reinforcements.[5]

After the "warmest kind of handshakes," Steele wrote, fifes and a side drum accompanied the veterans as they marched to the pioneer camp at the mouth of Emigration Canyon.[6] After two or three days Steele set up his white army tent on the northeast corner of the plot laid out for a temple, near City Creek. "I went out about two miles to Spring Creek east," he recalled, and "put in some guarden saus Buck wheat & turnips."[7]

As the first company settled in, the camp was assigned garden plots and the pioneers busied themselves planting potatoes, corn, beans, peas, and buckwheat.[8] Steele was rebuilding the Kingdom, and like his comrades, he identified the Mormon hegira with the flight of the Israelites and the pilgrims fleeing England.[9]

The evening Steele's group arrived in the Valley, Brigham Young, standing on an upside-down wagon box, laid out a fantastical, antihistorical conspiracy that the Battalion was recruited by the government "to destroy us from off the face of the earth" after having already damned President Polk. But what stuck in Steele's mind was Young's confident assertion to the Battalion that "you stand as sav[i]ours to this people."[10] Steele saw that as a covenant.

There were few drones in this group. Mormons sacralized work—the muscle-straining, sweaty, hard work that did the wash; gathered and cooked the food; made the dams; dug the irrigation canals, laterals, and ditches; plowed the land; shoed the horses; clothed and shod the people—the work of building God's Kingdom. As Leonard Arrington wrote, "the Kingdom of God . . . was to be realized by a thoroughly pragmatic mastery of the forces of nature."[11] William H. Dixon, an English historian and traveler, commented that in Utah "to do any piece of work is a righteous act; to be a toiling and producing man is to be in a state of grace."[12]

John didn't make another journal entry until Monday, August 9th, when he recorded the birth of his daughter Young Elizabeth, the first Mormon birth in what became Utah.[13] The baby was named for Brigham Young and John's sister Elizabeth.

Years later Steele claimed at a pioneer celebration, "I made the first last in Utah; I made the first shoe that was made on the last; I made the first foot that went into the shoe."[14] Steele also said he "made the first pair of gaiter shoes made in Salt Lake" for Scotchman John O. Angus.[15] (Gaiters are high-topped boots or a fabric worn over the lower pant leg and shoe, ideal for bad weather and in Steele's day part of the costume of Anglican bishops and archdeacons.)

The day before Elizabeth's birth an ailing Young—he'd suffered from fever during the last part of his sojourn to Salt Lake Valley—asked for volunteers to work in the adobe yard. Steele assured Young he could lay

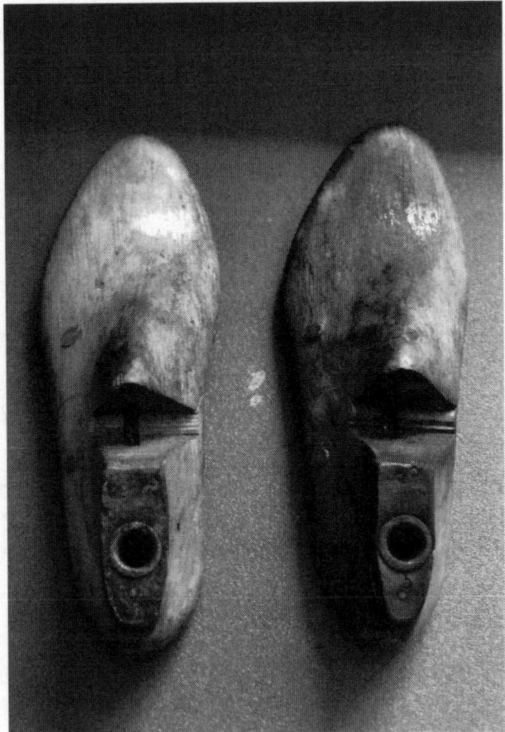

Shoe lasts. *Photo by author.*

adobes—undoubtedly emboldened by his close observation of adobe houses in New Mexico—and he became one of seventy-six volunteers.[16] He needed tools, and luckily, the ingenious blacksmith Burr Frost, inducted simultaneously with Steele into Masonry in Nauvoo,[17] made him a trowel from an old saw blade. "[T]he ingenuity of every man was taxed to the utmost," Steele remembered, and though many had no tools, "Bro. Burr Frost soon supplied us from his forge."[18]

Steele joined his companions in building homes into a three-foot-thick wall fortress, about seven feet high. He reminisced that he believed he built "about one half [of the Old Fort] with my own hands." He also claimed, "I built the first chimney that ever drew smoke, for Pres. Young." The fort was finished September 1st, and the next day "all hands moved down to the inside of the Stockade."[19]

The last Mormon conference of the year was held August 22, 1847, in preparation for the Twelve and many of the Battalion members to travel back to the Mormon camps in Iowa. Steele's report was succinct: "we had the Twelve to preach to us and Held Confarence the City was named the Great [Salt Lake] City of the Great bason of North America several Streams ware Named & other buisness attended to and Then ajourned for one year." Steele said Young told the remaining Battalion boys to "go to work for the wealth of the church was coming on and we would get bread stuff from them for our labour." Young also needed teams and wagons for his return trip, and John remembered that Young took seventy head of cattle.[20]

John and Catherine brought twelve pounds of flour into the Valley and started planting, even though they were expecting more pioneers with supplies. But Daniel Spencer's company came in on September 19th and didn't corral or guard their animals. Consequently, the field and the crops were devoured, including John's buckwheat, corn, and peas. Steele, expecting the social compact meant sharing, explained, "I have went time and again to ask them [those with supplies] to Sell to me, but the all refuse Saying the have not got enough for them selves." Luckily a ten-dollar cow they got when they crossed the Platte River began to give milk, but the "sarves [service] berries" they had dried before entering the Valley were soon gone.[21]

"I wrote a pettitan [petition] to the Councel for to do something for us as we knew well there ware plenty of provisions in our Camp." The petition, dated November 2, 1847, was addressed to Joseph Smith's uncle John Smith and the High Council. Steele rehearsed the sacrifices the Battalion had made to get to Salt Lake Valley, that once there they planted grain and were doing well until the first company let their cattle into the crops, "and of course devoured our means of subsistance."[22]

He didn't leave out the seventy head of cattle sent back, and argued that "to buy is altogather out of the Question and the little that can be bought the price would stare the Extortioner in the Face with astonishment 12 ½ dollars a hundr[e]d weight for corn meal and the lik[e] Ratiew [ratio]." Steele invoked Brigham Young and the implicit social contract, reminding the Council that Young had said, "none Could have come here had our Battalion not went and said he, you stand as sav[i]ours to this people." If brethren were not willing to share with their saviors, then they "are not worthy of the name of Saint or Brother and of Course no Confidence Can exist."[23]

The High Council decided to sell some wagons to help. But before that happened, James Brown returned with Battalion pay and "nocked all our arangements in the head," Steele wrote. He felt Brown's fee for getting their money was exorbitant, as was his demand they pay six cents a pound for all the U.S. beef they'd eaten since their discharge July 16th. Steele paid John Crandall five dollars for a hundred weight of meal and was so grateful, "I wish to remember [him] for good."[24]

But he felt Solomon Case was extortionate when he sold Steele cornmeal. Finally, "I was forced to the nessesity of digging Thistle Roots for a s^u^bsistance as buying is out of the Question." "[T]he only way we have to Get bread Stuff is by Exchanging Butter & milk for meal I also got from Brother Wm Brown[25] ^Dec 20^ 37 lbs of Corn for work which is the first Bread stuff I have got for work this winter I want to remember him for good for that."[26]

As time passed, "Many of the soldiers were literally starving," Steele recalled. "[O]ne poor boy, Daniel Brown and some others killed an animal and eat it. The matter was found out and he was condemned to receive ten lashes with a raw-hide, a cutting whip." After Brown was tied to a liberty pole, "John Nebeker administered the punishment when every blow brought the red."[27] Brown fled Utah for California, and John Nebeker became a "Mighty Man of Zion" to a lot of people,[28] but never to John Steele.

Steele, bitter at those who had plenty and flaunted it while sharing only with others who had plenty, surprised himself as he grew accustomed to the hardships. "It is very strange to say, but true that our stomachs were drawn to that extent that a piece of bread as large as my two fingers would satisfy me, and I can also say that I never suffered the severe pangs of hunger, and have ground all day for Solomon Case on his double hand corn grinder for 8 pounds of corn meal per day, and I have bartered some of these that I could outwork them, out jump them, or throw them down, who were fat and full of face, but they would not take me up." By February 1st he reported cold and stormy weather, which moderated and improved, but "there are a grait many of our cattle being destroyed by the Wolves or mountain Lions."[29]

Because of the stinginess of some of his coreligionists, Steele saw the irony that when Natives ran off some cattle, the "Battalion Boys" were called to the rescue. Steele named those who were stingy as well as those—like Charles C. Rich, Brigham Young's brother John, Jedediah M. Grant, and "Father" John Smith—who were generous. But "these men were not the wealthy of the church, and like ourselves were poor and as poverty sympathises with poverty, so those men sympathised with me."[30]

On "one occasion Brother Jedediah preached and told the people if they did not carry out President Young's counsel, and divide breadstuffs with the soldiers that the curse of Almighty God should rest upon them, and if grain was raised, many of them would never live to eat it." The High Council finally set prices, with wheat at five dollars a bushel, corn at four, and meat at four cents a pound. "This was very fair as many of the boys were working at $1.00 per day, but we did not find fault."

Despite the hardships, winter in the fort was enriched by socializing. "We visited out among our soldier families, but time brought us into contact with other families, both American, Scotch, and English," Steele remembered. "[A]s the Scotch are considered clannish we used to go into what is called the South Fort" to visit with several families with ties to Lanarkshire, where Glasgow is located.

By March, things began to improve. "Beef now began to be more plenty at 6 cts per pound," Steele remembered, "and Bishop Hunter was Commissary"—as Presiding Bishop, Hunter's responsibilities included the poor—"so I went to him and told him I wanted some meat. 'Well,' said he, 'what are you going to pay for it[?]' I told him I would pay money. 'Well' said he, 'that is good, you shall have some.'"

Steele bought forty-five pounds but when he got to his own door, he ran into Elijah Newman who said, "Well, me and my mess have not had anything to eat for the last three days." Steele drew out his butcher knife ("a thing that we each one carried in our belt") and split his meat in half. "From that time on I never knew what want was. God supplied me continually with something to eat."[31]

Just when things looked promising, there was another potentially existential worry. "June 4th 1848 Sunday this last week Grait Exitement prevails," John wrote. "the Crickets have come down in swarms and Eat up almost all before them and to mend the matter the frost came and cut Beans. Corn. Wheat &c and the Grait cry is to Californea." Settlers were afraid they'd starve and feared they wouldn't even have enough to get to a good seaport. A number of them left. It wasn't until July 15, 1848, that Steele felt encouraged, when new wheat came "& we then though[t] of begining to Live once more." But his seven acres of corn and other produce was cut down by crickets, early frost, and uncorralled cattle. All he got was "a mess pan of Ears of corn." He had to buy his flour for the next winter.[32]

Some did better. On August 23rd church leaders assured the still-absent

Brigham Young "our wheat harvest has far exceeded our expectations; green peas have been so plenty for a long time that we are becoming tired of them, cucumbers, squash, beets, carrots, parsnips, and greens are upon our tables . . . and no one has starved, and but few been much shortened for bread and meat."[33]

The winter of 1848–49 was easier on Steele, but it was much colder than the preceding year, likened to "a severe New England winter."[34] John hadn't raised much food, and famine was feared again. Careful inventories were made of foodstuffs.

By then the heavy hand of Young was back in the Salt Lake Valley and willing to do whatever it took to keep his people alive, including confiscation. "There is some of the meanest spirits here amoung the saints that ever graced this footstool," Young charged. Those not willing to share "maybe thankful that their Heads are not found wallowing in the snow." "They are too mean to live amoung the gentiles. The gentiles would be ashamed of them." But he was certain "the strongest side are willing to do right," and he was correct.[35]

John found a congenial occupation, for he "went to work and built houses, done the carpenter work, plastered and finished them from cellar to roof. This brought me in means sufficient to make me comfortable."[36] He had added housebuilding and contracting to his list of trades.

Steele wrote of 1848–49, "I spent my time all this Winter pretty well the Quorum ^29th^ that I belong to met in my house once a week and that gave me considerable enjoyment."[37] As he was becoming better known, and with a strong social bond to his fellow Battalion members, John was getting new opportunities. When the Nauvoo Legion was reorganized in Utah on April 27, 1849, he was appointed third lieutenant, but he had promotions ahead of him.[38] (All officers were former Battalion soldiers.)

These promotions must have been very fulfilling since his boyhood soldier drills by his father, his service in Macedonia, and the Mormon Battalion experience had convinced him and many others he had soldierly abilities. He wrote, "I received a commission from Jedediah M. Grant to raise a company of soldiers for the Nauvoo Legion, so on Saturday, April 27th, we all paraded on the public square." But "to our great disappointment Jed was elected a Brigadier General, as we expected he would have been our Captain, but we chose our own officers, so I nominated

GREAT SALT LAKE 10TH WARD –1849

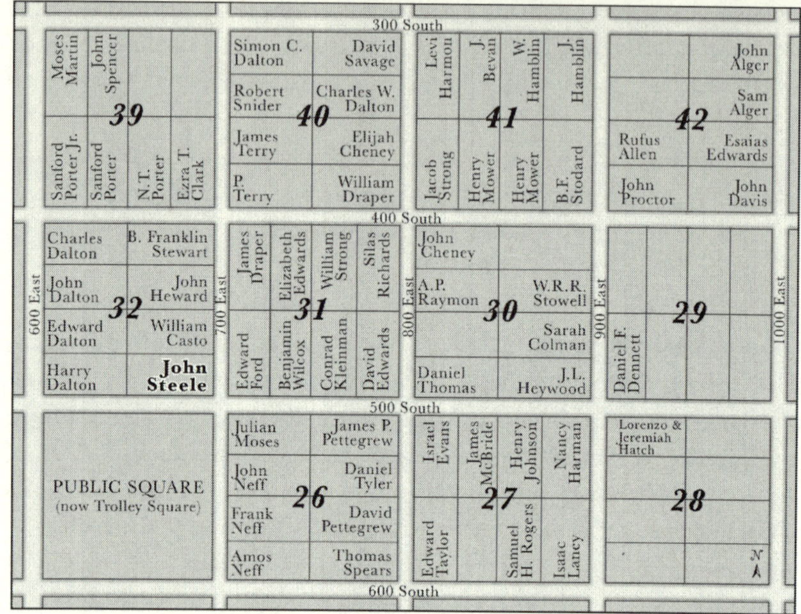

Great Salt Lake 10th Ward, 1849. *Map created by Chelsea McRaven Feeney.*

James T. S. Allred for Captain and I was First Lieutenant of a Cavalry Company."[39]

After lots were assigned, nineteen wards and bishops were set apart on February 22, 1849. (Steele had helped Henry G. Sherwood with the first city survey establishing the wards.) Battalion veteran David Pettegrew was chosen bishop of the Tenth Ward, where John lived.[40] Steele had a high opinion of Pettegrew, whose surname was a familiar one to Belfast residents,[41] and Pettegrew chose Steele as his clerk.

In the spring Steele moved onto his lot at the northwest corner of Seventh East and Seventh South and ploughed and planted wheat, built a house, and, having acquired a Spanish mare, made a two-wheeled, one-horse cart that met his needs.[42] On May 1, 1849, a son was added to his family, too: Mahonri Moriancumer,[43] named after the brother of Book of Mormon character Jared.

Steele's first record as ward clerk was May 31, 1849, regarding a civil dispute resolved by an ecclesiastical hearing. Charles Moore accused Moses

Martin of unchristian-like conduct for reneging on an agreement made in Iowa that in exchange for Moore's labor he would be supported in the valley through harvest. But after getting to Salt Lake, Martin turned him away, "homeless and destitute." Martin offered to take him back, but Moore refused. John recorded the verdict: "[I]t was then decided that Martin should devide his provisions equally with Moor[e] and give him one pr pantiloons one shirt & one vest."[44] Other cases included stealing; one motherless young man, John Brandon, was a repeat thief and ordered to be sold at public auction for twelve months.[45] In his role as ward clerk, Steele got some grounding in primitive justice, which proved helpful for his own later service as a judge, lawyer, and justice of the peace.

For Steele, "Nothing of any consequence took place I went to work poot in my wheat cropp & Maintained my self & Family pretty well," and he looked back later at this as a time when "Prosperity seemed at last to dawn permanently upon me." He felt blessed in his work, acquired horses and cattle, and "worked the day in and the day out, many times doing as much work as two men should do." By mid-September 1849 he was ready for winter.[46]

In addition to benefiting from his own sweat, communal cooperation, and irrigation, suddenly cheap goods and animals were available as well. The unexpected prosperity was because of the California Gold Rush.[47] The 1849 argonauts went through Utah by the thousands, selling goods and livestock at rock-bottom prices in their hurry. Brigham Young mocked those who jeered at Joseph Smith as a "money digger" but were giving all in hopes of California gold.[48]

But the winter of 1849–50 was challenging. "We had a very cold hard winter with much snow, and with wood very hard to be got," Steele remembered. "I went up into Millcreek canon and after wading in snow waist deep, and working so hard that my underclothes were wet with perspiration, and my outside clothes wet with snow, and on coming home I froze my feet so bad that I was laid up for six weeks." Pulling off his stockings, "the skin came also, but spring with its benevolent rays came at last, and I got to work again, getting my garden fixed up for crops as I had one of the best gardens in the country which almost kept my family."[49]

The Tenth Ward's New Year Celebration's Festival Committee for 1850 was diverse: Ulsterman and honorary Scotchman John Steele; Missouri-born Esaias Edwards, twice widowed, with his current wife on the verge of leaving him;[50] and Yankee Samuel Hollister Rogers, who claimed an ancestor in the Protestant martyr John Rogers.[51]

John luxuriated in the pomp, drawing up the program and then reciting his sixty-four-line poem on "the Murder of Joseph in Carthage Gaol." Like many folk songs, this represented the pain and anger of memory, not a historical monograph. "Dinner was then served up in good stile," Steele wrote, and named among those who prepared it his wife, "sister Steele."[52]

*

In 1849 an exploring party under command of Apostle Parley P. Pratt found iron several hundred miles south in Little Salt Lake Valley, and their excited reports to Brigham Young radically altered Steele's plans. In late 1850, Steele wrote, "The scene must now change as I was preparing to enjoy myself this coming winter, and had hauled up my winter's wood, and thought I was just going to have a good time with my old and tried friends, but alas! for man's calculations, it does not always carry out." He was "ordered out on a mission under command of Brother Geo. A. Smith to Iron County, and to sell out and go right away."[53]

The new settlement was to be where Pratt's group had unfurled their banner earlier that year—for the iron they discovered inspired Young's hopes to build a Pittsburgh in the south. The *Deseret News* called for volunteers July 27th, asking for "fifty or more good, effective men, with teams and wagons[,] provisions and clothing for one year," to leave their wives and children "for the Kingdom of Heaven's sake."[54]

But making iron was an unwanted mission. Provo Fort's president, Isaac Higbee, even after invoking the authority of Brigham Young, couldn't raise even ten men, and only a very late personal intercession of popular Apostle George A. Smith convinced Thomas Wheeler to go as a Ute interpreter.[55] After pleading failed (a later edition of the *News* taunted, "you could all go if a mob were at your heels"), a hundred men were called by name in the Bowery on October 26, 1850.[56]

Steele didn't volunteer, but his name, along with many others, was published in the *Deseret News* on November 16. It may be that his future mentor George A. Smith, the leader of the effort and a son of his friend John Smith, "volunteered" him. But even at that late date the newspaper asked for fifty more.[57]

These pioneers weren't chosen randomly. Building a Kingdom required specialized skills. The iron mission needed "1 mill wright, 5 carpenters and joiners, 2 blacksmiths, 2 shoemakers, and 1 surveyor, each with tools; 4 top and pit sawyers, with saws; 1 stone cutter, 2 masons," and numerous personal goods, such as one cow for every two people.[58] Some of the chosen didn't appreciate the opportunity, and some craftsmen weren't available. When Fillmore leader Anson Call failed to get a blacksmith, he advertised for one in the *Deseret News*.[59] But some occupations seemed incongruous, such as that of Iron County settler Benjamin R. Hulse, a ship joiner—a skill one would think not much needed in this arid valley.[60]

In preparation, Steele sold his Great Salt Lake property to his one-time teamster, Samuel I. Burgess, for $146.00 and a $225.75 due bill dated November 25, 1850.[61] He left collection in the hands of Brigham Young's secretary, Thomas Bullock, a man described by Elizabeth Cornelia Ferris as "short, round, dapper, and bustling, reminding one of a fussy, noisy little humble-bee."[62] But this humble-bee was never able to collect the debt.[63]

The Iron County mission vanguard was primarily male,[64] but Steele's wife Catherine had come far from the dress and shoe shops of Belfast and Glasgow. Despite being pregnant again, "My wife drove one wagon with one very large yoke of oxen on it, and the family and cooking tools in the wagon with stove in it. I drove the other wagon with one years fit out of flour, groceries and tools in it with three yoke of oxen and a yoke of cows on it"[65]—a far cry from his first night in the Mormon Battalion.

Steele had many friends and acquaintances among his fellow travelers, including Mormon Battalion comrades Orson B. and Susann Smith Adams, as well as Susann's stepfather, Priddy Meeks, an herbal doctor. (Meeks wrote that Orson Adams "was a good hand at almost anything he goes at." Well, except when he accidentally lopped off three fingers in a circular saw.[66]) Also part of the mission was astrologer John Sanderson, who had taught John that art; his first known horoscope was Sanderson's.[67]

The pioneers straggled south, catch-as-catch-can, but by the time they got to Provo on December 15th, many of them had rendezvoused, and George A. Smith organized the camp under the name "The Iron County Mission." He explained, "We are going to build up the Kingdom of God, prepare the way for the gathering of the Saints and establish Zion."[68]

Smith reported that on December 19th, in Peteetneet (now Payson), they "Completed the Organization of the Military of Iron County."[69] Steele recalled the specifics, writing that Smith "organised us into a Millatory force to do guard duty & be ready at a Moments warning for an Expadition against the Indians Should the Case require it." Like many trespassers, they expected and were prepared for violence. "I was appointed Liewtennant of the Light Infantry Company & pilot of my Ten," Steele wrote in his diary on December 15th, explaining that being pilot meant "I traviled in having always to go a head & break the road when our turn Came & Some times two feet of snoe to wade through."[70] Breaking a trail in summer meant avoiding all the dust for those following, yet in winter, with snow and other barriers, it was one of the toughest and most objectionable jobs, but his military assignment was a step up from third lieutenant.[71]

Smith wrote Brigham Young, "Our Military organization may appear strange to some of the Officers of the Nauvoo Legion, and in fact some of the Iron Co. Officers thought it rather odd. But it was organized to suit the needs of the Camp under our present circumstances." Maybe he was referring to a force of only 112 men being called a battalion and their surfeit of officers.[72]

The trail was already established and the company pilot was the experienced Joseph Horne, who had traveled the route with Pratt, though his most recent accomplishment was to advertise for a lost "Ladies' Boa" in the *Deseret News*.[73] He proved another excellent choice, taking the party astray only once when heavy fog obscured the route.[74]

6

PAROWAN

"This was a very snowy winter," Steele wrote. "Sometimes there was two feet of snow on our road and the pilots had to break the roads, but as I had a strong team I did not mind that."[1] He commented that on Christmas Day it was seventeen below zero and he froze his toes black.

Steele's journal is too brief to mention the social aspect of their expedition, but Henry Lunt, George A. Smith's private secretary, apparently kept his own and Smith's journals. He noted a peaceful, pleasant if cold evening Sunday, December 29th: "Camp in this snowey Desert presents quite a lively appearance, a number of Camp fires made of dry ceadar surrounded by Companies variously engaged, some listening to Violins, Accordions, Hym[n]s, relateing anecdotes Call of Guard &c. all serves to create a pleasant variety."[2]

At Corn Creek (now Hatton), Steele was probably finding journal-keeping and trail-breaking too wearing; he was succinct. "Thursday 2 [January 1851] Came 5 miles & Camped of big willow^5^."[3] Again it was the person keeping George A. Smith's journal who had time to give details: "The brethren found about ½ mile above the camp, the remains of an Indian village, they had planted about 2 acres of Corn wheat and beans, which from the stalks left on the ground, must have grown exceedingly fine, shows a very rich soil. This country is capable of sustaining a very extensive settlement."[4]

On January 13, 1851, they arrived at Little Salt Lake Valley, camping on Center Creek where just over a year earlier Apostle Parley P. Pratt and party had prematurely celebrated the founding of the town. They found a valley with sagebrush, greasewood, and rabbitbrush as well as something like bunchgrass. "We find large bodies of what our best Farmers call first rate farming land, covered with heavy coats of wire grass," Smith wrote, but some were determined to hate the country even before they got there, and "the result was many were disappointed, & almost thrown into the French Hysterics," explained company recorder John D. Lee.[5]

Steele later claimed a different reaction. As he lay face down in his tidy bed in his clean wagon, he "looked out [to the west], and had an open vision of a city there. I jumped out of the wagon and commenced preaching to the disaffected, and in a short time, I had made many converts." Astrologist John Sanderson, Dr. William Morse, and others "fell in with my views and as George A. Smith and a company of horsemen had gone on to Coal Creek to look for the right place, we were left in charge of the place, and when G. A. [Smith] came back, we were all converted that we were on the right spot."[6]

But Steele's contemporary journal does not confirm this marvelous story, and Parley P. Pratt had designated the site in 1849. Steele also didn't convince his fellow Mason. Burr Frost was oblivious to any merits Parley P. Pratt imagined in the area and hadn't weathered the trip well; a fellow pioneer, Edson Whipple, described him as a "sorry looking fellow not having shaved himself since he left home; his beard was long and his face was longer." Despite Frost's mechanical ingenuity, he was appalled at the proposed settlement site. "If any man said that he liked this country," Frost said, "if he had common sense that [*sic*, then] he was a liar; for, said he[,] it is not fit for any body to settle in, and for us to think of settling here, it was the height of folly, and he would venture to say as to iron ore there was none there."[7] (Frost's obituary noted that "He was open and fearless in his expressions."[8])

"Not one acre out of two thousand of the Territory of Utah can ever be cultivated until the mountains are leveled and the Lord sets springs in the desert," George A. Smith's father, John Smith, wrote in 1852, so finding those cultivable acres was important.[9] Steele wrote of looking for them and other necessities: "We proceeded up the [Parowan] canyon about 6 miles, where the snow was 3 ft. deep and found lots of the best kind of timber."[10] They also found gypsum and potential grindstones.[11] Steele said it took six hundred man-hours to open a road there; Smith said the road was completed—with six bridges—by January 28th.[12] Making the road was a reminder that the foreseeable future was endless work building the Kingdom. As Henry Lunt wrote, "It is a very toilsome job to break up new land, and to build new settlements."[13]

Having confirmed their location, they needed a town name. In short order they went through Cedar, then Louisa, until Brigham Young settled it by selecting Parowan.[14] (Steele's "Utah Indian Language" dictionary defines "parawanna" and "parawoona" as "a rainbow."[15])

Steele reported that they laid out the communal "Big Field" in black soil with what they misidentified as "wiregrass" (another name for Bermuda grass, which is not native to Utah). It was large enough to give every man 160 acres, but the actual acreage farmed was considerably less. As Aaron F. Farr put it, "the Brethren was too gready for Land."[16] More practical were the small garden plots just outside the fort.[17]

A long, breathless sentence from Iron County historians Morris A. Shirts and Kathryn H. Shirts beautifully captures the pioneers' energy.

> Surveying the fort site was the beginning of a sustained crescendo of activity, from building the road into the canyon, cutting and hauling timber for the council house and bastion, damming Center Creek and digging a two-mile irrigation ditch east of the fort site to erecting a blacksmith shop and making charcoal, building a sawmill in the mouth of the canyon, making and operating grindstones, raising a liberty pole, surveying farm lots, guarding the camp and stock, quarrying rock for the council house chimney and constructing a bowery and wickiup for a temporary school and meetinghouse.[18]

John saw himself building a city despite "all our foes" and the predominance of Satan,[19] redeeming God's Kingdom. "[W]e have had a fine time here lately the Spirrit of God like a fire is burning we have some of the finest meetings ^immagenable^ the people here are determined to do wright and not have them in their midst that would do wrong," John wrote, though he made allowance for six or seven bad characters who were "going to the gold diggons to worship there God unmolested."[20]

The Steeles did their part to grow the settlement. George A. Smith reported to Brigham Young on April 29th, "Since our last communication, two more children have been added to our number, and are doing well."[21] One was John and Catherine's daughter Susann Adams Steele, born the day before and named after Orson B. Adams's wife Susann. The elder Susann Adams likely served as midwife for she was "reared in the home of a doctor," her stepfather Priddy Meeks.[22]

Steele estimated he would get six bushels of wheat per acre from his first Parowan harvest but got much less: "I have raised 21 bushels of six acres Sone [some] done worse still & Some better we will make out neverthe less." Goods were so scarce by the end of 1851 he complained to Thomas Bullock: "[W]e are nearly naked all hands of us for want of Clothing and we are all day for want of some groceries & some Liquer there is no chance here to get any thing but buckskins and Uncle Sam's Laws prohibits us from trading So I sopose we may paint black & go naked." Another letter to Bullock gives Steele's pioneer shopping list, including tea, coffee, sugar, dried apples, rice, paper, cloth, thread, and pins and needles. His reminder not to forget to add "Some Alcoholl [and] send the groceries & licker" with Orson B. Adams confirms he'd abandoned his Rechabite beliefs.[23]

Steele's increasing prosperity was based on what we now call general contracting—"Hous[e] Biulding and any thing that Came handy," he explained.[24] He was also skilled at masonry and chimney construction. His contracting partner was Charles Hall, who with his brother Job was an original Parowan pioneer. Charles, like John, was a fine cabinetmaker and craftsman, his products including "barrels, tubs, chairs, tables, beds, cupboards, benches, spoons, and rolling pins. He also made adobes and brick blocks."[25]

Like the Puritans newly arrived to found Boston, craftsmen like Steele were in big demand.[26] For instance, on December 19, 1859, Steele and Hall presented a bill to the Iron County Probate Court for bridge work, and in 1860 did extensive repairs on the Council House.[27] But most of their work was probably for private individuals and doesn't show up in public records.

"I increased in property very fast," John wrote in 1854, and he valued his assets at $2,000.[28] Given general Mormon poverty, that was impressive. As late as 1858 a *New York Times* reporter, using a racist stereotype, claimed that outside Salt Lake City, "Not one woman in ten has a pair of shoes on her feet," and they were coarsely clothed while "their children [were] ragged, half naked, shockingly dirty, and rude as young Indians."[29]

City government was initiated on May 16, 1851, under Brigham Young's supervision. He began by reminding the settlers of the protocols of the Kingdom of God, where leaders were confirmed, not elected. "[S]hould we have two candidates & they have about eq[u]al votes," he asserted, "The United States would know we had apostiti^z[e]d^ from our faith & union or we were trying to deceive them."[30] Joseph Smith called this "theo-democracy," governance informally reliant on consensus, but where leaders could fire followers.[31]

Energetic but weak-willed William H. Dame was chosen as mayor, and Steele as city marshal despite being a British citizen.[32] "We have had hard worke to find Americans enough here to fill up the Elections so that rag tag & bob tale are now officers," he reported.[33]

Steele, thinking of but not eligible for the state legislature, got his citizenship in June 1852, one year to the day since he became Parowan's city marshal.[34] His naturalization gave him political rights he'd dreamed of as a Glasgow Chartist. Marshal was a minor office but gave him enforcement authority. Steele likely didn't strut around with a six-shooter on his hip—maybe he still had the butcher knife men carried in the early days in Salt Lake—and there were few drunken outlaws. But he was directed to "do his duty in effecting a union amongst the bands of horses."[35]

Parowan had an estimated five hundred head of horses and cattle in early November 1851, around the time a portion of the community left to settle Cedar City on Coal Creek, where the iron was to be manufactured. As Steele indelicately observed, they "are moving out to Coal Creek like a swarm of piss Aunts But the are poveriseing [impoverishing] paroan."[36]

Preteen boys generally cared for the common herd.[37] Steele wrote to Thomas Bullock about a Parowan herding case where things went deadly wrong and his marshal duties were needed. John Pugmire, age eleven, and Jerome Owens, twelve, were herding when Pugmire was shot and killed. Owens claimed the victim accidentally shot himself, but Steele wrote that "was proven false for several of us went to the place next morning and found that he was Shot at one place then he went 6 paces & fell then up & went 7 paces then made a square turn and went 9 paces & fell or rather sat down and fell backward." The trajectory of the bullet was down instead of up.[38]

Jerome Owens's trial was held in District Court before Judge Zerubbabel Snow in Great Salt Lake City; Steele took seven Iron County witnesses, undoubtedly in his role as city marshal. Owens was convicted on October 11, 1853, and sentenced to death.[39] Owens's frantic father, Robert, consecrated himself, his wife, his children, and all his property—carefully enumerated—"unto the lord" and sent the document to Brigham Young, who as governor had pardoning power. Jerome was pardoned, and Robert Owens found himself proselytizing in the "Hindostanee" (India) mission. Four years later Steele was still trying to get his witnesses reimbursed by the legislature.[40]

Much to Young's disgust, around thirty Parowan men wanted to go back to Great Salt Lake City in the fall of 1851, temporarily or permanently. According to Wilford Woodruff, Young lacerated them: "If you were now on a mission to France England or any other part of the Earth preaching the gospel you would not sit down & council to gather about going to get your families or go home untill your mission was ended." He added pointedly, "If my House, fields, flocks, wife or children die in my absence I say Amen to it."[41]

The stalwart suffered after the desertions, Steele complaining that "as soon as they could conveniently work up an excuse to get away they did it," eventually "leaving only 25 men out of a company of 113 to carry on the large enterprise," including finishing the fencing and irrigating the fields of their absconding compatriots. "This made us a great deal of trouble for those who remained," Steele wrote, "and as those who deserted were the most wealthy, the burden was now on the poorer portions of the camp."[42]

Maybe because of less competition, Steele began advancing in the military. The Territorial Militia records show that on August 4, 1851, he was a first lieutenant with impressive armaments: he had a horse with rigging, a rifle, a horse pistol, a sword, and a thousand rounds of ammunition. Steele got promoted November 5, 1851, to captain of Company B of the Mounted Rifles of the Nauvoo Legion. The muster roll reported he now had five thousand rounds of ammunition.[43]

The Iron Battalion mustered for Brigham Young in May 1852, after which Young held a meeting at the Cedar City Council House and organized Parowan Stake.[44] He selected as stake president an angular Yankee schoolmaster, John Calvin Lazelle Smith, known as J. C. L. or Calvin. John Steele became First Counselor, the second most powerful position in the county, with the calmer Henry Lunt named Second Counselor.

Steele was ordained by Apostle Orson Pratt, who at the same time "sealed" Steele to his wife Catherine. As that sealing originally happened in the Nauvoo Temple in 1846, this may be Steele's coded way of saying they were given their "Second Anointings," a privilege for the highest-ranking tried and proven members.[45]

Calvin Smith (unrelated to the Joseph Smith family) was in poor health, but he was described by his brother-in-law Joseph Fish as an enterprising man beloved by his people.[46] Yet only the most committed stayed in Parowan through the first year, and Calvin treated dissidence with fervor.

"Under his reign murder throve," claimed an embittered John D. Lee later, after being sentenced to death and blaming Brigham Young. Lee stated the same principles prevailed under Calvin Smith's successor.[47]

John Steele laid out his role in a revealing letter to townsman-turned-missionary James A. Little, Brigham Young's literary nephew: "This is truly the great thrashing-floor; you are the reapers in the field; we are the thrashers; the Perpetual Emigrating Fund is the means of bringing the sheaves into the garner." The flail, he wrote, is "the word of the Lord, as revealed to us from the authorities . . . and truly many that come here, as soon as the flail strikes them, jump off the floor, and bolt for some other country." Steele saw himself as the "thrasher," the enforcer. "Some who have stood the test for years, are tottering and moving out of their places, and others are stepping forward and filling up the ranks, so that there is not a vacancy but what is filled up," he wrote. "The day has at last come when one man leaving this work cannot militate against the progress of truth." Little was impressed enough with Steele's metaphor to publish the letter in the *Latter-Day Saints' Millennial Star* with the title "Deseret: The Lord's Thrashing-floor—Old and New 'Mormonism'—Progress of the Settlements."[48]

Steele's role as "thrasher" is murky, and most accounts report the community was unusually harmonious, though harmony was so prized by Mormons that leaders often felt compelled to claim it even when it was lacking.[49] Joel H. Johnson, a stalwart Mormon and the founder of Johnson's Fort, southwest of Parowan, wrote that "the Presidency of the Stake was constantly preaching the necessity of obeying counsel." After he was ordered to manage the community herd, Johnson wrote, "I thought I might as well be cut off from the church as not to do as they counseled," despite hating the job.[50]

Parowan's ill-mannered, hard-working, and disillusioned merchant James McGuffie remembered the early days as the equivalent of what we now call a police state. The town was very isolated, and guards were picketed day and night to watch for Native intruders; they also spied the untoward activities of settlers.[51] McGuffie said the post office was guarded and mail censored—and there's independent evidence of that[52]—and only Mormons were regarded as worthy to live among them.

After County Recorder James Lewis was called on a mission to China, Steele was appointed to replace him. He had also been chosen as mayor when William Dame's term expired in June 1853, and when Calvin C. Pendleton resigned as probate judge, Brigham Young chose Steele for that position as well. It was no wonder Steele wrote, "The year 1854 was a very busy year for me."[53]

The most unusual thing about Utah probate courts was they had original jurisdiction for both civil and criminal affairs. Mormons pointed out this meant timely administration of justice when federal judges were absent or far away. Gentile critics replied that because of Church control, all criminal cases were tried by leading Church members unlikely to deviate from Church wishes. Both were right.[54]

Steele presided as judge over a controversial case involving George W. and Sarah Ann Webber Braffett, who hosted Margaret Johns[t]on, wife of Lucian Woodworth, while her husband was preparing to go to California. Margaret, feeling she'd lose her soul if she abandoned Utah, asked for a divorce and sought George Braffett's protection. While Woodworth was recruiting his teams, Margaret was recruiting Braffett. He tried to hide her when Woodworth was leaving, but the gossipy little communities of Parowan and Cedar City with their perpetual picket guards found them out. Braffett was charged with "alienating the affections of Margaret Woodworth," luring her from her husband, and adultery. His wife Sarah was "charged with aiding and abetting."[55]

The accused pled not guilty, but in keeping with Brigham Young's blood atonement preachings, the court minutes report they "Wanted to [go] to Brigham, confess, and have their heads taken off." Despite the confessions and offers of their lives, the trial went forward, revealing homely details: as the plot was falling apart, Margaret Woodworth "scraped some potato skins at the door," and Braffett, his plans collapsing around him, was "lying on a bed his head tied up because of a headache." Jesse N. Smith got a fee as defense attorney, though Braffett "declined making any defense." The jury returned a verdict of guilty against him on all charges. The next day Sarah Braffett was found not guilty. Steele, as judge, "thrashed" the culprit, but he didn't order Braffett to have his head cut off. Instead, he sentenced him to twenty years of hard labor, a fine, and trial costs. Steele got five dollars a day for serving as judge and some additional remuneration as well.[56]

Braffett's property was seized to pay the fine, but it sold below value because, as John D. Lee remembered, "the brethren would not bid much for property taken from one who had broken his covenants."[57]

John D. Lee. *Alamy stock photo.*

According to Lee, after he took Braffett to Salt Lake City and got him a pardon from Brigham Young, he came back to find some of the brethren burning with anger over his mediation. He wrote that he was jailed for violating his temple covenants, which in a normal society would be a religious, not civil, offense. Lee's account, written in his angry deathbed "Confessions," said he was tried by the priesthood and threatened with a pistol to his head. Dislike of Lee may have played a factor; he wrote, "I expected to be assassinated in the dark, but for some reason it was not done."[58]

Late the next day, Lee recorded, "I looked out of the window of the chamber where I was confined, and saw a man by the name of John Steel. He was first Counselor to the President of that Stake of Zion"—and Braffett's judge. "I called to him and asked him to secure my freedom. After stating the case to him he promised to see what could be done for me, and went off. Through his exertions I was soon released."[59]

A probably apocryphal account by Steele's grandson Mahonri "Hon" M. Steele Jr. claims Steele got Lee's release by telling Isaac C. Haight, "If anything happens to that man I'll cut your goddam[n] throat."[60]

But as Col. William M. Wall recorded, Steele and other Parowanites were often sacrificially hospitable.[61] For example, on February 6, 1854, the lookout saw a group heading toward town and judged them to be Natives. The majority were: twelve were Delaware or Wyandotte, and nine were white. At least one of the white men, an expedition photographer named Solomon Carvalho, a Sephardic Jew, was so unwashed and unkempt, with starved, sunken eyes, frostbite, and symptoms of scurvy, he was mistaken as Native too. Probably most of the rest looked much like him. They were led by the famous explorer John C. Frémont, searching for a railway route from Missouri to California.[62] The expedition was intended to deflate enthusiasm for a route favored by the South and to scout out the country in the winter. Unfortunately, the game that Fremont expected to hunt on the way was nearly nonexistent.[63]

The starving men butchered some of their animals, cutting the hides in pieces and casting lots to eat them; after the bones were used to make soup, they were burned and carried along for lunch, reported Calvin Smith to the editor of the *Deseret News*. "The entrails were shaken, and then made into soup, together with the feet and eyes; thus using up the whole mule. They stated they had traveled for forty-five days living on this kind of fair." At the end they were eating ravens, dogs, and wolves.[64]

A few days before reaching Parowan, Carvalho wrote, they'd cached their "pack saddles, bales of cloth and blankets, the travelling bags, and extra clothes of the men, my daguerreotype boxes, containing besides several valuable scientific instruments," piling brush to hide them.[65]

"Although Colonel Fremont was considered by the people an enemy to the saints," Stake President Calvin Smith wrote, "and had no money, he was kindly treated and supplied on credit while at Parowan."[66] (Frémont was the son-in-law of Missouri senator Thomas H. Benton, whom the Mormons considered a vindictive enemy.[67]) According to Steele's future son-in-law Joseph Fish, some of Frémont's men were so hungry that, on the authority of Wilson G. Nowers, they were "confined under lock and key to prevent them from eating too much at first. There were many in the party whose feet were frosted and in bad condition."[68]

Jesse N. Smith scoured the town to gather supplies for the company while the townsfolk divided up their new charges. "[M]y sister, Sarah Smith, took care of Fremont," wrote Fish. "John Steele and others took some of the party," but it was several weeks before they recovered.[69]

Militia member James H. Martineau admired Frémont—"tough as a knot"—and confirmed that other members of his party said he never favored himself. Yet he looked to Martineau "as the best, physically, of any of the party." He also wrote that Frémont "appeared very grateful to the colonists for their kindly assistance and I believe that much of his former hostility to the 'Mormons' had ceased."[70]

Carvalho identified John Steele as the mayor, and said he played an important role in Frémont's remaining trek, despite being disgruntled: "About this Time John C Freemont Came along with some 25 Or 30 Men nearly starved to death we took them in and fed them and after staying some three weeks to recruit up they went on their way Exploring towards Californ[i]a." Steele wrote, "When he left he took from Me about 20 dollars worth of Mapps that I had loaned him to Coppy from. he also determin[e]d the Latitude of Parowan to be 37° 50' 41" we fited him out and he went on his way to the West."[71]

The maps were not Steele's but county surveys of Center Creek (Parowan) and Coal Creek (Cedar City). Steele groused in an affidavit some years later that Frémont promised "to return the said surveys to me. The said John C. Fremont did not return said maps but took said maps from the County, leaving me to replace said maps and surveys at a Heavy loss—I consider the said Fremont wilfully carried away said maps for his own profit—John Steele County Recorder."[72]

Frémont was more enthused about Steele, writing an interim report of this expedition for the *National Intelligencer* that was reprinted across the country. The explorer had not decided on the third and last part of his West Coast route but had two in mind: "one directly across the *plateau*, between the 37th and 38th parallels; the other keeping to the south of the mountains and following for about two hundred miles down a valley of the *Rio Virgen*—Virgin river—thence direct to the Tejon Pass, at the head of the San Joaquin valley." Frémont wrote, "This route down the Virgin River had been examined the year before [1853] with a view to settlement this summer by a Mormon exploring party under the Command of Major Steele of Parawan, who (and others of the party) informed me that they found fertile valleys inhabited by Indians who cultivated corn and melons, and the rich ground in many places matted over with grape vines."[73]

Frémont was familiar with the Tejon passes, and "Knowing the practicability of these passes, and confiding in the report of Major Steele as to the intermediate country, I determined to take the other (between the 37th and 38th parallels)" even though the Mormons said they'd tried several times to explore that country but "all failed for want of water."[74] His intuition about the proposed route was generally right: a railroad now runs from Pueblo, Colorado, into Utah, northwest to Salt Lake City but then south toward Parowan, and turns west into Nevada, following part of Frémont's line.[75]

A few of Frémont's men stayed behind, including Jose Chavez, who had been picked up "almost naked" en route after being abandoned by some hunters. He was a hitchhiker rather than an expedition member and, according to Carvalho, "perfectly worthless."[76] Indian interpreter George W. Bean claimed that the Ute chief Walker "sent his half-brother Ammon with the Mexican Chavez with ten pack animals" to retrieve Frémont's cache. They recovered valuable supplies but afterward Chavez was shot—Bean speculated by the Utes so they could keep all the booty.[77]

Many years later James McGuffie, described by the *New York Herald* as "one of the most canny, experienced and trustworthy apostates from the Mormon Church,"[78] didn't seem trustworthy with his confusing claims about Chavez (whom he remembered as Sherman). He claimed Simeon Howd got drunk, quarreled with Chavez, and after a mock trial Chavez was murdered by William Dame's "enforcers."[79] McGuffie amplified or clarified or confused his story a month or two later. In an article published in the *New York Herald* with the headline "Brigham Young's Infamy," he claimed, "John Steel, of Tokerville, who was ordered to assassinate poor Sherman [Chavez], one of Fremont's men, in 1854, and whose body was left for wolves to eat, was called by Brigham at last spring's conference to go on a mission to Europe."[80] Steele's response to the article in a letter to his wife Catherine was "I see James McGuffie has deigned to mention my name in Connection with pres Young and others, the Devil will get all his own by & by."[81]

The most one can draw from McGuffie's accounts is that he was malignant or confused, or the reporter was, and that at least one dissident looked back on the early days of Parowan as a time when religious fanaticism may have played out murderously and believed John Steele was involved.

Steele's grandson Mahonri "Hon" M. Steele Jr. confirmed a portion of this. "Steele says that Dame had a gang of cut throats to do his bidding, who were known as 'Dame's Avenging Angles [Angels],'" Carl A. Badger wrote after talking to the younger Steele.[82] (Historian Charles "Chas" Peterson said, "I doubt if any such group as 'Dame's Avenging Angels,' existed" unless it referred more generally to members of the Nauvoo Legion—where Steele had high rank, but Dame's in-laws, the Carters, were notorious for enforcing his will.[83])

*

"Henry Lunt was sent to preside in Cedar City, and for me to remain and help Calvin in Parowan," Steele wrote of his role as First Counselor to Calvin Smith.[84] Because of Smith's poor health, that left a lot of power in Steele's hands. Lunt was of a milder disposition. His charges in Cedar City don't seem to have been frightened of him, and a newspaperman who interviewed Lunt described him as amiable.[85] But Dr. Singleton Husted, having disappointed Steele, feared for his life if Steele found out.[86]

Some of Steele's counselor activities can be tracked in Henry Lunt's journal. Steele joined Lunt and Calvin Smith visiting settlements, holding meetings, monitoring progress, speaking, and sometimes hosting brethren at his home.[87] Once, when Brigham Young's party visited, Steele's Salt Lake City surveying mentor, "Old man [Henry G.] Sherwood," preached on his way to California and apostasy.[88]

The counselors listened to complaints and tried to resolve differences and build morale. A demonstration of Sunday School scholars, Lunt wrote, "was truly an imposing sight to hear the children sing so beautifully and the good order manifested." He noted that "Bro. Calvin [Smith] and Steele were well pleased at the order and the good singing and the spirit of God which was so easily felt. Bro James A Little Bro Steele and President J. C. L. Smith preached at the mornings meeting."[89]

Calvin Smith reported a trip with Steele and Dr. Calvin Pendleton to George A. Smith. They went to nearby Elkhorn Springs, stayed with Joel H. Johnson, and preached in his house. Always aware of the need to know their strength, they recorded five families living in the fort and eight men who could bear arms.[90] Being alert was sometimes more important than sermonizing, and although leaders were always exhorting Cedar City residents to produce iron, they were too often unable to ensure the iron mongers were clothed and fed.

At the 1852 Pioneer Day celebration William Bateman and Richard Benson sang a song Steele wrote "for the Iron Mongers of Iron County."

This was probably an untitled ballad in his papers that includes the lines "And melt & work the native oar to malible or steel / Or blast & drive our Iron shafts & make the mountain reel / And dig the Coal to melt the oar ^rich treasures to unfold^ & do as we are told / For these more precious are articles than ^silver or^ fare gold." (The phrase "do as we are told" seems a very Steele touch.)[91]

In 1854 Parowan also hosted a public ball for a group of Native missionaries heading to Harmony, south of Cedar City. Scotchman Thomas D. Brown was among them and appreciated the sumptuous treatment they received. In the evening the militia paraded "under Bror Steel, agreeable to the Instructions and orders carried from Genl. Wells by us. Here the Saints attend all their meetings under arms & seem always ready." Brown was impressed. "In Parowan I have witnessed the most peace, union, order, good feeling, cleanliness, &c., I have beheld anywhere on the road. All testified good in the circle, but hinted at some peculiar spirits we should meet with ahead especially at Harmony."[92] This probably referred to the turbulent John D. Lee, whom Brown was to find unbearable with his pretentiousness, prophesying, and preening.

Steele's new position put him in closer contact with Apostle George A. Smith, who had moved to Provo but regularly visited Parowan, where his wife Zilpha and sometimes his aunt, brother, and cousins lived. For instance, Cedar City's Henry Lunt found Saturday, November 13, 1852, to be a fine day, especially when visitors included "Messrs. and Mmes." George A. Smith, John Steele, James A. Little, and William Laney. The Steeles had supper with Lunt, and then the group met in council with Smith. The next day Smith, Little, and Steele all spoke at church, and afterward George A. held a meeting to hear the dissatisfactions of the iron workers.[93]

Pastoral care for Mormons included more than worrying about what others would consider spiritual ministrations. Iron was a must if Utah was to become God's self-sufficient Kingdom, and leaders took great care to address temporal concerns. John wrote, "[W]e Met in G A Smiths upper Room and I was Scribe we had no Candle but by the blaze of pine Chipps I Wrote on the harth Stone" the articles of incorporation of the Parowan Iron Company on November 19, 1852. He and his co-incorporators—George A. Smith, Calvin Smith, and engineer James James (called "Double James")—each pledged a hundred dollars in shares. But this effort lasted less than two weeks and was replaced by the Deseret Iron Company; Steele became a shareholder. Steele, Calvin Smith, and Lunt met with the new company to figure out the best way to get stone coal to the smelting site and appointed Matthew Carruthers "to let out the Job of driving the mine of coal out to the lowest bidder." This was capitalism put to communal purposes.[94]

John Steele and "Double James" also went to Cedar City to build a small air furnace in Henry Lunt's old house to try Little Creek Canyon ore. The results were mixed. The air furnace, Lunt concluded, "was rather too small, or would have done better."[95]

Despite iron failures, religious zealotry buttressed the miners, including Pentecostal-like spiritual manifestations; sometimes they spoke in tongues. But even without glossolalia, they enjoyed spiritual uplift. James H. Martineau recorded that he and his wife were rebaptized, and "I was confirmed by John Steele, who said I should do much good, bring thousands to Zion, should go and preach to a nation I have not yet heard of." Furthermore, Steele prophesied that Martineau would "have visions and dreams, and ministering of angels, be a very mighty man, and a great leader of the armies of Israel, to be terror to evil doers: no hand, tongue, or weapon raised against me should prosper, to be meek, humble and submissive."[96]

The Stake Presidency was also responsible for doctrinal affairs. Plural marriage, or polygamy, had been secretly practiced by at least some Mormons since Joseph Smith's time, but it wasn't until August 29, 1852, that the practice was publicly acknowledged. In Parowan in the latter part of December, with the weather so abnormally cold that it took half a day for two or three men to extricate the frozen wagon wheels from the ice, the plural marriage revelation was publicly acknowledged. "Prest J. C. [Calvin] L. Smith and John Steele preached on it," recorded James H. Martineau, "and Mrs. Samuel West also spoke in favor of it, being the first woman who ever advocated the plurality of wives in Iron County. May she be forever blessed."[97]

Pioneering had many enjoyable moments, and Steele loved it when they diverted themselves with spectacles and celebrations. When he read of plans for a Mormon Battalion Ball and Supper in Great Salt Lake City in 1855, he found that no representative on the committee lived farther south than Juab County. In a letter to George A. Smith, he wrote, "we see from the news paper that there was a Festival for the Mormon Battalion Boys and all was invited ex[c]ept iron County and I sopose we live so near Heaven that we could not be Reached without a ladder." Steele and others organized their own Battalion event, and as foreman of the committee, he invited Smith, explaining there were about twenty Battalion members in the area.[98]

Apostle Smith was too busy writing Joseph Smith's history to make the celebration but sent his apologies through Calvin Smith: "Tell Bro Steele & the managers of the party that I am greatly obliged for the ticket & kind offer."[99]

Capping Steele's satisfaction in leadership must have been receiving a commission as Nauvoo Legion major from Governor Brigham Young. He was commanded to "promptly and diligently" "discharge the duties of said office by doing and performing all things thereunto belonging" and those under his command required to obey. To outrank his soldier-father must have been incredibly satisfying.[100]

Steele was at the apogee of his responsibilities, and one suspects this was one of the most fulfilling times of his life: he could lead, command, rebuke, and proclaim his vision of the emerging Utopia.

7

EXPLORATIONS AND NATIVE AMERICANS

Most of the country southwest of Parowan would have looked to a farmer from the East like a tryout for hell. It is traversed by the Hurricane Fault and crossed with deeply gouged dry washes, uncultivatable red and white sandstone hoodoos, bluff-top volcanic rivers, extinct volcanoes, blue bentonite clay that turns to glue in a rainstorm, and shiftless orange Mohave Desert sand. To the west are mountains of chocolate cliffs among ruddy sandstone. George A. Smith led the first exploration of that area just after reaching Parowan. He found plenty of land, but as B. P. Wulffenstejn noted, "it stands edgewise."[1] This was landscape that would captivate artists like Maynard Dixon, while photographers such as Ansel Adams focused on the scarred, dry landscape, and Dorothea Lange, the scarred, dry people.

In early January 1852, just weeks after Jerome Owens allegedly shot John Pugmire, twelve men led by John D. Lee set out to explore this country. In an autobiographical fragment Steele recalled his part and claimed leadership despite Lee's contemporary account. He reported himself as "acting Journalist and Chief," so maybe he felt in charge.[2]

They traveled to the Virgin River, three feet deep, thirty-three feet wide, and entrapped in low hills. Half the party was left here while Lee, Steele, and five others headed west to the California road. Lee commented that though it was February, the temperature was like May.[3] On February 3rd, Steele wrote, they passed through the present locations of Harrisburg, Washington, and St. George: "[We] Explored ^to^ the South passing up the Valley where St George now Stands took dinner Where the Temple now Stands on the 2nd of February 1852."[4] They camped at what is now the town of Santa Clara.[5]

Steele didn't mention the Native Americans on the Santa Clara Creek, but Lee, who became a warm friend of Native peoples and a skilled interpreter, did. The Paiutes had about a hundred acres under cultivation, mainly squash and corn. "This tribe is numerous, and have quite an idea of husbandry," Lee wrote.[6]

We "went up the Clara to the old trail," wrote Steele, "then through the pass and down to the Virgin River Camped by the stream." Two of the brethren became lost and took three days to get back to camp, starving. The supplies of the rest, he remembered, ran so low, they had only a biscuit each for the last three days, but they reached Beaver Dam (now in Arizona) and named the Black Ridge on their way back to Parowan. "I will here say in behalf of the company, that they to a man were highly delighted with the climate and country," Lee wrote. "The natives say that snow does not lie on the ground in these vallies."[7] The climate was to earn the area the name "Dixie," and the success of Paiute farmers on the Santa Clara was encouraging.

In August the *Deseret News* published a letter co-authored by Calvin Smith and John Steele reporting two more expeditions. The first was at the invitation of Chief Quinnarrah (Kanarra)—to "Pang-quick" (Panguitch) Lake. Smith, Steele, Lee, and others left in early June and traveled up Parowan Canyon, then descended to the lake. They found an impressive amount of timber and were welcomed by Quinnarrah and his band of about a hundred Paiutes; they traded flour and bread for fish. Quinnarrah was indignant when they wouldn't trade gunpowder, but he would have been more upset if he knew how they coveted the country. "There is a good chance for a small colony to settle there, of some 50 or 100 families, who might wish to go into the lumber trade, as this is a good country for timber," Smith and Steele reported to Brigham Young.[8]

Another expedition followed. Besides Steele, Lee, and Calvin Smith, the group included blacksmith John Dart and Dr. Priddy Meeks; they left June 12th. This time they went north to what is now Paragonah, up Little Creek Canyon—"a rough, rocky place"—to the top of Cedar Mountain, and then descended into Sevier Valley near where Panguitch is today. They were explicitly taking notes for future settlements as they headed south. "I have been the first Mormon that ever explored the head watters of the virgen and Cevere [Sevier] along with some of My Breathren," Steele remembered.[9] Four days out they found themselves in a precipitous canyon, the bluffs checked by fantastic seams. In a small cave they inscribed their names in the soft rock, including "J. C. L. Smith," and the date, June 16, 1852.[10]

June 12, 1852 Expedition

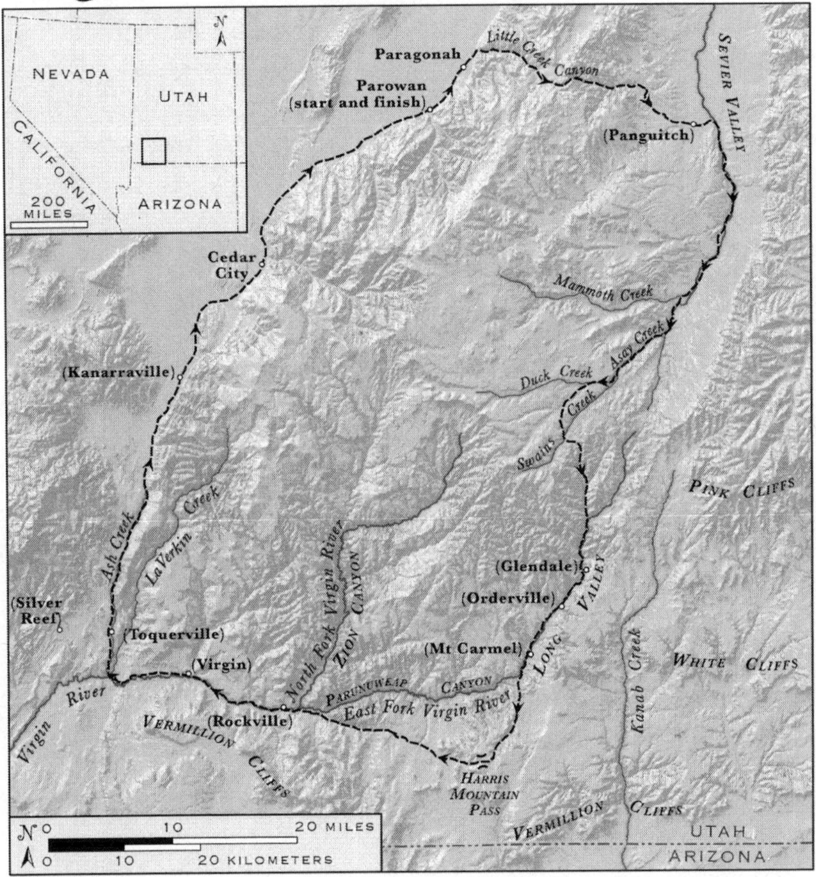

June 12, 1852, expedition circling Zion Canyon, now Zion National Park. *Map created by Chelsea McRaven Feeney.*

They then traveled to Mammoth Creek—which flows into the Sevier River—but instead of heading north, they followed it to the southwest, reaching Asay Creek, then Duck Creek, and then followed Swains Creek into the headwaters of Long Valley.[11] This valley, asserted British traveler Phil Robinson later, "rivals in beauty the scenery of Cashmere."[12]

Reaching this Utah Kashmir, they turned west and found themselves on a "perpendicular jump off clear away to the creek on the north and to the south it was no better," remembered Meeks. They thirstily looked at crystalline water in a valley far below but could find no way down. Stymied, they prayed in turn, beginning with Calvin Smith, then Steele. The prayers inspired Smith to prophesy "in the name of God that we would find water within three miles of that place." That energized the men, who took a forced march until dusk but failed to find anything. Retracing their route, about nine o'clock next morning the glare of the sun revealed a silver streak that proved to be "water issuing from the brow of the earth which sloped on the rock," Meeks wrote. "The water had not yet reached the foot of the rock which was some twenty rods below and looked like it had started to run sometime that night."[13]

They shoveled out the spring to find all the water they needed and found grass for their horses, too. But they were still stuck, so John D. Lee and John Steele left to find a way out. "They went on foot but did not get back that night and lay out in the mountains but the Lord was merciful unto them in bringing them at camp time to a basin in a rock, full of good water," Meeks wrote. "Here they fared well and thanked the Lord for it."

Meeks reported that "right here as the sun was going down in the west and tinted the tips of the mountains in the east with golden collors," Lee and Steele "stood on quite a mountain and with longing eyes and praying hearts wished to know how we could get out of that country. Inspiration seemed to burst forth as by vision. Look east see the lay of the country, that is the course to get out and it proved to be our only and best chance to get out and we had no trouble in getting out."[14]

They undertook probably the first documented circling of today's Zion National Park by following the Harris Mountain Pass and the Virgin Bottoms, and then were guided out by some Native Americans. Smith and Steele described these guides as "very smart, quick and active, almost naked, with bright intellects. We then proceeded along, followed by our new friends, who would not leave us; showed us all the curiosities they could think of, amongst the rest, a kind of weed that will quench thirst."[15]

When they reached the confluence of LaVerkin, Virgin, and Ash Creeks near Cane Beds, they were close to where Lee and Steele had visited earlier in the year. Again, they found "a number of Indians raising grain. Their corn was waist high; squashes, beans, potatoes, &c., looked well. They had in cultivation some four or five acres; their wheat had got ripe, and was cut." The explorers could see no tools and assumed all the work was done by hand. When the Paiutes talked about their destitution, Lee "told them we would learn them to work and raise breadstuff, make clothing, &c., at which they were well pleased, and wanted us to come soon and make a settlement among them."[16]

They had traveled 336 miles and found a number of places where they could settle, eventually displacing all the Native farmers, whose agricultural activities had been noted by Father Escalante in 1776 and had been going on for hundreds of years before that. Steele himself eventually took ownership of the Paiutes' Ash Creek farm.[17]

Steele studied the Paiute language, a Ute dialect that Parowan townsman George W. Brimhall said was hard to learn, "it being mixed with so many gesticulations of every conceivable position of body, arms, legs, feet, eyes and fingers." In early 1854, Calvin Smith reported, "We have day and evening schools at Parowan and Cedar City, for learning the English, Spanish, German, and Indian languages." One can imagine Steele in these classes. His daughter Elizabeth remembered, "Father learned to talk the Ute language"; how advanced he was isn't known.[18]

Robert L. Campbell wrote a brief Ute dictionary during the Parley Pratt 1849–50 expedition, and it may have influenced Steele's work. Steele's own "Utah Indian Language" was actually a Southern Paiute dictionary of 338 words, nearly a hundred more than Campbell identified. He noted that "Captain John Steele" was "Awitch Neager Ooish."[19] He doesn't give an interpretation, nor is one easily obtainable.

George Brimhall's claim that the Paiute language "consisted of about six hundred words and grunts" was disparaging and untrue, but suggests a few hundred words would go some way to understanding.[20] If so, Steele may have had the rudiments.

At first the Paiutes and their Ute cousins were friendly; an interest in learning their language couldn't hurt, nor, initially, did the high place Native peoples occupied in Mormon cosmology as descendants of Abraham, whose story was told in the Book of Mormon.

But soon the cheerful mutual curiosity became more complicated. By the summer of 1851, the first year of Parowan's settlement, George A. Smith was complaining their cattle were being eaten, they had to corral their animals, and "The indians seems quite saucy, and almost every day new faces appear among us."[21] Familiarity seems to have bred some disappointment on each side, and the colonists forgot the extent to which they were also sometimes seen as exasperating guests.

Brigham Young was committed to converting Native Americans, who, the Book of Mormon asserted, would then become "white and delightsome"—that is, European culturally and physically. Young and his followers spent enormous resources trying to turn Native peoples into nineteenth-century Mormon farmers, not appreciating that many were already accomplished agriculturalists. Some of the Natives that condescending settlers saw as restless wanderers showing up at the wrong time were actually rotating from one area to another for a livelihood. "The wrong time" for the settlers—when the pine nuts were ripe, fish were plentiful, and game accessible—was the right time for Natives engaged in hunting and gathering. Most Europeans weren't sophisticated enough to grasp the meaningfulness, success, and satisfactions of this lifestyle.

A crisis involving Parowanites and a traveling Ute band occurred in early December 1852, when the latter were more punctilious about etiquette. In late 1851 Parowan's then-leader, Zion's Camp veteran Elisha H. Groves, had provided a great feast, promising the Utes "that in twelve months, if they were good and honorable, he would give them another dinner."[22]

But when forty Utes under Green Jacket's leadership showed up late in 1852, the feast wasn't forthcoming; not only that, while Groves had invited the headmen to sit around his table, Calvin Smith offered no personal hospitality. The Utes were so offended, reported Joel H. Johnson six weeks later, "they still owe him a grudge and threaten his life."[23] Despite the lateness of the season, some of the grain in the Big Field was still in shock, so Green Jacket and his comrades turned out a hundred or so of their horses.[24]

There were few armed Mormons—Steele reported their force five months later as about thirty.[25] Despite their small numbers, the Parowanites drove out the horses—one account says they impounded them as strays—and repaired the fence. The Utes tore it down and put their horses back in the field. The Mormons then summoned the "head men" to ask what they meant by this. Steele, resolutely fearless, was a militia leader and involved. According to Joel H. Johnson, the Utes' answer was "they had a right too and the mormans wanted to fight and so did they."[26]

James Martineau wrote that the horses were kept out of the Big Field until Sunday, December 5th, and "the indians spent the night in the war-dance and yelling like devils. We spent the night in preparing for battle, running bullets, &c." The Mormons also repaired their cannon.[27]

Walkara and his brother Arapeen. *Utah Historical Society.*

But the Utes' position was compromised because their weaker (mostly horseless) cousins, the Paiutes, had allied with the Mormons as a counterweight to Ute slaving and stealing. Fifty-seven Paiutes had recently been baptized in Parowan; many members of Chief Quinnarrah's band lived outside the fort, and the Mormons hired them to herd, chore, wash, and blacksmith—building the kingdom.[28]

When the Paiutes ran into the fort to support the little band of settlers, Green Jacket and his band were outgunned and left roasting for revenge. According to Parowan folklore, smelling of campfire stories with its substitute of the fearsomely wily Chief Walkara for the lesser-known Green Jacket, the Mormon leader was "Captain John Steele." Steele is said to have parlayed unsuccessfully and then become confrontational: "See here, Walkar, you're a heap big Indian Chief, me heap big White man Chief. Now I'll fight you fist to fist, and if you win, you leave 'em in, and if I win, you take 'em out.' Then Walkar said 'Me take 'em out.' And he did."[29] That is, the Utes removed their horses from the Mormons' fields.

In any case, Green Jacket is said to have promised to keep the horses out of the field, but the Utes "watched ev[e]ry opertunity to plunder ev[e]ry deposit of vegetables and ev[e]ry threshing floor they could find," Joel H. Johnson wrote.[30]

In the folklore retelling of this confrontation, Walkara was so impressed with Steele's gumption that he later stayed with him for three days.[31] Steele's daughter Young Elizabeth Steele Stapley confirmed that Walkara came to dinner at her house "and how orderly her parents told her and her brother and sisters they must be while he was there."[32] It must have been an impressive sight, her fiery little father and Walkara, described as "tall, straight as an arrow, with features of Grecian mold rather than Indian, and a form full of gracious dignity and conscious power. His hair is slightly gray, and his eyes keen as the eagle's."[33]

William Leany, whom Steele recalled "helped many times to quell the Indians, and was never known to fail when called upon to assist in defending his brothers and friends,"[34] remembered a time when Walkara stood down. "[W]hile Indian Walker and his band had us hewed in the fort in the absence of pres. J C L smith," Leany wrote, Smith's "councilor Br. John steele put out guards all round and took a few of us into an upper room and We prayed twice and no good results and Br Steele rebuked some of them for the use of tobacco." Then James A. Little prophesied, "We could get the word of the Lord and it Must come through Br. Steele and Br steele arose and prophecied the spirit of fear would come on the Indians and they would leave in the night." He sent Little out in the morning to find the camp "desarted."[35]

Folklore gets mixed into these stories because confrontations over Native horses in Parowan fields happened more than once. Interpreter Nephi Johnson recalled another time, in May 1856, when Parowanites impounded Ute horses from a trampled grain field and "Majar John Steele," at the Utes' request, sent for Johnson to negotiate. Diplomacy and a few buckskins for compensation prevented bloodshed.[36]

Three years earlier, on April 10, 1853, Steele had written to Brigham Young about another potentially serious episode. A company of apostate Mormons from Salt Lake along with emigrants headed to California had a horse that, by its brand, appeared to be stolen. The local authorities confiscated the horse. The emigrants stayed a couple of days with Utes on Summit Creek, purchased a Paiute boy to sell to other slavers, sold and gave the Utes "rifles and a large amount of powder lead and caps. cloths &c."—and took the horse.[37]

When Lt. Col. James A. Little and his men got to Summit Creek to get the horse, they not only found the emigrants but about thirty Utes under Walkara. "[A]ll well armed and mounted, who with leveld rifles told them that they could not proceed that the Americans were good, but that the mormons were not good, ^and that Brigham Young was not good^," Steele wrote. "The boys being greatly surpassed in numbers and taking all existing matters into consideration thought proper to return to the fort."

After deliberation with church leaders and prayer, a letter was sent under Steele's name and signature (however, the extant copy in the Brigham Young letter files is not in his hand): "We are but about 30 strong in Parowan and in case of an Indian war would be obliged to extend aid and protection To our herd and the settlement at Elkhorn springs, (Johnson settlements,) Red creek settlement [Paragonah] could at best do no more than protect themselves," while Cedar City would have to look after itself and settlements further south.[38]

Young responded that he was sending some men down to talk to "Wacher" (Walkara) and hoped for an amicable resolution. It would be "better to conciliate, and make peace with the Indians." He said he planned to head south soon but advised his people to be "wise, and vigilant; forbearing and watchful" for the time being. That was wisdom in the circumstances. According to James Martineau, the stolen horse hoofed it back to Parowan.[39]

Other concerns about Natives intervened, and Young canceled his southern trip and issued a proclamation preparing for war. He sent Nauvoo Legion captain William Wall south to reconnoiter, inspect, and ensure inhabitants were on their guard. Wall found Parowan a model of "regularity, cleanliness, and good order" and recommended it as a pattern for all new Mormon settlements.[40] This, in part, reflected John Steele's leadership.

Interpreter Dimick B. Huntington told Young that Captain Wall's show of force was "the best teaching" the Natives had ever had. Apostle George A. Smith's aunt Mary seemed to agree: "we are prospering well here in this [Parowan] Colony no trouble with the Indians since the [Wall] Company came here they appear friendly bring fish now & then to trade for flour or shirts. We think them a treat."[41]

But skittishness is not subjection. The Utes, feeling cornered—with their fishing at Utah Lake disrupted by Mormon settlement, the ranges they used to run their horses reduced, the slaving which helped keep them in guns and ammunition under attack, and what must have seemed like piratical intimidation—weren't ready to submit.

The misnamed Walker War was mainly caused by Mormon efforts to outlaw Native slavery, and in the south tensions were already high. It was "not much of a war by most standards," wrote historian Howard Christy; the conflict was characterized by a series of intense skirmishes, rustling, and occasional shooting scrapes.[42] Brigham Young ordered consolidating settlements and "forting up" to protect settlers and their livestock.

Gwinn Harris Heap, passing through as a member of Indian agent E. F. Beale's expedition, agreed that Parowan was particularly appealing and made an oblique reference to John Steele's activities, noting that "parties of mounted men, well armed, patrolled the country; expresses came in from different quarters, bringing accounts of attacks by the Indians, on small parties and unprotected farms and houses."[43]

*

In what might have seemed like a sideshow to the Walker War, George A. Smith was creating havoc in Cedar City with his inflexibility. He was dissatisfied with Col. Peter W. Conover and complained to Brigham Young. Young put Smith in charge of the Southern Militia, and Smith visited every settlement, issued thirty of his own orders, and ruthlessly enforced Young's General Order no. 2, specifically: "All surplus stock that is not particularly needed for teams and milk must be driven to this city [Salt Lake] and placed in the charge of the Presiding Bishop of this city until further orders."[44] The purpose was to protect the extra stock of outlying settlements.

Though Parowan spawned Cedar City, the communities were quite different. Parowan had strains but was cohesive—and dissenters were driven out. Cedar City's residents had become impoverished trying to manufacture iron, and the hectoring by authorities had probably backfired.[45] The iron workers were discouraged, sometimes half-naked, and not always fed.[46]

"I have attended meeting this morning learned there that there is a great lack of bread stuff among the Miners [in Cedar City] a pressing Call on the Brethren here to divide with them with a great blessing annexed in case they comply Also the reverse portrayed in case of a refusal," wrote George A. Smith's aunt Mary Aikens Smith.[47] Taking "surplus" cattle to Salt Lake was resented everywhere, but only in Cedar did it provoke mutiny because unlike the agricultural communities, all the wealth the iron workers had was in their stock.[48]

Former Parowan alderman and current Nauvoo Legion major Matthew Carruthers was a Scotchman given to biblical language ("live humble, keep the commandments, and obey counsel, your souls will be like unto a well irrigated field of goodly soil"). He could proclaim that George A. Smith "will tell you words by which you may be saved," but he couldn't stomach the cattle confiscation. He shortly resigned his military command, though not until after taking part as a judge in a subsequent court martial.[49]

John D. Lee, who had been forced by the war to abandon Fort Harmony and move to Cedar, described the showdown to Brigham Young in his usual apocalyptic style and, like John Steele, wasn't above representing himself as a nearly lone self-righteous warrior for the Good Cause. He claimed to have "girded on my sword" and threatened shedding of blood of the "cursed wicked apostate ^fault finding^ wretches." He could bluster because he had James A. Little, John Steele, and their militia at his back. "Col. Little replied that he would not only back me up with his influence but his Pouder & Ball," and "Capt. Steel Said that he was on hand and the Parowan Boys to back him." The "wretches" were formidable. James H. Martineau wrote that "a large portion of the people of Cedar had rebelled," some even getting guns and threatening to shoot.[50]

"Aged men & young were put in Chains for resisting & had decapitation threatened," Thomas D. Brown was told; "was this the over officious acts of sub-alterns or how else? Well might they ask then, where can we find such cruelty oppression & tyranny?"[51]

George A. Smith tried twice before he was able to put down the rebellion. According to Martineau, "The military were camped half a mile from the settlement [of Cedar City], not feeling safe in it," and it wasn't until August 17th that Smith, "driving 280 head of surplus cattle from Parowan and Cedar," left for the north.[52]

Young got the animals but his representatives fined thirty-four men, including such stalwarts as Patriarch Elisha H. Groves, former Macedonia resident Joel H. Johnson, visionary Solomon Chamberlain, and Matthew Carruthers himself. Five men were court-martialed but community sympathy was so widespread that John D. Lee himself delivered a petition "in behalf of the prisoners."[53]

Carruthers abandoned God's Rocky Mountain Kingdom and found his Utopia as a farmer in El Cajon, California; he was replaced in the militia by John D. Lee.[54] If only Carruthers had abandoned God's Kingdom, the effect would have been slight. As John Steele said, there was a constant churn of burned-out Utopians replaced by eager new enthusiasts, but losing those in Cedar City with the courage to contest authority was to prove calamitous.

Young reacted with some patience, ostensibly upholding the leaders but quietly undercutting the punishments.[55] Yet he couldn't help taunt the dissidents: "In one of our orders issued lately, the Southern settlements were advised to send their surplus cattle to this Valley. No quicker had the news reached them, than our ears were greeted with one continued whine, which meant, 'We are afraid *you* want them.' So we did, to take care of them for you."[56]

The repercussions in the southern communities were profound. Steele spoke in the afternoon session of the September Parowan Stake Conference and like Lunt brought up the controversial General Orders. What they said can be guessed because the next day Stake President Calvin Smith took on the rebels, requesting that "all who did not feel to support the present organization of the Church not to vote for it." The vote for those authorities was unanimous, but that concealed unbridgeable rifts. John Steele, Elijah Newman, and William H. Dame followed Smith, all speaking "on the present condition of the Territory, our trials, blessings, &c and recommended those who could not stand it, to go to California or somewhere else."[57]

The disgruntled left: "the following persons gave their names for San Bernidino:- Joseph Bateman, John Gregory[,] Wm Cozens, John Smith, Wm Hewit, Wm Adshead, Wm Slack, David James, Wm Davis, Richard Varley, and Jas Bosnell; and Arthur Parks, E. Prothero and James Bullock uncertain whether to go or stay."[58] Many others followed, including John Dart, who had circumnavigated Zion with Steele and others in 1852; Dart family lore later claimed John D. Lee and John Steele planned Dart's assassination before he escaped Utah.[59]

Steele welcomed the expulsions. He told George A. Smith, "[W]e hope by next year that ma[n]y more of the same Class will turn their H[e]els to us as we do not want Whiners & Complainers & faultfinders amongst us defusing their Baneful influance among those who would otherwise do good."[60] A mass excommunication of the California-bound rebels followed.[61]

A year later Thomas D. Brown visited several who had stayed in Cedar, including Robert Wylie, Commodore Perry Liston, Samuel Pollock, and Samuel H. Rogers. "[A]ll seem still to remember their cattle, cows &c. during late Indians difficulties—[taken] against their will," he wrote, "more than the 'Surplus cattle' were sent north without their consent, and up to this time most of those cattle have never been returned nor their value," which was estimated as $12,000.[62]

*

The so-called Walker War had waned by fall. On November 24, 1853, Ammon visited Parowan on behalf of his brother Walkara to make peace. Steele must have been one of those consulted. According to Calvin Smith, the negotiations went well enough that Ammon and around two dozen others spent the winter in Parowan, at first bluffing the settlers for support but ending up trading buckskins and working for bread.[63] Except for a formal renunciation of war, peace was nearly at hand.

William C. McGregor, fearless enough to lead a successful rejection of Brigham Young's nominee Jesse N. Smith to preside over Parowan, recalled at the town's 1897 anniversary that "In early days Brother John Steele was the military leader of this place and led his minute company against the Indians whenever they were making raids against the settlers or against their stock." He also asserted that "we had such faith in our leader, that had Captain Steele given the command we would have fought all the Indians in the United States had it been possible."[64] We can pardon the hyperbole and honor the sentiment.

"About this tim[e]," Steele wrote with understated accuracy, "I had My hands so full that I Could not tell what to do first Indian troubles[,] troubles settling home Matters which are generally plenty in all new settlements."[65] He summarized those "Indian troubles": "I headed several expeditions against the Indians, always returning successful and the Indians considered I held a charmed life, as they had several shots at me and could not hit me. We had hard work to keep them quiet. They would steal and beg all we had if we would let them."[66] It seems he was oblivious to the roles he and his people had played as thieves and beggars.

8

LAS VEGAS

Ecstatic Pentecostal manifestations of the "Holy Spirit," speaking in tongues, and prophecies followed John Steele's removal from Parowan Stake leadership; townspeople weren't celebrating his leaving, but his and fellow townsman William C. Mitchell's mission call. He was set apart by Apostle George A. Smith to "lift thy voice even unto the wild Men of the wilderness." Acknowledging "the integrity of thy hart," Smith, who knew Steele better than his fellow apostles and was maybe thinking of Steele's volatility, promised "thou shalt be blessed in thy forbarence & long suffering" and concluded by sealing blessings in the name of Jesus Christ.[1]

The purpose of the mission, Steele wrote, was to build a fort between the Mormon settlement of San Bernardino, California, and southwestern Utah and to "make friends with the Indians."[2] He hurriedly planted his crops with trepidation because by late May the harvest was insect-infested. George A. Smith wrote that the grasshoppers "are far more numerous than the contending armies in the Crimea." Farmers planted potatoes as a backup, and gunsmith and doctor Calvin C. Pendleton expressed the hope "that the united efforts of men, women, and children, chickens, ducks, turkies, &c., &c., may save a sufficiency to have occasionally a little potato soup next winter."[3]

Many of Steele's fellow missionaries had been comrades in the Mormon Battalion, and he considered them "a first rate set of Boys."[4] A contrary view from federal Indian agent Garland Hurt, a competitor for Native goodwill, was that they were "a class of rude and lawless young men such as might be regarded as a curse to any civilized community."[5]

When they reached the Paiute band at Tonaquint (the Santa Clara), their hosts herded the missionaries' stock at night.[6] Steele did not record that the horses ate their wheat, which enraged them, and he placated them with a shirt, corn, and flour as restitution—the universal way of righting wrongs (except for Daniel Spencer's 1847 company, apparently). It was left to one-armed interpreter George W. Bean to write about that episode.[7] That evening, probably after making amends, Steele visited with the Paiute chief, who wanted some missionaries to, in his words, show "them how to work," which undoubtedly meant giving them access to new technology. They agreed they were friends, and the conversation concluded with the chief saying, "Taoy"—good.[8] (Or more likely, as Steele interpreted it in his dictionary, "Tah oy[:] enough Said it['s] a bargon."[9]) Their hosts warned them their Las Vegas destination had no timber, "and they said that the sun shou[n] down so hot that it would burn us"—the last still a good reminder for new visitors.[10]

At Las Vegas, Steele found a valley that seemed about fifty miles long and thirty miles wide, with a pleasant stream three miles above camp; "the head springs are about 25 yards long & about 10 wide boiling up most beautiful and strange to say a person Cannot sink," he wrote. On June 19th Thomas D. Brown, with Steele's help, drew the first Las Vegas map. A month later Steele wrote George A. Smith, "We have no instruments here for making surveys, and we have to do the best we can without them."[11] By October he had sent Smith two unscaled maps of the area so "you can form an Idea of the extent of our dominion."[12]

Richard Francaviglia's beautiful and useful book, *Mapmakers of New Zion*, credits Brown with teaching Steele some elements of cartography with that first Las Vegas map; Steele had also worked with Henry G. Sherwood on the Salt Lake City plat.[13] Francaviglia wrote that Steele was "a talented mapmaker" whose "informative map was also based on his keen observation of the site in the fall of 1855." The larger of the maps Steele sent Smith "is rendered very confidently, featuring heavily accented topography and bolder typography," with the Paiutes' sacred Sunrise Mountain a major landmark, as well as the Colorado River.[14]

They needed to establish boundaries because each missionary was to get a two-and-a-half-acre garden plot and five acres in the community field. Brutally thorny mesquite brush covered the land, so they cut it, placing it inside their fields with the butt ends out to keep cattle away.[15] Indefatigable Lorenzo Brown found it best to wear buckskin pants, a heavy shirt, and mittens when working with the prickly bushes.[16]

Steele didn't mention the nutritional value of this brush, but he kept a piece of Native-made mesquite seed bread. Seventy years later it was

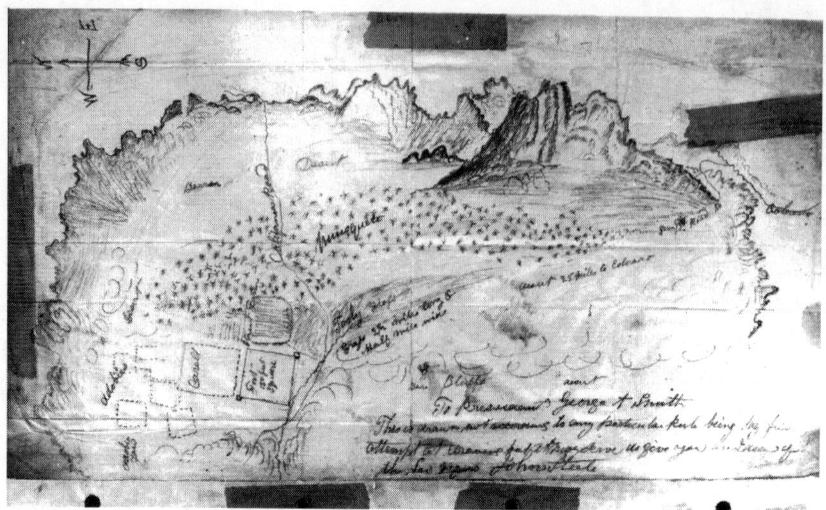

Las Vegas map by John Steele dated October 1, 1855. *LDS Church History Library.*

described by newspaperman Frank A. Beckwith as "about the size of a plump biscuit and even now retains a sweet smell rather faint. The texture of the food shows it to be of a coarse nature with large shiny flakes interspersed which I take to be the hulls of the grain whatever that grain may be. The slip of paper on it reads: Made of mesquite."[17] (Western trader Don Maguire said if you poured two gallons of sawdust over three quarts of sweetened glycerin and let it harden, you'd have the equivalent of "mescrew" bread.[18])

"We find that there are many more Lamanites in this Country than has been represented by travellers," mission president William Bringhurst wrote. "Almost Every day brings some strange Indians to see us." He said they were mostly honest and "many of them raise a little grain" despite their great poverty.[19] (The missionaries theorized the absence of lizards in the area was because the Paiutes had eaten them all.[20])

Steele saw how badly the Native people had been treated by some of the California emigrants, "as they have been shot at and drove away from the Camps of the Travelars who have been on the road for years the[y] will show us the bullet holes and marks they have received from white men."[21] What the missionaries may not have understood is that in Southern Paiute culture Mormon professions of friendship and brotherhood required sharing; gift-giving, whether Paiute labor or Mormon goods, "incurred an ethical obligation to share reciprocally with the donors whenever they in turn had excess bounty."[22] Stealing, as the Mormons understood it, wasn't recognized, and some missionaries felt the work the Paiutes did more than compensated for the price paid in produce, for the missionaries and Paiutes built canals, set out fields, and planted.[23] By August the tasseled corn was six feet high, potatoes were blooming, and they expected green peas in four weeks. The earliest warning sign of problems was saleratus (the main ingredient in baking soda), which began damaging their crops.[24]

The heat was a great help to their new fields ("we think that we can see the corn grow, at any rate it does grow one and one half inches in 24 hours," Bringhurst wrote[25]) but suffocating to the missionaries. Steele, fishing out wisdom from astrology and almanacs, blamed the weather on the moon becoming full,[26] and they soon adopted the sensible Spanish siesta during the day and worked mornings and evenings. Lorenzo Brown discarded his underwear to cool off and didn't put them on again until late August, while mules sometimes lay down and stuck their hooves in the air to get relief from the scorching sands.[27]

John wrote that by late July he and his brethren were not able to work as hard as they had, blaming this on the heat, not enough light clothing, worry that the home wheat crop was destroyed—"and the Last and principle fact is they have nothing (with a ve[r]y few exceptions) to Eat but dry bread and sometime a drink of watter & for a change they have watter & Bread as the Cows are mostly dry and some of us take it very hard to sit down to a hard crust who have been accustomed to the good things of this Life for 30 or 40 years."[28]

Steele saw that Native bands along the Colorado also practiced agriculture, but he was more interested in their war and hunting skills. The ones on the east side of the river didn't have bows and arrows but fought ruthlessly with large clubs, while some of those on the west side poisoned their arrows by teasing rattlesnakes to strike a piece of deer's liver, then burying it until it was putrid. The next step was to dry it, steep it, and then rub their arrows in it. "[W]here ever it Cuts the Skin It is sure to Kill and in this way they Kill their victoms."[29]

Ecclesiastical leaders such as Brigham Young (following Joseph Smith) encouraged missionaries to marry Native women, but despite several bands being in the area, Steele wrote the proposed missionary–Native American intermarriage plan was a dud: "I do not think there is Much Chance for they Mormons to become temperal F.athers in Isreal as they [the Native peoples] say they have no sisters to Spare." The slave-hunting Utes had seen to that.[30]

Indian relations were one of the reasons Steele soon grew disillusioned with Bringhurst's leadership. When William S. Covert took charge during the president's absence, Steele wrote, "Brother W S Covert is a great deal better Liked as a pressidant that Brothe[r] Wm Bringhurst."[31]

Acting President Covert ostensibly wrote a letter to Brigham Young about the lack of baptisms and other concerns, but it was in Steele's hand and undoubtedly reflected his feelings as well. Some Paiutes, they wrote, "have offered themselves for baptism & I thought we should Do So But the president [Bringhurst] thought oth[e]rwise therefore there has ^been^ none been baptised as yet." There was also a difference about whipping transgressing Paiutes—Bringhurst favoring it, Covert (and Steele) against it: "one word from you in reguard to the whipping," they wrote Young, "would ease they minds of some of they breathren."[32] Steele excused the losses to Native peoples because he didn't see anything in the country they could eat "Except musquete & Lizards." Even the wolves, he said, were as thin as starving greyhounds.[33]

The letter from Covert (and Steele) to Young also mentioned the Mormons were frustrated by the lack of support they got from the "chiefs." Steele may have thought of the power of Paiute chiefs the way he thought of the power of Brigham Young. If so, he and his comrades misunderstood the radically democratic Paiute society, which had no "chiefs" as Europeans understood the word. Their leaders were men of stature whose role included negotiating conflicts but not commanding.[34] (One "chief" trying to enforce white mores was pressed so hard he had to flee to the Mormons for protection.[35])

The Covert/Steele letter wasn't supportive of Bringhurst's leadership, and the comment "Brothe[r] Bringhurst does as well as he told you he would that is the best he can he is a man of Desision but he is like the rest of us he has not had experiance enough to be perfect in all things" wasn't flattering.[36] It is likely the cunningly crafted letter didn't fool Young, who once asked rhetorically, "Do you know that I have my threads strung all through the Territory that I may know what individuals do?"[37] A sampling of his voluminous correspondence confirms this.

Young was succinct in a follow-up letter to Bringhurst: "as regards administering the ordinance of baptism to the Lamanites, I should do it by all means whenever they desire it."[38] He also told Bringhurst of an incident in Green River where a white man flogging "an Indian" threatened hostilities, and rather than do that in Las Vegas, they should abandon the mission.[39]

Steele himself wasn't consistent about whipping. When Paiutes took his calf and butchered it, he insisted—through an interpreter, so his language skills must have been inadequate—the two culprits be whipped. In the end, and with promises to do better, the whipping was canceled.[40]

Both Native Americans and Mormons believed in magic and faith, and here was a way to win influence. Steele reported they had healed thirty-year-old Chief Oantump, who said "he was sick all over." A month later, while his people were waiting for Oantump to die, the ritual was repeated successfully with Steele being the "mouth" (speaker).[41]

While fort-building and Paiute friendship were their goals, missionaries also relaxed with entertainment and ritual. On July 4th "Capt Steele made a spirited speech concerning the causes of the Declaration of Independence & also of the policy [of] the U. S. Government towards this people."[42] If it was like Brigham Young's usual speeches about U.S. policy, Steele would have recited a litany of perceived abuses. It must have been anticlimactic to spend the next day plowing oats—until he had to stop to get his plow fixed. Exploring was more to his liking.

Letters usually gave Steele pleasure, but after receiving one, he had an unpleasant dream of home which he related at length in his journal. The most interesting part was when his father or Brigham Young—"I knew not which"—appointed him and others to preach.[43] Conflating his father—his earliest role model, supporter, and disciplinarian—with his religious leader suggests what a powerful hold Young had on him.

Despite confusing dreams on Steele's part, public improvements advanced in Las Vegas, but Utah crop failures and other home affairs affected his morale. In mid-September he got a letter from his wife Catherine saying things were hard without him and she wanted him to come home.[44] From an October 13th letter John wrote to her, one can infer her health wasn't good and the children had colds; she was also angry at someone, was worried about paying taxes, and felt like "Sis [Jane Gordon Bennett] Hulse"—whose husband Benjamin was in Las Vegas with John—had incited something. (John wrote, "as to Sis Hulse when she comes again stuffing you so as to alter your tone in writing show her the Hole in the wall.")[45]

He gave Catherine humorous assurances of his own welfare: "I get along first raite and wash make & mend like some old woman and taking all things into Consideration I get along very well." But the strangest part of his letter is unexplainable with the evidence we have now: "you say you are al without Spot as yet I believe that and also hope that you will Continue so." He claimed to be continually worried about her and the children's welfare and to pray to the Lord to "watch over you and keep you from going astray."[46] This shows his controlling personality and implies he had little faith in her decision-making.

These worries made Steele long to leave hot, dry Las Vegas. He wrote Apostle Smith saying he didn't want to neglect public affairs for private, "but when I hear that there is mo [no] meal in they barrel & they Bishop has now [i.e., none] and no money to Buy any with in the Treasury It Makes me feel as if: my little Babeys are hungary But I hope the Lord will Bless them & provide for them as it is not in my power to do it." He assured Smith of how satisfied he was and, by implication, accepted his lower religious status. "But upon the whole I am made to rejoice in the mission for it releeves my Mind of Many burdons that used to hang upon it when I was in Parowan." Now he had leisure to study useful books, enjoy God's spirit and the brethren's preaching, and benefit from prayers.[47]

By the third week of October the fort still wasn't finished, though Steele recorded, "My portion of wall work is nearly Completed and not having adobies enough we had to go again into the yard and make 4000 which we completed on the 19th." In an autobiographical scrap he wrote, "we built a fort[.] I built the most of it with my own hands," an unlikely claim and one his mission president would have disputed.[48]

Brigham Young sent Bringhurst a letter in the fall authorizing missionaries to go home for the winter so long as enough were left to attend to affairs. Those leaving included John Steele.[49] He was discouraged with Las Vegas; the saleratus killed all his crops except a few bushels of corn, and he didn't have confidence in the mission president. He left November 8th and reached home by the 17th, to find "all well but things in general was in a ve[r]y unsettled Condition."[50]

In December, Steele wrote to George A. Smith crediting his fellow missionaries with doing their best, but reminded him of the map he'd sent which showed how limited the farming area was and suggested Las Vegas could be a military or trading post—implying it was not fit for an agricultural settlement. He also reported that he couldn't promise to

THE RUINS OF LAS VEGAS.

Sketch of the Mormon fort at Las Vegas, made from memory and contemporary notes, by Thaddeus S. Kenderdine, in his book *A California Tramp*.

return by March 10, 1856, as some others did, because he was worried his family might be destitute. However, he was thankful to find that "so far as the Brethren & Sisters Could they have Ministered unto my family for which I thank them & the Lord who poot it in their hearts." Steele professed to want Smith's advice about whether he should return, but he also mentioned that his neighbor John Henderson, who could speak "the Indian language," wanted to go to Las Vegas.[51]

A few days later Steele wrote Young asking to be "exonerated from his mission" according to the clerk who catalogued Young's rough draft response to this missing Steele letter. Steele again cited the condition of his family caused by the 1855 crop failure, but Young's slightly impatient draft response advised he was quite aware of crop failures, but lectured it wasn't wise to leave the mission too short of men: "We say unto you remain and provide for your family during the winter" but return in the spring.[52]

*

That winter Steele forced his daughter Mary, age sixteen, to marry Thomas LeFevre, an eighteen-year-old emigrant from Lincolnshire, England. Joseph Fish, a competitor for Mary's attentions, wrote later that LeFevre "was rather a trifling person, and belonged to that worthless class of young men who were neither very good nor very bad." Fish recalled that Mary's "father was one of those stern characters who compelled their children to obey them in all things. He told her that I was too young and he wanted her to get married then," and she did so. The LeFevre marriage soon failed, and then Mary married her own choice, Joseph Fish.[53]

Maybe Mary was relieved when Steele, who had been promised the Las Vegas postmastership by President Bringhurst to entice him to return, went back in April 1856.[54] Bringhurst was temporarily in Salt Lake, William S. Covert absent, and Albert Miles readying to leave. Miles nominated Steele as acting president, and his brethren may not have found him oppressive because he was approved unanimously, though that sort of approval was a rarely challenged Mormon convention. Steele wrote of peace and goodwill between the missionaries and the Paiutes, and gave the departing brethren the courtesy of speaking.[55]

He apparently brought a different kind of leadership than Bringhurst, if we can trust the report in the official mission history (that is, if his "consultations" were not couched as commands). He gathered the men together to decide if they wanted to corral their horses at night—they unanimously decided they did—and when he thought they needed to hang a gate and build a ditch to prevent irrigation water from flooding the California trail, he called them together to discuss it. He also revived the Las Vegas Lyceum and the choir.[56] These last two fit with his own interests as a compulsive self-educator. He subscribed to newspapers, delivered by the California mail carrier, and besides hoeing and building, he read "some of the best bublecations that I Could find." He named Mitchell's geography, Peter Parley's generously illustrated *A History of All Nations*, a history of England, and others, noting "my mind has been employed in geting a knowledge of nations and at times studying the Indian Language."[57] He put this knowledge to work in at least one sermon.[58] Maybe that's why when his messmate Stephen C. Perry spoke in tongues, Steele felt able to interpret.[59] Lorenzo Brown wrote, "The brethren under the Presidency of John Steel from Parowan are kind indeed and take an active interest with their teams to assist our company across the desert."[60]

When Brigham Young heard reports of lead ore near Las Vegas, he wanted it investigated, and Steele led an exploring company. Paiute guide Koonah-Kibals took them to a likely spot with miles of promising ore, and they packed out 180 pounds of it. Steele confided to Catherine that they "found plenty of the best Lead oar and it exists in great abundance," which could be "a source of great welth for us." He believed the ore was impregnated with silver, explaining, "I send you a Small piece Let Brother [and blacksmith Francis T.] Whitney Smelt it and then you can see what it is I think the most of it is Silver Keep it still."[61]

He forwarded rock samples to Salt Lake, suggested there was silver in it, and asked Brigham Young to have it analyzed.[62] Young responded, claiming the ore was nearly ninety percent lead, with any silver "doubtless too Small to be worthy of attention." However, he encouraged Steele, writing he was "always gratified with descriptions of your travels, and with the Mineralogical Specimens you forward."[63]

By then Young had enlisted Nathaniel V. Jones, Philip Klingensmith, and Ira Hatch to prospect for lead and, maybe unsaid, silver. Jones, whom Steele knew as a Battalion officer, was described by an ex-wife as "a very fine looking man . . . over six feet in height, and in appearance was interesting and noble; but he was well known to be a hard, cruel man."[64] Klingensmith was the fast-talking, loud-voiced, tactless bishop of Cedar City.[65]

Jones, Klingensmith, and interpreter Ira Hatch, one of the few missionaries who had married a Native (Navajo) wife, arrived in Las Vegas on May 6, 1856. Steele moderated a meeting with the new arrivals despite having had some tensions with Jones, but Jones had a letter from Young authorizing him to conscript men, animals, and anything else needed. Jones asked for three men and five animals for thirty days. Several men volunteered, and Steele took Jones's party to Koonah-Kibals' ore. Jones thought there wasn't enough to justify working, but there were other promising veins.[66]

The missionaries provided Jones with thirty pounds of flour, the services of several men, and "boarded them all the time they ware here," Steele wrote. "I Started them on their Journey But they returned unsucksessful on account of the hot Season having begun."[67]

William S. Covert was back by mid-June. Steele gave up his presidency, confident he'd done his duty, and three weeks later Bringhurst, too, was back.[68] This triggered the most direct outburst in Steele's journal: "things began to Change the same old fashioned sermons was preached and arses threatned to be kicked if men did not do what was wanted of them this was one of the reasons I did not wish to be anoyed with the bustle of Compelling men on every ocation thinking that more mild treatment would do just as well."[69] His fellow missionary and Battalion comrade Samuel Thompson agreed. In a letter to Young, he dated the collapse of morale to the time of Bringhurst's return.[70]

When Bringhurst was in Las Vegas—between repeated trips to California and Utah on mission business—he lectured frequently, too often attacking other missionaries. This had begun soon after their arrival in 1855. When Bringhurst's counselor and clerk Ira S. Miles returned home, Bringhurst accused him of manifesting a wicked and contentious spirit and dropped him from leadership; soon Steele was auctioning off Miles's abandoned pig.[71] In late July that year Bringhurst lectured the missionaries on their selfishness and took a swipe at blacksmith Edward Cuthbert for not being accommodating in horseshoeing.[72]

After a year of this, it was a strained environment when Nathaniel V. Jones came back with a letter from Young authorizing him to take twenty men to finish their mission by working the lead with Jones. Bringhurst exploded. Steele wrote that there was "a great storm between them Calling each oth[e]r any thing but Gentliem[en]." They were so heated, Bringhurst professed Young's directions were unclear, and they postponed a decision until they could get further clarification. "Most of us responded readily although opposed by Bringhurst who manifested anything but kindness," Lorenzo Brown wrote.[73] The struggle, Young realized, wasn't about a dried-out little mission in the oven-hot Mohave, but about "an unrighteous desire to speculate in lead ore"—and, again unsaid, silver believed to be associated with it.[74]

The showdown came on September 19th, after weeks of increased tensions. John Steele played a significant role in the denouement, and luckily the mission recorder, William P. Jones (apparently unrelated to Nathaniel V.), outdid himself enumerating the details.[75]

"The time has come when the line must be drawn," President Bringhurst harangued the missionaries from the top of a wagon in overcast weather. Even if this wasn't a contest between good and evil, he pictured it that way, calling Nathaniel Jones disruptive and a liar for trying to undermine him. He charged there were men who had been working against the mission from the beginning, that he would give names, and then the brethren could speak their own minds.

William C. Covert, although privately critical of the Las Vegas mission, towed Bringhurst's line. (He had previously said some of the men were inspired by the devil in their wish to leave or break up the mission.[76]) William Riley chimed in, saying that "Jones came here full of the spirit of self-will and disorder," and E. K. Fuller "still felt to sustain Prest Bringhurst." Brother George Mayer agreed with Fuller.[77]

The phalanx of neutrals wavered. Miles Anderson "did not care whe [who] he labour[e]d under" (though he had written Brigham Young less than a month earlier that "thare is nothing heare [in Las Vegas] vary flattering except the lead mine" and the crop was "good for nothing"[78]). "Bro Hock" (William Hawk) "said he was for Jones & Bringhurst" and "he felt Jones was as near right as Bringhurst." But Bringhurst demanded allegiance: he "wanted men to take one side or the other if Jones[']s course was right his was roung." Covert spoke again, this time attacking Jones and accusing him of poisoning the minds of the Paiutes against the missionaries. That prompted Alexander Lemon and Albert Knapp to speak in support of Bringhurst.

John Steele was the first dissenter to speak and he was cautious. (He had been given permission to go home to attend to his destitute family provided he return as soon as practical.[79]) "Bro steel arose & said he did not feel like speaking in Bro Jones absence in conciquence of A little difficulty me & him had in the spring But said he did not fully acknowledge his cours[e.]" Edward Cuthbert, who had felt Bringhurst's lash more than once, was less equivocal: "It was [h]is duty to help Jones according to the authority of his writing said he felt that Jones was A honorable man." William Moss seemed confused; he had been sent to labor under Bringhurst but had done some work for Jones and "hoped he had not don roung."[80]

Edson Barney, a long-time Mormon who had been part of Zion's Camp, was not a Bringhurst supporter. He spoke of his disappointment in Las Vegas's farming prospects and said Bringhurst told the latest company to arrive in the spring that their mission was to dig lead. Bringhurst disputed that, and Barney was tactful enough to then qualify his statement to say that's what he had understood Bringhurst's meaning to be. But he went to the core of the issue: "Bro Jones came with the same authority" as Bringhurst and "he felt justifyed in going with him But if he had licked the rong Skellet it was the first time." In the end Bringhurst ordered Barney out of Las Vegas.[81]

Jacob Workman, who had seen worse adversity halfway across Iowa when he had to cut his wagon box into a coffin to bury his wife and son, "said he felt to justify Bro Jones in the course he had taken said he was for Jones."[82]

Bringhurst gave a qualified response to Barney and then attacked those he claimed "had used there influence against him from the commencement in every way possible." They were "father Hulet for one James bean for another & John steel for anoth[e]r said if they did not take A different course he wanted them to go to the vall[i]es of the mountains or any other place they wished for he would not suffer no such miserable cruses [curses] to stay here."[83]

Sylvester Hulet, part of John's "ten" on the way to Las Vegas and a close friend through their shared Mormon Battalion experiences, cowered under Bringhurst's attack, then "arose & asked forgiveness of Bro Bringhurst said he Knows he had don rong but he could not help the past. felt sorry that his Organization was of such A nature that had caused him to act in the way he had through life But he was determined to do better." James A. Bean challenged Bringhurst to name in what way he had used his influence against the mission from its commencement.[84]

John Steele became angry and "said Bro Bringhurs[t] was oppressive said when he talked with him in private he talked like A good fatherly man But when he apperd in publick it was wifs [end of line] cing all the time." Despite the incomprehensible word(s), Steele stuck to the heart of his complaint: Bringhurst was oppressive. Bringhurst's bullying, haranguing, and castigating of men in public are demonstrated in the mission record, and with that maybe Steele should have stopped. But Bringhurst must have also attacked Steele's work ethic, for he went on to claim he "had done more work then Bro Bringhurst sence he had been on th[e] mission" and attacked "old Blazzard" (John Hopwood Bleazard) for lying when he said Steele wasn't going to return from his September furlough. Then he "reiterated he had don as much for the mission as any other man. said he did Know he had done the best he could."[85]

William Covert, maybe thinking of the joint letter he and Steele sent Brigham Young, said "he believed men lied when they continually act contrary to there words said he would not give A curse for A mans long prays [prayers] when he don[e] nothing else worned men to be honest or the wrath of God would rest upon them." James T. S. Allred, whom Steele had nominated as a Nauvoo Legion captain in Salt Lake City in 1849, claimed he was glad for the showdown, that he supported Bringhurst, and "Bro Workman lied when he said Joneses company had not been useing there influance with the indians against this people."[86]

Bringhurst took them on one by one. He didn't have "much faith in Bro Hulet[']s acknowledgement for he had pled & praid for him till he had allmost lost all hope in him But yet he was wil[l]ing to try him again." He backtracked regarding James A. Bean, saying that rather than having been opposed to the mission from the beginning, that comment was in "referance to Bro Steel & Hulet." Bean, he said, "incouraged A spirit in him for the last 3 or 4 mounths that lead him to find fault with the grass water land & every thing else pertaining to this place said if he did not take A differant cours[e] it would sone lead him to hell."[87]

As for Steele, Bringhurst "was astonished that Bro Steel should presume to say he had done as much work as him. Prest Bringhurst said he had done more work in one mounth then steel had since he hed [*sic*] been on the mission." Always willing to call people dishonest, Bringhurst said, "Bro steel Know[s] he lied when he said he had done the best he could" and had been in opposition since they arrived. But, he said, "he did not call this meeting to try these men But mearley to Let them Know they must take A differant cours[e] or leave this place." (The record of public works up to February 27, 1856, shows that Bringhurst had contributed thirteen and a half days, and Steele just two. In fairness to Steele, Bringhurst stayed through the winter of 1855–56 and Steele did not, and Bringhurst valued Steele enough to lure him back with the promise of the Las Vegas postmastership.)

Hulet was crushed; he arose to acknowledge his sins and ask for forgiveness. James Bean was also contrite: "said he Knew he was wild rackless [*sic*] & had done roung in complaining of the bad grass water &c & trying to find falt with this place But asked forgiveness of Bro. Bringhurst & the breathren" and promised to do better.

Steele, however, was hardly conciliatory. He "said he did not know Bro Bringhurst had any feelings toward him But he felt in himself Bro Bringhurst had been trying to crowd him into the earth & he had maid up his mind that he would be dam[n]ed before he would be run over by any man." He was on understandable grounds there, but his claim that "his work was in the house & neither Bringhurst nor any other man Knew what he had don" sounds weak. When Steele went on to say "as far as preaching was concerned he had not felt like it for some time for he had heard it was considered that he was nobody anyhow," he sounded petulant. (His last recorded sermon was July 20, 1856.[88])

Steele was conflicted. Although he had written a verse about the iron mission that included the line "& do as we are told,"[89] and his course as counselor in the stake presidency included a continual demand for obedience to authority, he wasn't upholding President Bringhurst—he who believed God thrashed the recalcitrant, and he who relished dissenters being run out of the Kingdom.

But Steele offered an olive branch and "said if he had taken a roung v[i]ew of the matter he was ready to make all things right[.] Acknowledged he had done measurable wrong by let ing men speak against the authorityes here in his house."[90]

After these remarks Bringhurst seems to have calmed down or felt he had won. He moved that Hulet's offences be forgiven, which was carried unanimously, as were motions to forgive James Bean "of all past follies" and John Steele for "past offenses." Even with those reconciliations, when Bringhurst called for a vote, "J. Workman[,] E Barney[,] S[amuel] thompson gave th[e]re names against Prest Bringhurst[.] Meeting closed by prayer."[91]

When John Steele left for home two days later,[92] he must have felt especially angry and dispirited. Yet events tended to vindicate him. In December, Bringhurst got a letter from Brigham Young dropping him from leadership and disfellowshipping him.[93] Samuel Thompson, who had refused to uphold Bringhurst and ignored an order to leave,[94] was named as Bringhurst's replacement.

Thompson's reports to Young soon led to a letter that Thompson characterized as "liberating us from the Lasvegas."[95] Young could take a lot of setbacks, but with extensive crop failures in Utah in the fall of 1855 and again in 1856, he didn't feel he could support a mission that couldn't feed itself, let alone maintain morale. And so the Mormons were left out of the original riches of Nevada, the Silver State.

There are some similarities between Steele's disgruntlement and insubordination under Capt. James Brown in Pueblo and his resistance to President William Bringhurst. Undoubtedly part of it was his own untamed personality, which is why George A. Smith, in his blessing, had tried to instill in him "forbarence & long suffering."[96] And the first commandment of nineteenth-century Mormonism was obedience. But to whom? At

Pueblo, Brown was the military commander but that counted as nothing; it was religious authority one should obey, and there was no dominating priesthood rival to Brown. When Nathaniel V. Jones arrived in Las Vegas with instructions from Brigham Young making Bringhurst the de facto subordinate, Bringhurst's refusal to recognize that authority clouded the line of command.

There were differences. Brown was notoriously self-dealing and dishonest; Bringhurst was not accused of those crimes but of speaking softly with men one-on-one and then lambasting them in public. He destroyed the goodwill that, as a leader, he could have been treasuring up.

What comfort could be had for John Steele was that the records confirm the failure wasn't his fault. He wanted history to know he "took no part" in the Jones-Bringhurst quarrel and "soon the Evil among the heads Broke it up all togather until Nothing was left of it only the old walls that I had worked hard to help Build."[97]

Las Vegas eventually had a spectacular resurrection, and Steele is an integral part of its founding story; he would have been astonished, and maybe pleased. And as things happened, he found a silver mine in his own backyard.

9

INTERESTING TIMES

Mountain Meadows

"May you live in interesting times" is an apocryphal Chinese curse that describes John Steele's year after returning home from Las Vegas in 1856. In Parowan he found the expected scarcity of bread, corn, potatoes, and beets, and—unexpectedly—children afflicted with "diarrhea and bloody flux."[1] No wonder he and Catherine were in Salt Lake City that fall, when he got permission from Brigham Young to settle anywhere he liked—meaning release from the iron mission.[2]

Steele joined Salt Lakers in seeing the crop failures as a sign of God's dissatisfaction, but because Mormon prophets were considered infallible, the culprits had to be backsliding followers. One of Steele's exemplars, the charismatic, raw-boned Apostle Jedediah M. Grant, was a fanatic obsessed with body odors, cleanliness, and purity—and he was also an enthusiast for blood atonement. Grant started an out-of-control religious reformation: "I say, that there are men and women that I would advise to go to the President immediately and ask him to appoint a committee to attend to their case; and then let a place be selected, and let that committee shed their blood."[3]

Confessions, restitution of stolen property, mass hysteria, thousands of rebaptisms, a recommitment to plural marriage, the certainty of End Times, and some accusations of ritual murder followed. Steele, James H. Martineau, and others took the new crusade back to Parowan.[4]

Brigham Young wrote Steele in March 1857, "I say 'Go ahead' and dont be behind in this long tail of the 'Reformation'!" and concluded, "The more light, the more is made manifest, and I trust righteousness will increase among the saints, and in the Kingdom of God."[5]

Later Steele cryptically alluded to excesses when he wrote Catherine and said he'd had his fill of disagreeable men, "and like the Refirmation I have got through with it and I do not think of Going back over the past for improvement there has been many things of the past that has been forsed upon me by the Circumstances of the Case, But on my own account I have very few things on my own account to Blame Myself with,"[6] the "my own account" repetition suggesting he was unsettled.

Mormon focus abruptly turned from internal to external enemies when they learned in late July 1857 that President Buchanan had issued secret orders for 2,500 troops to be sent to Utah with a new governor to replace Young and suppress an alleged rebellion. This news came with wild soldier talk of hanging Young and other Mormon leaders. That didn't sound wild to those who had lived through the murder of the Smith brothers, while they were supposed to be under Illinois state protection, and had sworn temple oaths of vengeance.

Young declared martial law and sent the Nauvoo Legion (the territorial militia) to harry the federal troops. George A. Smith went south on a regional review but didn't preach restraint. He was in Parowan on August 8, 1857, where Isaac C. Haight of Cedar City said that "[William] Dame's attendants" included John Steele.[7] Smith reported that "in spite of all I could do I found myself preaching a military discourse."[8]

After two or three days, Dame joined Smith and others, possibly including Major Steele, to tour the south, review outlying militias, and make more inflammatory remarks. Mormons had long believed that Native peoples would be the "Battle axe of the Lord"[9] in conflicts with outsiders. That was in mind when the brethren talked to the Paiute chief Jackson and his band on the Santa Clara. According to John D. Lee's "confessions," George A. Smith was nervous and fearful around the Paiutes but happy they would help Mormons if enemies came that way. Lee claimed he told Smith that the Reformation left the people "still red-hot for the gospel," and immigrants "would be wiped out if they had been making threats against our people."[10]

Brigham Young directed Dame and others to find hideaways, so at Dame's direction, Steele joined or led a small party exploring to the northwest, looking for but failing to find a desert redoubt from federal troops; some went back to Las Vegas to get lead for ammunition while Steele's group stumbled upon it in Beaver County.[11] Steele was gone August 26–29 but back before his last child, Robert Henry Steele, was born. (The boy died young, allegedly from being overdosed with calomel, which can cause mercury poisoning.[12])

Two days after Robert's birth approximately 120 members of the California-bound Fancher party reached Parowan and camped about three-fourths of a mile from the town center.[13] Settlers, still suffering from food shortages, were ordered by Young to "save all their grain; nor let a kernel go to waste, or be sold to our enemies."[14] The anticipated U.S. assault was another reason to conserve.

This directive was unevenly enforced. Morgan Richards was only threatened with having his throat cut for selling supplies and had to retrieve them.[15] But when William Leany gave onions to a Fancher party member whose father had defended him from a Missouri mob,[16] Dame sent Barney Carter to punish him. Carter tore a picket off a fence and hit Leany in the head so hard he was never again of sound mind. Years later, in a letter to John Steele, Leany wrote, "you are far from ignorant of those deeds of blood from the day the picket was broke on my head to the day those three were murdered in our ward."[17]

Leany was a respected townsman who had held a number of minor offices, but he wasn't a cousin of George A. Smith, as Jesse Nathaniel Smith was. Jesse recorded in his journal under the date September 3, 1857 (though the entry was written later), "An emigrant train passed [Paragonah]. I went home and sold them some flour and salt."[18] He suffered no repercussions but then he was orthodox: "You know my feelings with regard to Californ[i]ans," he wrote. "Salt em at once rather than have them eat up the Saints but if you do, Salt em down so that their <---------> may not rattle bells to the no Small annoyance of Settlers."[19]

We are handicapped in knowing the sequence of what followed because, as historian Will Bagley noted, "Historians must reconstruct this event from the testimony of children, murderers, and passersby."[20] However, since Bagley wrote that, the Latter-day Saints have released valuable affidavits and other documents, some of which are more than the accounts of "passersby."[21]

The Fancher party camped west of Cedar City on September 4th, and according to local bishop Philip Klingensmith, Sam Jackson sold some of the party wheat and was excommunicated. It's said that some of them, not implausibly, cursed, threatened, and said "hard things about the Mormons."[22] It's also said they swore when they couldn't get what they wanted at the local store and ignored the fine imposed by city marshal John M. Higbee for swearing.[23] Reputedly, that same day, Isaac C. Haight talked to John D. Lee about arming the Paiutes to attack the party.

It's possible a hostile reception had been anticipated for them by George A. Smith in his recent visit.[24] One plausible version makes any actions by the Fancher party irrelevant because the Mormon leaders' plan all along was robbery. Mary S. Campbell remembered Cedar stake president Isaac C. Haight saying, "we wanted some stock and the intimation was to get the stock away from them [the Fancher party]."[25]

Whatever the genesis, implementation of the attack was dependent on two men: William H. Dame and Isaac C. Haight. Dame was Parowan stake president and Haight held the same position in Cedar City, but Dame was Haight's military superior.

Josiah Rogerson, who moved to Parowan later, was an admirer of John Steele and a close friend of Mahonri M. Steele and Joseph Fish; he also knew and had befriended Dame. Rogerson, like most witnesses, had personal blemishes, particularly with alcohol, but he was a skilled stenographer and sharp observer.[26]

Rogerson's characterization of Dame was not without praise, but overall it was scathing: "As a manual laborer [Dame] was a worker, from the rise to the setting of the Sun," and first to attend every church event. But "For him to be in-retain and possess office and position was the Feeding of his heart," and he was "as much a coward as a tyrant."[27] Fish confirmed Dame's timidity, but Rogerson's judgment was more vehement, maybe because he was defending the thesis that Dame had misled Brigham Young and allowed him to take blame for Dame's own actions regarding the massacre at Mountain Meadows.[28]

Stake President Isaac C. Haight was the kind of man who was called to leadership positions wherever he went, with forceful convictions and, more dangerous than Dame's wishy-washiness, excessive zeal.[29] George A. Smith told a bowery audience in Salt Lake that during his August military tour Haight told him that if six hundred cavalrymen came from the east toward Cedar City, he wouldn't wait for instructions: "he was going to take his dragoons and use them up before they could get down through the kanyons, for said he, if they are coming here they are coming for no good."[30]

Church councils were held in Cedar City and Parowan about the Fancher party, maybe even before they moved on to Mountain Meadows, fifty-two miles west of Cedar City. After these deliberations "a decision was made" to send territorial Indian agent John D. Lee to recruit white men and to arouse and lead the Paiutes to attack the immigrants. (Paiute technology, numbers, war methods, and social structure precluded sustained assaults on well-armed parties.[31]) Because of some hesitancy at the council in Cedar City, the attack was approved, apparently on September 6th, but a runner was sent to Brigham Young for guidance. During the attack on September 7th the Fancher party's resistance proved too formidable, and it soon became obvious the victims knew their attackers included or were led by white men.[32] Then "a decision was made" to call out the Cedar City Militia to murder the lot. No one in Parowan was called out, so Steele wasn't at the slaughter.

When men were sent to kill the Fancher party, where was independent-minded iron monger and Nauvoo Legion major Matthew Carruthers? And where were rebellious William Hewitt, Richard Varley, Thomas Machen, William Couzens, William Davies, James Easton, John Grant, William Henderson, William Slack, James Mitchell, Matthew Easton, James Thorpe, Samuel Kershaw, Isaac Perry, Harvey C. Ladd, John Dart, Edward Davies, David Davies, David Muria, and all their like? All in California and other parts, thrashed out in the great cattle rebellion of 1853.[33] Samuel Pollock and Robert Wylie had been angry about the cattle confiscation but stayed and learned to follow orders; they were both at Mountain Meadows.[34] So was the Paiute chief Jackson and his men, whom George A. Smith had met the previous month on the Santa Clara.[35] Major Carruthers had been replaced in the militia by John D. Lee. There was no moral force in the community able to counter orders to murder or the belief that a slaughter would honor their vengeance oaths.

Gulling the emigrants into surrendering with a white flag, the militia and their allies marched about a mile side-by-side with their victims. At a signal the perpetrators turned on their charges and slaughtered over a hundred of them on September 11, 1857. With a curiously strange moral punctilio, the older children were murdered but the smallest were spared; Mormon vows condemned shedding innocent blood.[36] Seventeen children who survived were distributed among Mormon families but were later reclaimed by the federal government and sent to their relatives.[37] The killers' religious vows did not prevent them from stripping and robbing their victims' bodies and sharing the booty.[38]

"A decision was made" is passive language that allowed the religiously motivated murderers to dodge responsibility. A plausible scenario of the decision-making process follows.

Haight got daily reports from Indian runners during the attack and learned the plan was failing because the Fancher party was well-armed and protected by their circled wagons. If the wounded and angry survivors escaped to California, their story could be used to raise volunteers—perhaps joined by federal troops—to attack southern Utah. As Dame's military subordinate, Haight needed his approval to call out the militia to reinforce the ragtag attackers. He also knew Dame could be bullied.

Cedar City's John Chatterley later testified that he carried a note to Parowan, where he waited while Dame assembled the High Council; he said this was around the time John D. Lee was in Cedar City—September 4th or 5th. Chatterley said he recognized the voices of Edward Dalton, John Steele, S. S. Rogers, Jesse N. Smith, and William H. Dame; there were two or three others.[39] Steele, with his Scotch-Irish accent, was probably particularly easy to identify.[40] The conference lasted into the night, and then Chatterley took a message back to Haight which, it is claimed, turned down his request for reinforcements.[41]

In this emergency, when the attack was faltering, Haight and stonecutter Elias Morris went to Parowan, apparently September 9th, in a light wagon, arriving about midnight at Dame's. Morris described Dame sending "For some of the leading men."[42] William Barton named those present as Dame, Morris, Haight, James H. Martineau, Jesse N. Smith, Calvin C. Pendleton, Elijah Newman, and Tarlton Lewis. This is not, and can't be expected to be, a punctiliously accurate roster given that Martineau was out of town on an exploring expedition September 4–11.[43] It is also a mostly different group than those at the meeting Chatterley remembered: Edward Dalton, John Steele, S. S. Rogers, Jesse N. Smith, and Dame. The lack of overlap tends to suggest there were at least two Parowan meetings.[44] Possibly the first, which included Major Steele, was a military one, and the second, including Dame's stake counselors, Jesse N. Smith and Calvin Pendleton,[45] was a meeting of the High Council. Massacre participant Daniel Macfarlane, Haight's stepson and son-in-law, later gave testimony that isn't reliable. But when he said that "a number of High Council meetings were held" and Haight, Higbee, and Morris made "several trips" to Parowan to consult Dame, that's possible.[46]

Barton confirmed Elias Morris's recollection that this meeting was "about Wednesday the 9th." The High Council—according to later reports, including from tainted witnesses who weren't there, such as Martineau and George A. Smith—rejected the plan to kill the emigrants. Martineau claimed that the response from Dame was "Do not notice their threats, words are but wind—they injure no one; but if they (the emigrants) commit acts of violence against citizens inform me by express, and such measures will be adopted that will insure tranquility."[47] This sounds like, and probably was, former newspaperman Martineau's literary language, not Dame's.

Barton also said the Council adopted a conciliatory proposition. He says it was made by Calvin C. Pendleton, to the effect that a Parowan company should be sent to Mountain Meadows to call off the attack, gather up the Fancher stock, "and let them continue their journey in peace." But after the meeting, Barton said, Haight, sitting outside on a pile of tanning bark, allegedly told Dame most of the emigrants were already dead and convinced him to overrule the High Council and approve murder (a meeting later referred to as the "Tan Bark Council").[48] Cedar City bishop Philip Klingensmith testified that massacre participant Ira Allen told him the doom of the emigrants was fixed at a meeting in Parowan.[49] Haight himself told William Barton about that meeting: "This is where I did wrong and I would give a world, if I had it, if we abided by the decision of the council."[50]

John Steele's role in the massacre is problematic, but his stature in the community, his likely participation in at least one if not two Parowan councils discussing the plan, and his general inquisitiveness make it certain he knew a great deal.

Steele's educated and politically connected grandson Mahonri "Hon" M. Steele Jr. talked to Delta newspaperman Frank A. Beckwith about Mountain Meadows. "Grandad came over to Panguitch once, when old," recalled Hon, "and said to me, 'Sonny, I haven't much longer to stay with you, and I want to talk with you.' Then Grandad took me out for a walk every day for several days, and all he talked about on each occasion was the Mountain Meadows Massacre. He gave me every angle of it." Hon asserted, "Grandad opposed it. Never did favor doing anything to 'em. The little men couldn't talk back, but Grandad was probate judge, and a lot of other things, and he did talk back and got away with it." This opposition, says Hon, was why his grandfather wasn't called to the slaughter.[51] Actually, as noted above, it was the Cedar City Militia, not Parowan's, that was called out. Further, everyone claimed to have been opposed to the massacre by the time Hon was taking walks with Grandpa.

Some of Hon's statements were inaccurate, but he confirmed his grandfather's well-known hostility toward Dame. A courageous man like Steele would have found it hard to respect the weak and waffling stake president, especially if the High Council had refused to approve the slaughter but Haight bullied Dame into authorizing it anyway.[52]

Hon also told Carlos Ashby Badger that Steele "always insisted that Dame at Beaver [Parowan], was the guiltiest party. It was said that Dame moulded the bullets that were used at the massacre."[53]

Frank Beckwith reported that Hon said of Dame, "I never knew him; but Grandad did, and never liked him. Always held him as the man who did it." Later in the same interview Hon said, "Grandad said Dame was the man who did it (the massacre); highest man there." In Steele's military mind, maybe Isaac C. Haight's unrelenting pressure counted as nothing since his military superior Dame blessed the attack. Hon also said, "Granddad told me that time, 'I know there is a lot said, but I want you to get the straight of it. I want you to know it as it was. Dame was the man.'"[54]

At least four things convinced contemporaries that the Mountain Meadows attack was not an "Indian" massacre. First, small children were not spared in such massacres. Second, the massacre was never reported in the territorial newspaper, the *Deseret News*. (A slighting reference was eventually made to it in a December editorial attacking hysterical California editors.[55]) As the *Salt Lake Tribune* editorialized years later, "Look at the files of *The Deseret News*, and you will see that every incident in Iron county was minutely reported. Things of a hundred fold less importance were carefully stated."[56] Third, the perpetrators and their accomplices slandered the victims, which would have been unnecessary if Natives were responsible for the murders. Fourth, Mormon participants talked about it; John M. Higbee even wrote a self-exculpatory account under the improbable name of "Bull Valley Snort."[57]

John Steele's surviving papers are almost bare of references to Mountain Meadows, except for three handwritten gray pages, the pencil lead smeared from large water stains on the left side, top, and bottom, making deciphering all of it impossible. It begins with what professes to be testimony from William Strong of Salt Lake City's Tenth Ward. He asserts that when the

Fancher party arrived in Salt Lake, people furnished them with vegetables and "Suplied the[i]r wants." Lyman Leonard sold them cornmeal.

The party then "moved down to the Jordan Whare they let down the fence and turned ther Cattle into the Hay fields of one of the Mormons." Upon being told to move their cattle, the group became "angary and with terrible Oaths" claimed "they had the Rifle and showed it tha[t?] Killed Joseph and Hyrum." They threatened Brigham Young, and one woman claimed she'd fed "Mormon beef" (that is, dead Mormons) to Mormon prisoners in Missouri and she'd do it again.

Next, Steele's document relates, they went to Corn Creek and poisoned some meat, killing "Indians," and poisoned a young man. They were said to have committed outrages in Beaver, and in Parowan they allegedly asked, "where does Your God Damned Bishop Leve?" In Cedar they had "the Same insulting Spurrit."[58]

Historians Ronald W. Walker, Richard E. Turley Jr., and Glen M. Leonard, noting Steele had been a judge (briefly, but a longtime justice of the peace), have suggested he interviewed some Salt Lake City residents about the massacre with the intention of drafting a formal statement. They also point out that "two of his informants, William Strong and Lyman Leonard, were known to have ties to the Salt Lake City neighborhood through which the emigration companies probably passed."[59]

Frank A. Beckwith quotes a lengthy speech that Hon Steele claimed his grandfather gave in an English pub during his 1877–78 mission slandering the murder victims to justify their killing.[60] It incorporated all the usual postmortem Mormon tropes, including some from John Steele's strange Mountain Meadows document: the death of Apostle Parley P. Pratt "by an Arkansan" and the emigrants being from Arkansas (Pratt's murder took place in Arkansas but his killer was not an Arkansan); the Missouri persecutions and members of this train "boasting that they came from Missouri"; one of the emigrants saying "they had the very pistol that killed the Prophet"; the belief that they'd raise an army in California to come back and "kill all the damned Mormons"; the threat from Johnston's army; martial law; the company's lack of a pass, as required by Governor Brigham Young; their insults to locals all along the southern route; the "snapping off [of] chickens' heads"; insults directed at "Old Lady Evans"; calling two bulls "Brigham" and "Heber" and lashing and cursing the animals by name in Mormon settlements; poisoning water and a beef carcass to kill Natives at

then Comes Wm Stone residing in
Salt Lake City in the 10 ward
[illegible] that when the company in
[illegible]
in the [illegible]
[illegible]
[illegible]
[illegible] been out with
vegetables and supplied the
[illegible] and Lyman [illegible]
[illegible] Corn Meal
[illegible]
the company [illegible] down
to the person where they let
down the fence and turned their
Cattle into the Hay field of one
of the Mormons and [illegible] to get on
to where there was more room
[illegible] the Settlers

Steele's water-damaged, penciled Mountain Meadows document, p. 1. *BYU Harold B. Lee Library.*

Corn Creek; poisoning Mrs. Tomkinson and a boy name Proctor Robison; and tearing down a fence in Cedar City and letting their cattle feed in the owner's pasture.[61]

These stories may have swayed an English audience and, as Hon asserted, entitled John Steele to a free pot in the alehouse, but that ale was worth a lot more than these specious justifications for murder. Most likely a few of the emigrants were provocative, as some in large groups can be, but not a single one of these charges against them can be substantiated, and nearly all, like the poisoning stories, are easily disproved, except possibly the insults directed at "Old Lady Evans." She was probably Elias Morris's mother, Barbara Thomas Morris, who was said to have been insulted on the streets of Cedar City.[62] One doesn't know if she had reason to feel aggrieved enough to want the death penalty for the whole party, but her son Elias, who accompanied Haight to the last meeting with Dame, may have.

The purpose of dragging the reader through the drudgery of these disagreeable, difficult, and unsubstantiated reports is to show that Steele knowingly joined his southern Utah compatriots in group solidarity and a cover-up.

James Haslam got back to Cedar City with a letter from Brigham Young after the slaughter. While instructing Haight "not to meddle" with the emigrants, Young wrote, "The Indians we expect will do as they please" and reminded Haight it was important to preserve good feelings with the them. Young advised that if any trains in the area "will leave, let them go in peace."[63] This was not a repudiation of the attack on the Fancher party, but Haslam testified later that Young told him, "don't spare horse flesh; these men must be spared; let them go in peace."[64]

*

The massacre at Mountain Meadows backfired spectacularly: rather than the Natives being the "Battle axe of the Lord," the Mormons were in the uncomfortable position of realizing they could motivate but not control their neighbors.

Young's idea of a Mormon-Indian alliance was always a mirage. In the case of the Paiutes, heavily put upon by their Ute cousins, the value of the Mormons as a counterweight resulted in a real though sometimes strained alliance. But Young was fooled by the oppressor's delusion: he believed his subordinates appreciated all the advantages that the oppressors dream they're giving and were ignorant of everything they took. "Experience shows that

Indians, like Congress-men and Government officials, have their price!" George A. Smith complained with surprise.[65]

As winter began to turn into spring, Young had to face some consequences. Whispers were going through his congregations about murder and bloodshed at the Meadows, and in March 1858 he felt compelled to announce that "it was not policy to shed the blood of our enemies and was better to leave our homes than to be driven from them."[66]

The prospect of several thousand federal soldiers in Wyoming fighting their way into the territory was sobering for both sides. With much back-and-forth and bluster and grief, and using Young's friend Thomas L. Kane as intermediary, an accommodation was reached with the new governor of Utah, Alfred Cumming, and Young accepted his successor and the troops.

George A. Smith's brother John L. was on a European mission when John Steele wrote to him on August 10, 1857, about the U.S. Army "invasion." Smith replied November 2nd from London. It must have felt like ancient news when Steele got John L.'s letter in late June 1858 and read, "when I think about Unkle Sam's raising his puny arm against the Saints of the most high, & Sending 2500 (as we are Informed) Soldiers to revolutionized Utah & hang up The leaders it makes my (shall I Say Smith Blood, or Mormon Blood) boil."[67]

Steele passed the letter on to George A. Smith and added, "I had the privelige of hearing a letter read last night from you to Brothe[r] James Louis [Lewis], stating that pease was restored and free pardon offered, which makes us Glad to think we have Lived so far through the days of Judgement, and have strong Expectations for the future[.] But one thing makes us rejoice above all ^the^ din of Warr, & that is that Mankind Can go no further than God will alow them."[68]

Evil was sown and calamities sprouted. California Mormons who had abandoned San Bernardino and were headed to settlements in southern Utah were shocked to see half-buried bodies as they went through Mountain Meadows, and to hear whispered stories about the crime. As time went on, more and more unsympathetic "new" immigrants moved into the southern part of Utah, discrediting local leaders.

The anguish for family members of the massacred was so horrendous that little has been written about the trauma experienced by the perpetrators, but James McGuffie claimed in 1877, "Many men who were in the massacre have died of broken hearts. It killed George A. Smith, and I know it from what he said to me."[69] Jacob Hamblin's adopted Shoshone son, Albert, witnessed the slaughter as a teenager and was haunted thereafter by "the devil or evil spirits."[70]

McGuffie also named Robert Wylie, a one-time Liverpool merchant and Utah legislator, who "never got over the horror of the massacre and it finally killed him."[71] Philip Klingensmith, the Cedar City bishop who testified against Lee, was reviled by everyone; a tortured man, after 1877 he disappeared from the historical record, with rumors he'd found a home among Native peoples along the Colorado and/or been assassinated by Mormons.[72]

Dame, who had a stroke, was remembered in his last years as a "gibbering idiot," riding around town leaning back in his carriage and weeping.[73] James H. Martineau's daughter Elvira Martineau Johnson said whenever her father spoke of the massacre, he would break into tears.[74] Nephi Johnson, an interpreter on the scene, died in delirium screaming, "Blood! BLOOD! BLOOD!"[75] Hon Steele's testimony shows John Steele was haunted by, and tried to lay blame for and yet justify, the massacre to the end of his life.

Support for William Dame was rickety; on August 9, 1858, one of his counselors, Jesse N. Smith, filed a list of complaints against him.[76] Every single Parowan church official except counselors James H. Martineau and Calvin C. Pendleton—the latter as wishy-washy as Dame—joined in.[77] That included the entire High Council, Bishop Tarlton Lewis, and John Steele.

Apostles and second cousins George A. Smith and Amasa M. Lyman held a trial for Dame August 10–12, but James H. Martineau's "minutes" are only a list of twelve charges. They include accusations against Dame of favoritism to his family, exploitation, and alleged swindling, but only oblique references to Mountain Meadows. One of those was "3d Also in relation to the case of William Leany who was brutally assaulted, and the men who assaulted him justified"—Leany having given onions to a Fancher party member. "8th In relation to the over bearing course of the Carter family upheld by him"[78]—Barney Carter being the one who attacked Leany. According to James McGuffie and John D. Lee, the Carters—Dame's in-laws—were notorious as his enforcers, and they were certainly disreputable.[79]

Dame was not overtly charged in connection with the massacre. Despite that, his leadership was at the heart of it, and by the time of his trial,

Mountain Meadows defined him. Isaac C. Haight, also deeply implicated in the massacre, was among those summoned.[80]

"I defended Br. Dame warmly during the whole trial," Martineau wrote. "Br. Pendleton said but little as no one could tell how the decision would be pronounced." But Dame had a great advantage: while Martineau wrote at least one whitewashed account of the crime, Apostle George A. Smith wrote several.[81] (Smith also, maybe inadvertently, pointed out a scapegoat when he wrote, "It is reported that John D. Lee and a few other white men were on the ground during a portion of the combat."[82]) Smith vigorously defended Dame, arguing, "Bro. Dame had not made half as many mistakes in the last five years as he himself had." Likewise, Apostle Amasa M. Lyman "said he had always thought well of Br. Dame," and the investigation "had raised him 100 per cent in his estimation."

Dame was not only officially exonerated but, according to Haight, "Much good counsel and instructions were given and some severe chastisement by Elders Smith and Lyman." Haight also wrote that "most of the charges proved to be not true," leaving us wishing for elucidation of that point.[83] In addition, wrote Martineau, "A paper"—in Martineau's hand—"was drawn up certifying that the charges had no foundation in truth, and all were required to sign it, which they did, finally."[84] The words "required" and "finally" suggest some signers were coerced. The ninth signer of twenty-three was John Steele. Jesse N. Smith was last. Four of the signers participated in the massacre; at least six others were officers in the Nauvoo Legion.[85]

But all the whitewashing in the world couldn't cover the crimes of the participants. "When I look back upon it now, sir," James McGuffie told the *New York Herald*, "it seems as if that little village of Parowan, where I lived so long ago, and through which you tell me you passed so recently, fairly smoked with blood offerings."[86]

When Cedar City's ironworks failed, demoralized townspeople fled. In 1858 traveler Thaddeus S. Kinderdine described the city as "half in ruins": "It was a sad sight to see so many dwellings, once thronged by busy inmates, going to decay; the roofs falling in, the walls crumbling." The remaining residents looked "lonesome and owlish amid the desolation."[87]

Parowan was affected, too. "The spirit that once reigned here has departed Stealing lying cheating &c drinking Whiskey seems the order of the day," wrote Judge James Lewis.[88] Internal divisions resulted in a widely signed petition against the fees at George A. Smith's gristmill, but John

Steele didn't sign the complaint.[89] Bishop William R. S. Warren apostatized, was excommunicated, and absconded, owing the sheep co-op $1,500, plus thousands of dollars in other debts, and leaving behind a pregnant wife and four children.[90]

Town members had reason to distrust each other. Mormon scout Ephraim K. Hanks said of Utah's new federal judge, John Cradlebaugh, "the judge possessed but one eye and that is a very good one." Cradlebaugh brought that good eye and a posse of soldiers to investigate Mountain Meadows in early 1859.[91]

Upon Cradlebaugh's approach, Dame directed anyone in authority in 1857 to flee to the mountains, but some fled secretly to the judge. The judge visited the Cedar City tithing office where the bloody bedclothes of the victims had been stored. The stench, he said, was "still offensive."[92] When Governor Albert Cumming withdrew Cradlebaugh's soldiers, justice failed. But Parowan's Miles Anderson said Cradlebaugh had the names of forty-five men who were at Mountain Meadows.[93]

The federal attention amplified paranoia and distrust. Barney Carter, Stake President Dame's enforcer, while admitting he had "a hard task to govern himself," warned "there were a good many amongst us that were not of us."[94] Happily, the Carters, including Barney's horse-stealing brother Atha, moved to California. "I fondly hope never to return," Calvin Pendleton commented.[95]

Miles Anderson, Steele's Las Vegas mission companion, had a love of liquor and a loose tongue. He was confronted in a High Priests' meeting for gabbing on the streets and talking to Cradlebaugh. Anderson was accused of asking "if he thought it right for people to suffer for things done by counsel of the authorities." John Steele came tepidly to Anderson's defense: "I considered the conversation among the brethren near the house of Jas Lewis was joking—on a pretty hard scale." The community was too divided to beat Anderson over the head with a picket or even excommunicate him. The charges were left pending but not taken up again.[96]

*

Despite having been released from the Parowan mission by Brigham Young, John Steele seemed committed to the area. He tried to dry-farm, developing fields near Red Creek and on Little Creek. James Martineau also surveyed a half-acre lot for Steele and the Hall brothers in Chimney Meadows, three miles northwest of Paragonah.[97]

Yet the Little Creek claim lapsed, and Steele experienced demoralizing conflict at the High Priests Quorum, where he'd once served as president pro tem.[98] William H. Dame used a Quorum meeting to sort out disputes he was having with John and his business partner, Charles Hall, over a contract to repair the Council House. An incensed Steele accused Dame of trying to "crowd him down," but things were papered over in part because of the tact of James H. Martineau.[99]

In early 1861 Steele accepted the priesthood nomination, along with millwright Nelson Hollingshead,[100] for Parowan alderman. Parowan's stingy miller, Richard Benson, joined with Steele's friend William Leany in getting up an opposing ticket: the crude, boisterous, and impulsive James McGuffie and a "Mr. Gregory."[101] This was remarkable for several reasons. First, contested elections were anathema to Brigham Young.[102] Second, McGuffie was by then an apostate and was even reported to have said the reason Cradlebaugh and the troops were in Parowan was "to straighten the people—set things to rights, and do away with iniquity."[103] We know nothing certain about Gregory except that when he and McGuffie won the election, before the era of secret ballots, it was astonishing proof that the brethren had lost control. John D. Lee wrote that George A. Smith and Brigham Young, "On hearing the news . . . felt somewhat grived at the folly of men who ought to know better."[104] Hollingshead consoled himself by taking an additional wife, seventeen-year-old Elizabeth Evans.[105] Steele had no such comfort.

Lee reported the failed election in his journal on February 16, 1861. By March 28th James Lewis wrote George A. Smith that he had just returned from a trip south and he'd like permission to move to Santa Clara. His postscript said, "Bro Steele wishes to go also."[106]

In June, Calvin C. Pendleton wrote that "Judge Lewis, John Steele, E. Newman, H. M. Alexander and others, are talking of making a home on the Rio Virgin above Grafton or Tinneys settlement. They have the Prests sanction I believe."[107] That sanction may have been reiterated—or iterated—when Brigham Young and George A. Smith visited Parowan in May 1861.

A large number of Dame's parishioners were moving on. James H. Martineau went north to Cache Valley but most went south, where W. E.

Dodge's lush orchards and vineyards in Washington County were boasting of "apples, peaches, apricots, nectarines, plums, pears, quinces, almonds, figs, English walnuts, gooseberries, currants, and Catawba, Isabella and California grapes."[108] Steele went shopping for real estate in the south while his family, attached to Parowan, fretted with resentment.

Josiah Rogerson, who bought William Leany's house, said Calvin C. Pendleton was the only confidante William H. Dame ever had, and named a host of admirable men Dame could have relied on. He included John Steele, "and fifty other brave hardy and intelligent frontiersmen as ever crossed the Rocky Mountains." He dated the mass exodus to "the fall of '61, and '62"; around forty left the little town, "having had enough of Dames peculiar regime, and prospered more exceedingly from the date of their exodus."[109] Former town schoolmaster Isaiah M. Coombs, visiting the town some years after, wrote, "Br Dame is still the presiding officer of the place and is as unpopular as ever."[110]

In June 1861 John Steele paid John D. Lee $700 for a house and a lot in Toquerville that included two hundred vine and fruit trees; the previous owner had been Mountain Meadows Massacre participant and Ulsterman Samuel Pollock.[111]

James H. Martineau, a man whose journal entries were generally cheerful, gave a happy public farewell, but after another provocation from the seemingly perpetually critical James Lewis, this usually good-natured man wrote angrily in words that may have spoken for others. He claimed he had left behind "a set of hypocritical leeches and scandal mongers."[112]

10

HOPIS, PAIUTES, AND NAVAJOS

On the way to their new home, the Steeles paused in just-settled Kanarra, located between Parowan and Toquerville, and named after the pliable Chief Quinnarrah. They waited as a biblical forty-day storm washed out Santa Clara, Seldom Stop, and Heberville, and Toquerville's Ash Creek flooded the town.[1] The rain toppled Harmony Fort, killing two children of John D. Lee, who versified on their marker, "Was it for sins that we have done" that "snatched from us those little ones?"[2]

After the rains the bedraggled Steeles got themselves to Toquer and cleaned mud and water out of the Pollock home. They "made the best of it but seemed to wish they were back in Parowan," daughter Elizabeth remembered.[3] But at least the floods increased the flow from the town spring.[4]

Steele used the Pollock house for a workshop after building a one-story, gable-roofed, three-room red brick adobe house—distinguished by short door frames reminding visitors that neither John nor Catherine Steele was over five feet, six inches.[5] By the time fall came around, John was called on a brief mission to the Moqui/Hopi. Soft-spoken Jacob Hamblin, "the Apostle to the Lamanites," was designated leader, so effective in Native relations he became a Mormon legend.[6]

"The foundational document for this expedition is an excellent diary by forty-one-year-old Mormon Battalion veteran John Steele," historian and award-winning biographer Todd M. Compton wrote.[7] A delightfully rich supplement is the memoir of Mosiah L. Hancock, son of John's Battalion companion Levi W. Hancock and a Battalion member himself.[8]

The twenty-five missionaries were accompanied by a "boat Company" that lugged a craft to the Colorado River. Steele, a one-time sailor, recorded his gratitude, relishing "a pleasant sail on the smooth water." The brethren buried the boat with enough cached provisions to take them back to St. George on their return.[9] This was "the first successful, practical crossing of the upper Colorado by boat, with animals, in modern times," wrote Compton.[10] The missionaries divided into two "messes"—Mosiah Hancock was cook for one, and Steele for the other,[11] which may explain why Steele was obsessed with supplies.

On December 1st, twenty-five miles from what they called Milkweed Springs, they met some Natives, apparently Hualapais. The chief gave a long speech, gestured with his bow, and promised friendship. "He finished his speech and sung us a song of his very best, which was certainly very interesting to us for we could not understand one word," Steele wrote, but shaking hands and sharing a cake was universally understood.

At Tutsegabbit's Spring their Shivwits guide turned back, warning the missionaries they'd die in the desert without water. That danger became clear after Mosiah Hancock's canteen burst when he ran into a cedar limb. After going thirsty for a day, he asked a man for a drink. "You are out of luck," he said. "I have none to spare you have no oil in your lamp"—recalling Jesus's parable of the foolish virgins who forgot their oil.

James Pearce offered him a quart canteen, saying, "Mosiah hang your lip over this and suck till it is all gone," but when Hancock shook the canteen, there wasn't enough water in it to make it worthwhile. The same with Ira Hatch's small flask.

"Please give me a drink," Mosiah asked another, who said, "You have enough of the good spirit to get along without it."

Steele, seeing how things stood, reached out to hand Hancock his three-pint canteen, laughed, and said, "Mosiah help yourself."

"I took the canteen and shook it and saw there was about a pint in it," remembered Hancock. "I saw that Bro John's Beard was beginning to look a little streaked so I returned it with the remark I will wait a little." He consoled himself by sucking on pebbles.[12]

Eventually they found snow and got water, and then Thomas Clark killed an antelope. Steele described the animal as "quite a treat" but it proved to be a laxative to some. Luckily Hancock had some general-purpose pills, though he was running low because the men had begun to rely on them. Noticing that ground squirrel droppings were quite similar, and realizing they were made of vegetable matter, Hancock picked up a quart, poured in some molasses, rolled them in flour on his saddle bag, and made all the "pills" the situation demanded. Since he and Steele were cooks of their respective messes, "I think I let him into the secret for he was a good Mormon Mason and some of our Boys had more faith in Pills than prayers So Some of the Brethren began to refer to me as 'I think he has a few left that he might spare.'"

Hancock also shared this joke with Hamblin, who kept his peace, and that was no doubt the reason Hancock described the latter as "wise and naturaly secretive in his Nature." He consoled himself over the deception by noting, "They, in no case that I knew of, ever proved fatal. I always believed in letting faith and works go together."[13]

When they got to the Hopi village of Oraibi, they were mistaken for a Navajo war party. "[S]everal hundred of them assembled on the points intending to give us a warm [hostile] reception," Steele wrote—before the Hopis spied Thales Haskell and realized their visitors were Mormons. "As soon as they found we ware their friends they reciev[e]d us very Kindly and gave us some peak [piki] a Kind of Bread and water in a Gourd also shoed us a house to take our packs into and envited us to go into their work shops and visit them which we did and found at once we ware at home," Steele remembered.[14]

The missionaries felt more affinities with the Hopi than with most other tribes and saw themselves in a people who farmed, raised livestock, and manufactured most of what they needed.[15]

The day after their arrival, Steele examined their farming land and found they had "Hirogliphise" (hieroglyphs) of what he interpreted to be the stars, sun, moon, and "the five points of frindship &c." Steele was seeing the Hopi images through the lenses of Masonry, Mormonism, and astrology—the sun, moon, and stars being powerful symbols to each—while the "five points of friendship" referred to the Masonic ritual phrase "Foot to foot, knee to knee, breast to breast, hand to back, and cheek to cheek or mouth to ear."[16] The ceremonies reminded Mormons of their own temple rituals.[17]

Hamblin advised the missionaries to socialize with the Hopis, accept invitations to eat with them, and avoid offensive behavior. But some of the missionaries were disrespectful—making comments like "They are only a lot of damned Injuns"—so the only Mormons allowed into evening meetings in their Council Hall were Jacob Hamblin, William Bailey Maxwell, John Steele, Ira Hatch, Jehiel McConnell, Thales Haskell, and Mosiah L. Hancock: seven of the twenty-five missionaries.[18]

Seated on benches in the terraced Council Hall, Steele admired the well-hewn ceiling timbers—some three feet in diameter—brought all the way from the San Francisco Mountains. They listened to a Hopi wise man whom Hancock identified by the Mormon name Lehi. "He looked somewhat ancient yet sturdy and dignified easy spoken keen eyed and as kind in his demeanor as could be wished," Hancock remembered. Lehi welcomed them and expressed the hope that all had a good purpose. Hamblin assured him they did, whereupon those present nodded approval, and then the Hopi men partly stripped, formed a circle, held hands as they circled to the left and danced by raising the left leg, bringing the left heel down on the right knee. "The[y] Bounced twice on the right toe—Then down quick with the left and up with the right in like manner and so on," Hancock recalled. They were praying for snow to wet the ground so their children would not go hungry.[19]

Steele, as mess cook, was worried about hunger, too. Provisions were becoming short, but their hosts "would rather give us a little than to sell it for they have been subject to great Famines here twenty four of their men and twenty two of the women having died through Starvation within the last two years."[20]

The Hopis had provisions—Mosiah Hancock remembered dried peaches strung on cotton strings and storage rooms packed crossways with rows of corn.[21] But according to Steele, the missionaries were able to cajole them into giving them only "one sheep some Beans, some peeches squash dried and some corn we got som[e] water-mellons but not enough of any of these to help us much."[22] "[T]hey have peech orchards, treese look bad," John wrote. "Never trimmed, do not Irrigate."[23] They did irrigate, but used water frugally.[24] The shiftless-looking, ragged trees relied on water traveling on the hard rock surface under the dunes and were actually prodigious producers.[25] The Hopi also raised beans, squash, cotton, and corn. Their piki bread was made of blue corn and culinary ash.

After a few days, Steele wrote, "we then thought of making a Start for our homes but they told us they ware about to make a Feast and we must stay untill it was over and then we might go." He described this feast in a follow-up report that historian Charles "Chas" S. Peterson described as "One of the best Mormon accounts of Hopi dances."[26]

A community feast was held, with every house offering food to their guests. Dancing was part of the festivities, again aiming to bring snow to water the ground at the new moon. After three days and nights a religious ritual was held in a structure described by Steele as a large cellar but was, in fact, a kiva: a circular underground room for ceremonies, and the only place off-limits to outsiders.[27] Steele thought the secrecy was because "they were ashamed of their works or thought our faith would operate against them,"[28] but it was because of the sacredness of their ceremonies.

Runners with a specially prepared corn husk went to each house, where it was breathed on and handed to their next neighbor to also breathe on and pass on. After everyone had taken part in this ritual several times, they gave it to the Mormons, "and when we found out what was wanting we Could perform the Ceremony as well as any of them we nex[t] ware presented a painted Stick with feathers tied on at several places and a handfull of Consecrated meal which was Distributed amongst us," Steele wrote.[29]

Following Thales Haskell, the missionaries marched through and out of town, where each one sprinkled his feathered stick with meal. These were pahos, Hopi prayer sticks. The purpose was "to incorporate our faith with theirs in order that snow might come down to water their land." Some of them also wet their hair and sprinkled it with meal to imitate snow.

The missionaries invited a few of their hosts to go back to Utah with them but were told "the[y] would go onley they ware affraid the Pah Utes would Kill them we told them we would defend them" Steele recorded. The Hopi also had an ancient taboo against crossing the Colorado River.[30]

Three missionaries—Thales Haskell, Ira Hatch, and Jehiel McConnell—stayed behind.[31] "[W]e need not be afraid to leave them for they would get plenty to eat," Steele wrote. The Hopi leaders said last year's crops had been good, which doesn't quite jibe with the difficulty the missionaries had when they tried to buy food.

The returning missionaries left Sunday, December 21st, by a new route, heading to the Crossing of the Fathers. Compton speculates that Hamblin chose this route because of the difficulty they'd encountered coming from Grand Wash, but it deprived them of their cached supplies. That choice also led to John Steele recording the first known circumnavigation of the Grand Canyon.[32]

The next day, apparently thanks to the Hopi snow rituals, there was a severe snowstorm and they sheltered in a cave. Despite the weather, the evening brought five Hopis with a letter explaining that four of them would go on to Utah after all: Ta-wa-ho-we, La-mo-e, Tu-wa-wat, and

Lye.[33] According to Hancock, part of their motivation was curiosity about white men's factories and technology.[34]

Steele felt that having Hopis along would ensure good treatment for Haskell, Hatch, and McConnell, and the net effect was the Mormons and Hopis had mutual hostages.

Christmas Day found the missionaries melting snow again, and their provisions were so low that Hamblin sent Steele and five others ahead to see if they could get supplies. "[I]n adition to our alredy short rations we have four of the natives to feed," Steele grumbled.[35] They did, however, find a few Paiutes and Navajos and were able to trade blankets and horses for some meat. Steele, maybe remembering the thieving by a few of his Parowan neighbors, wrote, "strange to say there was not one thing stolen by them although there ware both men and women in Camp."[36]

The Mormon parties reunited, and luckily some friendly Navajos caught up with them and traded more meat, though they were soon short again. Meanwhile Steele observed "the worst kind of a broken country," with steep cliffs, signs of "mighty eruptions," and detached table mountains.

The men were again on the verge of starving, and Steele's temper was frayed. He poured a small sack of flour into his pack and apparently announced the sack was empty. Newly married Tom Walker, formidable at six foot, two inches, and 260 pounds, looked in the sack and found maybe a half ounce of flour in one corner. Walker called Steele a thief, and when Steele tried to explain, Walker called him a liar. Steele, as mentioned, was no more than five feet, six inches, and even at sixty-six he weighed only 130 pounds.[37]

"Tom Walker," Steele rejoined, "you are a bigger man than I am, but powder and ball make us equal. Stand twenty steps off with your revolver, and we will see who is the best man!" The men cocked their guns and, according to witness Mosiah Hancock, would have discharged them, but Hancock tackled Walker to the ground and wrenched his revolver away while Jim Andrus put Steele "flat on his haunches and had his revolver too."[38]

The Colorado River was undoubtedly a welcome sight to the Mormons, but it frightened their Hopi guests, who considered turning back. While some tried to dissuade them, Hamblin was more practical: he sent their baggage across first, making it difficult for them to change their minds.[39]

They were all safely on the other side by noon, December 30th, but "there were only four tincupfulls of flour to a mess of thirteen per day," Steele wrote worriedly. The missionaries were so hungry that Mosiah Hancock ate the twelve Hopi beans he brought back with him.[40]

Hamblin again sent Steele and some others ahead for provisions, but after the advance party wrestled through "Mud Kanyon" and learned "our horses ware not amphebeous," they dragged their animals by their necks back to the main camp. Next morning the path was so bad they packed willows into bundles to cross the horses.[41]

New Year 1863 welcomed Hamblin's small party at the Paria River with a nighttime snowstorm; in the morning their New Year's gift was to find the pass had been washed away. Using their butcher knives, they carved a trail through the mud and rocks to get out of the canyon. Nephi Johnson's horse fell and rolled, but they were able to rescue it. When Steele's advance party got to the Tenney and Maxwell ranch at Short Creek, they sent a slaughtered sheep, bread, and flour back to Hamblin and the others. They themselves got a wonderful supper from Grace Tenney and one of the Mrs. Maxwells. It "was the first Good Meal we had had for the last two hundred miles and after being so long on quarter rations it seemed as though we could not get enough," Steele wrote George A. Smith.[42]

Nephi Johnson and Steele partnered the rest of the way home, reaching Grafton at dark but continuing to Johnson's home in Virgin City for supper. Steele left at 10 p.m. and got to Toquerville at midnight, walking behind his staggering horse to keep it moving; one suspects by then he wasn't too sturdy himself.

Historian Richard Francaviglia generously describes Steele's map of their route as an "imaginative depiction" that included details of peach orchards, farming lands, Hopi villages, vegetation, and mountains. "He uses a ladder-like symbol to depict steep cliffs," Francaviglia explains. "Although these symbols are unconventional and contribute to the sense that they are intuitive rather than scientific, they work extremely well." He also credits Steele with a perceptive understanding of biogeography. However, as Compton explains, "the big problem with the Steele map and diaries is that they give names to places that didn't catch on," and retracing the modern terrain is very difficult.[43]

Steele sent George A. Smith his map and a report, and explained that when Hamblin's company arrived home January 9th, "it was a joyfull meeting and the Breathren gave thanks to God and their Breathren for their

Kindness and even the Laymanites thanked God and the Mormons and said surely God had heard our prayers and the Mormons love one another.[44]

In his private journal Steele skipped that "love one another" stuff and wrote his real feelings. "This has been one of the hardest trips I ever took," he explained. "[W]e ware nearley starved to death by the improvident Management of Jacob Hamblin," who had asked the missionaries to bring too few supplies, "encouraged Indians around so that there ware 6 Men More than our scanty supplies would admit of," and then buried provisions in the boat "in a Cash (or Hole in the ground)" on the Colorado. Since they didn't go back that way, those supplies were lost. "[T]hat was the Caus of our Starvation—Well we got over it."[45]

This wasn't the first time Hamblin's poor planning had led to near starvation, but Steele's disregard for the well-being of their Hopi guests is one reason it was Hamblin, not him, who earned the nickname "Apostle to the Lamanites." And Steele himself had helped lead a similarly ill-prepared expedition in June 1852 into Upper Long Valley.

*

The Steeles' move to the new town of Toquerville and the settlement of nearby St. George were manifestations of the growing Kingdom. The desire for livestock range and an increasing population were drivers. In late 1863 Steele reported expansion had taken up "all the watering places of any account this Side the Buckskin Mountain," on the north end of the Kaibab Plateau.[46]

In early 1864 Mormons began moving into the Sevier country northeast of Parowan. John was by now so familiar with the area he was asked to take a group there. With or without him, settlers founded Circleville, Glenwood, Alma (now Monroe), Panguitch, Richfield, and Salina. These lands were attractive to the Mormons for the same reasons that local tribes valued them, but the ecosystem could provide for either Mormon agricultural practices or Native seasonal use—not both. These incursions disrupted Native life and led to starvation and fury.[47]

Mormons responded to Native grievances by arming themselves.[48] William H. Dame, commander of the Iron Military District, met with Steele and organized the Sixth Battalion from men in Toquerville and Harmony, two communities about twenty-three miles apart but separated by the steep

Steele's map of the Moqui/Hopi trip. *LDS Church History Library.*

Black Ridge. William W. Hutchings—a poor speller with worse handwriting, but thankfully diligent in keeping the "Battalion Book" of Steele's command—tells us in his "Minits of the organizedation of battalion" that on May 10, 1864, John Steele was elected major and Hutchings, adjutant.[49]

In theory a battalion was made up of three companies, and a company of five platoons, but Steele's actual command was two companies totaling eight platoons, half the size recommended. By December 7, 1866, Kanarra's militia company had been added to Steele's battalion, increasing its strength to the preferred three-company cohort.[50]

In May 1864 Steele set up guards for Toquerville and New Harmony, though serious hostilities didn't begin until April 1865 with the Black Hawk War.[51] Antonga, called Black Hawk by the Mormons, created a sophisticated multitribal and territorial alliance of Natives and a few renegade whites who were soon making a living from stolen Mormon cattle and horses.

At the same time Brigham Young and Col. Patrick E. Connor of the U.S. Army were feuding. Connor, based in Salt Lake, was looking for excuses to augment his Fort Douglas forces, and Young was looking for anything to keep Connor weakened. If Young acknowledged he had a full-fledged "Indian war" on his hands, it could strengthen genocidal Connor, who had slaughtered hundreds of Native people in the 1863 Bear River Massacre.[52] So Young, no longer governor and with no legal authority to do so, used the Nauvoo Legion—which the *Salt Lake Tribune*, with its exquisite sarcasm untampered by worries about accuracy, later described as "a rebel and Falstaffian militia"—to fight a war that he had no desire to publicize or escalate.[53]

Steele organized a cavalry and a review inspection on September 19, 1865.[54] Cavalry proved to be the Mormons' main force because they were facing clever marauders. Rumors from the Paiutes in late October claimed Antonga was going to invade Berry's Valley (now Glendale) or attack Kanarra, anywhere but contiguous.[55]

Maybe responding to concerns in the Kanab area, Steele held an inspection the day after Christmas despite the unseasonably cold weather. The sixty-six men had among them nine muskets, thirty-three rifles, sixteen Colt revolvers (presumably the cap and ball type used in the Civil War), three swords, thirty-four pounds of powder, and sixty-nine and a half pounds of lead. Besides that, John himself was well-armed: he had a rifle, revolver, sword, horse pistol, and one pound of powder with two pounds of lead.[56]

In early January 1866 there were reports that Navajos had crossed the Colorado and also suspicion that Dr. James H. Whitmore and his ranch hand Robert McIntire had been killed at Pipe Spring.[57] The militia was called up on January 10th, and the next day Steele was directed to send eight men with twenty days' rations, supplies, and shovels to Whitmore's ranch.[58] There they found the bodies of Whitmore and McIntire, which

JOHN STEELE – 1860S

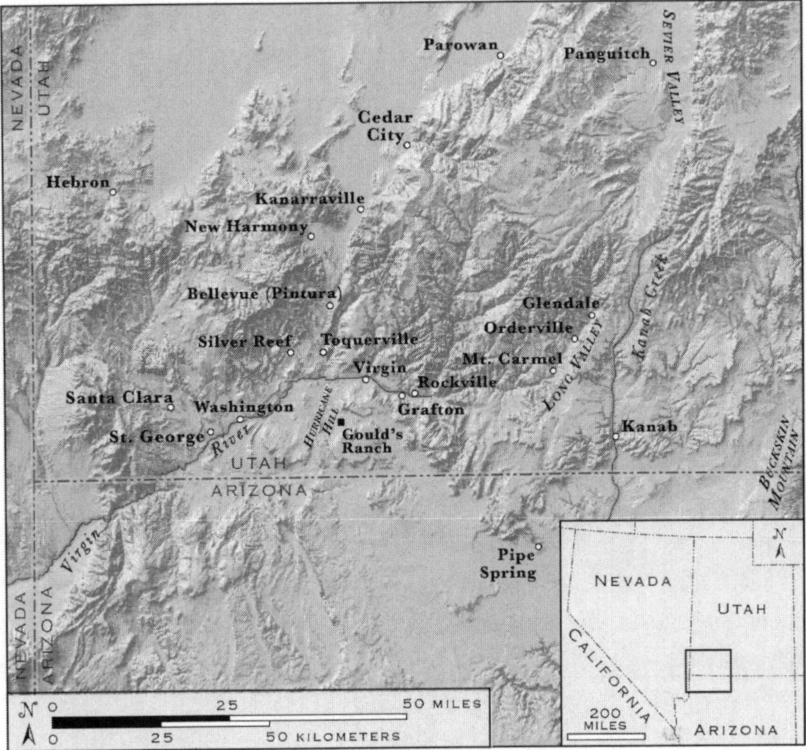

John Steele country during the Black Hawk War, 1865–1872. *Map created by Chelsea McRaven Feeney.*

were hauled through Toquerville on the way to St. George for burial. Steele reported to George A. Smith that the two men were shot while gathering cattle, Whitmore by a bullet in the breast, and McIntire with seven arrows.[59]

He also wrote that after finding the bodies, the militia came upon a camp of eight Paiutes with the ranchers' clothes and other goods, and after they "shoed [showed] fight," the militia slaughtered seven. But there was no fight: the Paiutes were tortured and then executed. Apparently, they had been given the murdered men's belongings by the mostly Navajo perpetrators.[60]

Steele was unfamiliar with how wily and versatile the Navajos were. They divided into groups of two or three, sneaking in on foot to steal stock.

Their tactics included cutting down and holding small trees while advancing toward Mormon stock, or hiding inside the hide and head and hoofs of gutted yearling calves to get into corrals.[61]

Steele had a blind spot regarding the Navajo role in the depredations and was convinced Whitmore and McIntire were not victims of members of that tribe: "[T]hey all prove to be pah utes and have been stealing all the time and laying the blame on the Navijoes." He thought preaching to them was worthless and wrote that if there was any good in them, "I Cannot see it."[62]

Apostle George A. Smith went south in 1866 to ensure there were sufficient protective measures.[63] He met with Toquerville citizens at the proposed site of their new social hall, made some remarks, and later inspected Steele's troops and others on a stormy day at Virgin City. Despite the weather, Col. Daniel D. McArthur had enough fortitude to drill Steele's men for an hour. Though a Nauvoo Legion general, Apostle Smith was so rotund he couldn't ride a horse; when he left Toquerville, Steele hauled Smith and Smith's cousin Jesse N. Smith in a lumber wagon as far as Washington.[64]

John was with Apostle Smith when he was sledded into Panguitch, visited outlying areas, and established Fort Sanford.[65] This was arduous, but as Joseph Fish recalled, "Our trip had been enjoyed by all, for Bro. George A. was a great story teller and always had one to tell."[66]

The original plan was for a permanent defensive settlement on the Sevier, and Apostle Erastus Snow wrote Steele about moving to Fort Sanford.[67] Steele replied, apologizing for not being at "the Cevier yet but am makeing haste to get there as soon as possible."[68] But the main import of Steele's letter was to report the deaths of Joseph and Robert Berry and Robert's wife Mary Isabella "about two Miles beyond Maxwells Ranch in the Cedars."[69] The Paiutes said the murderers were Navajos, but Steele argued, "We think here that the Piedes [Paiutes] are the Navijoes and this is Retaliation for the three that ware Killed by Capt James Andrews [Andrus]." Steele said there was no point hunting for the perpetrators over the mountains "when they are all around us." Part of the reason for his conclusion that the guilty were Paiutes is because they "Keep up a Constant Telegraph Communication and are apprised of all the movements that are going on on both sides when the Express arived here this Morning from Colonel Winsor stateing the Matter they Piedes Could Come and tell me all about it but not before."[70]

With trigger-happy and paranoid Mormon militiamen surrounding

George A. Smith, John Steele's mentor. *Utah Historical Society.*

them, and the Navajos and Utes seeing them as treacherous, the Paiutes would have been foolish not to amplify their communications and selectively cooperate with both sides.

Steele's son Mahonri, having turned seventeen, served under Capt. James Andrus, helping drive Kanab's two thousand stock to the foot of Hurricane Hill just before the town was evacuated. John's son John Alma spent ninety-five days of his fourteenth year stationed at Fort Sanford near the mouth of Bear Creek, nine miles below Panguitch. He furnished his own horse and afterward served under Capt. Albert Minnerly. By the time he was fifteen, he had earned the Indian War pension that would be his only income in old age.[71]

Some incident of perceived insubordination in June 1866 sent Steele into a tizzy, but we only have Erastus Snow's saintly response to infer why: "Yours of the 21st inst. has been received. In reply will say Bro John lift up your head and rejoice, and say 'get behind me Satan.'" Then Snow added the Bible verse he found most comforting when he was the victim of Brigham's sharp and sometimes cruel tongue: "Whom the Lord loveth he chasteneth."[72] He continued to fish up hopeful scriptures: "'every tree that beareth fruit he pruneth that it may bring forth more fruit.' Be patient and humble Bro. John and you shall yet triumph over all your foes." Snow added, "Your resignation is not accepted, at least not for the present, or until some further development. If any spirit of insubordination or disregard for your military authority manifests itself while you are in the line of duty fail not to report such case and I will further instruct you."[73] Steele stayed on as major, and Snow obviously valued his contributions.

Steele's role turned out to be mostly in logistics and commissary, maybe the least exciting but most important parts of warfare. He bettered Jacob Hamblin in coordinating and securing men, teams, and supplies for the patrols, pursuits, and occasional fighting. For example, Steele reported to Erastus Snow in late 1866, "Started from Virgen City at 6 30 a.m. 13 bushels corn 110 lbs Flour 3 ½ Gallons molasses 20 lbs beef 5 lbs Salt two frying pans 2 span mules and wagon 5 men mounted = Signal fires seen on the mountain due south of Virgen City at 9 oclock last night."[74]

Steele was ordered to furnish ten men and two teams to build a fort near Gould's Ranch. Perhaps as part of this, Capt. J. D. Pearce telegraphed "Maj Steele" December 30th: "You will rendisvous at the Troughs [by Gould's] tomorrow morning at 10 oclock and take Command of the forces and proce[e]d to Pipes springs to reconoitre & watch to prevent the Escape of Indians with stock and use caution & prudence. I will reinforce you at that Point." Pearce estimated the dragooned men would need eight days' rations.[75]

Steele had five men at Gould's in early February when his son-in-law Joseph Fish accompanied him on a visit there.[76] Raiders got thirty or so horses from Pine Valley, thirteen cattle at Washington, and then headed toward the Buckskin Mountain. When it was so warm in early 1867 that men were flushing flies out of their coffee, the militia from Toquerville and elsewhere—including Steele's men and perhaps Steele himself—were in pursuit. They surprised raiders near Whitmore's Ranch and killed three, mortally wounded others, and recovered all the stock but one horse, killed in the attack.[77]

The Mormon responses so far had been mostly ineffectual, but on January 15, 1867, a telegraph line was completed through Toquerville to St. George.[78] Within days George A. Smith sent Steele a telegram, to which he replied by the same medium on January 22nd, but worried by the relocation of the telegraph office when cotton donations pushed it out of the tithing office, he followed up with a chatty letter.

"We have had our share of Indian troubles lately," Steele explained, and he outlined what the militia had been doing and the alleged role of Navajos. But he remained skeptical: "It looked like Meal But Mischief Consealed under it which has been bitterly proven from last Friday night the Indians stole two horses from the Washington field." Then "the Indians" become "an Indian": the pursuers discovered a trail that looked like at least a hundred animals had been stolen, but when they ran into "him"—the single Indian—"he succeeded in making good his escape with the Horses" because he (or they) got the animals into an impregnable position in the Buckskin Mountains.

Steele eventually figured out that Antonga was much more sophisticated in his alliances than originally thought. On the back of a penciled telegram he received from St. George dated only "2"—probably November 2, 1869—he jotted the following (I've added brackets to clarify):[79]

Shiverats	or Read [Red] Lake Indians
Tabeeheats Tabeewats	on the other side th Coloread
Navajoes	

These were the main tribes aligned with Antonga. The "Shiverats or Read [Red] Lake Indians" were more commonly known as Sheberetches, the remnants of Walkara's powerful Ute band, based in what is now Moab. The "Tabeeheats/Tabeewats" were the Tabaguache ("People of Sun Mountain"), or Uncompahgre Utes, from southwestern Colorado.[80] Other tribes joined at times, sometimes even the Hopi. The Navajo, pushed ferociously by U.S. troops in the Long Walk of 1863–64, were rebuilding their wealth with Mormon stock, the Anglo encroachers reminding them of the profitability of robbery.[81]

The continual drain of horses and cattle was very discouraging to Steele and his neighbors, who in the best of times were often barefoot and hungry. Sixtus Johnson wrote that four out of five settlers had become impoverished, and when one group of militiamen were called out, eight had such poor horses they were sent back.[82] Steele himself reported that "in the years 1864-5-6 & 7 Stolen by Navvjos I lost a number of Head of Stock both Horses and Cattle, at one time in the Year 1865 I lost four 4 year old Steers three Cows and Calves, also Several head of Horses," and he claimed he had been under arms for a year.[83]

When Steele wrote to George A. Smith a few weeks later, he was taking "Indian" threats in stride and barely glanced on that subject: "The Indians still seems disposed to trouble us a little just enough to Keep us wide awake and on hand[.] our people wants to get themselves armed with Breech loading Guns as fast as they can."[84] Regimental drills continued frequently.[85]

Antonga himself, recovering from being badly wounded in a gun battle, made peace with the Mormons in the late summer of 1867. Peace continued into October—the Mormons had not yet learned that Navajo raids invariably took place in the fall and winter—and Steele telegraphed Brigham Young that they'd stopped posting a guard.[86] Young undoubtedly corrected Steele, though we don't have his message; almost immediately Anson P. Winsor of Rockville wrote Young that his recommendation to keep guard would be adopted.[87]

John's son Mahonri was promoted to first lieutenant under Captain Minnerly and assigned as his adjutant by February 1868.[88] In the summer there were raids in Beaver and Iron Counties, but when Steele dropped in to visit the editor of the *Deseret News* in mid-October, "Indian problems" weren't interesting; instead, the editor reported they talked about agriculture and grasshoppers.[89]

Steele was back in Toquerville in time for the 1868–69 winter raids, and things proceeded as in the past. Navajos stole stock; militiamen pursued them—mostly unsuccessfully—and Steele organized supplies and personnel to support the militia.[90] Telegrams and messages would come asking him for supplies and soldiers, and he responded as quickly as able. Sometimes the supplies needed were interesting. L. L. Adams wrote "Major Steel" asking for yeast powder, a spoon, a mess pan, and a small tin bucket to carry water. His postscript described even more urgent needs: "Please send mo[r]e tobacco to Col Pearce also some writing paper and a news paper and oblige." This note confirms they were low on paper since it was written on a tiny scrap.[91]

By now John knew the raids "Commensed in November, and ^lasted^ for about twenty days, we had all our Men and Horses that were fit for servace in the field, but did not find the Indians." They recovered a lot of stock, but "mostly by the help of our friendly Indians." These Paiutes were the ones Steele blamed for the raids earlier in the war. "[T]he Indians feel well and are willing to help our people Guard the Country," John added, "and expressed themselves willing to go out and look after our enomay as far as the Buckskin Mountain, but they ware afraid to go alone or without some of our folks with them." The Mormons were so grateful for this help that Erastus Snow held two special gift-giving ceremonies for the Paiutes.[92]

Since there was only one place where the Navajo raiders could get the animals across the Colorado River, Steele—who had been through there on his Moqui/Hopi mission—proposed a solution. Mud Canyon, where he had learned their horses weren't "amphebeous," could be dynamited and blockaded.[93] Steele's dynamiting recommendation was acted upon, though when isn't certain.[94]

The conflicts continued into late 1869 and Steele made a trip to the Black Ridge, where he found the "intrills of a beef" and was told fires had been seen on the West Mountain. "I still think there are Indians in the Country," he wrote Snow, and he organized a local militia in tiny Bellevue (now Pintura).[95]

This might have seemed an odd time for optimism, but Steele's Hopi mission companion Jehiel McConnell was wise in the ways of Native Americans. He wrote to George A. Smith from "Fort Canab" (Kanab) on December 17th that he had found about a hundred friendly "Indians" in good spirits, and John Mangrum was a capable leader. With the promise of intervention by Jacob Hamblin, he was sure "no man with whom I am acquainted will exert a better influence."[96]

McConnell was right: the adversary in the Dixie area now consisted of a few dozen Navajos. Some came back in February 1870 and made off with a few horses from Hebron, but the Mormons were prepared and had less stock to steal.[97] As late as October 1st, Daniel D. McArthur directed Steele to provide two mounted infantry, armed and equipped with one month's rations, for picket duty at Kanab, Paria, and Pipe Spring, and for hauling supplies.[98] This almost overshadowed the news that Antonga/ Black Hawk had died September 26th.

In February 1870 Steele's neighbor and friend Augustus E. Dodge, speaking for the Washington County Grand Jury, wrote to Indian agent John E. Tourtellotte of Arizona asking him to intervene with the Navajos. This sidestepped Brigham Young's demands that federal officials be left out of the conflict—and it was effective.[99] Tourtellotte ordered the arrest of marauders while the Utah territorial legislature appropriated a thousand dollars to build forts to protect Kane County—expanding the frontier, as Steele and others had recommended—and he called a meeting of Navajo leaders in November at Fort Defiance. Utah's interests were represented by explorer Jacob Hamblin and John Wesley Powell, who was amazed at Hamblin's skills with Native peoples.[100]

The peace that was agreed on recognized that individual tribal members might violate their pledges, but if so, federal troops would be sent in retaliation.[101] This effectively ended Navajo raiding. In early 1871 Mormons began reoccupying the ceded territory on the Sevier and in Long Valley.[102]

In his journal, John Steele summed up his service so briefly, it is misleading. It seems he was reluctant to speak of his role provisioning the militia and apparently would have preferred to be on horseback. He telescoped events and overlooked the complications of the war, as well as the subtleties of the peace, but he did finally recognize the primary role of the Navajos in the raiding of livestock.[103]

Steele's autobiography was shorter and more accurate, maybe aided by the unacknowledged editor who published the extracts from his journal in the *Utah Historical Quarterly*. "I soon had to take hold of the military of our part of the country, as Major in the 10th regiment of infantry under Col. McArthur and General Erastus Snow. I took quite an active part during our Indian wars."[104]

That's how he chose to remember it. Despite inflating his leadership by not detailing his actual logistical and other accomplishments, he undersold his own abilities and importance. It's ironic that he played an energetic role in organizing, arming, directing, and feeding the militia, but it was Jacob Hamblin's soft and patient guidance that helped make the peace.

11

PRACTICING ALL TRADES

"Our winters are very mild and pleasant," bragged prospector William T. Barbee from Utah's "Dixie" in December 1875. But by May, Wells Spicer reported, "Whew! Hot, hotter, hottest, hottenhot, hottentotter, hottenottentisimus!"[1] In August, John Steele's creative juices were so baked, all he could write was that when it got too hot, "a feeleng of Lassitude prevails among the most robust Constitutions, and feeling they would like to flee to the Snow Glad [clad] Mountains for a Short time."[2]

The heat, isolation, and water scarcity meant Dixie had the highest turnover of the expanding Mormon empire; prying a living out of the edge of the Mohave Desert, the driest in North America, was hit-and-miss. Between the late 1860s and his British mission call in 1877, Steele was building the Kingdom through agriculture, cobbling, carpentry, contracting, politics, lawyering, postmastering, expanding Mormon cooperative efforts, and mining silver. This was also a time of family changes, with his children marrying and Steele taking a second wife. And then he found himself peripherally entwined with the fate of John D. Lee.

Those who adapted to this desert were compensated by moderate, mostly snowless winters and exuberant crops "when," as Steele wrote, "we Can Get sand enough in one place, and Watter enough to make it ly still."[3] The challenges were serious though, as John Smith, George A.'s father, wrote: "The general topography of Utah is a succession of vast mountain ranges and impassable barriers to barren, naked rock; also desert plains that would do honor to Arabia."[4]

This was especially true in southern Utah. Rather than tidy flatlands waiting to be turned into farms, settlers were surrounded by startling but agriculturally useless geological wonders. The most famous, Zion Canyon, throws geology at the visitor with such force, one feels the need to duck from the sky-reaching buttes, mountains, and mesas that took 150 million years to carve, including the Navajo sandstone Great White Throne; the dirty yellow and white Checkerboard Mesa; the white stone–capped Court of the Patriarchs, with peaks named Abraham, Isaac, and Jacob; and Angel's Landing, stretching its rocky finger so high it invites a celestial touch while giving the bravest visitors a God's eye view of the canyon. What's more remarkable is this wasn't a lone phenomenon, for Toquerville is surrounded by unexpected geographical wonders—so much so, the most persistent challenge for Mormon incursion was the near-impossibility of making usable roads.[5]

Isolation counted as a draw for some of the first settlers in spring 1858. Mountain Meadows Massacre leader Isaac C. Haight selected the first town members. According to Steele, they included Philip Klingensmith, John Willis, Samuel Pollock, and Josiah Reeves, all implicated in the massacre. Nephi Johnson, the Native interpreter at Mountain Meadows, was in the "tokerville reserve" exploring Zion Canyon by fall. The first meeting house in the town was built by Robert Wylie, "used as an assassin at the Mountain Meadows Massacre." Other early settlers included massacre participants John M. Higbee, John Menzies Macfarlane, and a desirable witness for federal prosecutors, John Steele.[6]

"The appearance of the country to the first settlers was very forbidding and the thought was that they could live there all alone and none to molest nor make them afraid," Steele wrote in the first history of the town.[7] And what could be more fearsome for the murderers than justice for their Mountain Meadows victims?

Steele tackled the problem with limited agricultural land, reporting to the *Deseret News* that they had added to the town about a thousand acres of benchland, about half of which was to be planted in wheat in the late fall. A hundred-acre farm was being developed to the northwest of Toquerville, and the town itself was trying to expand west. Steele wrote to George A. Smith complaining about the terrible winds and noting, "when a day Comes that the Wind does not blow we think it is a pet and Means Something."[8]

Town members, including Steele, tried growing cotton, and in fall 1863 he wrote, "our Cotton Crop is nearly gathered."[9] His daughter Elizabeth remembered her mother made thirty-five yards of fabric.[10] But cotton proved unprofitable, and Toquerville's bishop, Joshua T. Willis, led the way for survival when he planted the first orchard. Fruit turned out to be

Steele's main source of income—"that is our Cash," he wrote in 1891.[11] In 1874 Toquerville claimed to produce 30,000 pounds of dried peaches that were shipped to major centers including St. Louis, St. Joseph, Chicago, and Burlington.[12] In good years Steele's orchards produced as much as five hundred bushels of apples, peaches, apricots, and currants. He often peddled his produce in Iron County, trading fruit, grapes, and wine for flour, potatoes, and other goods.[13]

John and Catherine Steele grew a lot of grapes—in 1868 John expected half a ton of them. When he was away in 1877, he wrote to Catherine in June to make most of their grapes into wine and dry what she could, and in September, "I am glad to hear you have got the peeches dried also the Wine made."[14]

"Dixie wine" was the name of the local product, and it had a distinctive taste and allegedly peculiar results. The *Pioche Record* speculated that Dixie wine was so toxic because of all the flies crushed in the wine presses, and more than once claimed its effect was so powerful, drinkers would steal their own clothes. One inebriate got so drunk he went home and ran off with his own mules.[15]

"I have a very fine place here," Steele wrote in September 1902. "A Good orchard & vine yeard with plenty of Lucern Grass to keep all the Horses & cows I care about keeping up, the rest runs upon the Range. We dont use much meat as we have So much Fruit and Vegitables." Despite there being plenty of Dixie wine, he claimed there were "But very few Drunkards as it is So Cheap few think any thing about it."[16] But he was writing to his niece in Australia and misrepresented the effects of the wine.

John and Catherine enjoyed the occasional glass of wine, but their son John Alma became an alcoholic. Dixie wine made "drunkards of a good many both old and young," wrote Steele's son-in-law Joseph Fish, who with his usual candor named several of them. John wrote his daughter Susann that wine was the cause of a good deal of evil in Toquerville.[17]

Besides tending his orchards and vineyards, Steele reluctantly continued cobbling, but advised his niece, "Shoemaking is a lost business and Evin if well followed, it don't pay."[18] When the "roving reporter of the Desert," Nell Murbarger, visited Toquerville in the 1950s, she interviewed eighty-nine-year-old Lorine Higbee, daughter of Steele's sometime business associate Edwin R. Lamb. Murbarger wrote that according to Higbee, Steele would trace "odd-shaped patterns on stiff sheets of the local leather,

John and Catherine Campbell Steele, April 4, 1873. *Family photograph.*

[and] he cut and fashioned these pieces into boots and shoes, the muted blows of his cobbler's hammer sounding along the quiet street until late each night."[19]

John's cabinetry, carpentry, and general contracting also kept him in work, especially since Brigham Young had two large public works projects in St. George. Besides repairing Appleton M. Harmon's cotton press for Bishop Willis, Steele was also doing carpentry work in 1867 that required at least 843 feet of lumber, most likely for the telegraph office in Willis's house.[20]

A scrap of paper that Steele's son Mahonri used to practice his writing recorded an exchange with William B. Lang for two and a half bushels of peaches as well as scribbled notes about a twelve-by-fourteen lean-to, a drawing of a "Joice" (joist), and a notation about hauling rock for an eighteen-inch foundation.[21] This incapsulated three occupations: Steele's fruit-raising, his carpentry, and Mahonri's future as a schoolmaster.[22]

Steele was also a member of what James Lewis, the former Iron County judge and now Kanab resident, derisively called "the Toker Ring," which controlled Kane County politics. John was rewarded with an almost continuous stream of county offices. Lewis was a sometime friend and sometime rival. ("I know the Devil is not Dead and I know James Lewis[, Edwin] Lamb & Logan but they must have their day as well as others," John wrote in 1877.)[23]

Lewis, defeated in his wishes to become Kane County probate judge, was reduced to sharing platitudinous nautical metaphors with Steele, his fellow one-time sailor. Lewis urged cautious retreat.

> Now John I will give you my advice—and that is to Keep close in Show these Stormy times do not venture do not get into the power of any one, do not Spread out beyond your Means so as to [e]ndanger your home do not trust to others take in Sail Reef down go slow, go slow the Rocks are around us, We are our own pilot to Steer our own Ship Keep Clear of the Rocks of the Sands there are Shoals ahead Sound often Keep off the Rocks, the Howling of the Storm is heard Reef down close Reef Topsails We shall have to S[u]ceed [?] by & by—Hear one of your friends, Keep in Show.[24]

Most likely Lewis was contemplating his own retreat as his political machinations fell short; the east end of the county, where he lived, was almost powerless against the larger population around Toquerville.

Steele didn't think he needed advice from Lewis to navigate politics, and putting down his head and closing reef topsails wasn't his method. In 1873 he became the Kane County surveyor, a position of importance as settlers in new country needed surveys, and when corners marked by the federal Surveyor General were lost, only county surveyors could reestablish them.[25] Some of Steele's surveys are in a small, blue-green-covered spring 1874 catalog of Hanauer, Kohn & Co., including surveys of Shonesburg and Springdale. He told Brigham Young both towns had the potential to grow.[26] The Springdale of today confirms Steele's prediction, but Shonesburg is a ghost town.

John was chosen assessor and collector of Kane County on March 5, 1874; his predecessor was William A. Bringhurst.[27] George A. Smith, writing to James Lewis about complaints against Steele's friend James H. Martineau, also a surveyor, captured the challenges for frontier officeholders: "As to his surveys, if he has been somewhat remiss, it is doubtful if he is the only one in the territory who has. Our public officers, or many of them, are called to office without much previous experience, and many of them no doubt make awkward work."[28] Despite the complaints, Martineau had a widely respected surveying career ahead of him.

Steele also lawyered, handling at least two divorces and other legal work.[29] His past service as a probate judge, his omnivorous mind, and maybe his long relationship with Judge Lewis helped prepare him. His most controversial case was representing his Cedar City friend George Wood, a one-time iron forger, who shot, beat, and killed Olive Curtis Coombs Chamberlain Higby, and shot and beat her daughter Emily Coombs. Wood, who was probably drunk, stated the reason was that Emily, who was between thirteen and sixteen, had seduced his nineteen-year-old son, Joseph.[30] At Wood's hearing Steele made a motion that his client be admitted to bail, which was denied; Wood was so reviled locally for his crime that Judge Silas Smith, Apostle George A. Smith's cousin, was worried that if he were released, he'd be lynched.[31] But George A. wrote Silas, "I think the killing of such a whore benefits the community enough to render the case bailable."[32] When Wood pled guilty and was "confined to hard labor for life," Steele was no longer his attorney. However, Wood was treated with unbelievable leniency at the penitentiary, including being allowed to wander the streets, and he was eventually pardoned because of a petition led by Apostle Smith and signed by both Mormons and Gentiles.[33]

Paralleling Steele's lawyering was another profession. "I have filled the office of Justice of the Peace in Washington County many times," Steele wrote (and, because of boundary changes, Kane County), "until I would get tired of it then I would throw it up and have Some one Else take it."[34]

His surviving justice records, from a later period, show that often the problems Steele faced were rooted in too much Dixie wine leading to swearing, fights, chicken stealing, bullying, and general mayhem. Steele was so unbending, he once insisted that Constable John Batty serve himself a summons for assault and battery. On the back, the little fighting constable wrote, "Served | John Batty."[35]

Judge-Bishop Joshua T. Willis appointed John prosecuting attorney for Kane County on March 9, 1873, when it was so cold St. George had four inches of snow, presaging a chilly spring.[36] But Steele's papers record only one case, a referral to the justice of the peace for an 1873 Christmas Eve fracas in which his son John Alma was attacked at 2 a.m. It must have been quite a party, and one can't help but speculate it was sloshed with Dixie wine. The record doesn't reveal the outcome of the case, but Steele got another term as prosecutor in 1879.[37]

Steele's role in the Toker Ring may have also helped him with another job reliant on patronage. His Greenfield cousins, James and Jane, were postmaster and then postmistress of Holywood for over forty years; John himself was the first acting postmaster of Las Vegas.[38] He became Toquerville postmaster on March 22, 1865, and served for ten years, but given his claim to have had sixteen years' tenure, he was probably assistant postmaster to Bishop Joshua T. Willis before that.[39]

In mid-June 1876 James Lewis's political antenna notified Steele about possible trouble: "our PM^s [postmasters] say they are afraid they shall lose their offices as they learn the whole Johnson fraternity is to go out who will be the Unlucky Man I do not know." Less than two months later John was replaced by William Lehi "Lee" Dykes, son of George Parker Dykes, Steele's Mormon Battalion nemesis. The elder Dykes had ridden into Toquerville the year before intending to settle and maybe pursue mining, as his son Lee was doing.[40]

Steele's loss of the postmaster job brought a letter from his talented Kanab friend William D. Johnson Jr.: "I see by the [Beaver] Enterprise that you have been removed from the P.O. am very sorry that your enimies have so much influence to use against you."[41] The fact that three other Kane County postmasters were replaced the same day as Steele suggests his political faction lost a patronage fight. He felt wronged, and ten years later he received $41.86 backpay.[42]

After he was dismissed, Steele was pressed hard for a missing piece of mail, and later he wrote his wife Catherine that he'd been too much bothered with "the Cursed post office and Every thing Connected with ^it^ and feel Glad it is Gone." He claimed, "I would not take it again for all Toquerville and John Nebeker and the Whole possy Could have had it years before but I did not want to be run by them but it was never any benefit to me."[43]

Meanwhile, the railroad was hustling its way to California to turn the West into a colony for Eastern money, and in response, Brigham Young began rolling out more of the communitarian ideals of Joseph Smith that had attracted Steele in the 1840s.[44]

Cooperatives, springing from the Owenite socialism Steele heard preached in Glasgow, were popular and successful in England.[45] They were Young's first major counterbalance, and the *Deseret News* in 1868 lauded "Co-operation": "In Great Britain especially they are entering largely into the system and great benefits follow its adoption." Young argued the alternative was "a community with a few rich men, and the rest poor and depending on the rich."[46] The anti-Mormon *Salt Lake Tribune*, jumbling Robert Owen with Karl Marx, complained the Mormon cooperative movement was "communistic," but the *Deseret News* cited Owen's son Robert Dale Owen as among "the benevolent school of philosophers" who recognized common stock possession "as the normal condition of society."[47]

Steele recalled that Toquerville's "first co-operative dry goods store was organized May 14, 1869, with a capital of $2,500, and now [1880] has a capital of running stock $5,000."[48] Called the Southern Utah Mercantile Co-Operative, it was organized by delegations from Toquerville, Rockville, Virgin, and Harrisburg; at the same time, they set up the Kane County Wool-Producing Institution. A year later the Canaan Co-Operative Stock Company was organized in Toquerville; in 1872, John wrote dunning letters to owners of "the Toquerville stock herd," which may have been another name for the Canaan Co-Operative. Efforts were also made to set up a Toquerville dairy cooperative.[49]

The Panic of 1873 jolted Brigham Young into taking the next step of Mormon economic millennialism, the United Order, because even cooperatives required stockholders, which meant participation was out of reach for the poor. This proposal was that men could more efficiently organize their labor, while women staffing communal kitchens and bakeries would allow other women time for factory work, clothing manufacture, and other needed tasks. Young claimed that "Half the labor necessary to make the people moderately comfortable" under the current system would make people rich through the United Order. This would be a society that "would never have to buy anything; they would always make and raise all they could eat, drink and wear." He recognized that only money rolls uphill, and countered that the poor could join United Orders through their labor.[50]

Young personally organized the Toquerville United Order, and the new bishop, William A. Bringhurst, was elected president. In this mostly cashless society, a board of appraisers was necessary since participants would be contributing goods, land, and labor. John's wife Catherine once held that position in the Toquerville Relief Society.[51] James Jackson and two others were appointed appraisers, but it proved unworkable because of Jackson's intransigence; maybe he'd been a peddler too long. He deadlocked the work.[52] The Order soon stopped working, and Isaac Haight wrote Brigham Young, gently and paternalistically faulting Bishop Bringhurst, nephew of William Bringhurst, former president of the Las Vegas mission: "Br Bringhurst is young with but little Experiance," and afraid to act with the dignity and independence his position demanded—lack of independence being a fault no one could charge on Haight.[53]

Steele was explicit when he wrote Brigham Young, claiming the Order failed because of lack of harmony among board members, and that even when the board was shuffled and reshuffled, the problems couldn't be resolved. He noted that after the United Order failed, Bishop Bringhurst told co-op members they could reclaim the property they had donated: "the people began to gather up the Harnice Waggons tools and all that Could be found of what had been turned in to the order and since that time there has been quite a standstill."[54]

Toquerville ended up with the same thing Orson W. Huntsman reported of the Hebron Order in Washington County: a "Disunited Order."[55] Lorenzo J. Slack, who joined at age seventeen, remembered, "I[t] wasn't much of a success"; his reward was a pair of oversized gaiters.[56] The Orders were hampered by human nature and particularly by the boldness of an experiment without enough successful empirical trials.

Though the United Order failed, many of the cooperatives survived for years, and Mormon devotion to communal values evolved but has never been abandoned.

*

A bullet hole in the Harrisburg Mining District record book hampers our understanding of John Steele's post–Las Vegas rendezvous with silver.[57] He served briefly as deputy to his friend Orson B. Adams, district recorder. One day Adams, soothed to a drunken stupor, hid his record book and couldn't find it when he sobered up. The whole district was in a panic, fearing their claims would be jumped. One company stationed a guard at its property, and it was only when Adams's wife Susann found the book under the mattress that the problem was solved.[58] Who later put a bullet through it may be an unsolvable mystery, but it challenges us in making full use of this source. (The temporary loss of the book may be why Adams lost the 1877 election for recorder by 83 to 130, and the 1878 election by 7 to 201.)

A prospector named John Kemple apparently boarded with Adams in 1866 and came back in 1868, intrigued by unexpected signs of silver in sandstone—generally considered a geological impossibility.[59] (Folklore says Kemple saw Adams's sandstone fireplace weeping molten silver.) In February 1871 he made a claim and, with others, organized the Union Mining District, soon to be renamed the Harrisburg Mining District, in the area that became known as Silver Reef. Speculators—including Adams, William Leany, and Samuel Pollock—filed at least five mining claims near St. George.[60] A few claims were filed in 1872, but it wasn't until 1874 that activity picked up. Then twenty-six claims were filed, including one by ten women who set up the Susann Company on the miles-long Pride of the West Ledge. (The Susann was named after Susann Smith Adams.)

Toquerville townsman Lorenzo J. Slack remembered that "Brother Steele and others thought there was silver at the reef and brought W. T. Barbee with a chemist [Thomas McNally] to find out."[61] Barbee made an exploratory visit in June 1875 and stumbled into petrified wood saturated with horn silver in sandstone at the north end of White Reef. He got the sensational story in the newspapers weeks before he staked his first claim.[62] Steele made two claims before Barbee, but the bullet hole in the record book obscures the locations. The strike was so new that in 1876 the *Pioche Record* informed its readers the place was named Silver Reef, not "Silver Wreath."[63]

It's clear that this was very early in the silver rush because Steele's Toquerville Company's claim was thirteenth of seventy-two filed in 1875 (he let it lapse the next year).[64] He made another claim in December, apparently south of Grapevine Springs.[65] His most successful effort was the Steele-Lamb (or Lamb-Steele) Mine, in association with Edwin R. Lamb.

Lamb's role in the mine is opaque; he and Steele each seem to have also had their own claims. In 1877 Steele denied Lamb was a partner, but

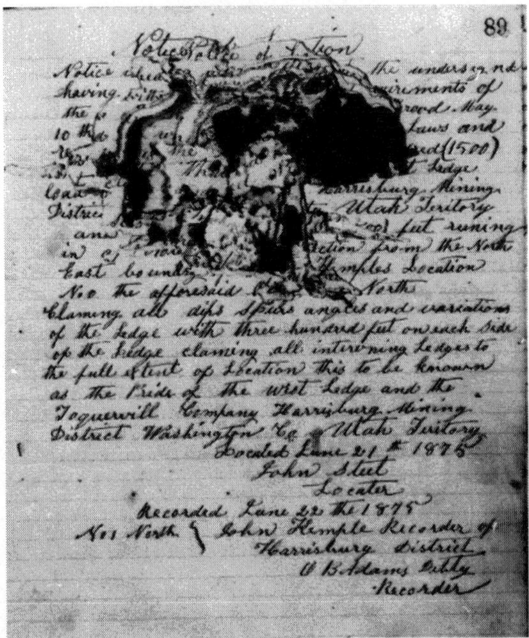
89

Claming all dips Spurs angles and variations
of the ledge with three hundred feet on each side
of the ledge claming all intervening ledges to
the full extent of Location this to be known
as the Pride of the West Ledge and the
Toquervill Company Harrisburg Mining
District Washington Co Utah Territory
Located June 21st 1875
John Steel
Locator
Recorded June 22 the 1875
No 1 North John Hemple Recorder of
Harrisburg District
O B Adams Deputy
Recorder

A bullet hole in the Harrisburg Mining District record book. *Utah State Archives.*

he wrote his wife Catherine, "as for the Mines," Lamb had "been Kicked out" because of his actions. Yet he later wrote that if the mines could be sold at value and expenses paid, he'd get his money out of Lamb's share and let him have the rest.[66]

The Steele-Lamb/Lamb-Steele Mine was on or near a farm Steele bought from Native people. (As late as October 1871, a band was living near Toquerville on Ash Creek, which is the general area of the farm and mine.) It was north of the Duffin Mine and south of the Dupaix and Spicer Mill and the Vanderbilt South Mine, several miles south of Silver Reef.[67] The Dupaix and Spicer Mill was so close, Steele filed a protest claiming the mill jeopardized his water rights.[68] Later claimants located the Dan Sperry Rip Van Winkle Mine north of the Steele-Lamb claim, and to the west a claim was made to the Argent Ledge, east of Grape Vine Wash.[69]

The *Salt Lake Tribune* described the "Lamb-Steele" Mine as "a good body of ore about four feet wide," but when a sample from the ore dump was assayed in August 1877, it produced only $67.54 of silver per ton, too little to be profitable. While others were hoping for stamp mills to process their ore, Steele went the poor man's route and paid Scotchman and ironworker David Barclay Adams to build him a horse-powered arrastra.[70]

"The whole face of the country for miles around is located and staked," wrote A. W. Nuckols to the *Salt Lake Tribune* in 1876. "Monuments and notices loom up in all directions, both up the hill and down the vale. Even the clay pastures and door yards are being dug up on the new addition."[71] Gentiles and Mormons including at least one Native American, Ebenezer Hanks's adopted son Albert—staked claims, while a good part of Pioche, Nevada, relocated to the new diggings.[72]

The mines became such an important source of cash for Dixie, the *Tribune* claimed that "Apostle [Erastus] Snow, on Sunday afternoon, while preaching, offered a prayer and blessing for 'Brother Barbee' and Brother [Lewis] Homan for their efforts in opening out and developing the mines in this vicinity."[73] That doesn't quite square with Snow's private assurances to Brigham Young that except for a few pockets, mining would probably "fizzle soon."[74] (Miners were willing to pay five cents each for early peaches and apples, which for orchardists like John Steele was as promising as silver.[75])

A correspondent for the *Salt Lake Herald* reported that "Steel's Arastra started up yesterday [May 28, 1876]" and expressed hope it would do better than Kirby, Pymm & Company's, but argued arrastras weren't adequate: "It is a mill we want and must have."[76] Because a lot of the ore had a high sulfur content, mill leaching destroyed as much as eighty percent of the silver, so arrastras could be more profitable in some circumstances.[77] However, "the Steele, by Steele & Co." was reported by Wells Spicer as one of many mines that could only be profitably worked with a stamp mill.[78]

Though categorizing the Steele-Lamb Mine as low-grade, in January 1877 the *Salt Lake Daily Herald* reported that it was doing "a quiet, steady business." Edwin R. Lamb's daughter Lorine Lamb Higbee claimed, "Many bars of silver about the size of a pound of butter" were produced by this mine; she said a bar was worth $300.[79]

While Steele was making some money and hoping for a lot more, Gentiles were moving in. James Lewis leered at the enterprise in a letter to Steele, writing, "I think Toker is getting like many other places of having their Celebrations graced by Miner Speculators Whoremongers." He envisioned, apparently scornfully, the town becoming infested with "Two or

An arrastra. *Alamy stock photo.*

three whorehouses & Saloo[n]s."[80] Actually, Silver Reef was a relatively quiet and orderly mining town.[81]

Prospectors weren't miners. Their goal was to sell their discoveries to someone with capital and find more ore, and in February 1877 John Steele found buyers in miner George Goddard and engineer David McKelvey, for $7,000.[82] He had long dreamed of helping poor converts emigrate to Utah and had even written Brigham Young in July 1872 on the subject. With this prospective wealth, and the cost of emigrating a single individual from England $100, his hopes might be realized.[83]

*

Steele's family life changed considerably in the 1860s and 1870s. His daughter Elizabeth married Australian-born James Stapley (brother of Charles Stapley, one of the town's most successful vintners and a member of the town bishopric) and became a formidable Kanarra midwife; residents explained her personality by reminding themselves "she was a Steele."[84]

"[S]ome of my Boys thinks of going up to the City this spring," John wrote George A. Smith in March 1869, "and if possable get their Endowments, one of them Mahonri Moriancumer, thinks of takeing him a wife, I wish you would help him a little, he thinks of Marying Bishop Edward Bunkers daughter" (Emily).[85]

Mahonri did marry Emily, but then went to St. George to help build the St. George Temple. Mary Ellen Jepson was there cooking, and during her month-long stay, she and Mahonri courted. They were married in the Salt Lake Endowment House in the spring.[86]

William Augustus Bringhurst, five feet, nine-and-a-half inches, with dark brown hair, was married to well-respected Selinda Dalby Palmer Bringhurst when he came to town. A year after his arrival, he married Steele's brisk daughter, sixteen-year-old Susann. Bringhurst was called as bishop after Joshua T. Willis was asked to resign, and he served until he died, picking up another wife, Mary Janet Stapley, along the way.[87]

John Peter Jensen was a half-orphaned Danish-Swede who'd nearly raised himself, working with a rough element freighting and carrying mail. (Maybe that's why his nose was conspicuously bent.) He had spent time in Toquerville in his boyhood (he was the unarmed private "Peter Yenson" in Steele's militia book) and returned about 1872 to board with the Spilsbury family and go to school. John's daughter Jane married Jensen on January 18, 1875, and in celebration their amiable friend Sheriff Ashton Nebeker inserted an announcement in the *Deseret News*.[88]

Steele's younger son, John Alma, never married and stayed at home throughout most of his parents' lives. He was a popular bass drummer in the town band and a dance caller. "Uncle Alma" was remembered by his niece Della Fish Smith as "naturally a very refined and gentelmanly man, large and strong." He worked at cowboying and odd jobs like undertaking. His addiction to Dixie wine too often entertained the town with mishaps and scrapes a soberer person may have avoided.[89]

Steele himself joined the newly-marrieds. In June 1869, after initially deciding against a Salt Lake City trip, he found himself heading to the metropolis with his friend William Theobald's stepdaughter, eighteen-year-old Mary Jane Ould. They left behind his orchard, stripped by grasshoppers of foliage and fruit buds.[90]

South African–born Mary Jane was part of a very large—and very poor—blended family. About a year earlier her mother had taken her eleven-year-old sister, Susie, to Elmeda Stringham Harmon and said, "Sister Harmon, we haven't enough to eat and you will have to take Susie and raise her."[91]

John Steele and Mary Jane Ould were married June 14th by Apostle Joseph F. Smith. The next day John had a surprise reunion with his Parowan friend James H. Martineau. In his journal, Martineau didn't mention the new wife, but he did say that he saw John for "the first time for many years. We were glad to see each other, and talk over old times." What was surprising about Steele's plural marriage is that it took so long. Steele and Calvin Smith had preached the first polygamy sermon in Parowan on Christmas Day, 1852, and he'd criticized those who refused to obey "the principles of the celestial law."[92] One suspects Catherine's cold disapproval had been at play.

There are only two records of this marriage left in John Steele's papers: an invitation to the 1869 Toquerville Christmas Social Parties from Isaac Duffin and Martin Slack addressed to "John Steele and Ladies"—fifty cents a couple and "Additional Ladies, 25 cents each"—and a scrap of paper labeled "DUPLICATE," which is a signed statement dated September 5, 1870, agreeing to dissolve their marriage. Brigham Young wrote that Mormon conventions were the wife asked for a divorce; in 1878 apostle and senator Erastus Snow introduced a bill to allow men to obtain a divorce from a wife in the same way a woman could get a divorce from a man, but it was defeated. It is therefore likely that ending the marriage was Mary Jane's idea.[93]

Besides acquiring sons- and daughters-in-law, the Steeles faced an irreparable loss when John found himself in Parowan at the bedside of his sociable and beloved daughter Mary Campbell Steele Fish, dying from what was believed to be heart disease but may have been eclampsia.[94] "Her father was with us when she passed away [December 12, 1874] and her mother was sent for at once and came up that day," wrote her husband, Joseph Fish.[95] Among the mourners was former apostle Amasa M. Lyman, who recorded her death in his journal and attended her burial on a cool winter day.[96]

With all the married children came many grandchildren, and several were drafted to stay with the Steeles and help with their orchard. "I am Glad you & James [Steele Stapley] went down to Toquerville and helped Grand Ma last peech cuting time," Steele wrote his eleven-year-old granddaughter, Kate Stapley. Granddaughter Della Fish remembered a rewarding visit with her grandparents, but "I did not regret saying good bye to the big patches of peaches I had helped to pick, cut and spread."[97]

*

While Steele's finances seemed to promise him a prosperous future, his friend John D. Lee was arrested in Panguitch by a posse including Thomas LeFevre, Steele's former son-in-law and now an apostate, and Franklin Fish, brother of Steele's son-in-law Joseph Fish.[98] (Franklin had graduated from horse and cattle rustler to federal marshal and had a future as a Silver Reef claim jumper.[99]) While Lee had been hiding, William H. Dame turned himself in voluntarily for his role in the Mountain Meadows Massacre.

Years of rumors had already convicted Lee and Dame but rumor isn't evidence; witnesses were needed, and most weren't volunteering. Residents of southern Utah were skittish of federal investigators. When Marshal William Stokes showed up one Sunday morning in Kanarra to find prospective jurors, churchgoers "instantly broke cover and fled to the hills."[100] Like Toquerville, Kanarra had residents with bloody hands. Indictments for seven men couldn't proceed because they were in hiding.[101] Curiously, no Natives were asked to testify, but one called "Beaver" told a newspaper reporter that a man named Moquepus said, "Lee came and asked them to help kill the emigrants" and complained that "these cowards have thrown all the blame on the Indians."[102]

Nevertheless, a few weeks after Stokes's failed mission to find Kanarra jurors, the feds had twenty-eight Mountain Meadows witnesses at Beaver, including John Steele. They were expected to testify in the anticipated trials of William H. Dame and John D. Lee.

The witnesses organized themselves with Orson B. Adams as chairman and Steele as clerk. As the proceedings dragged on, they became so dissatisfied that Steele and Adams wrote a letter to U.S. Marshal George R. Maxwell asking for means of subsistence while they waited for the trial because they'd left their harvest unattended. They also asked to be examined in chambers (privately by the judge) so those without relevant testimony could leave.[103]

Court officials, already stung by what they felt were such stingy federal appropriations that they didn't have the resources to track down other massacre participants, seemed insulted. Marshal Maxwell, who was later plausibly accused of embezzlement, replied tersely, "We did our duty when we summoned you; your duty was to attend," and it was up to prosecutors if they were examined in chambers.[104]

Eventually over a hundred witnesses were subpoenaed, and between a half and two-thirds were captured or showed up voluntarily, including the twenty-eight who signed the Adams-Steele letter.[105]

Steele was probably there as a witness in Dame's prospective trial. As mentioned earlier, according to John Chatterley, Steele was with Dame and the High Council when they debated the fate of the Fancher party.[106] But Dame was never tried, and Steele never testified. A reporter claimed all Dame's witnesses were present because he "is a Mormon in full standing," suggesting his witnesses weren't coerced into attendance.[107]

Lee was tried in July and August 1875, but the trial ended with a hung jury. He busied himself teaching a free prison school and wasn't tried again until July 1876. This time he was convicted and sentenced to be shot on January 26, 1877, but that was briefly postponed; the location ultimately chosen was Mountain Meadows.[108]

Steele followed Lee's case closely, met with him while he was in prison, and read his budding memoirs. When the prisoner was taken south to be shot, Steele jotted guardedly on the bottom of a retained copy of a letter to James Lewis, "John D Lee has been marched to the Meadows under command of a Company of Soldiers to witness the plase of former Exicutians."[109]

Some of Lee's family wanted him buried in Harmony, where Lee kin were awaiting the Great Resurrection. However, his wife Rachel, described by Army investigator James H. Carleton as "a simple minded person," had the body sent to Panguitch.[110] Lee was far from being a pariah there, and practically the entire town turned out for his burial. He "was highly esteemed as a neighbor and citizen. His disposition was peaceful and he was universally kind and obliging," reported the *Beaver Square Dealer*.[111] The victims were silent, but for Lee's friends it was time to remember his admirable work ethic, bone-breaking pioneering, and remarkable hospitality—and eventually he was acknowledged as a gifted diarist. His writings are basic to understanding the times and places where he lived.[112]

Mahonri M. Steele donated a burial plot for Lee, but when his daughter Nellie married Lee's grandson William Arthur Lee, "it hurt her parents greatly," remembered Nellie's brother, Mahonri M. Steele Jr.[113] By then

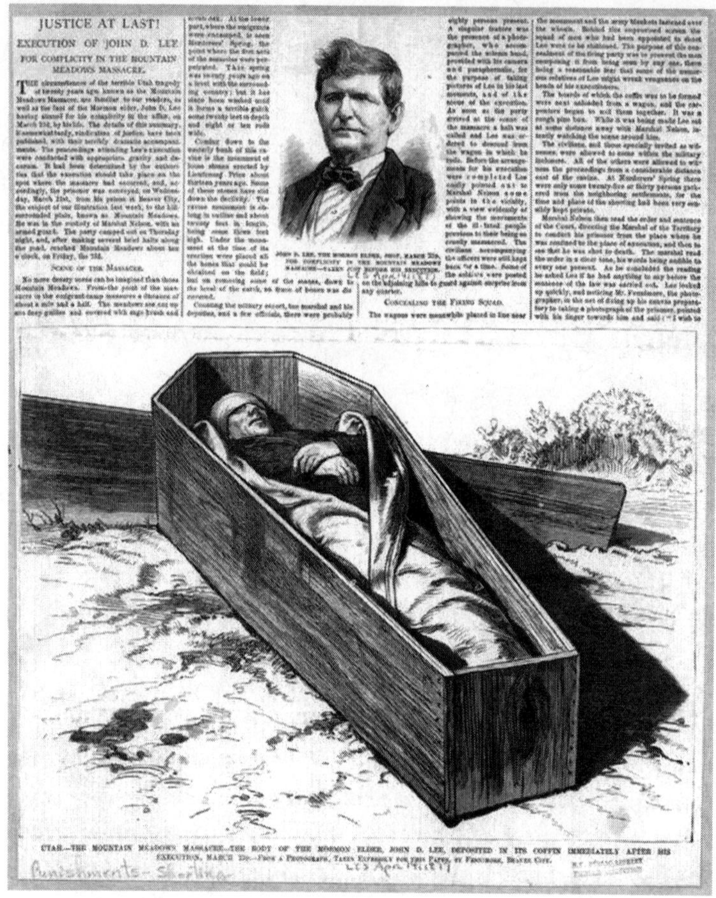

JUSTICE AT LAST!

EXECUTION OF JOHN D. LEE

FOR COMPLICITY IN THE MOUNTAIN MEADOWS MASSACRE.

"Justice At Last!," *Leslie's Illustrated Weekly, April 14, 1877.*

many southern Utahns felt the Lee family was cursed, but he has many accomplished descendants.

Curses on Lee or his family were secondary now in Steele's life. He was soon too busy witnessing and trying to counter the international revulsion to the Mountain Meadows horror, the terror raised by the name of John D. Lee, and the dead weight of polygamy on the reputations of his chosen people.

12

A BRITISH TRAMP

"Fifty tramps have been selected to scour the country in search of more Latter-day fools, and also to forage on the hen roosts of the Babylonian," proclaimed the *Salt Lake Tribune* when missionaries were called at the General Conference in St. George in April 1877.[1] John Steele and his son Mahonri were among those chosen, Mahonri later writing his mother with the same metaphor: "I am on the tramp all the while & truly as the Saviour said, 'without purse or scrip.[']"[2]

"The hands of several of these tramps are red with the blood of the Arkansas emigrants," the *Tribune* claimed, and later quoted the *Pioche Record*: "Most of the Mormons who figured in the massacre of the Arkansas emigrants are to be sent on foreign missions." The newspaper urged the federal government to "hurry up" if it expected to secure justice, but Mormon missionary records disprove a mass call-up of those implicated in the Mountain Meadows Massacre. After claiming Steele had a role in the murders, James McGuffie said he "was called by Brigham at last spring's conference to go on a mission to Europe. He is an Irishman and may be found on the Green Isle, where his mother is, if she is not dead," hinting Steele's call may have been to get him out of the country.[3]

Steele certainly had a more than keen interest in federal investigations and prosecutions. After arriving in Europe, he wrote in his journal that he got a "letter from Miss Sarah Amande Price telling of Jeter Clinton being put in chanes"; Clinton, a controversial justice of the peace, had been arrested in Salt Lake City for murder but was soon released.[4] In a letter to Catherine he wrote, "I hear there is 115 Indictments out against the Saints" and "Send me word if You Know who the Indictments are against."[5]

Before he left for Europe, Steele wrote his disgruntled deputy assessor, James Lewis, on March 22nd (the day before John D. Lee's execution), "I am going to conference and the talk is I Cross the Ocean as Soon after

Conference and Can get ready."[6] He gave Lewis a list of everyone owing taxes for 1875 and 1876, but didn't settle the county accounts before he left, giving Catherine no end of trouble with disgruntled bondsmen threatened by his default.

Steele dodged out of Toquerville at 9:30 a.m., May 8th. "I hope you and my family will excuse me for my abrupt Departure from home," he wrote Catherine two days later. "Knowing full well that my feelings would not Sustain me, I thought a sudden Retreat was the best part of Valor."[7]

He and his son Mahonri were soon on the train east. When they crossed the Missouri River to Council Bluffs, "I Knew the Place as soon as I saw it whare the Mormon Battalion started from," he wrote Catherine. "We Sean the old sight where the flag staf[f] stood and the big Slough I waded through to bring you to Sarpeas point[.] I knew it as soon as I saw ^it^."[8]

They stopped in Chicago to visit Catherine's childless sister, dressmaker Eliza Campbell Hamilton, and her husband James at 717 State Street.[9] They found the Hamiltons cool to missionary work, and Eliza quizzed Mahonri about how many wives they had.[10] In Philadelphia, Catherine's sister Mary Ann Campbell and the children of her sister Rebecca Campbell Boyd received them cheerfully and gave them a tour of Fairmount Park (John wrote "Fremont Park," thinking of his one-time Parowan guest and the first Republican candidate for president), but the *Philadelphia Inquirer* that day carried the headline "The Mormon Problem," and the Boyds were contentious about religion.[11]

On June 1st John and Mahonri arrived in New York City, where the *New York Herald* was entertaining the city with story after story about the Mormons. One extended headline from May read:

LATTER DAY SAINTS.

—

THE TRUE INWARDNESS OF MORMONISM EXPOSED.

—

A RELIGION OF CRUELTY AND HATE.

—

The Organization and Purpose of the Danites.

—

MURDER GIVEN NEW NAMES.

—

How the Blood of the Martyrs was to be Avenged.

—

Fanaticism's Victory of Ferocity.

—

Horrible Stories of Open and Secret Assassination.[12]

—

The *Herald* was making good use of its energetic young reporter Jerome B. Stillson, and by the time Stillson moved on to interview Sitting Bull, John Steele had been attacked in the *Herald* for his alleged involvement in killing "Sherman" (Jose Chavez) of John C. Frémont's party.[13] ("We had to fight the Mountain Meadow, newspaper slang, all the time we were in New York," Mahonri wrote.[14])

Catherine had an aunt and cousins—what Mahonri called "a whole nest of Knoxes"[15]—in New York City, and while they were hesitant about Mormons, they soon opened their arms and even debated religion.[16] "We get along very well about Lee that is not as bad as Poligama," John wrote.[17] He was as skeptical of the Knox business ventures as they were of his faith, but some of them acquired such great wealth, their twentieth-century lives were detailed in the social columns of the *New York Times*.

John and Mahonri were inquisitive New York City tourists, though John found the wine inferior to his own and was speechless when a man propositioned him: "I made no answer but thought of Sodom."[18] Another sign of the last days.

They were welcomed in Liverpool by the new mission president, Joseph F. Smith, who had performed John's marriage to Mary Jane Ould. John, forgetting those he came with, described Smith warmly as "the first honest face we had Seen since leaving Utah."[19] He didn't give his reaction to what Smith called "smoky, sooty, dark, dingy, drunken, degraded Liverpool."[20]

John preached his first mission sermon in the Liverpool Conference, but he reported that "Joseph F. thought it better for Mohonri and I to go and visit our friends and then return and labor in the Liverpool Conference." "Friends" meant relatives. They took a train to Bradford and he tried to pass himself off to his sister Jane McClelland as a Mr. Johnson. After looking at him for some time she asked, "Are you my brother?" When he confirmed it, she embraced him, wept, and sent for her children and neighbors. She was badly afflicted with rheumatism and dropsy, hardly able to walk. John had an alleged cure in one of his mission notebooks, but if Jane tried this, it wasn't effective, though his visit lifted her spirits.[21]

Soon they were in Belfast visiting Catherine's brother Robert Campbell at 65 Brougham Street.[22] This roomy four-bedroom house had two sitting rooms; it was off York Street in a respectable neighborhood.[23] Campbell, a carpenter-builder with claims to be an architect, was of a cheerful turn and accommodating enough that John, like other too-zealous enthusiasts, took politeness for acceptance. "Robert & his Good Wife are Strong believers," John wrote Catherine.[24]

Irish newspaper reports about Mormonism couldn't have helped the missionaries, who were still being dogged by the monstrosity of Mountain Meadows. John D. Lee's execution had drawn a headline in the *Belfast Telegraph*, "The Mormon Massacre," relying on New York newspapers to report Lee's last words. This was strategically placed over double headlines: "Horrible Case of Infanticide: Alleged Roasting of A Child."[25]

John was more genealogist than historian. When he visited his cousin Eliza Blake (which he spelled "Bleak"), he got papers that had belonged to his mother and kept a few, but burned the rest "as they ware of no use to me."[26] In Holywood they visited friends, including Rev. Charles James M'Alester, who "Received us very Kindly on account of old families times having known me when a Boy also on account of my Father & Mother," John wrote.[27]

He interrogated relatives for family records, copied gravestones, and searched unsuccessfully in the Episcopal parish register. This confirmed he was a capable genealogist, for so thorough was his search that not a single authentic name has been added to the pedigrees he developed for the Steeles and Campbells.[28] John visited his father's "old Field & House when he died and seen the great amount of change that took place since 1840 when I was there." But he left early for his brother-in-law Robert Campbell's "Orange" Masonic Lodge (which took its name from William III, known as William of Orange, who had terrorized and murdered Irish Catholics on behalf of Protestants). This allowed him "to preach to my Brother Free Masons in their Lodge, But Could not make an impression upon them, as they seem to think they have all that is nescessary for Salvatian."[29]

John and Mahonri, maybe because of the older Steele's interest in law, also attended the Belfast Assizes Court. They were allowed in, Mahonri wrote, "because we were American gentlemen." The scarlet-robed Right

Honorable Mr. Justice Robert Charles Barry—a *Vanity Fair* caricature shows a tall, thin man with narrow eyes, long, thin sideburns, a sloped hat, and a sloped nose to match—and the gray-wigged lawyers impressed Mahonri, who noted their attire.[30]

Sympathy for Mormonism was even more elusive in Ireland than it was for Catholic-Protestant ecumenism; the cross-religious alliances of the 1798 Irish Rebellion were dead and petrified, and John was anxious to leave. He claimed in his journal that President Joseph F. Smith had instructed him in a letter to give Belfast a good warning, but Smith's retained copy of this letter doesn't mention that. Instead, he encouraged Steele to "tarry awhile, and affect an opening if possible." Smith also recognized the difficulties: "May the Lord bless you both in your efforts . . . in that seemingly God-forsaken land."[31]

Personally, the visit was satisfying to John; he wrote Catherine, "there are Some here who does like me[.] if I was made of Jinger bread they would eat me up."[32] But there were none eager to gobble up his message.

Ignoring Smith's advice to tarry, the Steeles were soon back in Liverpool, where John set off with missionary companion Joseph Enos Cowley, son of a Manx shoemaker. They worked briefly in Cheshire, staying one night with Chester's presiding Elder, James Wallace, an Irish ragman; having nothing to eat, they went to bed after a supper consisting of singing and praising the Lord. Britain's great empire gave working people pride, not provisions. The next morning John rustled up "some bread dry and a heron [herring]," which with tea "filled up and felt well." He and Cowley got enough nourishment to hold services; Thomas Lounds, a whip maker and "an old Saint who is a little on the back ground through drink," took part with a few others.[33] Lounds's weakness apparently afflicted several members of their unsteady flock.

They then worked their way to Hawarden, Wales, seat of the notable Liberal prime minister, William E. Gladstone. Gladstone was home, writing letters and chopping down a great ash tree—his favorite hobby next to rescuing prostitutes—but they didn't knock on the castle door.[34]

The Welsh mission was difficult. "There are a great many in this part of Wales who cannot speak English and sometimes it is hard to understand those who can," John wrote to Catherine, noting that since he didn't speak Welsh, "it makes it very interesting."[35]

Joseph F. Smith knew of the language problem. In an 1877 letter to Brigham Young he wrote, "We are greatly in need of two or three good faithful Welsh Elders," and he later asked Henry W. Naisbitt, "Can you get one or two of the Welsh brethren into North Wales, the two brs. Howell for instance? Would bro. J. Steel do for S. Wales?"[36]

Steele and Cowley left New Market for Denbigh, stopping with Brother David Jones, a carriage and hearse driver. John described him as "a little smart man who had preached 20 years ago but like all the rest of the saints fallen asleep and forgot the Gosple." Steele attributed that to the long absence of Elders "to warm them up" but also made another passing reference to "Drink," which "seems to be the prevailing Evil all through this part of the countery." Jones's wife, Harriet, was hostile, and the next morning she gave them "a silent scanty meal," but she warmed up when they didn't beg. Jones had enough charity to give them a shilling as they left for Mold.[37]

Another David Jones with another hostile wife met them at Danby, but "when she got a few glasses of ale down," she told everybody that if Steele would take her to America, she would leave all her friends and go. That was a little too friendly; he lectured her on repentance and told her she'd have to take her family. It might have been a relief to flee to Edward Barclay's Mason's Arms Inn. Steele never forgot his Masonic connection, and on inquiry he was directed to Barclay's son-in-law for the night. That didn't work well because fleas monopolized the bedclothes.[38]

The following day, a wet Sunday, they explored Bailey Hill, saw the site of an alleged battle in the year AD 420, and visited nearby lead and silver mines. Steele got a piece of ore that he claimed had £100 of silver. He sketched a mud grinder that he thought "would make a good crusher for my selver ore," and he paid close attention to the economics of coal mining.[39]

Steele and Cowley skipped Gladstone's August 20th speech to an enthusiastic Hawarden audience of two thousand and instead walked through the rain twelve miles to Chester, where they found letters at the post office. One was an update from Joseph F. Smith, who concluded, "May the Lord abundantly bless you in your labors of love. & good will towards mankind," signing off, "With kind love I am your bro. in the Covt J. F. Smith." This was exhilarating from someone Steele saw as an apostle of Christ. But a letter from a Mormon apostle didn't get him a bite of the half loaf of bread he saw on J. Wallace's table (presumably the hungry ragman James Wallace); anyway, the children in the house looked starved, so they went elsewhere.[40]

"There are many Good Saints throughout Wales," he assured Catherine, and added with his often-spectacular lack of tact, "and they all wish to Emigrate as fast as the Can[.] two [wo]man told me the Same day that if I would take them they would leave their Drunken Men and Go with me." Then, with their wet clothes in a sack, Steele and Cowley "tramped home from Chester to Leverpool."[41]

There wasn't much of a respite in Liverpool; the missionaries went back to Runcorn, visited Widnes, and arrived so footsore that after supper Richard Brooks's wife, Mary Jane, gave John slippers and bathed his feet in hot water. Steele was rejuvenated and stayed up late talking and singing hymns.[42]

"DEATH OF BRIGHAM YOUNG," the *Liverpool Mercury* announced on August 31, 1877. The paper, after recounting a mostly accurate version of Young's life, reported that "he ruled over a region nearly a third as large again as Great Britain and Ireland, and a population said to amount to about 100,000 souls. He and his community have occasionally been brought into disagreeable conflict with the Government of the United States."[43]

Steele worshipped Young; he'd recently seen the Lord Lieutenant the Duke of Marlborough in Belfast and wrote, "I looked at him & he is not as Good looking to me as Pres B Young."[44] He wrote Joseph F. Smith and asked if there was any truth in the reports of Brigham's death.[45] Smith responded that he and Apostle Orson Pratt were leaving for Utah the next day, but "we have but little information in regard to our beloved Presidents death, and consequently cannot give you particulars."[46]

"How does the people take it about the death of Pres. Young?" Mahonri wrote his mother. But when Catherine reported Young's death to John, he responded, "We have all herd of the Presidant youngs Death Long ago and the Wire brings news here in a few hours of all the principle things of note as soon as it happiness [happens]." Mahonri the questioner, John a schoolmaster this time.[47]

A nineteenth-century Mormon mission was nothing without bigoted responses, and John faced that on Thursday, September 6th, in Runcorn's Forrester's Hall. The missionaries were warned of rotten eggs and "a row" but, John wrote, "we ware not frightened." He estimated the crowd at five or six hundred. Cowley prayed and John preached from Acts 17:26: "And hath made of one blood all nations of men for to dwell on all the face of the earth, and hath determined the times before appointed, and the bounds of their habitation," a choice anything but provocative. Nevertheless, after Steele had preached for a long time, clapping began, turning into a roar "like the rumble of a distant sea." As some of the crowd grew more moblike,

Steele was reminded of several verses, among them Luke 23:21: "Crucify him, crucify him."

Sympathizers moved to the stand to protect the missionaries. Sarah Ann Millington Gill intervened with a ringleader, Jim Cousins, hitting "him such a lick in the face that sent him back into the floor," Steele wrote admiringly. Someone shouted, "put out the lights!" Then in the dark a young man took Steele into the street, with the mob unwittingly parting right and left to let them out the door. When Cousins found Mrs. Gill outside, he pointed her out as the one who hit him: "Yes, and I can gee [give] thee another now if thee says ought about it."[48]

The mission president sent Cowley back to Runcorn, and John to Bradford to baptize his sister Jane. He reached there worn down with a cold, but a cup of warm punch and another of strong tea from Jane lifted his spirits. He was also grateful to get a letter from his sister Elizabeth in Australia. He interpreted her comments as a willingness to emigrate to Utah except for the cost and her poor health; tragically, she had lost six grandchildren in the course of a month.[49]

John preached in Bradford to a good crowd and on Sunday, October 7th, and baptized his sister and some of her family. Among them were her sons Washington ("black haired as a Raven and a Good Boy," he wrote) and Thomas, who had John's craggy brow and deep-set eyes.[50]

Steele later wrote that his nephew and namesake, John Steele McClelland, "is the best looking Man in Bradford but he has worked So much that he is nearly done over he has traviled for years 6 miles every morning to his work and back."[51] This man may have been handsome but there is a hint of tension among the brothers: William McClelland wrote, "Washington & James Henry are verry Kind to Mother [Jane Steele McClelland] as for My Brother John i have nothing to say."[52] Steele baptized his namesake nephew, but he died within two years, never making it to Utah. Three of Jane Steele McClelland's sons did; John helped finance at least one.

John was troubled with the lack of finances for emigration.[53] It took so long for converts to save passage money that it put many in what Steele called "on the back ground"—that is, no longer participating. A surprising number of the missionary baptisms were of lapsed Mormons; John looked at the Manchester Branch records and "found 51 names there who have been re Baptised besides several who are hanging on the fence neither on nor off."[54]

John thought of going back to Utah with the fall 1877 emigration, mainly because of domestic problems afflicting Catherine,[55] but Smith opposed paying travel costs of Elders who had served less than two years: "I should expect Elders John Steel[e], [Thomas] Barratt, and [H. O.] Riggs, if they come home next company—(which by the by leaves day after tomorrow) to pay their own fares and all or any other expenses throughout" because their short service would mean they weren't regularly released.[56]

John saw the problems caused by missionaries with shallow commitments: "there is Such a whining here by Some Sent out to preach to the English people[.] Just as Soon as Some Gets here and looks round about twice they want to turn about and Come [go] back Sick."[57]

Steele did record tourist diversions, but on October 19th he and Joseph Cowley boarded the *Monarch* for Douglas on the Isle of Man to missionize. Man is between England and Ireland, and the passage was so stormy even Steele was seasick. News of the execution of John D. Lee had reached this outpost, as had a review of "The Latest Dime Sensation," *The Mad Mangler, or the Terror of Murderer's Gulch*, where "The hero kills twenty Indians at one shot and rescues fourteen beautiful Mormon girls, all of whom he marries in the Endowment House at one clip."[58]

Joseph F. Smith was skeptical: "Bro J. Cowley has been about two months over on the Isle of Man, but has done but little. The Manx are a hard lot, bigoted, supersticious, self righteous, and concieted. At least so it seems to me."[59]

Smith's opinion is surprising given that the most gifted Mormon leader of the last part of the nineteenth century was a Manxman, Apostle George Q. Cannon; his extended clan had great influence in Utah, and his aunt was the first wife of Apostle John Taylor, who assumed leadership after Brigham Young's death. The Isle of Man was also the home of Cowley's parents, and eventually there were two Cowley apostles.[60]

Steele came away with two souvenirs of his time on the island. First, a handsome picture of himself by photographer T. Keig of Douglas. Second, the satisfying memory of a conflict and newspaper controversy he and Cowley stirred up. Assuring the school committee chair in Cronk-y-Voddy they would preach "sound doctrine from the Bible," they were given use of the school on a Sunday afternoon after the Episcopal chaplain of St. John's Church, Rev. Joseph W. Kyte, concluded his Sunday School meeting.[61] Kyte was a controversial figure, Irish-born and seemingly with all the arrogance of some of those Episcopalians (Church of Ireland) who lorded it over the Catholic Irish while forcing those unbelievers to pay their salaries. A critic charged that within fifteen months of Kyte assuming his rectorship, the entire choir abandoned the church and attendance dropped to three or four a week, with sometimes his wife the only worshiper. The Methodists in Lambfell or churches in Kirk Michael and Peel were suddenly more appealing.[62] The minister had neither charisma nor a prophetic voice, as a newspaper complaint makes clear ("ten minutes' mumbled reading").[63]

Kyte "wished to deprive us of the use of the Cronk y vaddy school house," John wrote. Sunday afternoon was proving to be a promising fight. On one side was dislike of the minister combined with dissenter and agnostic dissatisfaction with the established church and the popularity of the schoolmaster who connived at the Mormons' preaching. On the other was the disreputability of the Mormons. An anonymous writer recalled, "I think Mr Kyte ought to be thankful to the Mormons for their 'invasion,' because he had more people at his short service that night as they had wished to hear the Mormons afterwards."[64]

Maybe emboldened by the unusually robust congregation the Mormons helped deliver, Kyte tried to walk off with the key after his services, but the schoolmaster's mother snatched it from the door.[65] (Her son had conveniently gone to Peel.)

Thus, the *Manx Sun* reported, "the school was actually taken possession of by two Mormons, John Steele and Joseph Cowley, on Sunday morning the 18th November, while Mr Kyte was conducting his Sunday-school." Kyte argued that the Board of Education Act for the Isle of Man reserved "the school premises on all Sundays" and certain named holy days "for one half-hour of each day for religious instruction." He implausibly interpreted that to mean only he could grant permission for school use. According to the *Sun*, "The connivance of the School Committee and the schoolmaster made the two Mormons bold, and they stood at the church door in the evening inviting people to attend their meeting in the schoolroom and listen to their preaching."[66]

The minister "stood in the porch and tried to prevent people from coming ^in^" and howled about polygamy, Steele wrote. "But his whole Congragation was inside, and it made him very angary." Afterward the audience concurred that Steele preached the scriptures, yet Kyte wasn't done with his attacks and, Steele remembered, published "some Scurralous

Stuff about us," though most of the newspaper wrangling happened after the missionaries left the island.[67]

By December Steele was back in Lancashire giving a sermon at Wigan's Miners Hall.[68] The hall, established just over a year earlier with the Cooperative Societies Association shop on the first floor, could host 180 people: large enough for a congregation but not large enough for the mob Steele said he experienced in Chester.[69]

Mahonri wrote a summary of his father's sermon, and a reporter from the *Wigan Observer and Advertiser* also published an impression. The reports dovetail but the latter was critical: "There were large attendances of the curious, but if the afternoon service might be taken as a specimen of the others the visitors must have been sadly disappointed." The reporter noted that the sermon of "Elder John Steel, of Utah" "might have been delivered by any Methodist local preacher without in the least exciting the suspicions of his hearers" and seemed to find it curious that the ladies present appeared to be in full sympathy with the proceedings.[70]

Among Steele's comments in his sermon at Wigan's Miners Hall, those most obviously based on Mormon beliefs were missed by the reporter. Parley P. Pratt's *Voice of Warning*, a pamphlet that played a part in Steele's conversion, warned converts to be "prepared for persecution," and Steele reinforced that with his complaint about "the bayonet of persecution," something engrained into his being during the Illinois troubles.[71] Steele's call for prophetic witness may also have felt comfortable to a Methodist, but for those of Steele's faith it had a uniquely Mormon meaning. He was not referring to Old Testament prophets but to Parley P. Pratt's assertion that the Church of God must have contemporary "apostles, prophets, evangelists, pastors, and teachers, inspired from on high."[72]

Despite the reporter's impression of Steele as a generic Methodist, he was distinctive. In a letter to his mother, Mahonri wrote, "The people where father labors think every thing of him, but the presdents, are inclined to not think much of him: Well you Know he is not like other men= He has his way [of] doing things, and other mens ways are different to his, and so we go." In a subsequent letter he wrote, "The people like father splendid & when he & I are together I take a back seat." Mahonri confessed, "I am no preacher, but I can talk to the Saints, and sinners around the fire side."[73]

John Steele went to Bradford again but was soon back in Lancashire and in an especially cranky mood. His frustrations had been building, including a lot of anger at James Lewis, probably over the unresolved county tax issues. While John was in Europe, Lewis got 510 people to sign a petition to move the Kane County seat from Toquerville to Kanab; if successful, it would further Lewis's hopes of being probate judge but would considerably diminish Steele's chances for county office. Meanwhile, Steele's son-in-law Bishop Bringhurst was leading a petition drive to annex Toquerville and the upriver settlements to Washington County; if that happened, Steele would be competing against the considerably larger population of St. George.[74]

Catherine seems to have been boycotting her husband when he wrote her angrily in early 1878; unknown to him, she'd written two weeks before his blast. He complained she hadn't responded to the photos he sent, probably including the picture taken on the Isle of Man: "I sopose you never got them, if So why don't you treat them with common Sivility by acknowledging them, But I sopose it Makes no Matter is only Me." She must have been chary when he suggested that if she wanted him or Mahonri home, she should get Apostle Erastus Snow to "Send word."[75]

Other pressures from home probably irked: by the time he arrived in Belfast, he realized his buyers would likely walk away from the $7,000 silver mine sale. In a letter to his granddaughter Kate he wrote that failure to sell the mine "will stop me from doing what I would like to do," which was to help the poor emigrate. He explained there were over five thousand Saints in England and ten thousand in Europe who were held back because earlier beneficiaries of the Perpetual Emigration Fund hadn't repaid it.[76]

A recent district meeting cheered him, but then he went on to complain to Catherine: "I am sorry to hear of old Bp commiting him self so But he acted the S-t, a-c with me and he could not prosper"—presumably a reference to former Toquerville bishop Joshua T. Willis. His sign-off was kinder than the body of the letter: "God Bless you do the best you Can and all will be right . . . Your Affectionate Husband."[77]

In February 1878, Steele complained to his daughter Susann that he'd skinned his heel traveling through snow with a backpack and umbrella: "My Boot hurts very bad and I limp like a hen on a hot Griddle[;] you would laugh if you had Seen me." But "we are Making Saints nevertheless," and he found great kindness from the poor converts who "administer to our wants out of their Scanty Means and sometimes hand us a Shilling but very seldom."[78] (Mahonri, who wasn't used to European industrial conditions, wrote, "The poor, oh, how poor they are= The rich—oh how mean they are=."[79] Class differences like this didn't exist in Utah.) Steele went on to say they were living on "nick nacks, that is a nack when we get it and a nick when we Cant" and claimed he was getting fat—approaching 160 pounds.[80]

In the spring Steele got a new missionary companion, a friend and superior officer from Navajo raiding days, Daniel D. McArthur—"Brother Mac." When Steele next wrote Catherine, he commented, "Brother D D McCarthur and I are now writing on the Same table." He hoped Catherine could send him a hundred dollars but advised her to keep it from mission authorities; he anticipated returning and thought the mission should pay his fare. He also told her, "there is Some talk of the old Men being released next Summer," meaning himself among them.[81]

In his next letter, the hundred dollars apparently not forthcoming, he asked her to get Silver Reef merchant Joseph Birch's help selling his tank of quicksilver and mentioned he'd been talking to "messrs [H. W.] Naisbutt and Rush" about his mine but didn't have much hope. (Quicksilver—mercury—is needed to process ore, and was worth around forty to forty-five cents a pound.)[82]

Steele's shoes wore out, he replaced the mainspring of his watch three times, and the weather changed from freezing back to drizzling and then overheated. But it was the drizzling that he found worst. "I have slept in More than one hundred different beds Sence I Came to the Countary Some of them enough do [to] Kill a well man whare the water will run down the walls of your Sleeping Room," John wrote his grandson Jamie Stapley.[83]

John looked at the people with the same judgmental eye he cast on their crops and livestock: "there are Some as handsom Men and woman here as you would like to look at and others that you would think ware begoton in a wind storm and Set up against a Crooked Fence to dry and they Got badly warped while Soft." Their morals were, he felt, marred by tolerance of fornication and the subsequent illegitimacies.[84]

By May 1, 1878, John was hoping for release, possibly June 15th after a year of service. Mahonri's health had not improved despite all the variations of English mud and rain. After Henry Naisbitt saw off some emigrants on the ship *Nevada*, John talked to him about Mahonri. "I told him I did not think it would do to Kill an Elder and if the Climate did not suit he then said he could return in the next ship," he wrote Catherine. Soon Mahonri was released.[85]

John helped Mahonri and others board the *Montana* and lingered until he could no longer see the ship. Mahonri's absence probably prompted him to think again of home affairs. He commented to Catherine that son-in-law James Stapley "tells me nearly half of Toquer is bound for Arizona," and that "if that fellow pays for the mine I will buy [William Brown] Hill out across the street."[86]

Steele continued his proselytizing, writing Catherine an intemperate letter from Manchester in late May suggesting she dig a hole in the sand in Ash Creek to lodge her troubles and let a flood take them to the Gulf of California: "Should I Call around that way I will make Some inquiry." Besides being exhausted from travel, John could have been out of sorts because he found out he "Must remain until September." Furthermore, "the people here are not Gosple Greedy[;] War, Strikes, Lockouts, & So forth with poverty, and distress, is their Strong holds."[87] These signs of the last days were obvious to him but ignored by the mass of people in his mission.

Steele's complaints about Catherine not writing suggest she chose a passive-aggressive approach to his tirades. But despite the paucity of known surviving letters from her, she seems to have been a busy correspondent. "I have written Several letters to day," she wrote to Mahonri's first wife, and apologized, "Emily, this is an awful Scrib[b]le."[88] A few weeks later John wrote, complaining "It is a long time Since I herd from home, what is the matter with you all[?]"[89]

Steele's mood was considerably improved by summer for on July 16th he received a letter from Abraham A. Kimball saying that he and Daniel D. McArthur could return home in the fall. He felt his experience had matured and polished him: as he wrote Catherine, "Bro Kimble will feel the loss of Br Mac and me at the Same time Very Much as we have now got the Hang of the Barn nicely."[90]

It was in a happier frame of mind that Steele anticipated Toquerville's July 24th celebration: "it is now 10am and in Utah is about 4 oclock and in my immagenation Can hear the old anvil shout ^ring^ and can see the Bunting displayed at the Top of the pole and can imagin how they feel" celebrating Utah's holiday.[91]

"Bro Mc & Steele were rather excited on account of being released to return home," Kimball wrote on September 9, 1878.[92] John had anticipated this, having written Catherine on August 15th, "You must not write any more to me unless you think I will get it Either in Liverpool or S L City to be left until Called for." He was looking forward to peach dumplings and had already received a letter from Mahonri reporting Apostle Erastus Snow said Mahonri's labors were accepted.[93]

Despite the harassment Catherine was subjected to over John's unsettled county assessor accounts and other matters, she found peace in the new and nearby St. George Temple. "I am glad that you have had the priviledge of going through ^the Temple^ it will make you feel so good," Catherine wrote daughter-in-law Emily; "there is Such a good Spirit in the Temple the Angel's of peace dwel[l]s there." She was also comforted by visits from relatives, including several grandchildren. "Susy has got a ^another^ nice girl [Eleanor Campbell Bringhurst] and She had quiet [quite] a Serious time but She is all right now," Catherine wrote.[94]

John, with the same information, instructed Catherine, "Tell Susan I am thankful for Smal favors and if there is 5 more to Call me grandpa All I am Sory for is that my loom was out of order or I might have had a web in of my own." He wrote, "There are Plenty of Looms idle here and they go begging for Some one ^to^ fill them with warp and they will waft them & weave them themselves and not Charge a Cent how high is that."[95]

Steele's impending departure brought wistful congratulations from his fellow missionary Scotchman David Milne: "If there is one more than another ought to be at home to help his family it looks as if I am the fellow, but glad you are all getting out of it—only sorry I aint."[96]

Before leaving, John made another visit to his sister Jane, who was clearly dying. She was four-and-a-half feet in circumference—"as big as a Barrel from her brest to her toes," he wrote Catherine. "There is no Cure for her She Must Suffer it out."[97] He wrote in his journal on August 13th, "Bady [bade] my sister and her family good buy not Expecting to See her any more on this side the grave."[98] (Soon after Steele got back to Utah, the *Latter-Day Saints' Millennial Star* carried a notice that Jane had died on September 22nd.[99]) About the same time as Steele's visit to Jane his sister Elizabeth Steele Connelly wrote that she herself was of an enormous size, had very poor health, pain in her legs and feet, and "i cannot go far without my omberala for walken stick."[100]

Steele's last letter to Catherine from the British mission was written on September 1, 1878. He had reverted to bullying again ("I have not herd from you for a long time, and presuming you would like to here from me once again") but advised her of his release and that he would be returning on the

Elizabeth Steele Connelly. *Family photograph.*

Wyoming. He expected to be in Salt Lake in time for General Conference on October 6th and told her to write him there.[101]

John bought gifts as he made his last rounds, including scarves and thirty yards of fabric.[102] He also received presents from some of the converts he was leaving behind. On September 13th he signed a note for the cost of his passage home—later forgiven by President John Taylor—and boarded the *Wyoming* on the River Mersey. Newspapers, even the *Manx Sun*, as though to say good riddance to him personally, reported there were six hundred Mormon converts on board Capt. Henry Gadd's steamer emigrating to America, with "none having been obtained from Ireland."[103] Steele gave the shipboard prayer and they sailed September 15th into a rough sea, arriving at Sandy Hook, New Jersey, on September 24th, John's mission completed.

13

SIGNS OF THE TIMES

John Steele wrote in his journal that he was gladly welcomed home on October 20, 1878, but his worst premonitions were met: "[I had] 5 cents in my pocket, and that was all my wealth. I found on my return my fences down, and everything in a dilapidated condition, my former business all gone and poverty staring me in the face."[1] It couldn't have been a surprise since he had been receiving news while in Great Britain and knew his son John Alma would never meet his standards in maintaining the homestead. (The previous May, he had written irately from Manchester, England, declaring, "I think it strange if J Alma Could not find time to put a shingle over his own head to Keep out the rain."[2])

Steele also had to face his bondsmen and Kane County officials over his unsettled assessor and collector accounts. In December 1878 the county probate court gave him until March to settle.[3] In March they raised his compensation from 10 percent of collections to 12.5 percent, more in line with his successor's, but rejected his report. He stalled, but after being threatened with prosecution, he settled at the end of 1879 when James Lewis, his deputy assessor and also a county selectman, made a successful motion appropriating $74.43 to clear the account. (After Ashton Nebeker's subsequent five years as assessor and collector the county appropriated $269.28 to clear up shortages, and Nebeker also petitioned the territorial legislature in 1882 for $271.32 in "sundry" losses and was granted more.)[4]

The hard times of the 1870s and out-migrations probably contributed to Steele's challenges collecting taxes. On Christmas Day, 1878, he'd written to the *Millennial Star*, noting, "the Saints begin to think Utah too small for them and the Territories surrounding, Arizona, New Mexico, Idaho, Wyoming, and the States of Colorado and Nevada are receiving their quota of settlers from among our people."[5]

In the midst of growth through natural increase and immigration, Utah had such severe droughts that grain was "burnt up" at Summit and crops failed at Hamilton's Fort and Kanarra. Bellevue townsfolk had to haul their water from Toquerville, so Toquerville residents tunneled into the black hill hoping to increase the flow of their spring. Produce upriver in Springdale was attacked by squash bugs, ground squirrels, and grape flies.[6]

The winter of 1879–80 was bad, too, so cold it brought snow to St. George.[7] Kane County taxable valuation dropped between 1878 and 1879; by 1880 there wasn't even a notary in the county.[8] John sent his son Mahonri a map of south-central Utah and mentioned relocating. Mahonri wrote back that the map looked fine but that getting there would be difficult. He named some routes John could explore "till you find a nice piece of land, a beautifull spring Close by a beautifull mansion erected by your own hands." But, he wrote sarcastically, if John brought along drunken Toquerville cronies like Levi Savage or William Hill, they would "establish the Order (of Confusion) & go on to perdition."[9]

John found a temporary financial expedient in May 1880 when the *Deseret News* referred to him as "Dr. John Steele" in announcing the territorial census enumerators. Wags like Bill Nye, "The Laramie City Logician on the Weather," joked that questions included, "Do you remember George Washington, and if so to what amount? What is your fighting weight? . . . Are you single, and if so, what is your excuse? . . . Which side do you lie on while sleeping? Which side do you lie on during a political campaign?"[10]

The actual questions were more prosaic, and enumerators were paid three cents a person, so the three days he took to record Toquerville's 371 residents earned him $11.13; he was also assigned four other precincts. He was up to the task and went beyond his duty with his occasionally creative spelling. Shoemaker John Alder, for instance, was born in "Twitserland," which made him "Twitse." Despite phonetic spelling, he often went beyond census requirements to identify not just state or country of birth but city or province. In a few places he forgot or neglected to give all the information. Curiously, he didn't list the birthplaces of anyone in his own household; someone else wrote "Ohio" in dark pencil and dittoed that for the whole group. And he listed the Toquerville family of Loram and Frances Pratt twice.[11]

Steele again took up surveying, keeping a brief 1881 survey diary that highlights the varied nature of his work and interests. Southern Utah chronicler James G. Bleak credited him with the first proper survey of

Bunkerville, Nevada.[12] According to family lore, Steele intended to move there, but Catherine replied, "I've moved as far as I'm going to. I'm not moving another step," and told him, "You can go where you want to but I'm not going any further."[13] In surveying Bunkerville, John saved out 160 acres for "Steele & Co.," lending some credence to the story.[14]

Steele hadn't lost enough cast as Kane County assessor and collector to prevent him from becoming Kane County surveyor again. The Kane County Probate Court records show his predecessor had been busy; maybe he didn't leave much for Steele. His notebooks reflect a few jobs, but the probate court records don't. He later surveyed and laid claim to "Steele's Spring" with forty acres of surrounding land.[15]

One source of income that wasn't subject to slumps enticed John. The holy grail for aging soldiers was a military pension, like his father had. Before leaving for his mission, Steele had written to George Q. Cannon, the Utah representative in Congress (so charismatic and polished the *Tribune* nicknamed him "Smoothbore Cannon"[16]) to ask about a Mexican War pension; he wanted more than the Mexican War badge of his fellow soldier and friend David Wilkin.[17] It appears he didn't qualify because nothing came of it except a courteous response.[18]

What may have triggered Steele to try again was signing a pension affidavit for his Toquerville neighbor, the lean and lanky (six feet tall, 165 pounds) Augustus E. Dodge.[19] Nine months after signing Dodge's affidavit, Steele hired Dodge's pension attorney and made his own claim. He had waited so long because he was "located in the Deserts of the West so far from sources of information, and not knowing until recently that a pension could be obtained for the injuries he received while in actual Service."[20]

Steele claimed that on or about November 24, 1846, a large house log was "let go upon him" in Pueblo, Colorado. Because he was "standing on a twist," it injured his kidneys and he'd never recovered. He emphasized he was "very much disabled."

He also solicited statements from various doctors and Battalion comrades Lyman Stevens and Orson B. Adams, who testified they witnessed the accident. Even Steele's sometime Battalion nemesis, Capt. Nelson Higgins, confirmed Steele's account. Augustus E. Dodge and Levi Savage favored Steele with an affidavit. Both were American born but claimed they'd known Steele for two years before he joined the Battalion—generously rounding up the sixteen months he'd then been in the United States.[21]

After Steele's application was approved on July 31, 1882, he began a lifelong quest for increases. As he wrote lawyer T. H. Kennedy six weeks after he had the bird of the pension in hand and was anticipating the promise of an increase from the bird in the bush, "I think it Very ungenerous, after a man has helped take as good a Country As this Western portion of the united States had turned out to be, with all its mineral wealth, and been injured in the Servace, and for 36 years had had to pay his own Dr's bills, and then turn him of with the mear pittance of $6" a month. That and the lack of more back pay "don't speak well for the most Magnamimous and powerfull government in the world."[22]

One of the physicians who examined him for a potential increase was doubtful. Dr. Singleton Husted, an 1879 graduate of Columbia's College of Physicians and Surgeons, practiced in Silver Reef but had been Provo's quarantine physician until leaving after he threatened a reporter over an editorial he interpreted as a slur. The press, naturally, didn't take to this; the *Deseret News* correspondent called Husted "Our belligerent golden-haired little Dr." His practice in Salt Lake City resulted in more controversy before he ended up in Silver Reef.[23]

Dr. Husted's Christmas Eve, 1887, examination caused him to conclude Steele's disability was from "Diabetes & resulting inability to use the right leg for work." He also suspected an enlarged prostate. Instead of accepting Steele's self-report of being five feet, six inches tall, Husted, a small man himself, measured and found him five feet, four and a half inches. He recorded that Steele's pain was on the right side of his spine in the small of his back and extended to the right side of his groin.

Steele told Dr. Husted his appetite was "Very poor," "Eat scarcely anything," and when it came to thirst, he might have "one, possibly two cups of tea at meal time." Steele said his eyesight had deteriorated and now he had to wear glasses. He still had most of his front teeth but had lost the back ones.

"It is my opinion," Dr. Husted wrote, "that the ^slight^ lameness was caused by a subsequent accident. He injoys traveling around a horse back & walks with a slight limp." Although he assured the War Department that Steele had no vicious personal habits, Husted concluded that he wasn't entitled to a pension increase. Then he wrote a brief, private letter:

STORMONT MINING COMPANY,
SILVER REEF, UTAH Dec. 28th 1887

% The Hon. Mr Black.
Commissioner of Pensions.

Dear Sir

In this case of John Steele, I have made an adverse report to his wishes. He is a Mormon and in this part of the country my wellfare and life would scarcely be safe, should he know of the nature of the report. It is for this reason that the document has not been forwarded by the Justice of the Peace Mr Julius Jordon to the County Clerk at St George who is also a mormon and the whole matter would then become known. Furthermore as I have made this report in good faith I would ask that you keep my name sub rosa

Faithfully Yours
S. Husted M.D.
Col. Phys & Surg. N.Y.C.
Class 1879.[24]

Steele didn't get an increase and was resentful for years, but he might have had some satisfaction by how much he frightened the doctor.[25]

While his good health wasn't steady—one July he fell out of an apricot tree and then fretted his fruit was going to waste—he was not the incapacitated pauper he represented to the pension authorities. He painted his situation in rosy colors to nonmilitary correspondents to prove he was flourishing in the Kingdom of God. He had a reputation in southern Utah for liberality,[26] and he played the grand seigneur with Rachel Connelly, his friend since his earliest days in Holywood. He sent her a little money, confirming his prosperity.

Steele continued to write periodically to pension officials about his disabilities, but in July 1889 he and Levi Savage, as members of Toquerville's Fourth of July Committee, were trying to get the Liberty Pole set up for the holiday. Savage wrote in his journal that after asking several of the young men for help and getting nowhere, "Mager [Steele] himself, a man well onto 70 years olde, clam [climbed] some 30 feet and helped to properly adjust and secure the top pole in place."[27]

Some of the most informative letters from Steele's later years were to his Australian niece, Letisha Connelly Todd, though she had to plow through almost endless religious dogma to turn up family news. "I am pretty wel[l] off in this worlds goods," he wrote her.[28]

But by the mid- to late 1890s John sometimes admitted to his niece that he was slowing down. Yet even in 1901, he claimed, "My Health is very good for a man of my years now 81 and Can Climb a tree faster than any of the Boys & Ride a Horse over the plains at top Speed when I am hunting Cattle."[29]

*

Federal pressure on Mormons over polygamy became intense in the 1880s, and for those like Steele who studied warnings, prophecies, and the stars, these were ominous. For example, Revelations 11:13 warned of earthquakes. John had been on the lookout for them for years and in April 1880 reported a very satisfactory one to the *Deseret News*.[30] Following the earthquake, water from Toquerville's spring dropped by two-thirds—another sign.[31]

On the back of Steele's retained copy of his *Deseret News* earthquake report he worked out horoscopes because he believed stars provided guidance to the future. In 1879 the *Deseret News* reported that Professor C. A. Grimmer expected tribulations because of the perihelia of Jupiter, Uranus, Neptune, and Saturn. The reporter claimed that the results "will be felt on this globe from 1880 to 1887. Among them are plague, pestilence, earthquakes, tidal waves, tornadoes, shipwrecks, mountains sinking, valleys rising, great conflagrations, wars, civil strifes, anarchy, accidents, and, to use the language of [Professor] Grimmer, 'one universal carnival of death.'" But the reporter was also confident the Lord would watch out for his people.[32]

Zadkiel's Almanac for 1881 (along with *Raphael's*, favored by Steele) reinforced the predictions of the aptly named Grimmer. *Zadkiel's* projected a partial eclipse of the sun on May 27, 1881, which would be visible in Salt Lake City and could cause "brain fever, sunstroke, diphtheria, and acute fevers." According to Zadkiel, other signs threatened "a change in the marriage-laws and a great amount of vice and immorality." He speculated that "it looks as if there would be a complete overthrow of the Mormon ascendency . . . within the next four years."[33]

Levi Savage. *Family photograph.*

An overthrow of the Mormons seemed presaged when Gentile power entered remote places like Toquerville. After abusing Bishop Bringhurst for allegedly celebrating the first murder of a "Gentile" in Utah, the *Salt Lake Tribune* admitted that Toquer was "a very pretty place in the Spring" and assured its readers, "The people of this little town are noted for their liberality and freedom from the prejudice against the new comers, or Gentiles, as they call them, (The priesthood always being excepted)."[34] And a Pioche miner claimed the best wine in Utah was found in Bishop Bringhurst's cellar.[35] But Steele's son-in-law Joseph Fish was advised by assistant St. George temple president David H. Cannon to avoid Toquerville "on account of apostates."[36]

More traumatically for the Mormons, in reversing a long-standing precedent, the Supreme Court asserted in *Reynolds v. the United States* that the federal government could overrule local power and standardize "American" marriage practices. This was ironic because it was governmental inability under pre–Civil War federalism that prevented the United

States from interceding for the Mormons in the Midwest—though they were threatened with the bogeyman of federal cooperation in expelling them from Illinois.[37]

The 1882 Edmunds Act disfranchised polygamists; disqualified them and believers in polygamy, as well as violators of the 1862 anti-polygamy act, from jury service; declared all Utah elective offices vacant; set up a presidentially appointed five-member Utah Commission to oversee elections; and put in place vigorous laws to ensure the successful prosecution of those engaging in polygamy and cohabitation (marriages had to be proved to prosecute for polygamy; cohabitation required only evidence of marital-like relations).[38]

John Steele had spent his Utah life enjoying his service in various local offices. Despite the Edmunds Act, Steele's future looked hopeful. The Utah Commission chair, Alex Ramsey of Minnesota, who was also President Rutherford B. Hayes's former secretary of war, signed Steele's commission as Kane County's chief voting registrar on August 30, 1882; his selection was exceptional because two-thirds of the new registrars were reportedly Gentiles.[39] Steele filed his bonds and selected deputy registration officers for Kanab, Johnson, Paria, Mt. Carmel, Orderville, and Glendale and designated five election judges.[40]

The oath required Steele to testify, "I am not a bigamist nor a polygamist; that I have not violated the laws of the United States prohibiting bigamy or polygamy."[41] However, Steele's brief plural marriage to Mary Jane Ould in 1869 had violated the 1862 act, and since his commission was published in the *Deseret Evening News,* Beaver's *Southern Utonian*, and the *Ogden Daily Herald*, there was the possibility he could be turned in by someone who knew the facts.[42] Mary Jane herself was living with her new husband, Amos Harmon, in nearby Silver Reef and doesn't seem to have been enamored of Mormonism: her 1910 burial service was performed by a Baptist minister.[43]

Steele did the prudent thing. He wrote to John Sharp, a shrewd Scottish businessman who began life as a coal miner but wrestled successfully with the deadbeat Union Pacific Railroad on behalf of Brigham Young. Sharp carried those skills into his role as chairman of the Peoples' Party, a creation of the Mormon Church.[44]

Steele had two questions. First, "if a man has married a wife in 1869 and Divorced her in 1870 and has still otherwise Kept the Law of 1862 will this debar him from holding the office of Register." The second apparently wasn't relevant to his own situation: "if a mans plural wife is Dead five years ago having taken her Since 1862 will that hinder him from acting as Register or from the Poles please answer."[45]

Sharp must have telegraphed John that it would be better to resign because four days later Steele wrote to Kanab rancher John Riley Stewart stating that "in consequence of Changes made by the Ruling of the Commissioners for Utah in Registration Matters I have been disquallified from Continuing in office as Registration officer for Kane County." He explained that he'd forwarded Stewart's name to replace him, outlined the appointments he'd begun to make and the hours he had worked so far, and suggested he be paid $32 for eight days' service. He signed off, "John Steele Rigestration officer Defacto."[46]

The rebuff left Steele angry. He'd written Stewart relinquishing his position on September 9th, and on September 23rd he had a chance to vent when he read a negative story about Mormons in one of his favorite newspapers, Montreal's *Family Herald and Weekly Star.* It was mild compared to the general run of these kinds of reports, and even avoided mentioning John D. Lee and the bloody red flag of Mountain Meadows. Headed "The Mormons," the paragraph claimed that secret instructions were given by "the Mormon priesthood" asking bishops to sit with precinct registrars overseeing voting registration and concluded, "The Gentiles are much incensed at this interference."[47]

Steele wrote the *Star*, identifying himself as a Mormon, "(So Called by our Enomays) otherwise a latterday Saint," who earned his living as a working man, and he rehearsed the missions Mormon elders like himself had undertaken to educate the world about their faith. He hauled out his own credentials and history, having "faught the Mexicans to obtain this Countary have fought the Indians to retain this countary and have helped make the Roads and bridges for men to travil through this Countary."[48]

In the recent election George Q. Cannon received over 18,000 votes for congressional delegate while his opponent, Allen G. Campbell, received around 1,300—this despite, as the *Tribune* wrote, the ladies of Gentile Frisco—who had just been given the vote—turning "out on election day almost 'to a man.'"[49] (The *Deseret News*, in mocking, tiny type, called the failed candidate "minority campbell."[50]) Nevertheless, the territorial governor, Eli H. Murray, awarded an election certificate to Campbell because

Cannon had obtained citizenship by allegedly misrepresenting the length of his residency in the United States.[51] Steele couldn't pass up attacking that outrage on democratic sensibilities by relaying one of his quaint stories: "when 1,300 Counts more than 18,000 we have caus[e] to fear, it is like the fable of the Cat roled up in the meal, when the young rat wanted to go and get some, the old Experianced rat Said, true it may be meal but there may be misChief consealed under it."[52] (Steele's county cast 607 votes for Cannon, none for Campbell.[53])

Steele pointed out that Mormon bishops—who he said wouldn't have time to sit with registrars—"have a perfect right like any other Citizan to look after their people and see that they are not imposed upon." Yet Steele liked the newspaper, and his conclusion was conciliatory, asking only that his people be spoken of truthfully and judged on their own merits. "If you have not a good word for us as a people pleas[e] touch the Mormons lightly and oblidge your Correspondant."[54] Here he was anticipating the Mormon policy of bribing newspapers to publish positive stories, or at least not negative ones.[55]

The Edmunds Act triggered the "Raids," when federal marshals, relying on informants ("Spotters"[56]) arrested suspects, put them before "Gentile" grand juries, usually convicted them of cohabitation, and—unless they repudiated their marriages—fined them $300 and gave them six months in the penitentiary.

The self-styled "Saints" were angry when their leading men were forced underground or imprisoned. It had been almost a requirement to have plural wives in order to serve in higher church offices—Steele having been an early exception—and as the polygamists fled, hid, or moved away, the territory suffered a loss of experienced leaders. The business affairs of those living in plural marriage also suffered, and Mormon communalism retrenched and sometimes collapsed.[57]

Toquerville's Levi Savage was arrested, but the great prize was Bishop Bringhurst. In a "cohab secret code," Toquerville was known as "Cloudy," and Bringhurst as "Awake." The message "Come home" was disguised as "Pike"; federal judges Boreman and Zane became "Herod" and "Nero."[58]

Bishop Bringhurst had a close call and fled the "deps" in his underwear in the middle of the night. Shortly after, Mahonri took a son to the Murdock Academy in Beaver, where the Second District Court was. "I heard of W. A. B. taking through the lot in an undress uniform. Well he had better go slow, for they have his case in B[eaver]-. & five years is not so funny."[59]

Steele's Battalion comrade John Conrad Naegle had the largest collection of wives and wine in Toquerville. The lower level of his barrack-like home was a huge wine cellar, and the upstairs housed some of his seven wives and twenty-nine children. He ended up in Mexico, where, the *Deseret News* reported, adultery couldn't be prosecuted unless one of the conjugal partners complained. It's ironic that if the Mormon Battalion and other Mexican War soldiers had failed to wrest the Southwest from Mexico, polygamy might have flourished.[60] (The suggestion that Mormons should emigrate to Turkey, where polygamy was accepted and Christianity tolerated, didn't entice the brethren.[61])

Steele found himself acting as financial agent for two polygamists: Ashton Nebeker, who had taken his families to Arizona, and Oscar S. Bocker. Bocker was so skittish about directly giving money to his Toquerville wife Anna, he sent the money to Steele to distribute anonymously. In 1886 he was bold enough to sign his real name, but by 1889 he had become "S. Rekob."[62] Nor was this excessive caution on Bocker's part: cohabitation was so broadly defined that regularly providing food, shelter, or cash to a woman could be construed as an offense even if the man never saw her.[63]

After the Supreme Court struck down the test oath that forced John to give up his Kane County registrar position, a satisfactory substitute soon replaced it—at least satisfactory to him. He was again elected Toquerville justice of the peace. In 1887 his name was also drawn as a juror for the May term of the Second District Court. But the *Salt Lake Herald* warned that many names were drawn, "mainly that men professing any sort of allegiance to the Mormon Church are to be seriously discouraged from taking the new oath" and challenged for their religious beliefs.[64]

Mahonri considered accepting Apostle Erastus Snow's invitation to move to Mexico.[65] His sister Jane Steele Jensen was enthused. "If Mahonri is talking of going to Old Mexico," she wrote her mother, "there is a good chance now." Jane had incorrectly heard that the Mormons had a 120-square-mile tract in "Senora" (Sonora) where anyone with a Mormon recommendation was invited.[66] John was also interested in Mexico, eventually working out the horoscope for "Mexican | Grant | Jany 8, 91 | 12M."[67] But Church President John Taylor dissuaded Mahonri and he stayed put.[68]

Eventually the "deps" served papers on Mahonri for cohabitation, and his wives and his son Mahonri Jr. were summoned to Beaver for the May 1887 court term. John readied himself to go there at the same time for jury duty. His granddaughter Josephine "Josie" Fish Barraclough wrote from there to her grandmother Catherine, "Grandpa will have to be here the first of May." Mahonri wrote his mother, "I am intending to stay it off till fall if I can," adding, "Josie is intending to go home with father when he does."[69] On the expected date Mahonri, his wives, and son faced Joseph Henry Dupaix, sitting in for the regular U.S. commissioner, who was considered by the prosecuting attorney too drunk to do his job. (Dupaix was also part-owner of the mill Steele complained had impinged on his water rights.)

Mahonri waived examination, was bound over, and, as he hoped, was due back in September. That may not have been generosity on the part of the court; Beaver attorney and Battalion historian Daniel Tyler, a long-time friend of Steele's, said he suspected Mahonri had to return to Panguitch without a hearing because "there were too many of his real peers on the jury."[70]

To be sworn in as a juror, John was up against Judge "Herod" (Boreman). The judge harangued his prospects, saying he "did not see how any honest, conscientious Mormon" could take the required oath, and the Steeles left Beaver with nothing done except Mahonri's postponement.

Mahonri's plural wife Mary Ellen Jepson Steele died a few weeks later in Panguitch giving birth to her last child, Emily. "Hope that M. M. will get through with his troubles all right and will avoide going to the 'Pen,'" Steele's son-in-law Joseph Fish wrote. He supposed "the cause of Mary Ellens death was the fright she got from the 'Deps.'"[71]

Fish, who developed a sideline as a Western historian, kept informed about Utah events. "I see by the News," he wrote, "that arrests still goes on and hear they have got Wm. Bringherst suppose they will be quite severe on him if they can."[72]

Bringhurst pled guilty to unlawful cohabitation, and John wrote Wilford Woodruff that "we are trying to hold the fort while our Bishop Wm A. B[r]inghurst is in prison."[73] The bishop was sentenced to "the usual penalty of six months," a $300 fine, and court costs.[74]

Upon his release Bringhurst was met by Levi Savage and John Steele two miles from town; when they got to Ash Creek, town members gave their bishop a "warm salute of welcome home again" and honored him with music, speeches, recitations, and a picnic that lasted until midnight. Soon the multitalented bishop was pulling some of Savage's aching teeth.[75]

"Well, Prest., Taylor has passed away," Mahonri wrote John in early August 1887, "and he will rest in peace while his enemies will go to hell Cross lots."[76] John Taylor had died July 25th while hiding from prosecutors underground, the death a reminder that the pioneer generation was aging—like John himself. Eighty-year-old Apostle Wilford Woodruff replaced Taylor; Erastus Snow, the "Apostle to Dixie," died May 27, 1888, and John was on hand to speak at Toquerville's memorial service for him.[77]

*

It was obvious to the Millennial-obsessed Mormons that the events of the 1880s were the prelude to cataclysm and the Second Coming of Christ.[78] Apostle John W. Taylor, son of former president John Taylor, spoke to that sentiment in a St. George sermon in 1888 when he said members of the congregation before him "would see the Savior come."[79] Joseph Fish wrote, "the fifty six years are up that the Prophet said would wind up the Scene so we may look for a change soon,"[80] referring to Joseph Smith's prophecy that "the son of man will not come in the clouds of heaven till I am eighty-five years old," and his proclamation in 1835, "Even fifty-six years shall wind up the scene."[81]

Steele saw Mormon troubles as rooted in machinations of "the Father of lies," and he didn't have to search far beyond Montreal's *Family Herald* for those lies. The newspapers were titillated in late 1889 by Martin D. Wardell's testimony under oath that lately deceased William H. Dame had years earlier ordered the killing of an immigrant named Green twenty miles west of Green River. Green was called out by three men: "one caught him by the hair and another cut his throat; they got $5000 from him; some of us began to object, and John W. Young[82] said if we did not shut up, we would be served the same." Wardell said, "my son and the Gentile took Green's outfit to the Tithing yard." One of the killers, Wardell said, was Bill Hickman, "the captain."[83]

William Green of Spanish Fork was the Green referred to, and he shyly waved his hand and signed an affidavit admitting he had no recollection of having been killed by Danites or anyone else. He added, "I am not a

Mormon, nor have I been for several years." The *Deseret Weekly News* was so impressed by his non-blood-atoned status, they reprinted his affidavit over and over.[84] But by then, entire novels slandering the Mormons were being palmed off as factual.

John didn't see honest differences. In a partially retained copy of a letter presumably to a newspaper, he wrote, "the Priests and Editors, Judges, and lawyers, found that if they let those people alone their Craft was in danger the[i]r trade in Mens Sowls would fail and they would have to go to work and Earn an honest living." This led to plunder and murder, "Which is the Same argument that Satan has always used against the People of God Even their half Brother Herrod Who found out Jesus was born Sent out and murdered all the Young Children of two years Old."

Who would know better than Steele? "I am now 70 years old and have been privileged to hold a standing in the Church of Jesus Christ for 50 years and know of what I speak, there is no danite band only the wicked flee when no man persue and the remorse of their own Evil acts haunts them at Every step." He recalled William Green: after "all that has been said about those murders is like Mr Green that was killed But is living yet and this Lucifer the father of lies Goads on his Children to be lik[e] their Father."[85]

Steele, or anyone, could see the Kingdom was shaking under the assaults. In 1887 non-Mormons were elected to the Salt Lake City school board and won five seats in the territorial legislature; in 1889 they took over Ogden City and had a majority in Salt Lake City, capturing the capital city mayoralty in 1890. Steele was so concerned about the latter, he worked out the horoscope of the Salt Lake City election. Also in 1890 the Supreme Court upheld an Idaho oath that barred all Mormons from voting.[86]

Historian Patrick Q. Mason has noted that the last quarter of the nineteenth century saw even more heated Mormon rhetoric "that the fury of God" would be unleashed because of the prosecutions and persecutions.[87] The events of the 1880s were so traumatic for church leaders that a hundred years later some apostles were still in a terrified crouch at historians exploring their remarkable and richly documented story.

Steele's papers confirm Mason's assertion. He didn't find the official sermons blood-curdling enough to satisfy his thirst for vengeance against Satan's dupes. More satisfactory were folk prophecies. His handwritten copy of the anonymous "Predictions of a Seventy," dated July and August

1887, included Millennial warnings: "In 1888 there will be anarchy in the States which will bring terror to 34,000,000 of people, it will grow worse in 1889." Nor would the Lord's revenge stop there: he "is about to arise," and an earthquake before October 8, 1891, would destroy at least two-thirds of Butte City, Malad City, Carson City, Virginia City, and Park City.[88]

John added notes to himself on this document: "Find the date of the destruction of New York, Boston & Albany," and reminded himself to "analize the word Albany[.] B A N Y are the initials of Boston Albany and New York[.] A L means all or points with the prophetic finger to these three Cities and their Common And almost Simultanious destruction and abolishment."

Then he added:

> "S.U.S.A.N B. Anthony
> "Susan 7 or 87, 88, 89, 90, 91, 92, 93"[89]

Susan B. Anthony had a long-term alliance with Mormons because Utah Territory was the first in the United States where women voted, though Wyoming granted suffrage a bit earlier. She was upset the Edmunds-Tucker Act had just revoked Utah women's suffrage, but why John used numerology on her name is unknown.[90]

Steele wrote about another vision received in Salt Lake City on December 14, 1879. This was in Steele's handwriting and even more gruesome. The anonymous visionary foresaw desolation and murder across the country. At the thirty-nine-foot-high Battle Monument in front of Baltimore's St. Charles Hotel, "I saw the Dead piled up to fill the Square, I saw Mothers cut the throats of their own Children for the Sake of Their Blood"—and, gruesomely, much more of the same. It's hard to know how seriously Steele took this: on the back he penciled some math calculations, wrote his name, and drew what appeared to be a map with lots labeled "Isom" and "Cornelius," Virgin City surnames. He was always thrifty with paper.[91]

Steele kept another folk prophecy by his Mormon Battalion comrade Newman Bulkley, this one drenched in visions of revenge. Senators were hurled from their seats so violently, some were killed; the survivors had "Edmunds" on their foreheads, referring to the infamous U.S. senator George F. Edmunds, who sponsored the anti-polygamy legislation bringing on this apocalypse.[92]

These were the folk cries of a weakened people in shock and gave them hope of an apocalyptic rebalancing. Wilford Woodruff captured the essence in his journal: "Thus Ends the year 1889 And the word of the Prophet Joseph Smith is begining to be fulfilled that the whole Nation would turn against Zion & make war upon the Saints[.] The Nation has never been filled so full of lies against the Saints as to Day[.] 1890 will be an important year with the Latter Day Saints & American Nation."[93]

All the signs showed that the immediate future was bleak for Mormons, but John was sure the sinners were facing Apocalypse for their embrace of Satan's agenda.

14

MAD INTERLUDE

While God seemed to be waiting with unsettling patience to send the Apocalypse, John Steele, Toquerville justice of the peace, was judging his friends and neighbors with considerably less restraint. The work suited his authoritarian nature and seems not to have been resented since he served repeatedly.[1] This was a change from Tenth Ward days, when church courts took care of discord.

But Steele's term as justice was winding down when President Wilford Woodruff wrote in his journal on September 25, 1890: "I have arived at a point in the History of my life as President of the Church of Jesus Christ of Latter Day Saints whare I am under the necessity of acting for the Temporal Salvation of the church."[2] After prayer, assisted by what he felt was inspiration, Woodruff, one of the most enthusiastic Millennialists of his quorum (his patriarchal blessing from Joseph Smith Sr. promised him he would "remain on the earth to behold thy Savior Come in the Clouds of heaven"),[3] signed an "Official Declaration" affirming the Church of Latter-day Saints would obey the laws enacted by Congress and "pronounced constitutional by the court of last resort." He declared his intention to honor those laws and use his influence to ensure others did as well.[4]

At first this astonishing concession to end plural marriage wasn't especially noticed by Mormon adversaries, but when it was ratified by Church members in Conference on October 6, 1890, it marked the beginning of a profound shift in God's Kingdom. Thomas G. Alexander, Woodruff's able biographer, wrote, "Had Henry Lawrence and Charles Varian not decided to press confiscation of the church's temples and other houses of worship, polygamy may have survived."[5] But the situation was so complex, it's hard in hindsight to see how the Church could have persevered as a public institution without this about-face.

Steele's Millennialism was too engrained for him to recognize, at first, the extent of this change, but he felt it when his son-in-law Bishop Bringhurst announced he was putting aside Steele's daughter Susann in conformity with the law; Mahonri described Bringhurst's decision as "villinay."[6] Within five years Utah's religion-based political parties were replaced by Democrats and Republicans, the territory became a state, and thanks to extraordinary efforts on both sides, a considerable if imperfect reconciliation took place. Steele adjusted to the new order and found himself cheerfully astonished at a parade celebrating the fiftieth anniversary of the Mormons' arrival in Salt Lake Valley when he marched with Mormon Battalion survivors behind federal cavalry, infantry, and artillery soldiers who "gave us a rousing Salute, by Waving their Caps and three Cheers for the Utah pioneers."[7]

Steele prepared himself politically for the new regime. Despite Republicans having led the anti-polygamy crusade, many Republican principles were compatible with Mormon kingdom-building values, including tariffs to protect home industries like the Garfield County sheep business so important to Steele's son Mahonri.[8] Steele collected political tracts on both sides of current events and studied the issues, becoming a member of the Republican Club of Toquerville—whose draft policies are in his hand and among his papers. He also put his utopian energies into dreams of reforming the federal government, creating old-age pensions, and making constitutional changes.[9]

*

Catherine Steele was the center of attention at the family's 1890 reunion. "This day is her Birth day 75 years ago She first Saw the light of day in that Beautifull Town Called Straban[e] in the County Tyrone Ireland nine miles from the City of Londonderry," John wrote his niece Letisha Todd. "We are making a Birthday for her when her Children, and Grand, and Great Grand Children Several of whom will be present, but it would take a larger house than I have at present to hold them all as there is about 80 of them all told." He assured his niece that Catherine was "right Smart looking" despite having had nine children.[10]

"I am very pleased to know that mother is improving & hope she may be able to weather the storm for many days to come," Mahonri wrote in early 1891,[11] but as Levi Savage noted, "her age is against her."[12] She got weaker and died on June 15th.[13] Relief Society sister Eliza A. Slack said of Catherine, "blessed are they that die in the Lord for they shall have eternal life." And the Toquerville Relief Society's records reported, "She left a Husband and 9 Children 4 dead 5 living (Absent but not Forgoten)."[14]

Steele expressed sorrow over his wife's death in some jottings on the back of a letter from *The Contributor*, recalling that despite her cares and woes, she gathered "with the saints of God and help[ed] with her small mite, to rear a kingdom where the will of God might here on earth be done as it is in heaven."[15] He honored her request to be buried in Parowan beside their daughter Mary and son Robert Henry, and their old friend William Campbell McGregor wrote her obituary, assuring readers, "All who had the pleasure of an acquaintance with Sister Steele speak of her as a kind, self-possessed, brave and noble woman. The blessings promised in the Gospel will be her eternal reward."[16]

After Catherine's death, John wrote, "[I] was lonely and all my numerous family had gone to make Homes and work out for themselves."[17] His friend Joseph L. Heywood, a one-time federal marshal who had been much-married, wanted to help. "After my last conversation with you upon the subject of matrimony a personage was presented to my mind," Heywood wrote. He recommended Wandle Mace's widow Rebecca, living in Kanab, "a most estimable lady & true Latter Day Saint. Sister Mace may be something over Fifty years of age, has never had any children, I have had some Corispondence with her of late as she has been making up her husbands History."[18]

But there's no evidence that Steele ever met Mrs. Mace, and the lonely widower apparently told his friend David Milne that he had struggled to get his fruit dried without Catherine.[19] "I plodid away alone and made the best of my lot," he wrote in his journal.[20]

On April 6, 1893, a great celebration was planned to lay the capstone and dedicate the Salt Lake Temple,[21] though the astrological prognostications Steele jotted down for April weren't encouraging: the United States would be troubled with "much Evil, Anarchests, and great fires." His sources didn't predict anything good happening the whole year, and in August "wife murder will prevail."[22]

Steele went to Salt Lake for the temple dedication and looked up John Drakeford, who had been presiding elder in Leek, Staffordshire, England,

and had given Steele a tour of a braid factory when John was on his mission.[23] Now he gave Steele his picture, one of a mustachioed man so plump only the top button of his jacket was closed. On the back Steele wrote "Elder John Drakeford 91 Oak Street S L City April 6th 1893."[24]

April 6th was temple dedication day, but Steele's mind was diverted. That same day Drakeford reintroduced him to Matilda Kirk Booth. She knew John as the missionary who'd been at the baptism of two of her children and confirmed one, Tamar Elizabeth Booth, known by the family as Lizzy but who usually signed her name "Tamar."[25]

Prosperity had refused to make house calls on the Booths; Matilda's husband, Elijah Booth, a railroad engine driver in the old country, had died the year before in Salt Lake City and was buried as a pauper.[26] The family was large—between the two marriages of Elijah Booth and the two marriages of Matilda they had twenty children.

Steele saw Matilda's daughter Tamar, who had been eleven when he confirmed her, and had asked him to take her to America. Now she was twenty-five and clear of sin, having been rebaptized in the Tabernacle font two days earlier.[27] Despite his seventy-two years, he was interested. "Her mother gave her to me while in England," John claimed in a reminiscent account, but his contemporary journal mentions no such promise.[28]

Steele represented financial stability with his pension and his Toquerville fruit farm. "I thought he was just the man[,] I thought he was a good Latter day Saint and a man of experence and I still hold the same opinion," Tamar's mother, Matilda, recalled.[29]

John wrote, "[A]s soon as I saw her I knew her and told her saying my girl I will take you home with me she said she was willing to go, this was on Thursday, April 6."[30]

Drakeford warned that Tamar had a bad temper, but John was convinced he could overpower that, and that she would be a cure for his loneliness.[31] With no time to arrange a temple ceremony, they were married two days later before a probate judge "according to the Law of the Land."[32] Later he explained the rush: "I was In Company with others who had left their Teams at Milford I was Oblidged to be on time," and he learned they had to be married for him to take her. He found she had two children, "Which up to that time I was not aware off, or Even of her being married."[33]

Her children were six-year-old Albert Henry, called Cheetham, and blue-eyed, blond-haired Charles Edwin Cheetham, age three. John may

"Elder John Drakeford 91 Oak Street S L City April 6th 1893" Steele wrote on the back of this picture. *Family photograph.*

not have known that Albert Henry Cheetham was Tamar's illegitimate son, born Albert Henry Booth.[34] Charles Edwin was indeed a Cheetham, the son of James Albert Cheetham (sometimes spelled Cheatham). Another incumbrance was that the previous May, Tamar had married Frederick A. Rennick, allegedly a soldier, but that marriage was brief, and it's unclear when Steele learned about it.

Milford was the southern terminus of the railroad, a primitive desert freighting station on the edge of the frontier. There they picked up John's team and drove to Toquerville. John's son John Alma had moved to Tropic in Garfield County, where he was road supervisor, so John and Tamar were able to start married life without that distraction.[35]

A photograph that belonged to Elizabeth Steele Stapley, with the same provenance as Steele's John Drakeford picture, shows a young woman seated in a spooled wooden rocker. She's wearing a long dark skirt with side pleats from waist to ankle. A dark, heavy shoe peers out from under her pleated hem. She has a white collar and a medallion on a heavy chain slightly off-center, probably so it wouldn't be blocked by the baby's head. She looks rather stylish—slim and pretty. She has a pleasant face, well focused, with her hair braided and wound behind her ears. She holds a blond baby boy in a frilly nineteenth-century dress with black boots and a white lacy collar, a fringe of white undergarment showing. His hair is short, and there may have been an attempt to part it in the middle. To her left, standing on a box so the top of his wide head almost reaches the top of hers, is a dark-haired older boy in high-topped boots, a big bow tie, and a jacket with three buttons. It appears his eyes are light-colored and his gaze is very steady. This may be the picture she intended to send John when she wrote, "I Payed an extra 2 bits" to have her photo taken with the boys.[36] But this may also be a picture of some missionary's wife and sons. It was printed by William Hill of Manti, Utah, who also specialized in copying and enlarging, and the mediocre quality may indicate it's a copy, though it is not known if Tamar had affiliations with Manti.[37]

On Sunday, April 23, 1893, Tamar was accepted into the Toquerville Ward, and Steele was one of those who spoke of the temple dedication. "Their account of the cerimonies, the magniffìcient building and other improvements in the city were very interesting," Levi Savage wrote. Then, in probably the only near-censorious entry he ever made regarding John Steele, Savage clucked in his journal about his Battalion comrades who'd never enjoyed three simultaneous wives: "I am informed that John Steel, a high priest, and Augustus E. Dodge Senior President of the 9th Quorum of Seventies each took a wife and the marriage ceremonies were performed by a Gentile Judge. This is contrary to the rule of the Church in such matters and excites unfavorable comment with many of the Saints."[38]

Not all comments were adverse. John's daughter Jane Jensen wrote from Taylor, Arizona, "I am delighted beyond expression to think you have got you a house Keeper I am sure you did not get her before you needed one I hope you will enjoy your selves togather & see meny pleasent hours" and concluded. "Give my Love to my new Ma."[39]

Maybe it helped his community standing when they were promptly married in the St. George Temple and her sons adopted to him through sacred Mormon rituals.[40] But soon Tamar showed a temper daunting even to John; on May 1st they quarreled and she smashed the dishes, threatened his life, and broke his windows and doors.[41]

Possibly Tamar Elizabeth Cheetham and her sons Charles and Albert Cheetham. *Family photograph.*

In late August or early September—around the time his astrology sources said wife-murder would prevail—John wrote to Tamar's mother. Matilda reported that the contents made her heart sink, that she found it heart-rending, and told John, "You Say that you Can not stand it much longer." She reminded him that Drakeford had warned him about Tamar's bad temper, and Steele had said he "Could get along with that." Matilda added, "I Presume she has got the Best of you." Talk of a divorce was

Matilda Booth, Tamar's mother. *Family photograph.*

unwelcome, and what would become of Tamar? Matilda couldn't take care of her.

Then she aimed at Tamar. "She ought to be ashamed of herself to think she had such a chance of a good home and has gone through the House of the Lord." Matilda couldn't tell what kind of spirit "layed hold of her." "Now Lizzie I want you to repent at once ask your husband['s] for giveness of all your hard speeches and tell him that you will from this time hence forth and for evermore do Right, and be one with him and make him happy." She concluded by asking for a better letter next time as another like she'd just received "will finish me right out."[42]

John also wrote to Boston astrologer Oliver Ames Goold about his marital problems and received a discouragingly insightful and succinct reply. Goold, Maine-born, fifty years old, a one-time manufacturer who invented an indelible ink and was an occasional lawyer, also knew something about an unconventional marriage: he'd married a forty-four-year-old widow when he was thirty-three.[43]

"Your letters both Received," Goold wrote. "I note all you Say and understand the Situation very well, owing to the presence of Saturn in the

7th House of the Heavens." Goold warned Steele bluntly, "you do not Seem to be destined to much good fortune in marriage, take it all in all, a woman whom you would care enough for to want to keep her, you would [no] doubt loose by Death, while one whom you would not care for permanantly you Could not get rid of as Soon as you might choose."

It was all very scientific: "Inasmuch as the Moon occupied the Sign Cancer, a prolific Sign, you would be likely to have more than one wife in your lifetime," Goold wrote, but "had I been advising you Early in life I Should have counciled you to have nothing or not married any woman in the world and now when you get rid of the one you have do not take any other. I do not expect the one you have to go through your life with you."[44]

John had delayed answering Matilda because he "was waiting to see if things would take a better turn, which oft it does, and at other times it returns with all the fury of a maniac." He didn't hold anything back: "It is tru I Took your Daughter, not knowing or Caring particularly [if] she was a saint; what She had passed through, and as Brother Drakeford Said she had a bad temper, But as I have had considerable Experience in handling different bad tempers and believing my own one of the best to Control others with, I thought it must be bad indeed if I could not manage it."

He continued, "when it Comes home to me in my own House, where I have every thing for comfort and convenience, bread, meat, milk, butter, wine, & Honey and fruit in abundance (if taken Care of) to make a Family comfortable," and to have that disrupted, leaving him without control of the house and being assaulted by "all manner of billingsgate, no man alive could Stand it." (It must be said that Steele was so inflexible that when Catherine once made a cuff too long, he tore it off, handed it to her, and demanded she fix it.[45]) Tamar, with two young boys, was up against a martinet.

"You Say She has asked my forgiveness very true," Steele went on. "She did once, But it did not last a few days until she was as bad or worse than before, and Every trifle that takes her toe she flares up." She called him a liar, whoremaster, black-hearted scoundrel, and other names, which "are titles I dont Claim and would not allow any man to use them under the penalty of having his head badly hurt."

Then there were Albert and Charles. They disturbed his careful arrangement of things and were destructive. And Tamar didn't just have a temper either. She was violent: "when she gets one of her Trantrums on, which is very often Every Thing she takes hold of is dashed to pieces. She threw a bucketfull of water about me and then threw a Stone about three pounds weight, which by good luck just missed me, or Another Time She threw a washbasin of water about me as I was leaving the house to get away from her noise and abuse." He didn't name all of his grievances, writing, "These are only a few of her pranks."

That military precision he'd learned at the knee of his aging soldier-father didn't make room for compromise: "I wish you and Every Body else to understand that I control my house and all that belongs to it, and will not tamely Submit to any body man woman or child to run over me[.] If they do it will be at their own risk." He acknowledged the temple marriage, "but that does not argue that I should be controlled by one of the worst Tongues that ever stuck in a womans head, and were it not for that sealing I Should have parted from her long ago. To be tortured by the Tongue of a termigant [a harsh-tempered or overbearing woman] just because She can, I could not stand it."

Divorce was still an active consideration, and Steele didn't care much what Tamar told her mother, as "Every body round here has heard her voice In the street and you may believe what I say or not But all the people will bear testimony to its truth." As for him asking "her forgiveness that is simply nonsense[.] There is no compromise I am Either Right or I am Wrong, and if she has any Concessions to make I am ready to hear them otherwise There is a Stand off." Steele wrote that sometimes Tamar was cheerful, and "it would be all Kisses and in one hour it would be all curses, which made me think that a Lunatic Asylum were the proper place for her just then." He was catching some signs of her bipolar disorder, but not that she didn't have agency to control her symptoms.

Since Tamar "always talks of writing when she is boiling mad," Matilda perhaps didn't get the full picture, but Steele wrote, "As you say, it is hell to me. I have offered her her freedom, but no She seems to want to make me miserable and to form on [an?] Excuse. She is not so young being a Widow Twice, and Should have some good Sence by this time to Know which Side her bread is buttered on."

Steeled admitted that "True, I have taken her and her family to Support I am not old as some may call me, as I can out run or Throw down many much younger in years, I have had many good Chances for wives but because of former communications I felt myself measurably bound to take her"—which was a pretense that a comment in 1878 when he confirmed her as a Mormon was a formal engagement to an eleven-year-old—"and if She would only stop her bad talking I would not desire a separation as in herself I still like her and would be to her all she could desire." He concluded by thanking Matilda for her previous kind letter, "but I dare not trust it in her hands until she promises she won't tear it as she did your last one"—which had been written in late October or early November and partly survives in John's papers.[46]

There was no news until December 17th, when Matilda wrote that she had been expecting a letter from John and hoped she hadn't offended him. She also gave Tamar a staccato list of commands: "cheer up and don't be so despondent keep a bridle on your tongue don't worry keep your mind calm and take care of your health," and more in that line.[47]

One suspects some kind of truce, however sullen, when Matilda wrote on January 26, 1894, that she was planning to visit. Tamar may not have been feeling well since her mother directed her to "take care of yourself take plenty of cooling medicine I want you to tell your husband how you are for he is a fine doctor and perhaps he will give you something that will do you good."[48]

Steele did, in fact, have a medical concoction for Tamar's condition that included whisky and cannabis.

> For nervious Debillity, in Females, Take Some puruvian Bark, (Cinchini) Indian (or ^2 ozs^ Common hemp) Cannibis Sativa 2 ozs Blue Vernine (verbena Hastata) [2?[49]] Drs Elecampan 3 Drs Latan name Inulin 3 ozs with one pind good Whiskey one pound loaf Sugar and fill a 3 pind bottle by adding water. = then ad if need be some Mother wort Blue Cohosh Some nervine Some Golden Seal Some Blood [r]oot this taken in moderation.[50]

Maybe that had kept Catherine calm, but if Steele tried it on Tamar, he was disappointed.

Matilda added a postscript to Tamar because just as she was ready to mail her letter to Steele, another came with stories of more trouble. Matilda had decided not to visit after all and wrote that she would be obliged if Steele would send Tamar home straight away: "I begin to think marriage is a failure tell him I would like him to Reliese you honowrably as you have not committed the unpardonable sin tell him we told him you had a very bad temper and we heard that he had another."[51]

They made it through their first anniversary, maybe partly because Steele had other distractions, including continuing to build the Kingdom. He'd done lawyering for James Jepson Jr., who thought he'd found a way to bring water onto the Hurricane Bench. Steele measured Jepson's proposed canal route with his spirit level, found it feasible, and they recruited others to bring the water that established one of the last Utah Mormon pioneering efforts, the town of Hurricane.[52]

Steele also inserted himself into a discussion about who was "the first white boy" born in Salt Lake Valley[53]— and spent one Ides of March casting a horoscope to determine the right time to plants peas ("put in peas ʘ [Sun] in ♄ [Saturn]").[54] Things mellowed with Tamar, at least if we judge by a March 9th letter from her mother, who described herself as highly pleased with their last report. Matilda's note was quite short, and she probably had some doubts their accommodation would hold without a little maternal prompting, so she tried, warning Tamar to obey and honor and respect her husband, and "keep a guard on your tongue for it is an unruly member." She was jaunty enough to once again imagine a trip to Toquerville to visit her elderly son-in-law.[55]

In another letter, dated April 13th, Matilda was still considering a trip south, though "money is so scarse I cant get a dollar from anyw[h]ere," yet by July she'd decided she wouldn't be able to stand the southern Utah heat.[56]

Tamar had a plan for that; she nagged John to send her back to Salt Lake.[57] He eventually sent her on July 19th, and thanks to this visit, we hear Tamar speak in her own voice. She wrote John and sounded like anything but a scold or a mad woman: "you must Pardon me for not writing sooner for I have been considiring how I Can get home for I ca-nt see my way clear" because she needed money. She lectured him on the needs of the boys he had adopted through Mormon ritual in the St. George Temple. Their clothes were nearly worn out, and "I want you to send me as much money as you can for I can get clothes cheap here and the children are wanting clothes both winder and op[58] clothing." Next, she commanded, "dont dissapoint me for I want to come as soon as Possible. before the school starts as I want Albert to go to school this winter." She mentioned that her mother would take Albert, but she didn't have a bed for him, and also that her mother said if John would get something to help the children pass the time, they'd be less troublesome.[59]

Matilda also thought that with some training Albert—who was developing excellent handwriting and was described in 1913 as "a bright, intelligent man"—could be a great help.[60] Meanwhile, Tamar wrote, "I would like ^to know^ weath^ar^ you have Got alright again As I know you must have had a hard time of it but you never miss a wive till she gone but I hope I will soon be with you and do my best to cheer you." She promised, "I will bring you a drop of the Crater [bowl] and then I will help you to drink it. so cheer up. and dont die in the shell, live in hopes. if you should have to die in Despair."

She outlined her wishes as though there'd never been a disagreement. "Dear Husband, I would like you to make ^some^ Different arrangment coming home. I dont want to be know longer on the road going than I was coming." With nights cooling off—maybe in Salt Lake, but in Dixie it would still be hot in late August—she worried she could take a cold. As for where she would stay when she got off the train at Milford, she wrote that instead of paying for a room, "I would much rather, you bring your Team, and the loan of that waggon I came in and fetch me yourself, or otherwise one of your Grandsons for I am sure he was Good Company." She signed off, "I Conclude with my very best love from your Dearest wive, Tamar," wrote a row of *x*'s, added some inconsequential comments along the side of the last page, and asked him to write soon.[61]

"I sent her money to come back," Steele wrote in his journal,[62] and a fragment of a subsequent letter from her mother shows Tamar left Salt Lake in a hurry with a bad cold, and Albert went with her because his grandma couldn't keep him.[63]

Whether Tamar was a help or hindrance on Steele's next adventure is unknown, but at age seventy-three, he found himself the sacrificial Republican candidate for Washington County surveyor, losing to St. George's Isaac Chauncey Macfarlane by 174 to 492 votes.[64] It probably didn't boost his pride when the *Deseret Weekly* referred to him soon after as "the late John Steele, of Toquerville, Utah."[65]

Matilda's next letter implies Steele was on to some of the facts of Tamar's marriages. She wrote that Tamar's first husband, James A. Cheetham, hated the Mormons and said he'd never come to Utah. Frederick Rennick deceived Tamar by promising to get a divorce before their marriage, so he had no claim on her. As for Albert and Charles, "Children will be children and if they are trained it will be a great blessing both to you and your husband."[66]

John and Tamar seem to have faced their second anniversary in another standoff. The rigid old man and his sometimes manic wife were still together, but by summer their relationship was worsening.

On Sunday, July 7, 1895, Levi Savage was at Toquerville's visiting teachers' meeting to talk about issues among families in the ward. He wrote in his journal, "Brother Steel and his wife quarreling was mentioned. Some proposed to arrest them for disturbing the peace, others thought a better way could be adopted. The matter rested here."[67]

John and Tamar's conflicts were heightened because he'd confirmed she'd not been divorced from either previous husband. John wrote President Wilford Woodruff, stating, when "I found the particulars [of her unfamiliarity with divorce courts] I Sent her home to her Mother in Salt Lake City."[68] In his more contemporary journal he was more circumspect: "after a while she wanted to go to Salt Lake again to see her mother so again on August 15 1895 she left once more for the city. She still kept crying to come back But I could not think of it and so I did not send for her again."[69]

Before Tamar left, John enlisted Garfield County lawyer John F. Chidester, a family friend currently campaigning for the Utah state senate, to draw up divorce papers.[70] This brief document didn't mention polyandry and didn't elaborate on all of John's grievances, but did state "That Since the Said Marriage the defendant has treated plaintiff in a cruel and inhuman manner and in particular as follows on the firs[t] day of May 1893 the Defendant did Strike and beat plaintiff and did break up dishes belonging to plaintiff and threaten plaintiff's life and did break the windows and Doors of plaintiff." He added the generic argument that Tamar "is in the habit of abusing plaintiff and anoy him to the Extent of Causing plaintiff Great mental Suffering." The paper was signed by the Garfield County clerk, who happened to be Steele's grandson Mahonri M. Steele Jr.[71] The uncontested divorce was granted November 19, 1895.

Tamar wrote John on August 27th, before she got the divorce papers. Her crazily erratic misuse of periods as she progressed in this letter may reflect a backfiring mind, and certainly leaves the reader feeling like they'd chewed on dried corn on the cob: "My Dear Husband this comes with kind love to you, hoping to find you ^arrived well all safe & sound^." She had a cold, her mother wasn't well off, and she was living in a place so small they couldn't fit two beds in it. Furthermore, "I am sorry to tell you that my baggage went astray." She thought Isaac Nephi Duffin was to blame because when he took her to Milford, he didn't tie down her trunk. "[A]ll the family. says if you had acted wise. you. would. have got a divorce. and not thrown so much. money away." She was received coldly because the family lost a watch they had expected John to redeem when they pawned it to send Tamar money. Matilda was very discouraged. Tamar wrote, "mother says she his tired of seeing us knock around. we. are. knock. around. like a chip. on. a. ocean," and Matilda wanted to know where Tamar was going. "[Y]ou know full. well that i aint got a cent to get a divorce with. my brother.s ^are^ all disguisted because you dont come to some settlement. and, make me a home it would. only cost you 18 dollars to get me ^a divorce^.[72] but if you dont maintain me. I shall have to throw myself on the church no one can help me here."

John Alma, who was back, seems to have been part of the problem. Tamar wrote, "Let me know in Your next if alma is living with you Yet. and how long is he going to remain with you." She was interested in John's fruit, wished he'd send her a sack of grapes, and said, "mother is Ex tremely. obliged for that good wine. she said it was number one. I would like you to keep a little wine on hand for our own use please to put suggar in it the next time." She wished John would visit them in Salt Lake at the April or October Conference, and "I wish you would try and sell some of your stock and buy a little home up here. and with your Carpenters tools you could Make a Good living you know that I dont like South. nor never will feel at home."

Surely the courageous old pioneer was offended when she counseled, "I wish you would have some Spunk about you and Show the old Business that you are the head and. and that you make your own laws and that you-ll not be Circumscribed by none of them and Just let every body see how much you respect your wive and family."[73]

Eventually Tamar got the divorce papers, and Steele got a scolding from his friend John Howcroft, who accused him of turning her and her children "on a crwel world on a poor crippled mother."[74]

At some point Tamar sent John an undated Valentine's card and wrote, or more likely copied, the following:

When Rocks and Hills
Divide us and you
no more Ill—see
When of others
you are thinking will
You sometimes think
of me.
Tamara E. Steele[75]

They continued to correspond and Steele sometimes sent her money. She wrote on April 3, 1896, from "Stevenes Row in the area of Lake st.," addressing him as "My Dear Husband." After expressing perfunctory concern about him being sick, she reported her health was improving but her mother's worsening. Changing wards hurt because the new bishop was stingier than the last. Her family did what they could, but meanwhile the house was drafty, cold, and in a swampy area with blowing winds. She outlined some of her hardships and wrote, "if any one has suffered more than I since I left home I sincerely Pity them but I have learned a lesson which I shall not easily forget. I have had a hard experience not that I want to throw any Responsibility on you for I could be free but I dont consider i am." Still, their temple marriage had great meaning, and even if they were separated by civil law, they were still married in the eyes of God. She knew she left Toquerville with tongues a-wagging: "I feel sometimes I would not dare to come back after so much scandal and If any one was to upbraid it would effect me very much not withstanding if you want me to come home."

Since Tamar and the children couldn't see John, she sent her picture and promised to follow up with pictures of her and the boys. She mentioned Conference and referenced the celebration of his recent seventy-fifth birthday: "You must have had a great old time together 2 think they did not share the music. I wish i could have been there it must have been lovable. I drank my own health last birthday Party . . . I am ever so much obliged for the 5 dollars."

Bitterness seems to have abated for her mother since Tamar wrote, "all the family sends their best regards." After signing off she added a postscript, including an update on his little stepson Charlie, who "is often talking about you, he says his pa can mend shoes and make shoes and I don't know what his pa ca-nt do in his estimation." The last sentence was, "Write soon and let me know what you think or what you mean to do."[76]

Steele looked for astrological meaning in this letter, working out a horoscope for "Lizzies Letter | April 27 1896 | 10 am | Monday."[77]

Levi Savage noted in his journal that John was keeping busy with his religious duties and had dosed him for a kidney ailment, but he was also puzzled about Tamar.[78] At the advice of St. George's David Cannon, Steele wrote President Wilford Woodruff to explain the marriage/divorce/polyandry dilemma. Assuming part of his story was already notorious—"I Should make the Subject as plain as posible part of it you no doubt have heard"—he explained that after his wife Catherine died, he met Tamar in Salt Lake, sixteen years after her mother promised her to him, and they promptly got married. He acknowledged the later temple ceremony and wrote that when he found out she was still married, he sent her back to her mother and they legally separated. All this was preparatory. His main point was that Tamar wanted to come back, made promises to do better, and "I have been living alone in my House now over a year and it has become Monotonous and lonely and I need Some one to be with."[79]

Woodruff's efficient secretary, George Reynolds—the Reynolds in *Reynolds v. the United States*, in which the Supreme Court ruled against polygamy—had spent time in federal prison and he answered from experience: the Mormon faith no longer claimed its ideas of marriage made civil law irrelevant. He wrote, "[T]wo things appear: One, that, in the eye of the law, you are a single man and therefore can marry any woman who is in the same condition as yourself, who would be willing to accept you. Second, that if you wish to receive back your former wife it will be first necessary for her to obtain a divorce from her legal husband, and then for you to re-marry."[80]

In the summer of 1897 the secretary of the Pioneer Jubilee Commission sent Steele and his daughter Elizabeth free train tickets to the great celebration in Salt Lake City of the fiftieth anniversary of arrival in the valley.[81] John used a *Pierce's Memorandum Account Book* for a journal of this trip, including writing two addresses for "Mrs Elizabeth Booth," one on Ninth South and Seventh East, Stevens Row in the rear of Lake Street, and the second at 65 Grape Street. This was his ex-wife Tamar; maybe he listed her as Booth because he didn't know which of her four potential surnames she was using.[82]

John visited the Lagoon amusement park in Farmington, took in the sights, and at a tabernacle ceremony he and daughter Elizabeth were among the 1847 pioneers who "obtained a Badge and gold meddle" that entitled them to free admission at all the events. There were lots of them—an "Indian" band at Saltair, bicycle races at Beck's Hot Springs, a Grand Concert in the tabernacle, and a special orator, Democratic presidential candidate William Jennings Bryan, a renowned champion of silver.[83]

Steele and some family members found time to go to C. R. Savage's gallery for several photographs, including one with him and several of his children.[84]

John and other family members toured the Salt Lake City and County Building, including climbing to the clock tower for "a good view of city and Surrounding Countery."[85] He doesn't mention, and may not have known, that his wife Catherine's face was carved into stone on the east side of the building, commemorating her role as mother of the first Mormon born in Utah.[86]

More astonishing, and surprisingly gratifying for John, was "my Wife Elizabeth Booth Steele Came and walked with me in the procission and I took Supper with her that Night."[87] He didn't report the conversation but later said she begged to go back to Toquerville.

The Jubilee vindicated John Steele's life, for he'd seen the movement he'd joined almost in its infancy "Extend from Cannady on the north, to Mexico on the South, and from the Small handfull of pioneers of 148 in number, it was reported there ware 600,000 [*sic*] people ther[e] on July 24 1897." He bragged to his niece, "All this [was] by the industery of those who Came into this Desert land 50 years ago, and got no help from any Source but their own Strong arm, and the Blessings of the Almighty."[88]

Steele was soon back in Toquer but his loneliness overcame his experience, and he sent for Tamar and Albert. Naturally, that didn't work out, so he took her to Milford to catch the train back to Salt Lake City but was still in touch with her as late as April 1898.[89]

This was a mad interlude for John, but the dénouement for Tamar and her boys was heartbreaking. She was soon destitute and sent to Salt Lake County's poor farm, and then, with her mother's no doubt reluctant endorsement, committed to the insane asylum in Provo in late 1898. The doctors reported, "Mrs. Rennick was found to be suffering from melancholia superinduced by poverty."[90]

From left, Mahonri M. Steele, Young Elizabeth Steele Stapley, Susann Adams Steele Bringhurst, and John Steele, 1897. Elizabeth and John are wearing their 1847 pioneer ribbons. *Family photograph.*

But Tamar's story had more twists than a Silver Reef mine; the *Salt Lake Tribune* called it "a strange tale, tinged with sadness and romance."[91]

More than ten months after she was committed, her first (and legal) husband, James Albert Cheetham, now a successful Manchester fishmonger, came to Utah and claimed her. He posted $500 bond to release her from the asylum, and a fairytale "happily ever after" story appeared in the newspaper. Except the story's headline probably tipped him off to some of her subsequent marriage adventures, giving him an additional surname: "James Albert Cheatham-Rennick comes to Salt Lake on Hearing that Mrs. Rennick, Whom He Had Not Heard from for Years, had Become Crazy—Gave a Bond for Her Release, and Brought Her to this City Yesterday—Her Indigent Condition."[92]

Cheetham soon disappeared but he didn't have a right to be concerned about Tamar's other husbands: he had left a wife behind in England named Mary Hannah. After he left Tamar, Mary Hannah met Cheetham in Boston, and they sailed together on a Cunard steamer back to England.[93]

Catherine Campbell Steele sculpture on the east side of the Salt Lake City and County Building. *Photo by author.*

Although John's granddaughter Cassie (Catherine/Cathern) Steele (later Riding) was employed at the state mental hospital in 1903 while Tamar was there, there's no record of any interaction between them. After being abandoned by her first husband, Tamar returned to the hospital and remained institutionalized until her death on October 18, 1914, from apoplexy, with "Manic Depressive Psychoses" as a contributing factor.[94]

During her manias, Tamar's children so repulsed her that they were left at the poor farm. Albert lived out his public career in the newspapers, from boyhood robberies to San Francisco's Chinese opium dens. The last mention of him was in March 1913, when he was back in Salt Lake making news as "Red Doc," a recovering addict, his slavery to "hop" (opium), morphine, and cocaine hopefully a thing of the past.[95]

After working as a waiter, Tamar's elder son, Charles Cheetham, enlisted in the Army and was stationed at Fort Douglas for several years, but by World War I he'd lost a leg, and he died in jail on July 19, 1922, after drinking poisoned alcohol; his death certificate listed his residence as "City jail most of the time" and the cause of death as acute alcoholism.[96]

Authoritarian bullying may have forced Mormons to relinquish polygamy, but Tamar's story reminds us that not all difficulties can be beaten into submission.

15

LEECHDOMS, WORTCUNNING, STARCRAFT, AND FATE

John Steele's worldview is best reflected in Thomas Oswald Cockayne's book of preconquest Anglo-Saxon magic charms and medicine, *Leechdoms, Wortcunning, and Starcraft of Early England* (1864).[1]

Leechdoms refers to medical skills; *wortcunning* was from the words *wyrt*, meaning herb, plant, root, or vegetable (*wyrd*, interestingly, means inescapable destiny); and *cunnan*, whose meanings include to know how to, to have power to, and, in the context of magic, secret esoteric knowledge or a person with that knowledge: an adept. *Starcraft* is the ability to read the stars; that is, astrology. These arts protected the folk in the dark, wet forests of Anglo-Saxon England from monsters like *Beowulf*'s Grendel, malignant elves, Æsir (ancient German gods), and witches who tormented people with disease.[2] Steele added fate to that list in the context of divination, such as determining when one was most likely to die.

When Steele set himself up as a doctor, it was a calling, not a livelihood. In 1876 a *Salt Lake Tribune* correspondent wrote that Leeds, near Toquer, "now has two doctors, but if they were to follow their profession, both would starve to death, as this is the 'most painfully healthy' region in the West."[3] Steele would have concurred. In an 1867 letter to Apostle George A. Smith, he wrote, "The health of our settlement as usual is good," a sentiment he repeated as late as 1901.[4]

"Weather permitting," wrote Toquerville historian Dr. Wesley P. Larsen, Steele "always wore a blue cape with a red lining and carried a cane. On call to help the sick and wounded, he always rode a fine white horse, 'Charlie.' One of Toquer's most prominent citizens, he looked like a dignified Southern Colonel on a white horse."[5]

In a letter to his niece Letisha Todd, Steele confided, "I take great delight in Doctering up our Sick and wounded and don't charge one cent for it. . . . I am called all round to help them . . . my Daughters ar[e] good nurses & midwives and we have plenty to do."[6]

Steele probably learned many of his medical precepts from two of Parowan's first settlers, the "professor of herbology," Dr. William A. Morse, and Thomsonian doctor Priddy Meeks. (Thomsonian medicine was a series of natural and herbal remedies prescribed by Samuel Thomson, a self-taught Connecticut farmer and botanist; it reached its apogee as the Mormons first migrated to Utah.) Meeks and Morse were both admired friends of Steele's.[7]

In 1870, the same year the census recorded Steele's profession as "doctor," a new system was peeking over the horizon. In February *Deseret News* editor George Q. Cannon reported that Professor John Tyndall's new germ theory of disease was "likely to overthrow long established ideas."[8] Tyndall's speculations were buttressed by a series of incredible discoveries: in 1876 anthrax bacilli were identified; in 1877, the cause of malignant edema; in 1878, traumatic infection; in 1880, streptococcus and staphylococcus bacteria and typhoid bacillus; in 1882, tuberculous; in 1883, diphtheria bacillus; and in 1884, cholera bacillus.[9]

*

Among the medical skills, or leechdoms, that Steele studied was uroscopy, an ancient practice, though it was looked on with some disfavor in seventeenth-century England: herbalist Nicholas Culpeper called such practitioners "piss prophets," yet he wrote *Urinalia*, a pamphlet on the subject.[10]

Steele's regimen was to warm a glass of urine ("watter") by a fire, then examine it with a magnifying glass. In a list of concoctions in the back of his first journal he wrote, "[I]f the watter settles to the bottom the Liver is effected (tending to consumption) & if it rises half way from the bottom the hart is effected But if the Sparks rises up lively there is a good Chance of a cure[.] If you Shake the glass and the watters settles very quick it is a nervus Complaint."[11]

Reviving the drowned was another specialized skill. When Jane Hanks Sylvester was swept out of her wagon trying to cross flooded Ash Creek on Christmas Eve, 1889, Edward Batty lassoed her and pulled her out of the stream unconscious with a beat-up face and head, horribly swollen and apparently drowned.

"The men worked over her a long time trying to revive her," Jane's daughter Gladys recalled. Then John Steele, perhaps with knowledge from witnessing drowning resuscitations on Belfast Lough or Glasgow Green, took command, "and through determination and perseverance brought her back to life to her husband and four small children." But the accident was blamed for the arthritis that killed her some years later.[12]

When I visited Toquerville in 1984 with a tape recorder under my arm, I confirmed Steele's bonesetter skills: I interviewed ninety-year-old Charles Andrew Olds, whose arm had been set by "Doc Steele." He remembered him as a bearded "little fellow" and a nice old man.

Olds broke his arm climbing over a rock wall with a big watermelon; he hid so his parents wouldn't know, but someone spoke up: "Andy broke his arm!" "So they all surrounded me," Olds remembered, "and rolled my sleeve up and it was broke. Picked me up and took me up there, and that old man [John Steele] got a—them days all the boxes they had were made out of wood. Now you don't see so many of 'em. Broke the slats off that, put it down and put it along there, and you can't tell it was broke, it was right along in there, [you can] feel it."[13]

You could.

Another case made it into the local newspaper. "Victor Sylvester came to town the other day from the Danish ranch with a broken arm," the *Washington County News* reported. "Bro. Steel[e] set the broken limb."[14] Victor, it turned out, was a son of Jane, the woman Steele had resuscitated nearly eleven years earlier; the high-spirited boy had decided to go to Toquerville despite parental forbidding and was thrown from his horse trying to escape. He bragged later that by breaking his arm he got to town anyway.[15]

*

Steele's herbal remedies represented the "wyrt" in wortcunning. He had ingredients and recipes to treat 105 conditions. Alphabetically they ranged from abdominal pain—as distinguished from abdominal swelling—to whooping cough. In between, one can find applications for such things as bruises, cancer, convulsions, diabetes, epilepsy, frozen limbs, gangrene, glaucoma, hives, intoxication, joint weakness, kidney problems, loss of consciousness, migraine, neuralgia, paralysis, rashes, scalp troubles, and warts.

Steele drew from more than two hundred substances, most of them botanical, many with pre-Christian pedigrees. Some, like hemlock, went back to at least Socrates in 399 BC; others, like Euphrasia (Eyebright), known to the Anglo-Saxons as ægwyrt (eye-wort), also had an ancient history.[16] Henbane, or nightshade, was "good in Convulsions brain fever &c.," Steele wrote, and recommended it to produce drowsiness. This remedy goes back at least to the late sixteenth century, and probably further.[17] "Atropine and scopolamine, powerful hallucinogens, can be found in plants in the nightshade family, among them mandrake, henbane and thorn apple," reported the *New York Times*, and these substances were found in three-thousand-year-old Bronze-aged human hair in Minorca.[18]

Steele listed twenty-six of Thomson's seventy "Medica Materia," or necessary herbs.[19] Thomson's Medica Materia No. 1 was lobelia, a plant almost never used for medical purposes before he recommended it. Dr. Priddy Meeks thought lobelia's efficacy almost supernatural.[20] Steele has five references for use of this poisonous plant, including to treat diphtheria and yellow fever, to stop bleeding, and for use as a general emetic. Steele also included it as part of a hot pack for the neck and, combined with other ingredients, a croup treatment.[21]

If a patient had yellow fever, Steele told them to drink herbal tea, then "tak[e] a lobelia emetic and vomit yourself for an hour or more. As nearly to death as you can and live."[22] This was believed to purge the body of the so-called mismatched humors (a Greek concept that didn't fall out of favor until about 1850), and vomiting "As nearly to death as you can and live" was a central thesis in the concept of restoring internal humoral balance. It also seems suspiciously similar to the principles behind chemotherapy and radiation treatment.

Journalist Nell Murbarger reported that Steele used local plants, but his written recipes reference no Indigenous medicines. That rich tradition should have been known to him, for he was well acquainted with Paiutes. Maybe he was misled by the Thomsonians, one of whom claimed that despite using several herbs traceable to Native Americans, Native people had "no remedies worth notice" and "no medicines."[23] However, historians Gary Tom and Ronald Holt point out that Paiutes were "highly sophisticated botanists" whose remedies were used by many practitioners: among other plants, they used agave, Brigham (Mormon) tea, buckthorn, creosote, dock, Indian corn, mesquite, prickly pear, sego lilies, and squawbush.[24]

Steele was aware of the excellent medicinal qualities of some other American plants and herbs. He writes of "China, peruvian Bark, [for] weakness of animal fluid, intermittant fever and all kinds of fevers stomaches, bowels, skin diseases chilliness hot skin diseases."[25] This South American plant, also known as Jesuit's bark, contains quinine and is excellent for malaria. If he'd had it in Nauvoo in late 1845, it may have saved his children's lives. (Quinine was among the "simple medicines" required of a well-equipped nineteenth-century traveler in the West.[26])

As already noted, Steele found various uses for cannabis. In his herbal directory he writes, "Cannabis, Hemp Good in Kidney Blader Rheumatisms occationed By fatigue ulcerated pains in Kidneys Catarrh inflamation of Chest &c.,"[27] and it does have positive effects for arthritis and can help nervous women—or men.

The "doctrine of signatures," or sympathy, was one of Steele's practices and represents the "cunning" or magical part of wortcunning, the belief that all things are linked, and so resemblances of disparate items can be a key to solving health problems. When the Chinese recognized that ginseng root looked something like a human body, they relied on signatures to use pieces of the root to heal the corresponding body parts.[28] Botanist Dr. Wesley Pratt Larsen, who for some years owned John Steele's home, found *Phallus impudicus* (sixteenth-century botanist John Gerard called it the "Pricke Mushrom," an edible penis-shaped fungus) growing on Steele's homestead. Larsen theorized Steele grew it for its alleged aphrodisiac qualities; it isn't native to the area.[29]

Steele's cunning practices also included magic charms, an Anglo-Saxon practice. His cure for ringbone—arthritis creating a bony proliferation in a horse's coffin joint and pastern (between the fetlock and the top of the hoof)—shows the lack of boundaries between medicine and magic. The cure required one to ride the horse as fast as possible after the full moon and stop at a place where a horse had died, then take a similar bone from the dead horse, repeat a magic charm, and lay the bone in its place.[30] He also had a charm to find stolen property and make the thief return it, as well as two charms to destroy witchcraft.[31]

Steele himself had black magic spells, such as one for making people hate each other using waxen images in fighting mode.[32] Whether he used these is not known, but one was similar to punishing a waxen image of the person you want to injure, generally associated with voodoo but an

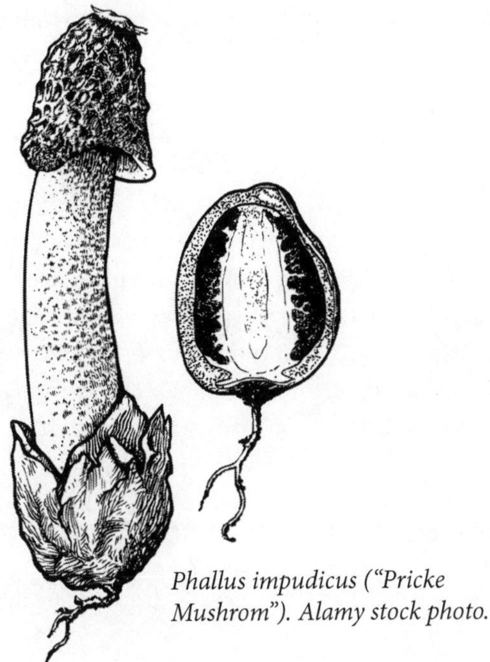

Phallus impudicus ("Pricke Mushrom"). Alamy stock photo.

ancient worldwide practice. His spell involved waiting until the moon is afflicted by Saturn, Mars, or a new moon, and then sticking a copper nail in the image and burying it.[33]

Like Joseph Smith, Steele was interested in "crystal prophesying."[34] His *Raphael Almanacs* advertised "Crystal Balls for the Use of Astrologers, Seers, and Mediumistic persons."[35] Steele's scryer charm has careful instructions for how to prepare oneself for the ritual and invokes the Trinity, heavenly hosts, and angels for guidance.[36]

Steele probably also had an interest in a newer "science," phrenology: his library included Samuel R. Wells's *New Physiognomy, or, Signs of Character as Manifested Through Temperament and External Forms, and especially in 'The Human Face Divine.' 'With more than One Thousand illustrations.'*[37] Wells specialized in publishing about phrenology and other contemporary medical fads.

Steele had an interest in numerology, and just as he sought to establish the meaning of Susan B. Anthony's name by ascribing numbers to each letter, he did the same with his own. "John" totaled 47 and "Steele" 93, which, he noted, made a whole of 140. He doesn't explain how he interpreted these numbers.[38]

*

Starcraft—astrology—is at least as ancient as the first written records. Babylonian astronomical diaries were written on mud, and a court astronomer in 652 BC reported, "Mercury's last appearance in the east behind Pisces, and Saturn's last appearance behind Pisces; cloudy days, I did not observe."[39]

Nicholas Culpeper, drawing on ancient English practices and perhaps even older ones, explained how starcraft was related to herbal medicine, or wortcunning. Steele echoed Culpeper when he wrote that herbs were under the influence of various celestial bodies. Moist and pale-colored plants were under the influence of Venus, he explained, listing dandelions, featherful, and motherwort. Poison herbs were under the influence of Mercury, "Prickly & stinging things" under Mars, mild herbs under Jupiter, and comfrey under Saturn.[40]

For Steele and many of his contemporaries, astrology and astronomy were the same science. His motherless granddaughter Della Fish remembered helping dry peaches in Toquerville and that "Grandpa did lots of outdoor work yet found time to teach me many things about astronomy." He used his astronomical instruments "to teach me many lessons about the heavens which were so interesting to him," lessons she felt sure made her later moonlight strolls with young men more entertaining because of the stars they saw.[41]

John gave starcraft serious attention, explaining the etymology of *astronomy* as from "Astor meaning a Star, Onomy a Sciance and the word Combined meaning the Sciance of the Stars." He explained the diameter of the sun, its rate of revolving, and its density compared to earth, and went on to describe other planets and the earth's moon in the same detail.[42] This was a self-taught man comfortable with math and awed by the immensity of the solar system.

Despite the astrological interests of founding prophet Joseph Smith and his brother Hyrum, starcraft was condemned by Smith's successors. "Some dabble in astrology and gather thoughts of misery from it," the *Deseret News* wrote, charging that their predictions "are always postponed as the calculations prove incorrect."[43] The *News* also repeated the argument that there

A leaning tower of Steele's *Raphael Almanacs. Author's photo.*

was no need for astrology because Mormons had the priesthood.[44] In 1898 the Mormon magazine *Improvement Era* published an article invoking the Buddha to argue against "divination, interpretation of dreams, palmistry, astrology, crystal prophesying, [and] charms of all sorts"[45]—all of which, except for palmistry, Steele had instructions for or engaged in.

Steele was an avid collector of astrological texts, so much so that Brigham Young University's L. Tom Perry Special Collections register of Steele's papers says his astrological publications "constitute the largest such private collection yet discovered for pioneer Utah."[46]

In a 1900 letter to astrologer "Mr. Azrael" in New York City, he wrote, "I have worked in the Science [of astrology] for the last 40 years."[47] His first known horoscope was of his astrology teacher John Sanderson in Parowan in late 1851, which means by 1900 Steele had been dabbling in this practice for at least forty-nine years.[48] (That winter there'd been a group of Parowan men studying under Sanderson's guidance, but most gave up after being discouraged by Brigham Young.[49])

Steele's magic spells were written next to Sanderson's horoscope, so the latter may have provided them to Steele, as he did a remedy to James H. Martineau.[50] Steele's collection of astrological almanacs goes back to at least 1849 and includes six published by a fellow Mormon, William W. Phelps.[51] Steele worked out his own nativity many times. The profile he got according to his *Grammar of Astrology*, like most horoscopes, describes some relevant characteristics.[52]

Steele also put these skills to work for family and friends. He told his daughter Jane Steele Jensen about some worrying astrological implications for her son Leonard Peter Jensen and steps to protect him.[53] Olive DeMille Stevens was very happy with the calculations he did for her, while Mahonri had a mixed response, but David Milne gave Steele all the indulgence he should have been giving his disgruntled, angry ex-wives: "I believe you hit it pretty close in your Horoscope business."[54]

*

In 1894—at the instigation of "graduates of the orthodox [medical] schools"—the Utah legislature passed a medical licensing requirement. Laws like these had been on the books earlier in the century, but the Thomsonians led a drive to repeal them. The new law made provision for individuals who had been practicing medicine but had not graduated from medical colleges: they would have to pay a $25 fee, get twenty-five legal voters in their area to sign a petition, and pass a test administered by the Board of Medical Examiners.[55]

Excluded from the Board of Examiners were practitioners of the "Physio-Medical, Allopathic, Homeopathic and Eclectic" schools of medicine. Soon a few long-time practitioners were convicted of practicing medicine without a license.[56]

Steele did get an application for a license and partly filled it out, but then apparently gave up. Instead, he thought of getting help from his Democratic legislator, Isaac and Mary Duffin's mustachioed boy James G. Duffin, with a penchant for bow ties and more education than Toquerville provided.

On January 31, 1897, Steele wrote Duffin a letter eloquent enough to serve as the last lament for dying prescientific medicine: "Dear Sir, as there has been Great Discrimination among a Certain Class of Docters, who profess to monopolise the healing Art, and who have amalgamated themselves togather As a Board," he opened.[57] This and much else echoed Thomsonian complaints.[58] This board, he wrote, excluded "Every other person who have not been, or are not able, to answer Certain Questions of Greek, And Latin, in medical practice, from practising the healing art, although they may have Served the public for Twent[y], or Forty years."

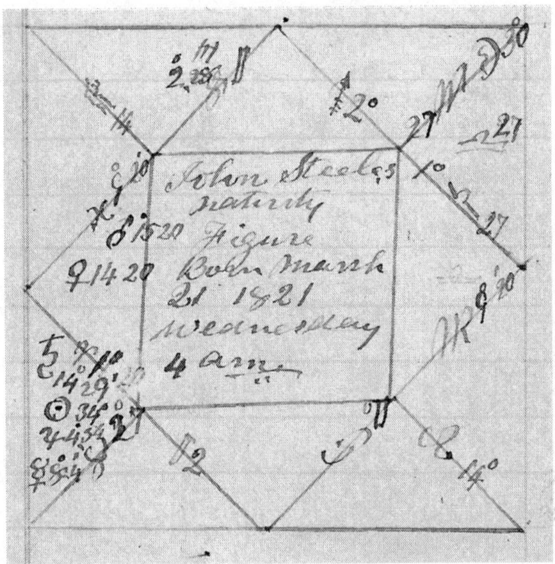

John Steele's horoscope for himself. *LDS Church History Library.*

He repeated most of the arguments of the Thomsonians from two generations earlier: "Neither a dose of mathematics nor knowledge of Greek or Latin ever reduced a fractured limb, healed a lacerated wound, explained dropsy, or cured consumption."[59]

Steele insisted that self-taught doctors like himself were "doing much good, and in Curing diseases of various Kinds, going among the people by day, & by night, and in many Cases without fee, or reward, and furnishing medicine from their own private Medicine Chest." He continued a line of argument familiar to the Thomsonians in the 1830s: "[H]eretofore the History of Medicine Legislation, and its Enforcements in this State, whereby a Ring of professionals, have held Controle, Shutting out from practice all who Could not understand Alpha, Beta, Gamma, Delta, Epsilon, Zeta, of Greek, Or the Latin, ah, bay."

What was the practicality of all that schooling? Those approved by the "Medical Ring" were working the public for "the Fee they can obtain, Having Spent a Couple of years in Some institution of learning, Come out a full fledged Docter with a Diplona [diploma] as long as your arm, with the privilige of Charging a Fee as long as your leg."[60]

If he heard from Duffin by letter, it has gone missing; more likely they talked after the legislative session.

Duffin didn't change the law, but the Thomsonian bogeymen of the 1820s and '30s were dead: bleeding, calomel, antimony, and other poisons hated by the Thomsonians were proven to be as bad as the herbalists said they were. Steele didn't get a doctor's certificate but continued his practice; he was listed in the *Utah State Gazetteer and Business Directory, 1903–04* as "Steele John, physician."[61] Doctoring also sometimes helped with loneliness: "I have plenty of Company at times more than I want," he confided when he reiterated his doctoring role.[62]

Steele could argue he accepted the new sciences despite no evidence that he accepted germ theory; he sent his nephew George Connelly the *Scientific American* and wrote part of his autobiography on the back of an 1875 blank subscription list for that magazine.[63] His library was replete with a mix of quackery and the latest discoveries: for instance, he got a correspondent course degree in hypnotism and had a flyer for "Three Messages by Mental Vibration,"[64] but also owned the empirically based *Medical News: A Weekly Journal of Medical Science*, which in at least one of the issues he owned had a scientific report on typhoid.[65]

*

John Steele seemed to thrive with all these activities. When the *Washington County News* reported Toquerville's "Old Folk's Day" in 1899, seventy-eight-year-old Steele was one of three who reminisced about his life experiences, and he came in second for a recitation. Besides that, he was voted best step-dancer.[66] Three years later, a *Deseret News* reporter who attended Parowan's 1902 Pioneer Day commented that "Father John Steele of Toquerville, 82 years of age, was among the most agile and active."[67]

Steele continued to exercise his mind and devour newspapers, collecting subscriptions for the *Family Herald and Weekly Star* of Montreal and outlining the free gifts each of his subscribers wanted—mostly subscriptions to *The Little Sweetheart*. (Steele himself preferred *Old Favourites, The Cottage Barometer*, and *Pitmanic Shorthand*.)[68]

As he aged, Steele worried about the afterlife for his sister Jane Steele McClelland. He wrote to President Wilford Woodruff about what he could do to ensure Jane had a worthy eternal husband: "[H]er Husband [John

McClelland] was a drinking man and often acted bad to her So that She would not have him for Eternity but wished to be Sealed to me when She died." He said he told her he didn't know if that could be done, though it had in the past. She said if not, she wanted to be sealed to his son Mahonri and her children adopted to him.[69]

The letter sent in reply, signed by Woodruff but perhaps written by someone else, recounted Steele's questions and then stated, "Of course, I am not conversant with what information you may have on this subject; but I am not aware of any such sealings or adoptions in this Church," and claimed, "It is not any more proper for your sister to be sealed to you as her husband, now that she is dead, than it would be if she were alive; neither should she be sealed to your son, because such a marriage is too near of kin." The letter suggested that if John's sister didn't give any other preferences, "you should make a choice in her behalf, and have her sealed to some faithful man in the Church, either living or dead, and have her children adopted into his family."[70]

Woodruff was eighty-two at that point and may have forgotten some of his own history despite his magnificent journals: he himself was sealed in marriage to his own deceased sister, Eunice, on June 15, 1867. He also would have known that Brigham Young's secretary, George D. Watt, was sealed to and had children by his half-sister Jane Brown, the precedent cited being the patriarch Abraham and his half-sister Sarah. Given these omissions, it's probable a young clerk unfamiliar with the evolution of Mormon marriages answered Steele's letter, not Woodruff himself.[71] Regardless of who wrote the letter, the problem was solved by sealing Jane to the late apostle George A. Smith, with Smith's son's approval.[72] Steele was also concerned with religious adoptions, having been "sealed" as a son to Joseph Smith and Eliza Snow. He sought advice and L. John Nuttall wrote on behalf of George Q. Cannon to "let it alone as it is."[73]

Another project was Steele's autobiography. "I have just finished Copying all of your mothers [Elizabeth Steele Connelly] letters to me, also yours, and George [P. Connelly]'s and filed them away for my history when Completed," he wrote his niece Letisha Todd in February 1893.[74] A censored version of his autobiography was published in the 1930s, with editor J. Cecil Alter privately assuring Frank A. Beckwith, "The owners may be sure that the Church will be shielded from every possible reflection, by the elision of undesirable matter."[75] The original has not surfaced. At about the same time Steele again took up efforts to write a great Mormon ballad; this writer would have preferred the autobiography.[76]

By now Steele was well-known. When the *Washington County News* reported one of his visits to St. George, it described him as "one of Dixie's old standbys," and the *Salt Lake Telegram* remarked he was "A pioneer well known in Salt Lake City."[77]

Given Steele's reputation, it wasn't surprising that an eloquent and energetic Mormon apostle was drawn to him. Mathias F. Cowley was a forceful preacher. Like his apostolic fellows, he traveled to the quarterly stake conferences in Mormon country. One Gentile observer described a typical apostolic sermon (not Cowley's) as a "curious admixture of present farming and future salvation, business advice and pious exhortation."[78] Mormon kingdom-building always included the spiritual and the secular.

Cowley spent the first months of 1903 attending conferences across the state. He and his party, which included John's son Mahonri at least as far as Kanarraville, reached Toquerville in time to hold a 10 a.m. meeting on March 13th. Apostles selected patriarchs and, maybe influenced by Mahonri's stories of Steele, Cowley ordained him a patriarch, meaning "father"—a title similar to pope, but unlike in the Eastern and Catholic Churches, Mormon patriarchs do not have executive functions.[79]

If Cowley knew of Steele's unorthodox occult practices, he was unmoved; Steele's respectful neighbors didn't see the need to raise an alarm. Patriarchs gave blessings considered revelatory, with the prophecies predicated on faithfulness; they were inspiring to the recipients and often served as life guides as they puzzled their present and future prospects.[80]

Patriarchs were respected and devout men, usually older; the small fee for the blessings helped some avoid penury. When Steele planned a trip to visit James Jepson in Virgin City, he wrote offering to provide blessings to those who wished one; the practice of limiting blessings to once in a lifetime wasn't yet established.[81]

*

Fate, in the sense of divination, was another specialty of "Raphael" and of interest to Steele.[82] He was reminded of mortality when his forty-seven-year-old daughter Jane died in 1903 in Arizona. She had been sick for four months and left nine children.[83] John himself had a lingering illness in the spring

John Steele, 1897. *Family photo.*

of 1903; his granddaughter Josie Fish Barraclough wrote from Beaver that she hoped he was better and invited him to visit in her cooler climate ("last week we had snow on the ground").[84]

But Steele was soon prancing around like a man twenty years younger. A letter from Mahonri shared the news that John's grandson and namesake, John E. Steele, had left to be a Rough Rider (a cavalryman in the Spanish-American War), leading one to suspect the old man's grit was inherited.[85] Soon after, however, John lost his long-time neighbor, and his wife Catherine's attentive friend, Fannie Smith Spilsbury, whose obituary he wrote for *El Progreso*.[86]

Steele's daughter Elizabeth and her family left Kanarra on July 22, 1903, for their usual summer stay at their Cedar Mountain ranch, where they made butter and cheese.[87] John joined the family to give Elizabeth a surprise fifty-sixth birthday party. He was in a fine mood and afterward reported to Mahonri what an enjoyable time he had and mentioned singing "Oh My Father"—this despite being packed in "like sardines in a can."[88]

In 1900, John had written to "Azrael" asking for his own fate. He wrote, "[N]ow I would like you to send me the nature of the Disease or accident that will terminate my Existance here," and he enclosed his horoscope and some personal information, including he was subject to falls and had broken bones in his arms, back, head, and feet, and had served in the Mexican War. "But the main point is what is the nature of the trouble that May Cary me out of this world[?]"[89]

"Azrael" responded, "Your health will be severely tried in January, Sept. and Dec. 1901. Passing those periods you come under affliction again, in April 1902, and in December of the same year. If you escape those afflictions you might live to see your 87th birthday."[90]

Even a drought in Toquerville didn't seem to slow him down—until, in late 1903, as his great-granddaughter Reba Roundy LeFevre explained, "He stepped on a nail an they didn't do it right an it turned to gangrene." Possibly the diabetes Dr. Childs Mantor of Silver Reef had diagnosed in 1882 was an underlying cause.[91]

Daughter Elizabeth went to Toquerville to take care of John while other family members gathered around. "He had to take so many drops of medicine," Reba recalled. She speculated that it might have been some kind of painkiller. "But, now you—they didn't have a medicine dropper. Now you count them drops an you make jest exactly what they are, no bigger, nor no littler. The drops has got to be the same size. Then he would take his medicine. If he didn't, he wouldn't take it. An he's very strict. You done this. You done that." Reba confirmed that Steele was impossible to please unless people "done it exactly as he said," which she credibly attributed to his military background. "I think that's where Granma [Stapley] got her strictness from."[92]

Steele had his own cures for gangrene: "Cantharis, Spanish Fly good in burning, itching of Skin rawness, Soreness of the whole body inflamation, gangrene of the parts Convulsions of limbs pains in Kidneys & Bladder"; another was hemlock. These nostrums may have delayed competent medical care; he didn't rally. On December 6th he gave Elizabeth a patriarchal blessing with his son Mahonri as scribe. Steele assured her, quite accurately, "You shall live Yet Many Years upon the earth"—and she outlived all her siblings. He also promised, "The Lord will give unto thee in his own due time the Holy Priesthood in fullness." Not only would she be especially blessed with spiritual powers, but so would her posterity.[93]

On December 26th, the *Iron County (UT) Record* reported, "We are pleased to recall the statement in last week's issue concerning Gran[d]father Steele, and say: He is surprisingly smart at the age of 82 and were it not for his foot he could no nout [doubt] as he says, walk a mile in ten minutes. He is now at the [Kanarra] residence of Jas [and Elizabeth] Stapley of this place." The same article reported that "Father and son George Wood, were down to see their old friend, Jno. Steel and try to console him if possible."[94] The older Wood and John Steele had more than fifty years of shared memories, from the settlement of Parowan, to Wood serving under John in the Nauvoo Legion, to John acting as Wood's lawyer at the preliminary hearing for his murder of Olivia Coombs Higby and taking addresses to look up Wood's English kin in 1877.[95]

By late December Steele knew his end was near. Under a Kanarra byline the paper had announced, "Grandfather Steele is gradually climbing the ladder to the other side. His sons and daughter have been telegraphed for."[96] But he hung on until the year's end, dying December 31, 1903. The *Deseret Evening News* reported that Steele had "always led an active life," and that despite having lived in Toquerville, "his wife was buried in the Parowan cemetery" and he wished to be buried next to her. Speakers at his funeral included his old friend William Campbell McGregor, who had written Catherine's obituary, as well as Charles Adams, whose boyhood horoscope had been drawn by Parowan's John Sanderson, and William C. Mitchell, John's fellow Las Vegas missionary.[97]

Utah's weekly papers subscribed to a "Utah News" column, and Steele's death was included, so it was reported throughout the state. This story mentioned his membership in the Mormon Battalion, his early arrival in Salt Lake, the distinction of being the "father of the first baby girl born in Salt Lake," and his role in the settlement of Parowan. Although the column item asserted Steele was eighty-three, he'd fallen a few months short of that birthday.[98]

In early February 1904 the *Deseret News* published an excellent summary

Hemlock. *Alamy stock photo.*

of John Steele's career, complete with precise dates. The byline was Panguitch so the author was undoubtedly John's son Mahonri, who inherited John's trunk of books, letters, and personal memorabilia. The elder Steele would have appreciated the precise correction to his age: he was "aged 82 years, 9 months and 10 days." Furthermore, "He was quick and decisive in his actions, and through his promptness in action, among the Indians in Iron County, and its early settlement, there is no doubt but much bloodshed was averted. . . . He held many official positions in political and military affairs, as well as ecclesiastical, and held a commission as major of infantry."[99]

*

John Steele spent sixty years building the Mormon Kingdom, arriving in the United States when the movement seemed shattered by the deaths of the prophetic Smith brothers and the loss of Mormon political power in Illinois, which had been slaughtered with them. At the time of John's death, some five hundred communities were in the Mormon corridor.[100]

Economist Richard T. Ely, founder of the American Economic Association and the Christian Social Union (the latter with the goal of applying Christian principles to social problems), was an admirer of Mormon organization. In the last year of Steele's life, Ely wrote that the Mormon empire encompassed some 400,000 people, most centered in Utah but spreading "north and south along the Rocky Mountain range from Canada to Mexico, and going beyond the boundaries of the United States, even, into both these last named countries, with settlements in Alberta, Canada, and Chihuahua, Mexico." This was not paradise or a Utopia, and there were casualties—especially among Indigenous people—with this remarkable expansion, but Steele's many talents and trades, and those of tens of thousands of others, including Native and other peoples, built the primary infrastructure of today's secular Rocky Mountain Kingdom and beyond, including roads, dams, canals, farms, lumber and flour mills, mines, cities, and towns.

Ely suggested Mormon communalism had regressed by his time, but added, "cooperation floats before the minds of all the leaders as a goal, and they expect to advance much beyond any past achievements."[101] He was right: Mormon social aspirations were never abandoned. Mormon bishops still provide assistance to those in need, and members find the most spiritual uplift in communitarian service, building the Kingdom in old and new ways.[102] The new and old historical convergence is illustrated by the statehood centennial history of Iron County, subtitled *Community Above Self*.[103]

Once impotent nationally, the Mormons at the time of Steele's death had representatives in the U.S. House and Senate, and a sympathizer in the White House—enough political power that the old-time coalition

Steele's trunk, with his self-repaired copy of Thomas Andrew, M.D., *A Cyclopedia of Domestic Medicine and Surgery* (Glasgow: Blackie and Son, Queen Street, 1842) on top. He signed the inside cover "John Steele's Book Glasgow Scotland 1841 [*sic*]" and added a black nameplate with gold lettering, "JOHN STEELE." The repair is more like a shoemaker's than a bookbinder's.

that had powered federal anti-Mormon legislation a decade earlier proved unable to prevent the sitting of Utah's new senator, Apostle Reed Smoot. Respectability for the outcast religion had not yet been achieved, but it was knocking on the door.

APPENDIX

William Leany's February 17, 1883, letter to John Steele

Leany's letter to Steele, with its references to three "murdered in our ward," and Dr. Wesley P. Larsen's conjecture that they might refer to the murders of three members of the John Wesley Powell expedition have caused some stir, but serious historians discount that possibility.[1] The letter is in the John Steele Collection (box 1, folder 30, Vault MSS 528), L. Tom Perry Special Collections, Harold B. Lee Library, Brigham Young University, Provo, Utah. I have read this transcript against the original, and also benefited from a three-page typed transcript in the folder with the original. Written on the last page is "Letter to J. Steele Esq.," but that is not in Steele's or, apparently, in Leany's hand. Leany wrote about John Steele with admiration in his disjointed reminiscences, and he also dreamed about him,[2] while Steele referred affectionally to Leany and wrote his obituary.[3]

Harris burg Utah Feb. 17th 1883

Mr. J. Steele Dear Bro.

After my love & a thousand thanks for your kind letter of Dec. 11th allow Me to say that your first statement that We had been acquainted for over thirty seaven years[4] & not ane [any] jar betwen Us[5] tells the whole story and here I might say the Berrys, the Adamses the Meekses, the Hendricks, the Lewises[6] & ^others^ have known me much longer Some of them over sixty five years & not a jar & it all shows that if Pres. Snow had been and honest fair Man that would ^hear^ heard both sides the same might be said of he & I but all this & all other proof shows that he has been led by bill smiths dog & a few other drunken adulterous murderous wretches[7]

And as to your idea of my repenting & confessing all to get those blessings in the house of God We so much value I must say that I think that would wholy unfit Me for there for God shall bear me witness that I am clean of all of which they accuse Me & they guilty of all that I accuse them & Much More & here let me ask you to join

Me & let us sanction, ratify & confirm that unholy ungodly curse of Pres. snows with two or three provisos, first that the inocent go free & the curse fall on the guilty though it be I & Mine, he & his, they & theirs, even Lewis & all the dogs wherewith he has doged Me & Mine for the last thirty years.[8] And I cannot see that for me to confess to a lie would make me more worthy or they less guilty & here let me say that my object is & has been to stay the overwhelming tide of thieving whoredom Murder Suicide & like wickednesses & abominations, ^that^ threaten to dessolate the land & you are far from ignorant of those deeds of blood from the day the picket was broke on my head[9] to the day those three were murdered in our ward & the ^murderer^ killed to stop the sheding of more blood[10] & you know too much of the raising those texbills [tax bills] & the deal with Capt. Hooper[11] & much more that I might mention. But it has long been my mind asid[e] from these deeds of blood that my life would be well spent if laid down to establish one or all of the principles that no court Quorum Council or Conference is fit to hear any case unless they have the power & the will to fetch in the witnesses & protect them from insult insted of Making parties into charges & through mock trials without the shadow of preparation as the reccords & all other proofs show has been done with me & I will not only forfeit My last drop of blood but those holy ordina[n]ces of which you speak to establish said principles rather than go through the house of God as Many are[12] doing & if you had heard the prophet Joseph tell as I did how Uriah would get even with David & how Many of the crushed of Our day would get even with their oppressors I think you [would] side with me

And as you speak of my often use of hard words I will refer you to the fact that I only recently told you of jim Lewises career with G J Adams & bill Smith[13] though I had known it for thirty years & if this is not enough proof of my reserve in connexion with Our long intimacy & uniform peace please name one time or place that I spoke out of place or out of season for I think I can endure the rebuke of a friend. But here let Me say that the fact of My hard speeches being so true & appropas that none dare deal with me notwithstanding their high possitions until kicked into it by Br. Taylor[14] & then bulldog out all my witnesses & promising Me a transcript & the council guilding & lying and it for over a year & then denying my right to call for the transcript all show just ^what^ I knew for years & what many of my friend[s] have hinted to me that I must be sacrificed to maintain the dignity of the priesthood but remember Br Taylors promise that he would cleanse the inside of the platter if he began at the Quorum of the twelve & his career certainly gives hope though Pres. Young Said he could not touch the big lions for the less lions that surrounded them & Many old prophets said the shepherds would not judge between fat & lean cattle but if Br. Taylor will only allow their own reccords the lions are all so much worse than Judges A. A. King Turman Esqs Black & Mann[15] that worse is no name for their measures and until we right up these wrongs we May lay hands on our Mouths & ceas[e] to bray about gentile Courts Committees & Congresses for God would cease to [be] God unless he made good the sayings of Moses & Jesus that if you devour one another you will be devoured one of another & Jesus said the Measure you mete shall be meted unto you etc. etc. & as the old prophets said if the blood & violence in the city & blood toucheth blood[16] if that was not fulfilled in the Killing the three in one room in our own ward[17] please say what it was & for all this & much more unrighteous dominion shall We be cast out of the Court unless We arise cleanse the inside of the platter & then will it rest from its blood & have its sabbaths which I, you, & God knows it does not enjoy now. And though I have not hinted at half your points or half the points on my mind yet I must close hoping you will be so good as to carefully scan this & note on the back any faults you may find in it. But be assured that I will God being My helper clear my skirts of the mobing robing stealing whoredom murder suicide infanticide lying slander & all wickedness & abominations even in high places

So No More but remains your Bro. In the Gospel

Wm. Leany Sr

Testimony of John Steele about the Mountain Meadows Massacre

John Steele's testimony about the massacre is in his handwriting; written in pencil and badly water damaged. It is in box 2, folder 8, Vault MSS 528, in the John Steele Collection, 1847–1936, L. Tom Perry Special Collections,

Harold B. Lee Library, Brigham Young University, Provo, Utah. Besides the originals on three numbered gray pages, there are two transcripts or partial transcripts. For a discussion of these charges see Will Bagley, *Blood of the Prophets: Brigham Young and the Massacre at Mountain Meadows* (Norman: University of Oklahoma Press, 2002), 99–122.

1

then Comes Wm Strong residing in Salt Lake City in the 10 Ward[18] Saying that when the Company in question who was murdered in the Mountains - when they came first upon the Bench East of [three or four illegible words] the People [two or three words; possibly 'sent there'] Children out with vegatables and Suplied ther[e] wants [one word, perhaps 'and,' as it ends with a 'd' written with Steele's distinctive loop] Lyman Lenard[19] sold [one or two words] Corn Meal [perhaps two words, which might be 'He wanted'] for [partial unintelligible word]ls per lb the Company then moved down to the Jordon Whare they let down the fence and turned ther[e] Cattle into the Hay fields of one of the Mormons and ^~~when~~^ told to Get on to where there was more room and not damage the Setlars

2

The Compan[y became very[20]] angary and with terrible Oaths [said[21]] they had the Rifle and showed it th[at?] Killed Joseph and Hyrum and said with a terrible Oath that its the Rifle kill [one or two words missing] Sh[all?] Kill Brigham [a word illegible] and [one word, perhaps possible letters: 'Gn..g'] the Woman [one word illegible seems to end with 'rc'] She had fed Mormon beef to the ^Mormon^ prisoners in Missouri and by her Maker She Could do it again then th[e]y Moved on and the Same Reckles Manner went with them and whare ever they went the[y] Abused the inhabitents in the Vallies until they arrived at Corn Creek

3

Whare the[y] Poisoned a animal that died. and when the Indians took Some of the Meat & Eat it Several of them died—this made the rest of the tribe [Mad[22]] and they pursued after [illegible word the transcriber/s read as "them"] the[y] also poisoned A Spring and a Young Man by the name of Robinson Died by the [two illegible words] Said poison they then Cane [Came] on to Beaver Co [perhaps a very short illegible word or "Co" is part of a word, the rest of which is unintelligible] Where Seve[ral[23]] Outrages [two or three words illegible] –mited And When they Came to Parowan the first [two illegible words, possibly 'gued' and 'turn'] Asked was whare does Your God Damned Bishop Leve the[y] passed on to Cedar City Whare they G[?od G . . .] done by Miller [blank for a name, presumably] and the Same insulting Spurrit was Made Manifest as on all former Ocations

Letter from Catherine Steele to Emily Steele, February 20, 1878

This is only the second letter from Catherine Campbell Steele I've seen.[24] It was written to her daughter-in-law Emily Bunker Steele, wife of Mahonri M. Steele, while Mahonri and John Steele were on British missions. It was posted by Gayle Workman on FamilySearch on May 28, 2020. Mrs. Workman's notes have helped me annotate this letter.

Toquerville Feb. 20th. 1878

Dear Daughter Emily

I received your welcome letter. I was very glad to hear from you. I thought you had gone to the flat you were so long in answering.[25] I wish you would write to me before you go and tell me if Eddy[26] can take a Barrel of wine for me and dont Stay too long down at the flat. I want you to make a longer visit with me before you go to Panquitch. I hope that ~~A~~ Aurthur[27] is better and that the other Children are well. I have not heard from Mohonri but once Since you left here. Susy has got a ^another^ nice girl and She had quiet [quite] a Serious time but She is all right now and Selinda has a gathered breast it broke this morning and Johny had a great boil on his neck under his chin. you may think what a time what we have had.[28] I am very near tired out but they are all on the mend now. I hope you are well and that your mother is better tell Grand Ma[29] that I will write to her Soon. I have written Several letters to day and my hand hurts and I have got a very poor pen but that is the way with all poor work men they always get bad tools. I am glad that you have had the priviledge of going through ^the Temple^ it will make you feel so good there is Such a good Spirit in the Temple the Angel's of peace dwel[l]s there well give my kind love to all the folks Susy Jane and Alma[30] Send their love to you please write Soon to your ever loving Mother C Steele.

[written upside down on the bottom of the page:] Emily, this is an awful Scrib[b]le

NOTES

Abbreviations

BYU Brigham Young University, Provo, Utah
CHL Church History Library, Church of Jesus Christ of Latter-day Saints, Salt Lake City, Utah
LTPSC L. Tom Perry Special Collections, Harold B. Lee Library, Brigham Young University, Provo, Utah

Page and column numbers for newspaper articles are separated by a slash (e.g., 408/2).

Introduction

1 "Labor Fighting Capital," *Deseret News* (*DN*), August 1, 1877, p. 408, col. 2.
2 For more on John's wife Catherine, see *The Women: A Family Story* (Salt Lake City: University of Utah Press, 2016). It covers her life and those of selected women in the family to 1949.
3 John Steele to Wilford Woodruff, July 30, 1888, CHL; partly published as "Pioneer Reminiscences," *DN*, August 8, 1888, 16/2–3.
4 Death certificate for Elizabeth [Tamar] Renick Cheatham (with "Cheatham" partly erased; she's indexed as "Renick, Elizabeth"), Utah State Archives, Salt Lake City.
5 Diane Noble, *The Veil* (Colorado Springs: Waterbrook, 1998).

Chapter 1

1 Text between the symbols ^ ^ means it was above or below the line in the original.
2 John Steele reminiscences and journals, 1846–1898, [frame 10], MS 1847, CHL. This and frame 9 are pages torn out of Nancy Kennedy Steele's Bible.
3 Samuel Lewis, *A Topographical Dictionary of Ireland* (London: S. Lewis, 1837), 2:6; "Holywood Cattle and Grain Show," *Belfast News-Letter* (*BNL*), October 27, 1840, 1/3; John P. Gordon testimonial to John Steele, February 6, 1821, attached to pp. 2–3 of *Raphael's Astronomical Ephemeris 1821,* copy in author's possession.
4 H. Brown, War Office, to John Steele [Sr.], March 11, 1830, copy in author's possession; transcript made by Iona J. Poling from personal records of John Steele, copy in author's possession.
5 Elizabeth Steele Connelly to John Steele, September 2, 1873; January 18, 1878; August 21, [1878?]; photocopies in author's possession.

6 UK, Royal Hospital Chelsea Pensioner Soldier Service Records. WO 97: Royal Hospital Chelsea: Soldiers Service Documents > Piece 0589: 43rd Foot: Sas–Wal (1760–1854) > S > Steele, Jackson; UK Royal Hospital Chelsea Pensioner Admission and Discharge Records, WO 116: Disability and Out-Pensions, Admissions > Piece 018: 1814–1815 (Cavalry and Infantry) > Page 121; Jos. Wells, December 9, 1814.

7 Benjamin Grob-Fitzgibbon, *Turning Points of the Irish Revolution: The British Government, Intelligence, and the Cost of Indifference, 1912–1921* (New York: Palgrave Macmillan, 2007), 18; Thomas Pakenham, *The Year of Liberty: The Great Irish Rebellion of 1798* (London: Abacus, 1997), 35.

8 Regimental Description Books, WO 12/308, report in author's possession.

9 Charles Dickson, *Revolt in the North: Antrim and Down in 1798* (London: Constable, 1997), 241–42; Pakenham, *Year of Liberty*, 284; W. A. Maguire, "Arthur McMahon, United Irishman and French Soldier," *Irish Sword* 9, no. 36 (Summer 1970): 208–9.

10 Frank A. Beckwith Sr., "Valuable Relics Found in Old Trunk," *Millard County (UT) Chronicle*, July 24, 1930, 1/1, 8/4: "A sword used in the East Indian War by a Great Grandfather [John Steele Sr.]."

11 Discharge certificate in regular soldiers' documents, WO 97/237; "Pensioner's Affidavit," April 27, 1816, box 1, folder 11, Vault MSS 528, John Steele Collection, 1847–1936, LTPSC, Harold B. Lee Library, Brigham Young University, Provo, Utah (hereafter Steele Collection, LTPSC).

12 Robert Campbell to John Steele, January 6, 1888, copy in author's possession.

13 John Steele, journal entries, [frames 88, 61], MS 1847, folder 2, vol. 2, CHL. "Kennedy, Wm., Holywood (shoemaker) 1818," Down Wills, 1646–1858: the original will was destroyed in the 1922 conflagration of Irish records. The year of probate matches the death date on Kennedy's gravestone in Holywood. Rachel Connelly to John Steele, January 18, 1889, box 1, folder 26, Steele Collection, LTPSC; "Deaths," *BNL*, December 24, 1888, 1/1.

14 Photocopy in author's possession.

15 WO 97: Royal Hospital Chelsea: Soldiers Service Documents > Piece 0589: 43rd Foot: Sas–Wal (1760–1854) > S > Steele, Jackson; UK Royal Hospital Chelsea Pensioner Admission and Discharge Records, WO 116: Disability and Out-Pensions, Admissions > Piece 018: 1814–1815 (Cavalry and Infantry) > Page 121.

16 From John Steele's retained copy of a biography questionnaire for J. H. E. Webster's "The History of Utah Project" (hereafter referred to as Webster questionnaire), box 2, folder 6, Steele Collection, LTPSC.

17 John Steele to Mrs. "Latitia" [Letisha] Todd, August 2, 1897; transcript provided by Ileen Judd Johnson in author's possession.

18 David Hackett Fischer, *Liberty and Freedom* (Oxford: Oxford University Press, 2005), 81.

19 "Military Punishment of the Old School," *BNL*, December 15, 1835, 2/2.

20 Frank A. Beckwith, "From the Journal of John Steele," *Millard County (UT)*

Chronicle, August 25, 1932, 6/2; Steele, "Extracts from the Journal of John Steele," ed. J. Cecil Alter, *Utah Historical Quarterly* 6, no. 1 (January 1933): 4. Alter improved the spelling of "kane" to "cane." The autobiography that Beckwith and Alter drew on is missing.

21 Reba Roundy LeFevre, oral history interview by author, May 23, 1987, 6.

22 John Steele to Mrs. "Latitia" [Letisha] Todd, September 12, 1902, copy in author's possession.

23 Webster questionnaire, box 2, folder 26, Steele Collection, LTPSC.

24 "Heroical Humanity," *BNL,* March 11, 1823, 3/5. It is my assumption that the sailor James Davison who helped save the *Marcella* passengers at Holywood was Steele's sailor uncle of that name, married to a Holywood girl ("Married," *Banner of Ulster*, November 5, 1850, 2/7).

25 John Steele, journal entry, [frame 7], MS 1847, folder 2, vol. 1, CHL.

26 Webster questionnaire, box 2, folder 6, Steele Collection, LTPSC.

27 "Education of the Poor," *BNL*, July 7, 1826, 3/5.

28 Beckwith, "From the Journal of Elder John Steele," *Millard County (UT) Chronicle*, August 25, 1932, 6/2.

29 *BNL*: [untitled], November 6, 1829, 2/5, regarding the Carrickfergus Lancasterian school (Carrickfergus is opposite Holywood across Belfast Lough); "Frederick Street Lancasterian School," June 1, 1830, 4/2; "Lancasterian School," June 18, 1830, 2/2; "Lancasterian School," June 22, 1830, 4/2.

30 Charles Andrew Olds, oral history interview by author, October 11, 1984, 7–9.

31 This list is based on the inventory I took of John Steele's trunk on April 22, 1987, when it was in the possession of Gary Hall Callister of Hurricane, Utah; the photocopied title pages (and sometimes additional pages) in box 3, folder 25, Steele Collection, LTPSC (mostly if not entirely made up of books from the Callister collection); books mentioned in Steele's journals; books identified in WPA record forms that were in the collection in the 1930s (box 2, folder 10, Steele Collection, LTPSC); and Beckwith, "Valuable Relics," *Millard County (UT) Chronicle*, July 24, 1930, 1/1, 8/4.

32 *BNL*: "In the Matter of William Hanna, an Insolvent," October 30, 1827, 2/5; "Married," June 14, 1833, 3/2; "Died," September 23, 1834, 2/5.

33 "Valuation Books for Holywood, co. Down, c. 1832," Public Record Office of Northern Ireland, VAL IB/318.

34 John Steele, journal entry, 1 [frame 7], MS D 1847, folder 2, vol. 1, CHL.

35 *BNL,* November 29, 1836: "The Bakers," 2/3; "Wanted Immediately, Fifty Journeyman Bakers," 3/4.

36 Raymond Gillespie and Stephen A. Royle, *Irish Historic Towns Atlas No. 12, Belfast, Part I, to 1840* (Dublin: Dublin University Press, 2003), 14–15, 19; this is a meticulous reference with beautiful maps. *BNL*: "New Upholstery Warehouse," February 25, 1831, 3/1 (Greenfield's Court); "Belfast Quarter Sessions," January 28, 1834, 2/5 (Squeeze-gut).

37 "Marriage," *Newry Telegraph*, September 24, 1844, 3/5. Robert S. Agnew (husband of Elizabeth Greenfield) had a brother, Sir James Willson Agnew,

who became premier of Tasmania ("The Late Sir James Agnew, K. C. M. G., M. D., M. E. C.," *The Mercury* [Hobart, Tasmania], November 9, 1901, 144).

38 "The Theatre," *BNL,* October 15, 1833, 2/3.

39 *BNL*: "Road to Holywood," January 3, 1824, 2/4; "Dangerous State of the Long Bridge," February 12, 1830, 2/3; "The Long Bridge," March 2, 1830, 4/2.

40 Gillespie and Royle, *Irish Historic Towns,* 1–6; *BNL*: "Holywood Agricultural Society," October 20, 1837, 1/2; "Cattle and Grain Show of the Holywood Agricultural Society," November 26, 1839, 1/6.

41 Webster questionnaire, box 2, folder 6, Steele Collection, LTPSC.

42 *Martin's Belfast Directory, for 1840–41* (Belfast: 10, Hercules-Place, 1840), 159. Josephine Kay Garfield, oral history interview by author, May 26, 1989, 14; Reba Roundy LeFevre, oral history interview by author, October 6, 1989, 15–16. In 1989 Mrs. Garfield still had a handsome little chest made by Steele that was painted white.

43 John Steele, journal entry, [frame 7], MS 1847, folder 2, vol. 1, CHL.

44 "Kennedy, Wm., Holywood (shoemaker) 1818," Down Wills, 1646–1858. For Robert M'Clure (McClure) see *The Covenanter* 8 (1852–1853): 320. *BNL*: "Wanted. 150 Boot and Shoe-Makers," November 4, 1834, 3/1; "Trades' Combination," April 26, 1836, 2/2; "Boot Makers and Boot Closers," April 26, 1836, 3/1; "Shoemakers' Turn-Out," May 17, 1836, 4/4.

45 *Belfast Directory for 1831–32* (Belfast: Robert Donaldson, n.d.), 41. The Robert M'Clure, shoemaker, at 2 Matier's-court, Belfast, in 1840 may be William's father and John Steele Jr.'s uncle (*Martin's Belfast Directory 1840–41,* 186).

46 *Martin's Belfast Directory 1840–41*, 186, 223 .

47 John Steele, journal entry, [frame 7], MS 1847, folder 2, vol. 1, CHL.

48 Steele, July 23, 1847, penciled journal, box 1, folder 2, Steele Collection, LTPSC. BYU library staff were kind enough to have this difficult-to-read journal enhanced for me. The second version is in the rewritten journal, [frame 70], MS 1847, folder 2, vol. 1, CHL.

49 John Steele, "Forbidden Fruit," February 11, 1901, box 3, folder 6, Steele Collection, LTPSC.

50 John Edgar, "Prostitution in Belfast," *BNL,* August 13, 1839, 4/2.

51 "Belfast Quarter Sessions," *BNL,* November 1, 1839, 1/5–6.

52 Alphabetical lists of convicts with particulars for 1788–1825 and 1840–42, Colonial Office and Predecessors, National Archives Microfilm Publication CO 207/9, p. 222, National Archives of the UK (TNA), Kew, Surrey, England.

53 *Belfast Commercial Chronicle*: "Police," September 21, 1816, 2/4; "Police-Office," June 2, 1827, 2/4; "Convictions and Sentences," October 29, 1827, 4/1; "Police Office," October 22, 1831, 4/4; "Belfast Quarter Sessions," July 7, 1838, 4/4; "Belfast Quarter Sessions," January 15, 1840, 3/1. *BNL*: "Police Office," October 21, 1831, 2/3; "Belfast Quarter Sessions," October 29, 1839, 2/1. *Northern Whig* (Belfast) (*NW*): "Belfast Quarter Sessions," July 5, 1838,

2/6; "Belfast Quarter Sessions," October 31, 1839, 1/6; "Belfast Petty Sessions," January 4, 1840, 2/5. *Vindicator* (Belfast): "Belfast Quarter Sessions," October 30, 1839, 1/6; "Belfast Quarter Sessions," January 18, 1840, 4/3.

54 "Belfast Petty Sessions," *BNL*, May 17, 1839, 4/3; "Belfast Petty Sessions," *NW*, May 14, 1839, 1/2.

55 "Belfast Quarter Sessions," *BNL*, July 9, 1839, 2/6, 3/1; "Belfast Quarter Sessions," *NW*, July 9, 1839, 2/3; "Belfast Quarter Sessions," *Vindicator* (Belfast), July 13, 1839, 4/2.

56 Matthew Martin, *Martin's Belfast Directory 1839* (Belfast: Matthew Martin, 1839), 133.

57 "Belfast Quarter Sessions," *BNL*, July 9, 1839, 2/6, 3/1; "Belfast Quarter Sessions," *NW*, July 9, 1839, 2/3; "Belfast Quarter Sessions," *Vindicator* (Belfast), July 13, 1839, 4/2.

58 Alphabetical lists of convicts with particulars, 1788–1825; 1840–1842, Colonial Office and Predecessors, National Archives Microfilm Publication CO 207/9, p. 222; New South Wales Government, *Butts of Certificates of Freedom,* NRS 1165, 1166, 1167, 12208, 12210, reels 601, 602, 604, 982–1027; State Records Authority of New South Wales, Kingswood, Australia Marriage Index, 1788–1950, accessed on Ancestry.com.

59 "Belfast Petty Sessions," *BNL,* December 6, 1839, 4/3.

60 "Death from Intemperance," *Banner of Ulster* (Belfast), March 13, 1846, 3/6.

61 Rev. W. M. O'Hanlon, *Walks Among the Poor of Belfast* (1853; reprint, East Ardsley, England: S. R. Publishers, 1971), 23; Gillespie and Royle, *Irish Historic Towns,* 15 and accompanying maps.

62 John Steele, journal entries, 1–2 [frames 7–8], MS 1847, folder 2, vol. 1, CHL.

63 John Steele, journal entry, July 11, 1877, in *Journals of John Steele and Mahonri Moriancumer Steele,* (Cedar City, UT: self-published, 1967), sec. 2, p. 86; *Martin's Belfast Directory 1840–41*, 34, 104.

64 *Martin's Belfast Directory 1840–41*, 36; Matthew Martin, *Martin's Belfast Directory, for 1842–3* (Belfast: Matthew Martin, 1842), 38; John Henderson, *Henderson's New Belfast Directory, and Northern Repository, for 1843–44* (Belfast: John Henderson, 1843), 250; John Henderson, *Henderson's New Belfast Directory, and Northern Repository, for 1846–47* (Belfast: John Henderson, 1846), 225; *Henderson's New Belfast Directory, and Northern Repository [1850]* (Belfast: John Henderson, 1850), 188; James Alexander Henderson, *The Belfast and Province of Ulster Directory for 1852* (Belfast: James Alexander Henderson, 1852), 222. The marriage record of Catherine's brother Robert Campbell identifies their father Michael as a tobacconist, which is key to distinguishing him from other contemporary Belfast Michael Campbells (1848 Belfast Marriages 2:763, 24 April 1848). Family records show Michael Campbell died September 14, 1852, and his wife, Mary Knox Campbell, died February 8, 1854, both in Belfast.

65 Gillespie and Royle, *Irish Historic Towns*, 7–8.

66 [Untitled], *BNL*, November 11, 1831, 2/4.

67 *BNL*: "Police Office," November 5, 1824, 1/5; "Belfast Quarter Sessions," November 5, 1824, 3/2–3; "Stripping Children," May 1 1829, 2/2; "Stripping Children," September 28, 1829, 1/4; "Stripping Children," May 17, 1833, 4/3; "Belfast Quarter Sessions," July 6, 1838, 2/4; "Belfast Quarter Sessions," October 29, 1839, 1/5–6, 2/1.

68 Quote is from Emily Steele Jensen's 1933 application for membership in the Daughters of the Utah Pioneers, http://johnsonfamilyhistorystories.blogspot.com.

69 *BNL*: "Attempted Highway Robbery," March 17, 1829, 4/5; "County of Down Assizes," April 3, 1829, 1/5; "Conspiracy in Armagh Jail," April 24, 1829, 2/3; "Belfast Quarter Sessions," May 4, 1830, 4/2–4; "The Late Robberies," February 7, 1834, 4/3; "Belfast Quarter Sessions," October 29, 1839, 2/1; "Quarrelling Amongst the Military," November 29, 1839, 2/5, quoting the *Newry Telegraph*.

70 "The Poor Female Soldier!," *BNL*, October 29, 1822, 3/3. At least one "husband" proved to be a woman ("A Female Husband," *BNL*, April 20, 1838, 1/2; this husband was a bricklayer).

71 "J. Steele" pension file for Mormon Battalion service, Utah State Archives, Salt Lake City: examinations by Dr. Israel Ivins, March 4, 1882; Dr. C. Mantor, June 20, 1882; Dr. Oris B. Estes, September 18, 1883, and September 14, 1885. When Dr. Singleton Husted examined Steele on December 27, 1887, he likely actually measured Steele's height and reported it was five feet, four and a half inches. It is likely the earlier statements were self-reported to the doctors. On March 18, 1897, Dr. Frederic Clift found John to be five feet, three and a half inches. Dr. J. T. Affleck reported Steele was five feet, five inches on May 10, 1895. Mahonri Moriancumer Steele Jr. suggests John "was about five feet eight inches tall," which is wrong (*The Memoirs of Mahonri Moriancumer Steele Jr.*, ed. Ileen J. Johnson and Wanda S. Cox [mimeographed, 1963], 5).

72 Steele, *Memoirs of Mahonri*, 5.

73 Steele, *Memoirs of Mahonri*, 6. The text actually reads "seemed to be to be a" [*sic*]; I have corrected it.

74 For details see Kerry William Bate, *The Women: A Family Story* (Salt Lake City: University of Utah Press, 2016), 8.

75 "Wants a Situation," *BNL*, October 25, 1839, 3/1.

76 Carol Cornwall Madsen, *An Advocate for Women: The Public Life of Emmeline B. Wells, 1870–1920* (Provo, UT: Brigham Young University Press, 2006), 70.

77 John Steele to George A. Smith, February 16, 1855, "Incoming Letters 1855," 8, MS 1322, G. A. Smith Papers, CHL.

78 John Steele to Catherine Campbell Steele, December 18, 1877, box 1, folder 12, Steele Collection, LTPSC.

79 John Steele to George A. Smith, December 2, 1855, MS 1322, G. A. Smith Papers, CHL.

80 Catherine Campbell Steele to Emily Bunker Steele, February 20, 1878. I want to thank Gayle Workman for posting this letter—and a transcription—on FamilySearch.org.

81 Announcement of opening of Fisherwick from the *BNL*: "New Presbyterian Meeting-House," September 4, 1827, 2/2. This announcement ran again on September 7 (2/3) and September 11, 1827 (2/2), followed by [untitled], *BNL*, September 28, 1827, 1/2.

82 "John Steele and Catherine Campbell: 1840 Marriage: Ireland, Antrim, Belfast," marriage record of Fisherwick Place Church, Synod of Ulster, Belfast, by mail, received June 24, 1955, copy in author's possession; John Steele, journal entry, [frames 7–8], MS D 1847, folder 2, vol. 1, CHL.

83 "The Blue Book," box 1, folder 4, Steele Collection, LTPSC.

84 John Steele, journal entry, [frame 8], MS D 1847, folder 2, vol. 1, CHL.

85 *BNL*: "Tremendous Hurricane in Belfast," January 8, 1839, 2/5; "Additional Particulars Respecting the Late Storm," January 11, 1839, 2/5; "Riot Near Newtownards," January 25, 1839, 2/4; "Export of Potatoes Prevented," January 29, 1839, 4/4; "County of Down Assizes," March 15, 1839, 1/1; "County of Antrim Assizes," March 15, 1839, 1/2; "The Potato Riot in Belfast," March 15, 1839, 1/2; "Crown Court," March 19, 1839, 4/4. "A Boy Missing," October 25, 1839, 4/4; "Child Stealing," October 29, 1839, 4/2. *Chronicle*: "Child Lost," February 21, 1840, 4/3; "County of Antrim Assizes," March 13, 1840, 1/3; "Child-Stealing," September 11, 1840, 4/3; "The Storm," *NW*, January 8, 1839, 2/6; Gillespie and Royle, *Irish Historic Towns*, accompanying maps.

86 Hubert Howe Bancroft, *Retrospection, Political and Personal* (New York: Bancroft, 1913), 21.

87 "Cattle and Grain Show of the Holywood Agricultural Society," *BNL*, November 26, 1839, 1/4–6, 2/1; Holywood is reported to have had strong institutions to assist (or persecute) the poor. *BNL*: "The Committee of the Holywood Mendicity Association," August 4, 1826, 2/4; "Charity Sermon," August 4, 1826: 3/4; "Holywood Mendicity Society, March 2, 1827, 1/3; [untitled advertisement], July 17, 1827, 1/4; "Charity Sermon," July 17, 1827, 2/2; "Charity Sermons," July 24, 1827, 2/1; "Holywood Mendicity Association," September 16, 1828, 1/5 (this society was still active after John moved to Belfast).

88 Elizabeth Steele Connelly to "My Dear Brother John Steel," December 6, 1877; photocopy in author's possession.

89 "8 Am" is written above the word December.

90 John Steele, journal entry, [frame 8], MS D 1847, folder 2, vol. 1, CHL.

91 "State of the Thermometer at Belfast, in the Shade," *BNL*, December 29, 1840, 2/5, shows that it was 39.5 degrees at 9 a.m. and 40.25 at 3 p.m. on Friday, December 23.

92 John Steele, journal entry, [frame 8], MS D 1847, folder 2, vol. 1, CHL.

93 Samuel Carter Hall and Anna Maria Fielding Hall, *Hall's Ireland: Mr. and Mrs. Hall's Tour of 1840* (first published in 1841–43) (London: Sphere Books,

1984), 334–35; William Shaw Mason, *Statistical Account, or, Parochial Survey of Ireland* (1819; reprint, Arkos, 2015), 3:206.

94 R. F. Foster, *Modern Ireland, 1600–1972* (New York: Allen Lane and Penguin, 1988), 73.

95 The *Glasgow Chronicle*, quoted in an untitled article in the *BNL*, June 15, 1824, 2/1; C. A. Oakley, *The Second City* (London: Blackie & Sons, 1946), 70.

96 Alexander Wilson, *The Chartist Movement in Scotland* (New York: Augustus M. Kelley, 1970), 4.

97 Oakley, *Second City*, 68–69, 70–71.

98 *BNL*, February 5, 184: "Belfast Ship News,", 3/2; "For Glasgow," 3/6; and "The Moon," 4/6; *BNL*, February 12, 1841: "Belfast Ship News," 2/6; "State of the Thermometer at Belfast, in the Shade," 3/1.

Chapter 2

1 J. G. Kohl, *Travels in Scotland* (London: J. & D. A. Darling, 1849), 15, 19; "The Weather," *Glasgow Herald* (*GH*), February 15, 1841, p. 2, col. 1.

2 Alexander Wilson, *The Chartist Movement in Scotland* (New York: Augustus M. Kelley, 1970), 5; Mrs. Cobden [Emma Jane Cobden] Unwin, introduction to *The Hungry Forties: Life Under the Bread Tax* (London: T. Fisher Unwin, 1904).

3 Kohl, *Travels in Scotland*, 27. This phrase is not in the excerpt in "A Foreigner's Impressions of Glasgow," *GH*, April 29, 1844, 4/7.

4 Wilson, *Chartist Movement*, 6, 24. *GH*: "Distress Among the Handloom Weavers," June 7, 1841, 2/4; [untitled], June 11, 1841, 2/3; "Strike, Mobbing and Assault at Mile-End," August 15, 1842, 2/5.

5 Steele, "Extracts from the Journal of John Steele," *Utah Historical Quarterly* 6, no. 1 (January 1933): 3.

6 David Milne to John Steele, August 27, 1878, box 1, folder 29, Steele Collection, LTPSC. Steele wrote of his uncle, "I think he called his name Greenfield on account of being drawn to serve in the Millitia and did not want to serve the government as he was a Strong presbyterian and his forefathers had suffered much as Covenanters from the English Government." Michael was a son of Athur Steele's second wife, Jenny Higgins and took his surname from his father's previous wife, Elizabeth Greenfield. John Steele, journal entry, *Journals of John Steele and Mahonri Moriancumer Steele*, ed. Ileen J. Johnson and Wanda S. Cox (Cedar City, UT: self-published, 1967), sec. 1, p. 52. Curiously, Michael's sons, at least by his second wife, took the surname Greenshields.

7 John Steele, journal entry, [frame 8], MS 1847, folder 2, vol. 1, CHL; Census of Scotland, 1841, 19 Great Dove Hill, St. James' Parish, Glasgow, Lanark, Scotland, parish number 644/1, accessed through Ancestry.com.

8 James Burn Russell, *Public Health Administration in Glasgow: A Memorial*

Volume of the Writings of James Burn Russell (Glasgow: James Maclehose & Sons, 1905), 7; "Condition of the Dwellings in the Wynds of Glasgow," *GH*, September 5, 1842, 4/5.

9 *The Post-Office Glasgow Annual Directory 1841–42* (Glasgow: John Graham for the Letter-Carriers of the Post Office, 1841), 79, 106, 162, 250, 263, 317, 365, 395; *The Post-Office Glasgow Directory for 1842–43* (Glasgow: John Graham, 1842), 78, 104, 157, 161, 214, 241, 244, 256, 345, 357, 387, appendix (pagination starts over), 27; *The Post-Office Glasgow Annual Directory for 1843–44* (Glasgow: John Graham, 1843), 102, 116, 155, 162, 225, 238, 241, 253, 305, 342, 345, 348–49, 352–53, 380, appendix (pagination starts over), 27; *The Post Office Annual Glasgow Directory for 1844–45* (Glasgow: Edward H. Khull, 1844), 116, 131, 173, 235, 250, 252, 264, 280, 291, 326, 335, 376, 380, 384, 421, 475, 481, 483.

10 Robert Campbell to John Steele and Catherine Campbell Steele, November 3, 1890, box 1, folder 27, Steele Collection, LTPSC.

11 Thomas Hamilton, "James Morgan," *The Dictionary of National Biography*, ed. Leslie Stephen and Sir Henry Lee (Oxford: Oxford University Press, 1960), 13:918–19.

12 Steele, "Extracts from the Journal of John Steele," 3; *GH*: "Opening of Cooke's Circus on the Green," February 16, 1844, 3/2; "Cooke's Circus.—Carter, the Lion King," February 26, 1844, 2/5; "The Penny Shows on the Green," July 26, 1844, 2/3; James Denholm, *The History of the City of Glasgow and Suburbs* (Glasgow: R. Chapman, 1804), 139–41.

13 "Trial of the Rebeccaites," *GH*, January 12, 1844, 4/3; Richardson Campbell, *History of the Rechabite Order* (Manchester, England: Board of Directors of the Order, 1911), 10.

14 "Glasgow.—Great Procession of Teetotalers," *Northern Star and Leeds Advertiser*, July 31, 1841, 11/3; Campbell, *History of the Rechabite Order*, 100 (the latter source claimed 10,000 participants); [untitled], *GH*, June 18, 1841, 2/3.

15 John Steele, journal entry, [frame 8], MS 1847, folder 2, vol. 1, CHL; "Burial Clubs," *GH*, April 14, 1844, 4/7, quoting the *Quarterly Review*, claims there were cases of infanticide to collect burial fees.

16 *GH*: "Rebecca Riots," June 26, 1843, 4/4; "Rebecca and Her Daughters," June 30, 1843, 1/4; "Committal of 26 Rebeccaites," November 24, 1843, 4/3; "Trial of the Rebeccaites," January 12, 1844, 4/3.

17 The Rechabites claimed biblical precedent for their name but the society was founded in 1835.

18 Steele, "Extracts from the Journal of John Steele," 3.

19 John Steele, journal entry, [frame 8], MS 1847, folder 2, vol. 1, CHL.

20 *GH*: "Colliers' and the Miners' Strike," August 8, 1842, 2/5; "Strike, Mobbing and Assault at Mile-End," August 15, 1842, 2/5; "Fearful Riots in the Potteries," August 19, 1842, 2/1; "Disturbances in the Mining Districts," August 19, 1842, 1/6–8; "The Rioters at Dunfermline," August 19, 1842, 2/7; "Weavers'

Strike," August 29, 1842,2/4; "Strike of the Dandy-Loom Weavers," September 2, 1842, 4/4.

21 Steele, "Extracts from the Journal of John Steele," 3.

22 John Steele, journal entry, [frame 8], MS 1847, folder 2, vol. 1, CHL.

23 *GH*: "Glasgow, April 12," April 12, 1841, 2/4; [untitled], May 17, 1841, 2/3; [untitled], August 23, 1841, 2/5.

24 *GH*: [untitled], August 23, 1841, 2/5; also see [untitled], April 8, 1842, 2/4; [untitled], June 27, 1842, 4/5.

25 J. F. C. Harrison, *Quest for the New Moral World: Robert Owen and the Owenites in Britain and America* (New York: Charles Scribner's Sons, 1969), 46; Michael Robertson, *The Last Utopians: Four Late Nineteenth-century Visionaries and Their Legacy* (Princeton: Princeton University Press, 2018), 241. Robertson's quote from Daniel T. Rodgers suggests that the late twentieth-century's conservative fetishization of free markets was another utopian project.

26 I. G. C. Hutchison, "Glasgow Working-class Politics," in *The Working Class in Glasgow, 1750–1914* (London: Croom Helm, 1987), 106; "The Birmingham Meeting," *BNL*, August 14, 1838, 2/3; also see Wilson, *Chartist Movement*, 43–58.

27 "Chartist Meeting on the Green," *GH*, August 29, 1842, 2/5.

28 "The Birmingham Meeting," *BNL*, August 14, 1838, 2/3.

29 "Rich and Poor," *GH*, August 14, 1843, 4/5, quoting the *New Monthly Magazine*.

30 Wilson, *Chartist Movement*, 160. *GH* (April 25, 1842, 2/3) reported Crawford's motion to inquire into Parliamentary representation—a key Chartist demand—was rejected 226 to 67.

31 "Dinner in Holywood, to Wm. Sharman Crawford, Esq., M.P.," *BNL*, November 6, 1835, 4/3; "The Crawford Family of Crawfordsburn, Co. Down," 1, https://bloomfieldbelfast.co.uk/crawford-family-1798-1831.php. Crawford's birth surname was Sharman; he took the name Crawford from his wealthy heiress wife.

32 John Steele, journal entry, [frame 9], MS 1847, folder 2, vol. 1, CHL.

33 Wilson, *Chartist Movement*, 124–25, 138–50; *GH*: "Chartist Church," April 23, 1841, 4/4; "Rev. Mr. [Patrick] Brewster," May 7, 1841, 4/5.

34 Wilson, *Chartist Movement*, 12; Andrew Wallace, *A Popular Sketch of the History of Glasgow From the Earliest to the Present Time* (Glasgow: Thomas D. Morison, 1882), 122–25.

35 These beliefs mirrored early Mormonism; see J. S. Fullmer, "Letter of J. S. Fullmer," March 1840, *Latter-Day Saints' Millennial Star* 4, no. 1 (May 1843): 6–7.

36 Peter Norberg, introduction to "Nature," in *Essays and Poems by Ralph Waldo Emerson* (New York: Barnes & Noble Classics, 2004), 9.

37 Steele, "Extracts from the Journal of John Steele," 3.

38 *BNL*: "Extraordinary Sect of Fanatics in America," October 26, 1838, 4/4,

quoting "Publicus," "Philadelphia, Oct. 4," *Morning Chronicle* (London), October 19, 1838, 3/4. Also see "Mormonites," *BNL*, December 18, 1838, 4/5.

39 "Extraordinary Sect of Fanatics in America," *BNL*, October 26, 1838, 4/4; "Mormonism in America," *Belfast Commercial Chronicle*, October 27, 1838, 4/2.

40 Steele, "Extracts from the Journal of John Steele," 3; Susan Easton-Black, comp., *Membership of The Church of Jesus Christ of Latter-day Saints, 1830–1848*, 50 vols. (Provo, UT: Brigham Young University Religious Studies Center, 1989); Census of Scotland, 1851, Glasgow, Lanark, Scotland, Graham Douglass, accessed at Ancestry.com.

41 Mark Twain (Samuel L. Clemens), *Roughing It* (Berkeley: University of California Press, 1995), 106.

42 Steele, "Extracts from the Journal of John Steele," 3.

43 For a sermon on this theme see Jeffrey R. Holland, "'Are We Not all Beggars?'" https://www.churchofjesuschrist.org/study/general-conference/2014/10/are-we-not-all-beggars?lang=eng. I thank my sister Sara Jo Bate Merrill for drawing my attention to this text.

44 Gary Topping, *Leonard J. Arrington: A Historian's Life* (Norman, OK: Arthur H. Clark, 2008), 181; Leonard J. Arrington, Feramorz Y. Fox, and Dean L. May, *Building the City of God: Community and Cooperation Among the Mormons* (Salt Lake City: Deseret Book, 1976), 1–40.

45 Parley Parker Pratt, *A Voice of Warning* (Salt Lake City: Deseret Book, 1979), 1; this book begins with Pratt's *Key to the Science of Theology* and then begins over at p. 1 with *A Voice of Warning*.

46 John Steele to Letisha Connelly Todd, November 16, 1890, copy in author's possession.

47 John Steele to Letisha Connelly Todd, November 16, 1890, copy in author's possession.

48 Daniel T. Rodgers, *As a City on a Hill: The Story of America's Most Famous Lay Sermon* (Princeton: Princeton University Press, 2018), see especially 58.

49 Rodgers, *As a City on a Hill*, 94.

50 John Steele, journal entry, [frame 9], MS 1847, folder 2, vol. 1, CHL.

51 John Steele, biographical form, CR 100 18, 17:06:16, CHL; John McEwan diary, August 28–29, 1853, 5–6, MS 1051, BYU; "Died," *Deseret News*, March 6, 1878, 65/5 (obituary of McEwan).

52 Steele, "Extracts from the Journal of John Steele," 3.

53 An interlinear addition, the birth and death dates of his daughter Margaret, has been removed from this quote.

54 John Steele, journal entry, [frame 9], MS 1847, folder 2, vol. 1, CHL.

55 Reuben Hedlock to Willard Richards, October 16, 1843, box 20, folder 4, MS 2183, Brigham Young Correspondence, CHL.

56 Reuben Hedlock, U.S. Passport Applications, 1795–1925, accessed through Ancestry.com.

57 John Steele, journal entry, [frame 9], MS 1847, folder 2, vol. 1, CHL. Steele's original ordination certificate as "preest" is in his papers (box 3, folder 3, Steele Collection, LTPSC).

58 For the Rutherglen fairs see "Rutherglen Beltane Fair," *Perthshire Advertiser* (Perth, Scotland), May 11, 1843, 3/6; *Caledonian Mercury* (Edinburgh, Scotland): "Rutherglen Luke Fair," November 9, 1843, 4/6; "Rutherglen 'Cauld Fair'"; "Rutherglen Martinmas Fair," *Stirling Observer,* December 5, 1844, 1/6; John Steele, journal entry, [frame 9], MS 1847, folder 2, vol. 1, CHL.

59 "Threatened Turn-Out of the Colliers in Lanarkshire," *Perthshire Advertiser* (Perth, Scotland), September 14, 1843, 2/2.

60 "The Colliers Movement," *Northern Star and General Leeds Advertiser,* November 4, 1843, 8/5–6.

61 "Died," *DN,* March 6, 1878, 65/5; "Emigration," *Latter-Day Saints' Millennial Star* 4, no. 1 (May 1843): 14; Frederick S. Buchanan, "The Ebb and Flow of Mormonism in Scotland," *BYU Studies* 27, no. 2 (April 1987): 27–52.

62 "War Against the Mormons," *Dundee Warder and Arbroath and Forfar Journal,* July 23, 1844, 1/6–7; originally published as "Philadelphia, June 30," *Morning Chronicle* (London), July 15, 1844, 3/5.

63 War Against the Mormons," *Dundee Warder,* July 23, 1844, 1/6–7.

64 GH, "United States &c.," August 2, 1844, 1/7; also see: "United States &c.," August 9, 1844, 1/5; "Joe Smith, the Mormon Prophet," August 12, 1844, 4/3; "United States &c.," August 16, 1844, 2/1; "United States," September 16, 1844, 1/8; "United States," October 25, 1844, 1/8, "Respect for Law," 4/4; "Religion in America," November 11, 1844, 1/8.

65 Frank A. Beckwith Sr., "Valuable Relics Found in Old Trunk," *Millard County (UT) Chronicle,* July 24, 1930, 1/1, 8/4.

66 John Steele to William McClelland, August 16, 1878, retained copy in Steele journal, [frames 109–12], MS 1847, folder 2, vol. 2, CHL.

67 Mrs. [Nancy Kennedy] Steele, August 1, 1844 to "Dear [presumably son John]," photocopy of letter in author's possession; W. Anderson to John Steele [Sr.], October 21, 1823, as transcribed by Frank Beckwith. Anderson writes of William Steele "that it appears that he died at Berbin 10 May 1823," but Beckwith's typesetter was often faulty (Beckwith, "Valuable Relics Found in Old Trunk," *Millard County [UT] Chronicle,* July 24, 1930, 1/1).

68 Photocopy of letter in author's possession. Steele didn't inherit anything directly from his father as the older man left everything to his wife; the will was dated at Holywood, January 6, 1841 (copy in author's possession).

69 John Steele, journal entry, [frame 10], MS 1847, folder 2, vol. 1, CHL; Conway B. Sonne, *Ships, Saints, and Mariners: A Maritime Encyclopedia of Mormon Migration, 1830–1890* (Salt Lake City: University of Utah Press, 1987), 164; "List of Passengers Arrived from Foreign Parts in the Port of New Orleans," March 11, 1845, *New Orleans, Passenger List Quarterly Abstracts, 1820–1875,* accessed through Ancestry.com. As of 2011, the passenger list did not include the Steeles unless their surname was mangled and they were the "J. Stub" and

"Cath. Stub," the former a laborer, the latter no occupation, both twenty-four. Neither Amos Fielding nor Ann Pitchforth, other known *Palmyra* passengers, is mentioned. Woodruff, *Wilford Woodruff Journals*, vol. 2: *1845–1855* (Salt Lake City: Signature Books, 1983), 11–12; Reuben Hedlock, Liverpool, to Brigham Young, January 16, 1845, box 30, folder 13, MS 2183, Brigham Young Correspondence, CHL.

70 Ann Pitchforth, "To the Saints in the Isle of Man," *Latter-Day Saints' Millennial Star* 8, no. 1 (July 15, 1846): 12–13. Steele entered the number 3 on the back of a commercial letterhead for subscriptions to *The Scientific American* dated 1875 (box 2, folder 6, Steele Collection, LTPSC).

71 *Scientific American,* box 2, folder 6, Steele Collection, LTPSC; "List of Vessels in the Port of New-Orleans," *Commercial Bulletin, Price Current & Shipping List* (New Orleans), March 13, 1845, 4/1; "Arrived," and "Memoranda," *Times-Picayune* (New Orleans), March 9, 1845, 4/6; "Loss of Brig Camilla," *Buffalo (NY) Courier*, March 21, 1845, 2/2.

72 *Scientific American,* box 2, folder 6, Steele Collection, LTPSC.

73 John Steele, journal entry, [frame 10], MS 1847, folder 2, vol. 1, CHL.

74 *Scientific American,* box 2, folder 6, Steele Collection, LTPSC.

75 John Steele, journal entry, [frame 10], MS 1847, folder 2, vol. 1, CHL.

Chapter 3

1 William R. Polk, *Polk's Folly: An American Family History* (New York: Doubleday, 2000).

2 "From Washington," *St. Landry Whig* (Opelousas, LA), March 20, 1845, p. 2, col. 1.

3 Steele, "Extracts from the Journal of John Steele," *Utah Historical Quarterly* 6, no. 1 (January 1933): 3–4; Raymond Lee Hill, "When Mark Twain Worked the Mississippi," *Travel Magazine* 15, no. 7 (April 1910): 334; George D. Watt, *Liverpool to Great Salt Lake: The 1851 Journal of Missionary George D. Watt* (Lincoln: University of Nebraska Press, 2022), 45.

4 Steele, "Extracts from the Journal of John Steele," 3–4.

5 John Steele, journal entry, [frame 98], MS 1847, folder 2, vol. 1, CHL; Andrew Karl Larson, *Erastus Snow: The Life of a Missionary and Pioneer for the Early Mormon Church* (Salt Lake City: University of Utah Press, 1971), 93.

6 Steele, "Extracts from the Journal of John Steele," 4, 7.

7 John Steele, journal entry, [frame 16], MS 1847, folder 2, vol. 1, CHL; Steele, "Extracts from the Journal of John Steele," 4; Glen M. Leonard, *Nauvoo: A Place of Peace, A People of Promise* (Salt Lake City: Deseret Book, 2002), 489.

8 Now in the Steele Collection, box 3, folder 30, LTPSC.

9 John Steele, journal entry, [frame 12], MS 1847, folder 2, vol. 1, CHL.

10 William Clayton, journal entry, December 14, 1845, *An Intimate Chronicle: The Journals of William Clayton* (Salt Lake City: Signature Books, 1995), 213.

11 Steele, "Extracts from the Journal of John Steele," 4.

12 Michael W. Homer, "'Similarity of Priesthood in Masonry': The Relationship between Freemasonry and Mormonism," *Dialogue: A Journal of Mormon Thought* 27, no. 3 (Fall 1994): 30–33.

13 Minutes from June 5, August 8, and August 18, 1845, "Freemasons Minutebook, 1841 October–1846 February," MS 3436, CHL.

14 August 8, 1845, entry, "John Steele 3.00 to L. N. S. [Lucius Nelson Scovil]," "Freemasons account book, 1842–1845 [*sic*, 1846]," MS 3433, CHL.

15 Homer, "'Similarity of Priesthood in Masonry,'" 72–73.

16 Thomas Ford, *History of Illinois* (Chicago: Lakeside Press, 1946), 2:171. For a Mormon view of lawlessness in Nauvoo see Kenneth W. Godfrey, "Crime and Punishment in Mormon Nauvoo, 1839–1846," *BYU Studies* 32, nos. 1–2 (1992): 195–227.

17 Ford, *History of Illinois*, 2:237; Susan Sessions Rugh, "Conflict in the Countryside: The Mormon Settlement at Macedonia, Illinois," *BYU Studies* 32, no. 1 (January 1992): 165–66; Harold Schindler, *Orrin Porter Rockwell: Man of God, Son of Thunder* (Salt Lake City: University of Utah Press, 1966), 144–46.

18 Ford, *History of Illinois*, 2:297; from the *Warsaw (IL) Signal* on the dates mentioned; also see "The Election—Great Doings in Warsaw," August 13, 1845, 2/1; "Another Mormon War," August 20, 1845, 3/1–2. Rugh, "Conflict," 165.

19 Ford, *History of Illinois*, 2:294; Leonard, *Nauvoo: A Place of Peace,* 525.

20 Godfrey, "Crime and Punishment," 205–6; Rugh, "Conflict," 159–60; "Joel H. Johnson Autobiographical Sketch," MS 12931, CHL.

21 Thomas Callister, autobiographical notes, September 7, 1845, MS 5112, CHL.

22 W. G. Perkins and Isaac Clark to Brigham Young, September 22, 1845, box 20, folder 15, CR 1234 1, MS 2183, Brigham Young Correspondence, CHL.

23 The note from Young was written on the bottom of the letter from W. G. Perkins and Isaac Clark dated September 22, 1845, cited in previous note.

24 John Steele, journal entry, 1 [frame 11], folder 2, vol. 1, MS 1847, CHL.

25 [Frank A. Beckwith], "FILLMORE CELEBRATES STATE DAYS ON 24TH," *Millard County (UT) Chronicle*, July 31, 1930, 1/6.

26 Steele, "Extracts from the Journal of John Steele," 4.

27 John Steele, journal entry, [frame 11], MS 1847, folder 2, vol. 1, CHL.

28 Steele, "Extracts from the Journal of John Steele," 4–5; Hosea Stout, diary entry, September 22, 1845, *On the Mormon Frontier: The Diary of Hosea Stout* (Salt Lake City: University of Utah, 1964), 1:71; Norton Jacob, record entry, September 22, 1845, *The Mormon Vanguard Brigade of 1847: Norton Jacob's Record* (Logan: Utah State University Press, 2005), 49.

29 Steele, "Extracts from the Journal of John Steele," 4–5; Frank A. Beckwith, "From the Journal of John Steele," *Millard County (UT) Chronicle,* August 25, 1932, 6/1–3. See also Andrew Jenson, *Latter-day Saints Biographical Encyclopedia* (1914; reprinted, Salt Lake City: Western Epics, 1971), 2:429–30.

30 Steele, "Extracts from the Journal of John Steele," 3–4; Beckwith, "From the Journal of John Steele," *Millard County (UT) Chronicle*, August 25, 1932, 6/26/1–3.

31 Leonard, *Nauvoo*, 535–39.

32 Leonard J. Arrington, *Great Basin Kingdom: An Economic History of the Latter-day Saints, 1830–1900* (Lincoln: University of Nebraska Press, 1968), 19.

33 "Bill of Particulars," *Nauvoo (IL) Neighbor*, October 29, 1845, 3/1.

34 John Steele, journal entry, [frame 11], MS 1847, folder 2, vol. 1, CHL.

35 Beckwith, "From the Journal of John Steele," *Millard County (UT) Chronicle*, August 25, 1932, 6/1–3. Beckwith capitalized all the letters in "four years," which I suspect was his own addition.

36 Thomas Bullock, journal entries, September 20–October 31, 1845, *Thomas Bullock Nauvoo Journal* (Orem, UT: Grandin Book Co., 1994), 10–24.

37 John Steele, journal entry, [frame 17], MS 1847, folder 2, vol. 1, CHL.

38 Beckwith, "From the Journal of John Steele," *Millard County (UT) Chronicle*, August 25, 1932, 6/1–3; William Clayton, journal entry, December 10, 1845, *An Intimate Chronicle: The Journals of William Clayton* (Salt Lake City: Signature Books, 1995), 199.

39 September 10, 1845, "Crockery Munroe & Steele 6.25," 60; March 19, 1846 "ac/- p^{r} J. Taylor John Steele 3.10," 147; May 9, 1846, "1 Pr. of small shoes John Steele .50," 151; March 10, 1846, amount brought forward, "John Steele 2.50," 169; March 19, 1846, amount brought forward, "John Steele 1.92," 171, Trustee in Trust Ledgers, 1841–1846: Ledger B June 1845 to September 1846, CR 5 70, CHL.

40 Persecution was a major theme of Mormonism, and for some good reasons. See, for example, Dan Erickson, *"As a Thief in the Night": The Mormon Quest for Millennial Deliverance* (Salt Lake City: Signature Books, 1998), 57.

41 John Steele, journal entry, [frames 17–18], MS 1847, folder 2, vol. 1, CHL.

42 Steele, "Extracts from the Journal of John Steele," 7.

43 Steele, "Extracts," 5.

44 David John Buerger, "The Development of the Mormon Temple Endowment Ceremony," *Dialogue: A Journal of Mormon Thought* 20, no. 4 (Winter 1987): 101–3; Richard E. Turley Jr. and Barbara Jones Brown, *Vengeance Is Mine: The Mountain Meadows Massacre and Its Aftermath* (New York: Oxford University Press, 2023), 8–9.

45 "Minutes of the General Conference," April 6, 1853, *Deseret News*, April 16, 1853, 146/5.

46 John Steele, journal entry, [frame 18], MS 1847, folder 2, vol. 1, CHL.

47 B. H. Roberts, *History of the Church of Jesus Christ of Latter-day Saints Period II* (Salt Lake City: Deseret Book, 1978), 7:438.

48 Steele, "Extracts from the Journal of John Steele," 6; Leonard, *Nauvoo*, 552.

49 Steele, "Extracts," 6.

50 John Steele retained two fragments (box 3, folder 15, Steele Collection, LTPSC). These appear to be the first parts of the "Yanky Blade" letter dated February 8, 1890 (box 2, folder 11).

51 This lamentation for Catherine is dated June 15, 1891. The first part is in box 1, folder 12, Steele Collection, LTPSC, and the full document is in *Journals of John Steele and Mahonri Moriancumer Steele*, ed. Ileen J. Johnson and Wanda Steele Cox (Cedar City, UT: self-published, 1967), sec. 1, pp. 55–57.

52 John Smith, Charles C. Rich, John Young, and High Council, "An Epistle of the Presidency & High Council of this Stake of Zion," to D. C. Davis and Jesse D. Hunter, November 16, 1847, MS 20384, CHL.

Chapter 4

1 John Steele, journal entry, 12 [frame 18], folder 2, vol. 1, MS D 1847, CHL; John Doyle Lee, entry for June 8, 1846, *The Early Journals of John D. Lee: Nauvoo to Nebraska 1840–1847*, ed. Verne R. Lee (self-published, n.d.), 343. Lewis Zabriskie (1796–1884) was the bishop but his nephew Lewis Curtis Zabriskie (1817–1872) was also at Council Bluffs (Elden J. Watson, ed., *Manuscript History of Brigham Young, 1846–1847* [Salt Lake City: self-published, 1971], 261 [July 17, 1846]); I have assumed that the Lewis Zabriskie whom Steele interacted with was the older man because he was a bishop who would become responsible for Steele's effects. *BNL*: "Indian Letters to the Pope," June 1, 1832, p. 1, col. 4; "The American Indians," November 10, 1837, 1/4–5; "Characteristic Traits of the North American Indians," *Northern Whig*, April 19, 1838, 4/3; *Belfast Commercial Chronicle*: "The Chippewa Indians," April 13, 1835, 4/4; "Indian Jealousy and Elopement," August 23, 1837, 4/1.

2 *BNL*: "Indian Letters to the Pope," June 1, 1832, 1/4; "The American Indians," November 10, 1837, 1/4–5; "Characteristic Traits of the North American Indians," *Northern Whig* (Belfast), April 19, 1838, 4/3; *Belfast Commercial Chronicle*: "The Chippewa Indians," April 13, 1835, 4/4; "Indian Jealousy and Elopement," August 23, 1837, 4/1.

3 This tribe had been described in the *Northern Whig* (Belfast): [untitled], November 22, 1832, 2/2; "Stoics of the Woods," October 21, 1837, 4/4.

4 Thomas Burnell Colbert, "Poweshiek," *Biographical Dictionary of Iowa* (University of Iowa Press, 2009), accessed online.

5 Steele used commas in some places in this document where he wanted apostrophes. I have silently corrected them to apostrophes even where grammatically an apostrophe is not warranted.

6 John Steele, journal entries, July 10–11, 1846, 14–15 [frames 20–21], MS 1847, folder 2, vol. 1, CHL.

7 J. Brown Horey to G. A. Parsons, June 23, 1846; L. Marshall to President James Knox Polk, July 4, 1846; Governor J. C. Edwards to William L. Marcy, August 11, 1846: all in Henry Standage, *The March of the Mormon Battalion*

from Council Bluffs to California Taken from the Journal of Henry Standage (New York: Century Co., 1928), 94–99.

8 Thomas Ford, *History of Illinois* (Chicago: Lakeside Press, 1946), 2:309–10; Robert Selph Henry, *Story of the Mexican War* (New York: Da Capo Paperback, 1950), 84; Sherman L. Fleek, *History May Be Searched in Vain: A Military History of the Mormon Battalion* (Spokane, WA: Arthur H. Clark, 2006), 52–54.

9 John Steele, journal entry, 7–8 [frames 13–14], MS 1847, folder 2, vol. 1, CHL; Steele, "Extracts from the Journal of John Steele," *Utah Historical Quarterly* 6, no. 1 (January 1933): 7.

10 Steele, "Extracts," 6–7.

11 Watson, *Manuscript History of Brigham Young* (Salt Lake City: self-published, 1971), 197–98 (June 27, 1846).

12 John Steele, journal entry, July 18, 1846, 15 [frame 21], MS 1847, folder 2, vol. 1, CHL; Norma Baldwin Ricketts, *The Mormon Battalion: U.S. Army of the West, 1846–1848* (Logan: Utah State University Press, 1996), 16.

13 Steele, "Extracts from the Journal of John Steele," 6–7. Watson (*Manuscript History of Brigham Young* [Salt Lake City: self-published, 1971], 221) shows that July 7, 1846, was the likely date this happened.

14 Fleek, *History*, 137–38.

15 John Steele, journal entry, July 18, 1846, 15 [frame 21], MS D 1847, folder 2, vol. 1, CHL.

16 Ricketts, *Mormon Battalion*, 28, 30–33.

17 John Steele, journal entry, July 22, 1846, 16 [frame 22], MS 1847, folder 2, vol. 1, CHL.

18 Lee, *Early Journals*, 343 (June 8, 1846).

19 Fleek, *History*, 100.

20 John Steele, journal entry, [frame 4], MS 1847, folder 2, vol. 1, CHL.

21 John Steele to Thomas Bullock, August 18, 1851; November 7, 1851; November 18, 1851; January 8, 1852; May 13, 1852; pre-August 10, 1852: all in Correspondence: Letters, box 1, folder 11, MS 27307, Thomas Bullock Collection, CHL.

22 John Steele, journal entry, July 12, 1846, 15 [frame 21], MS 1847, folder 2, vol. 1, CHL.

23 Fleek, *History*, 138–39; John Frank George Yurtinus, "A Ram in the Thicket: The Mormon Battalion in the Mexican War" (PhD diss., BYU, 1975), 56. It's surprising Yurtinus's superb dissertation wasn't published.

24 Steele, "Extracts from the Journal of John Steele," 7; Steele, journal entry, August 4, 1846, 15–16 [frames 22–23], MS 1847, folder 2, vol. 1, CHL.

25 Yurtinus, "Ram," 59, citing Willard Richards's journal entry of July 18, 1846, CHL.

26 Elijah Elmer, "The Mormon Battalion Portion of the Journal of Elijah Elmer, Sergeant, Company C," August 1, 1846, typescript, Compilation of Mormon Battalion Journals, MS 13956, CHL.

27 John Steele, journal entry, July 23, 1846, 17 [frame 22], MS 1847, folder 2, vol. 1, CHL.
28 John Steele, journal entry, July 24, 1846 [frame 23–24], MS 1847, folder 2, vol. 1, CHL.
29 John Steele, journal entries, MS 1847, folder 2, vol. 1, CHL.
30 Watson, *Manuscript History of Brigham Young* (Salt Lake City: self-published, 1971), 264 (July 18, 1846).
31 Blackburn, *Frontiersman: Abner Blackburn* (Salt Lake City: University of Utah Press, 1992), 39.
32 Steele, "Extracts from the Journal of John Steele," 9.
33 Fleek, *History*, 149–50.
34 John Steele, journal entry, August 7, 1846, 26 [frame 26], MS D 1847, folder 2, vol. 1, CHL.
35 John Steele, journal entry, October 17, 1846, 35 [frame 41], MS 1847, folder 2, vol. 1, CHL.
36 John Steele, journal entries, August 19 and 27, 1846, 21–22 [frames 27–28, 31], MS 1847, folder 2, vol. 1, CHL; Ricketts, *Mormon Battalion*, 42–43 (August 19, 1846).
37 Henry Standage, journal entry, August 19–20, 1846, *March of the Mormon Battalion*, 147–48.
38 John Steele, journal entry, August 23, 1846, 23 [frame 29], MS 1847, folder 2, vol. 1, CHL.
39 Steele, "Extracts from the Journal of John Steele," 8.
40 Yurtinus, "Ram," 137.
41 Steele, "Extracts from the Journal of John Steele," 9.
42 John Steele, journal entry, October 6, 1846, 32 [frame 38], MS 1847, folder 2, vol. 1, CHL; Steele, "Extracts from the Journal of John Steele," 10.
43 John Steele, journal entry, October 9, 1846, 33 [frame 39], MS 1847, folder 2, vol. 1, CHL; Steele, "Extracts from the Journal of John Steele," 10.
44 John Steele, journal entry, October 12, 1846, 33–34 [frames 39–40], MS 1847, folder 2, vol. 1, CHL.
45 Steele, "Extracts from the Journal of John Steele," 10; Henry Standage, journal entry, September 10, 1846, *March of the Mormon Battalion*, 161.
46 Joseph Smith et al., *History of the Church of Jesus Christ of Latter-day Saints*, ed. B. H. Roberts (Salt Lake City: Deseret Book, 1964), 3:190–91; Fleek, *History*, 106–7.
47 Philip St. George Cooke, *The Conquest of New Mexico and California, an Historical and Personal Narrative* (Albuquerque: Horn and Wallace, 1964), 91.
48 Steele, "Extracts from the Journal of John Steele," 12.
49 Cooke, *Conquest*, 91.
50 John Steele, journal entry, October 12, 1846, 34 [frame 40], MS 1847, folder 2, vol. 1, CHL.
51 Yurtinus ("Ram," 68n38) points out that George P. Dykes may have been

maligned because he later left Brigham Young's Mormonism for that of Joseph Smith III.

52 Steele, "Extracts from the Journal of John Steele," 11.

53 Florence C. Youngberg, *Conquerors of the West: Stalwart Mormon Pioneers* (Salt Lake City: National Society for Sons of the Utah Pioneers, 1999), 2:1081–88.

54 Steele, "Extracts from the Journal of John Steele," 11.

55 P. St. George Cooke, entry of February 5, 1847, "Report of Lieut. Col. P. St. George Cooke of his March from Santa Fe, New Mexico, to San Diego, Upper California," *Utah Historical Quarterly* 22, no. 1 (January 1954): 18n9.

56 John Steele, journal entry, October 12, 1846, 34 [frame 40], MS D 1847, folder 2, vol. 1, CHL; Wanda Wood, "John W. Hess, with the Mormon Battalion," *Utah Historical Quarterly* 4, no. 2 (April 1931): 51.

57 Steele, "Extracts from the Journal of John Steele," 11.

58 Otis E. Young, *The West of Philip St. George Cooke* (Glendale, CA: Arthur H. Clark, 1955), 93–94.

59 Steele, "Extracts from the Journal of John Steele," 11–12.

60 Cooke, "Report," 18n9.

61 Fleek, *History*, 235–37.

62 Young, *The West*, 189.

63 Cooke, "Report," 19. Cooke also expressed concern for the laundresses in his October 15, 1846, Order No. 8 directing Capt. James Brown to take a group to Pueblo (Daniel Tyler, *A Concise History of the Mormon Battalion in the Mexican War* [Glorieta, NM: Rio Grande Press, 1969], 166–67).

64 Steele, "Extracts from the Journal of John Steele," 12. Fleek (*History*, 202–3) gives a useful description of oxen and the wagons they pulled.

65 Cooke, "Report," 19–20.

66 The ballad "Trip to Pueblo" is in box 1, folder 2, Steele Collection, LTPSC.

67 Steele, "Extracts from the Journal of John Steele," 13.

68 John Steele, journal entry, November 6–7, 1846, 37–38 [frames 43–44], MS 1847, folder 2, vol. 1, CHL. This is the first journal entry where Steele clearly writes retrospectively. Almost all references to Brown by his fellow soldiers are uncomplimentary or worse.

69 James H. Glines, John Steele, and William Walker to Heber C. Kimball, October 15, 1846, Mormon Battalion letters, 1846, CR 100 696, box 2, folder 23; Brigham Young history documents: Mormon Battalion letters, 1846 September–December, MS 2183, Brigham Young Correspondence, CHL.

70 Francis Parkman, *The Oregon Trail* (New York: Library of America, 1991), 274.

71 John Steele, journal entry, November 19, 1846, 45 [frame 39], MS 1847, folder 2, vol. 1, CHL.

72 "Thursday" is written over Tuesday in black ink.

73 John Steele, journal entry, November 20–24, 1846, 45 [frame 39]), MS 1847, folder 2, vol. 1, CHL.

74 John Steele, journal entry, December 21, 1846, 45 [frame 39], MS 1847, folder 2, vol. 1, CHL.
75 J. Steele pension file for Mormon Battalion service, General Affidavit, June 24, 1881, signed by Lyman Stevens and Orson B. Adams; Declaration for an Increase of an Invalid Pension, October 3, 1882; Dr. J. T. Affleck, Physician's Affidavit, May 19, 1896: in Utah State Archives, Salt Lake City.
76 J. Steele pension file, Dr. Frederick Clift affidavit, March 18, 1897, Utah State Archives, Salt Lake City.
77 J. Steele pension file, Nelson Higgins, "Proof of Disability," March 23, 1882, Utah State Archives, Salt Lake City.
78 David L. Bigler and Will Bagley, eds., *Army of Israel: Mormon Battalion Narratives* (Logan: Utah State University Press, 2000), 116–17.
79 John Steele to Heber C. Kimball, December 28, 1846, "Mormon Battalion letters, 1846," partial transcript in Andrew Jenson, "Manuscript History of Pueblo, 1840–1850," box 3, folder 3, MS 4029, reel 2, CHL.
80 Steele to Kimball, December 28, 1846, "Mormon Battalion letters, 1846."
81 Steele and Glines to Kimball, December 28, 1846, "Mormon Battalion letters, 1846."
82 Steele, "Extracts from the Journal of John Steele," 14.
83 John Steele, journal entry, January 19, 1847, 43–44 [frames 49–50], MS 1847, folder 2, vol. 1, CHL.
84 John Steele, journal entry, January 11, 1847, 41–42 [frames 47–48], MS 1847, folder 2, vol. 1, CHL.
85 Bigler and Bagley, *Army of Israel*, 27.
86 John Steele, journal entry, March 18, 1847, 52 [frame 58], MS 1847, folder 2, vol. 1, CHL.
87 John Steele, journal entry, March 4, 1847, 49–50 [frames 55–56], MS 1847, folder 2, vol. 1, CHL.
88 Yurtinus, "Ram," 306.
89 George Deliverance Wilson, unpaginated journal typescript in author's possession.
90 John Steele poetry, box 1, folder 2, Steele Collection, LTPSC.
91 Yurtinus, "Ram," 298.
92 John Steele, journal entry, January 25, 1847, 45 [frame 51], MS 1847, folder 2, vol. 1, CHL.
93 Quoted in Yurtinus, "Ram," 300–301.
94 John Steele, journal entry, February 13, 1847 [frame 222], MS 1847, folder 2, vol. 1, CHL.
95 John Steele, journal entry, March 18, 1847, 51 [frame 57], MS 1847, folder 2, vol. 1, CHL.
96 John Steele, journal entry, March 21, 1847, 52 [frame 58], MS 1847, folder 2, vol. 1, CHL.
97 John Steele, journal entry, June 11, 1846, [frame 64], MS 1847, folder 2, vol. 1, CHL.

98 Bea W. Barton, *The Mormon Battalion: Mississippi Saints and Pioneers, Douglas County, Colorado: Honorable Remembrance to the Latest Generation, 1846–2005* (n.p.: Johnson Printing, 2008), 290.

99 John Steele, journal entry, June 13, 1847, 58 [frame 64], MS 1847, folder 2, vol. 1, CHL. Steele wrote "he had" twice; I've eliminated the repetition. Lyman was blessed in having such a talented biographer—Edward Leo Lyman (*Amasa Mason Lyman, Mormon Apostle and Apostate: A Study in Dedication* [Salt Lake City: University of Utah Press, 2009]); see 141–42 for an account of Lyman and the Pueblo Mormons. Lyman's journal has a lacuna between June 15 and December 28, 1847 (*Thirteenth Apostle: The Diaries of Amasa M. Lyman, 1832–1877* [Salt Lake City: Signature Books, 2016], 82–83).

100 Steele, June 20, 1847, penciled journal, box 1, folder 2, Steele Collection, LTPSC.

101 John Steele, journal entry, June 20, 1847, 51 [frame 66], MS 1847, folder 2, vol. 1, CHL.

102 Amasa M. Lyman to Brigham Young, June 28, 1847, CR 1234 1, MS 2183, Letters from Church Leaders and Others, Brigham Young Correspondence, CHL.

103 Steele, July 16, 1847, penciled journal, box 1, folder 2, Steele Collection, LTPSC.

104 Steele, "Extracts from the Journal of John Steele," 16–17.

105 John Steele, journal entry, July 25, 1847, 64–65 [frames 70–71], MS 1847, folder 2, vol. 1, CHL.

106 John Steele, journal entry, July 28, 1847, 65 [frame 71], MS 1847, folder 2, vol. 1, CHL.

Chapter 5

1 Steele, "Extracts from the Journal of John Steele," *Utah Historical Quarterly* 6, no. 1 (January 1933): 17–18.

2 Steele, "Extracts," 17.

3 John Steele to Heber C. Kimball, December 28, 1846, Brigham Young history documents: Mormon Battalion letters, 1846 September–December, CR 100 696, box 2, folder 23, CHL.

4 Steele, "Extracts from the Journal of John Steele," 17.

5 Woodruff, entry, July 29, 1847, *Wilford Woodruff Journals*, 2:234.

6 Steele, July 30, 1847, penciled journal, box 1, folder 2, Steele Collection, LTPSC.

7 John Steele, journal entry, August 1, 1847 [frame 72], folder 2, vol. 1, MS 1847, CHL.

8 Woodruff, entry, July 29, 1847, *Wilford Woodruff Journals*, 2:234.

9 Leonard J. Arrington, *Great Basin Kingdom: Economic History of the Latter-Day Saints, 1830–1900* (1958; reprint, Lincoln: University of Nebraska Press, 1968) is the classic study of the Mormon economy.

10 Steele, "Extracts from the Journal of John Steele," 20; Woodruff, journal entries, July 28 and 30, 1847, *Wilford Woodruff's Journals*, 2:233 and 235; John Steele, journal entry, November 2, 1847 [frame 78], MS 1847, folder 2, vol. 1, CHL.

11 Arrington, *Great Basin Kingdom*, 25, cited in Topping, *Leonard J. Arrington*, 64.

12 William Hepworth Dixon, *New America* (Philadelphia: J. B. Lippincott, 1867), 199–200.

13 John Steele, journal entry, August 9, 1847 [frame 72], MS 1847, folder 2, vol. 1, CHL.

14 Badger, journal entry, September 26, 1905, in journal dated "September 9, 1905, to January 23, 1907," Carlos Ashby Badger Papers, MSS 1298, LTPSC.

15 Steele, "Extracts from the Journal of John Steele," 18. Alter misread Angus's name as John "Dangus."

16 Woodruff, entry, August 8, 1847, *Wilford Woodruff Journals*, 2:238.

17 "Freemasons Minutebook, 1841 October–1846 February," MS 3436, CHL.

18 Steele, "Extracts from the Journal of John Steele," 18.

19 Steele, "Extracts," 18; John Steele to Wilford Woodruff, July 30, 1888, copy in author's possession.

20 John Steele, journal entries, August 22 and November 2, 1847 [frames 71, 77], MS 1847, folder 2, vol. 1, CHL.

21 John Steele, journal entries, July 29 and September 19, 1847 [frames 71, 75], MS 1847, folder 2, vol. 1, CHL.

22 John Steele, journal entry, November 2, 1847 [frames 76–79], MS 1847, folder 2, vol. 1, CHL.

23 John Steele, journal entry, November 2, 1847.

24 John was apparently the only Crandall who was an 1847 pioneer (Utah Mormon Pioneer Overland Travel Database, accessed April 15, 2023).

25 Iona Poling, who was expert at reading Steele's handwriting, read this surname as Brown; it looks like "Brurn" to me. William W. Brown (1824–1899) of the Mormon Battalion may be the one referenced.

26 John Steele, journal entries: on or after September 19, 1846 [frame 76] and December 20, 1847, 74 [frame 80], MS 1847, folder 2, vol. 1, CHL.

27 Steele, "Extracts from the Journal of John Steele," 20.

28 "Pvt. Daniel L. Brown" (1822–1899), Findagrave.com; "Died," [Daniel Brown], *Evening Sentinel* (Santa Cruz, CA), October 28, 1899, 2/3; Joseph Irwin, Laketown, Rich County, Utah, to Editor, November 14, 1886, *Deseret News (DN)*, November 24, 1886, 707/3–4.

29 John Steele, journal entry, February 1, 1848, 75 [frame 81], MS 1847, folder 2, vol. 1, CHL.

30 Steele, "Extracts from the Journal of John Steele," 21–22.

31 Steele, "Extracts," 21.

32 John Steele, journal entries, June 4 and July 15, 1848, 79 [frames 84–85], MS 1847, folder 2, vol. 1, CHL.

33 Parley P. Pratt, John Taylor, and John Smith to Brigham Young, August 23, 1848, in William S. Harwell, *Manuscript History of Brigham Young, 1847–1850* (Salt Lake City: Collier's, 1997), 117.
34 Harwell, *Brigham Young*, 185 (April 9, 1849).
35 John D. Lee, diary entry, February 9, 1849, *A Mormon Chronicle: The Diaries of John D. Lee, 1848–1876* (San Marino, CA: Huntington Library, 1955), 1:88.
36 Steele, "Extracts from the Journal of John Steele," 22.
37 John Steele, journal entry, on or after July 15, 1848, 79 [frame 85], MS 1847, folder 2, vol. 1, CHL.
38 Harwell, *Brigham Young*, 205 (May 26, 1849).
39 Steele, "Extracts from the Journal of John Steele," 23.
40 Harwell, *Brigham Young*, 160 (February 22, 1849).
41 John "Pettecrew" is in the 1631 muster roll of "Holliwood," County Down, with sword and pike, as is a Robert Steele ("Muster Roll of the County of Down. 1631"; typescript in the Family History Library, Salt Lake City.
42 Steele, "Extracts from the Journal of John Steele," 23.
43 John Steele, journal entry, May 1, 1849, 79 [frames 85–86], MS 1847, folder 2, vol. 1, CHL.
44 Salt Lake City Tenth Ward, Record of Members 1849–1866, Historical Record 1849–1855, 8, LR 9051 11, reel 1, CHL.
45 Salt Lake City Tenth Ward, Record of Members 1849–1866, Historical Record 1849–1855, 19, 32–35, LR 9051 11, reel 1, CHL.
46 John Steele, journal entry, undated [frame 86], MS 1847, folder 2, vol. 1, CHL.
47 Harwell, *Brigham Young*, 187 (April 9, 1849); Brigham D. Madsen, *Gold Rush Sojourners in Great Salt Lake City, 1849 and 1850* (Salt Lake City: University of Utah Press, 1983), 19.
48 Madsen, *Gold Rush Sojourners*, 19; Harwell, *Brigham Young*, 312 (June 1850).
49 Steele, "Extracts from the Journal of John Steele," 23.
50 "Esaias Edwards Journal," typescript, 23–24, Utah Historical Society, Salt Lake City; Esaias Edwards to Willard Richards, June 1, 1851, box 4, folder 6, Willard Richards Journals and Papers, MS 1490, CHL. Edwards's letter is dated 1850 but an attached prospective advertisement is dated 1851; Edwards's journal shows he didn't move to Tooele until "the fore part of October" (1850), so the letter would have been written in 1851.
51 Samuel Hollister Rogers's journal can be found at https://www.familysearch.org/photos/artifacts/9095845.
52 Salt Lake City Tenth Ward, Record of Members 1849–1866, Historical Record 1849–1855, 21–31 (January 1, 1850), LR 9051 11, reel 1, CHL.
53 Steele, "Extracts from the Journal of John Steele," 23.
54 "Little Salt Lake," *DN*, July 27, 1850, 50/2.
55 Smith, journal entry, December 16, 1851, journal not paginated, G. A. Smith Papers, box 2, folder 5, MS 1322, CHL.

56 "Volunteers," *DN*, November 16, 1850, 156/2–3; Morris A. Shirts and Kathryn H. Shirts, *A Trial Furnace: Southern Utah's Iron Mission* (Provo, UT: Brigham Young University Press, 2001), 16–20.

57 "Names of the Company and their outfit for Little Salt Lake," *DN*, November 16, 1850, 154/2–3, 155/1.

58 "Names of the Company," *DN*, November 16, 1850.

59 By spring 1852 colonists were advertising for "Two good blacksmiths" for Parowan ("A Blacksmith Wanted," *DN*, May 29, 1852, 3/6; [untitled], *DN*, April 3, 1852, 1/5).

60 George A. Zabriskie and Dorothy L. Robinson, "The U.S. Census of Utah, 1851," *Utah Genealogical Magazine* 29, no. 3 (July 1938): 132.

61 John Steele, journal entry, undated, 81 [frame 87], MS 1847, folder 2, vol. 1, CHL; Steele, "Extracts from the Journal of John Steele," 23–24.

62 Mrs. B. G. [Elizabeth Cornelia] Ferris, *The Mormons at Home* (New York: Dix & Edwards, 1856), 178.

63 John Steele to Thomas Bullock, November 7, 1851, box 1, folder 10, Correspondence, Letters, 1851, Thomas Bullock Collection, CHL.

64 Joseph Fish, *The Autobiography of Joseph Fish* (n.p.: Lulu, 2009), 35–36.

65 Steele, "Extracts from the Journal of John Steele," 24.

66 Priddy Meeks, "Journal of Priddy Meeks," *Utah Historical Quarterly* 10 (1942): 168; "Elder Orson B. Adams," *DN*, April 1, 1857, 28/1–3.

67 John Steele, journal entry [frame 212], MS 1847, folder 2, vol. 1, CHL.

68 Smith, journal entry, December 15, 1850, MS 1322, G. A. Smith Papers, CHL.

69 Smith, journal entry, December 19, 1850, MS 1322, G. A. Smith Papers, CHL. John D. Lee implies the organization didn't take place until this day (entry dated December 19, 1850, "Journal of the Iron County Mission," *Utah Historical Quarterly* 20 [1952]: 119–20), but Steele lists the officers, including himself, in his journal entry of December 15.

70 John Steele, journal entry, December 15, 1850, 82 [frame 88], MS 1847, folder 2, vol. 1, CHL.

71 Lee, journal entry, December 19, 1850, "Journal," 120. Lee gives Steele the middle initial "C."

72 George A. Smith to Brigham Young, December 20, 1850, box 42, folder 4, MS 2183, Brigham Young Correspondence, CHL.

73 Shirts and Shirts, *A Trial Furnace*, 26; "Notice," *DN*, November 16, 1850, 157/3.

74 Lee, journal entry, January 3, 1851, "Journal," 257.

Chapter 6

1 Steele, "Extracts from the Journal of John Steele," *Utah Historical Quarterly* 6, no. 1 (January 1933): 24.

2 Henry Lunt describes himself as "assistant Clerk & Pres. G.A. Smith private secretary," [frame 12], MS 15781, CHL. This manuscript is a modern handwritten transcript of Lunt's original journal.

3 Steele, journal entry, January 2, 1851 [frame 89], 83, folder 2, vol. 1, MS 1847, CHL.
4 Smith, journal entry, January 2, 1851, journal dated December 1850–April 1851, not paginated, box 2, folder 5, MS 1322, G. A. Smith Papers, CHL.
5 George A. Smith to Brigham Young, January 17, 1851, box 42, folder 4, MS 2183, Brigham Young Correspondence, CHL; John D. Lee, journal entry, January 19, 1851, "Journal of the Iron County Mission," *Utah Historical Quarterly* 20 (1952): 355.
6 Steele, "Extracts from the Journal of John Steele," 25.
7 Quoted in Morris A. Shirts and Kathryn H. Shirts, *A Trial Furnace* (Provo, UT: Brigham Young University Press, 2001), 69.
8 "Another Veteran Departed," *Deseret News (DN)*, March , 20, 1878, p. 105, col. 4.
9 [John Smith], "Territory of Utah," *Weekly Journal of Commerce* (New York), Thursday, May 3, 1852, vol. 1, no. 20, 3/6.
10 Steele, "Extracts from the Journal of John Steele," 25.
11 Lee, journal entry, January 17, 1851, "Journal," 278.
12 Steele, "Extracts from the Journal of John Steele," 25; George A. Smith to Brigham Young, January 28, 1851, box 42, folder 4, MS 2183, Brigham Young Correspondence, CHL.
13 Lunt, journal entry, May 1, 1852, 60/11 (double pagination in original), "The Life of Henry Lunt," BYU typescript, LTPSC.
14 "Fifth General Epistle," *Latter-Day Saints' Millennial Star* (*MS*) 13, no. 14 (July 15, 1851): 212; George A. Smith to Brigham Young, January 28, 1851, box 42, folder 4, MS 2183, Brigham Young Correspondence, CHL; Woodruff, entries for May 10–13, 1851, *Wilford Woodruff Journals*, 2:468–69.
15 John Steele, "Utah Indian Language," December 4, 1851, box 1, folder 3, Steele Collection, Brigham Young University, L. Tom Perry Special Collections. William R. Palmer wrote that the word *Parowan* meant "mean or evil water" ("Indian Names in Utah Geography," *Utah Historical Quarterly* 1, no. 1 [January 1928]: 9–10).
16 Aaron F. Farr to George A. Smith, July 27, 1851 (misdated 1850), G. A. Smith Papers, 1834–1877, MS 1322, CHL.
17 Shirts and Shirts, *A Trial Furnace*, 97.
18 Shirts and Shirts, *A Trial Furnace*, 82.
19 John Steele poetry, box 1, folder 4, Steele Collection, LTPSC.
20 John Steele to Thomas Bullock, January 8, 1852, box 2, folder 11, Correspondence, Letters, 1852, Bullock Collection, CHL.
21 "Letter from George A. Smith," April 29, 1851, *DN*, May 17, 1851, 259/1–2.
22 "Death of Susann Smith Adams," *Deseret Weekly News* (*DWN*) 44 (February 27, 1892), 807/1.
23 John Steele to Thomas Bullock, November 7, 1851, and August 18, 1851, box 1, folder 10, Bullock Collection, CHL.
24 Steele, retained copy of biography questionnaire for J. H. E. Webster's "The History of Utah Project," box 2, folder 6, Steele Collection, LTPSC.

25 Theresa Flake Johnson and Iris Flake Farr, "Charles Albert Hall," FamilySearch.com.

26 Rodgers, *As a City on a Hill*, 101–2.

27 Minutes 1853–1868 Iron County Probate Court, 23 (December 19, 1859). James Henry Martineau, "Parowan Stake History Book," January 3 and 6, 1860; minutes for January 5–6, 1860, Parowan High Priests Quorum Minutes, 1855–1887, LR 6778 13, CHL.

28 Steele, "Extracts from the Journal of John Steele," 27.

29 "One Week Later from Utah," *New York Times,* August 13, 1858, 1/1–3.

30 Woodruff, entry for May 16, 1851, *Wilford Woodruff Journals,* 2:470.

31 Joseph Smith, "The Globe," *Times and Seasons* 5, no. 6 (April 14, 1844): 510.

32 Steele, journal entry [frame 92], vol. 1; "Extracts from the Journal of John Steele," 25. City marshal was such a minor office it wasn't reported in the newspaper ("President Young's Visit," *DN*, June 28, 1851, 284/1). Elections for county officers and territorial representative were held before the town site was chosen.

33 John Steele to Thomas Bullock, November 18, 1851, box 1, folder 10, Bullock Collection, CHL.

34 Steele, "Extracts from the Journal of John Steele," 26. A copy of Steele's citizenship paper attested by Martin Slack on September 23, 1896, is in box 2, folder 1, Steele Collection, LTPSC.

35 Minutes for June 15, 1851, Parowan Priesthood Minute Book 1851, reel 1, folder 1, LR 6775 11, CHL.

36 John Steele to Thomas Bullock, November 18, 1851, box 1, folder 10, Bullock Collection, CHL.

37 "Herding," *DN*, October 12, 1859, 252/2. The *Deseret News* denounced boys herding as "a nursery of vice" and costly to crops through carelessness. The Parowan Priesthood Minute Book 1851 reflects a rate of three cents per head per day per cow (September 14, 1851, item no. 1, LR 6775 1, CHL).

38 John Steele to Thomas Bullock, January 8, 1852, box 1, folder 11, Bullock Collection, CHL.

39 Hosea Stout, diary entries, January 3 and 5, 1855, *On the Mormon Frontier: The Diary of Hosea Stout, 1844–1861* (University of Utah Press: Salt Lake City, 1982), 2:539–40.

40 Robert Owens to Brigham Young, October 12 and November 4, 1852, box, 22, folder 18; Zerubbabel Snow to Brigham Young, November 28, 1852, and to Thomas Bullock, November 28, 1852 (both in box 53, folder 20): all in MS 2183, Brigham Young Correspondence, CHL. Stout, *On the Mormon Frontier,* 2:540n36. *DN*: "Foreign Correspondence," April 18, 1855, 46/1–3; "News from Elders," October 31, 1855, 269/2–3; Nathaniel Vary Jones, "Hindostanee Mission," December 19, 1855, 334/1–3.

41 Woodruff, entry, May 12, 1851, *Wilford Woodruff's Journals,* 2:469.

42 Steele, "Extracts from the Journal of John Steele," 25.

43 Muster rolls for August 1 and November 29, 1851, Utah Territorial Militia Records, series 2210, reel 10, doc. 3288, Utah State Archives, Salt Lake City.

44 Muster roll for May 12, 1852, Utah Territorial Militia Records, series 2210, reel 10, doc. 3301, Utah State Archives, Salt Lake City.
45 David John Buerger, "'The Fulness of the Priesthood,'" *Dialogue: A Journal of Mormon Thought* 16, no. 1 (1983): 11–44.
46 Joseph Fish, *Autobiography of Joseph Fish* (n.p.: Lulu: 2009), 45.
47 "Latter Day Saints," *New York Herald*, May 13, 1877, 9/1–3.
48 Steele to Little, January 7, 1855; published as "Deseret," *Latter-day Saints' Millennial Star* 17, no. 21 (May 26, 1855): 334.
49 Henry Lunt to Brigham Young, August 3, 1862, MS 2183, Brigham Young Correspondence, CHL.
50 Quoted in Louise Parkin and Beulah Gibson, *A Voice from the Mountains: Life and Works of Joel Hills Johnson* (Mesa, AZ: Joel Hills Johnson Arizona Committee, 1982), 38.
51 "Mormon Rascality!," *New York Herald,* May 10, 1877, 4/1–2.
52 "Mail Irregularities," *Salt Lake Tribune*, February 21, 1875, 2/1.
53 Steele, "Extracts from the Journal of John Steele," 27.
54 James B. Allen, "The Unusual Jurisdiction of County Probate Courts in the Territory of Utah," *Utah Historical Quarterly* 36, no. 2 (Spring 1968): 132–42.
55 John Doyle Lee, *Mormonism Unveiled* (St. Louis, MO: M. E. Mason, 1891), 275–78.
56 Minutes for "Special Session of the Probate Court held at Parowan Jany 19 & 20, 1854," "Minutes, 1853–1868," Iron County Probate Court, series 17477, Minute Book A, June 3, 1851, to June 5, 1854, Utah State Archives, Salt Lake City.
57 Lee, *Mormonism Unveiled*, 275–78.
58 Lee, *Mormonism Unveiled*, 275–78.
59 Lee, *Mormonism Unveiled*, 275–78.
60 Conversation between Mahonri "Hon" M. Steele Jr. and Frank A. Beckwith, reported in Beckwith, "Shameful Friday: A Critical Study of the Mountain Meadows Massacre," unfinished, partly paginated MS, insert A; copy in author's possession. I'm very grateful to the late historian Will Bagley for sharing this.
61 William Wall, "To the Editor of the Deseret News," May 28, 1853, *DN,* May 31, 1853, 3/3–4.
62 Solomon Nunes Carvalho, *Incidents of Travel and Adventure in the Far West*, ed. Bertram Wallace Korn (Philadelphia: Jewish Publication Society of America, 1954), 201.
63 Allen Nevins, *Fremont in the Civil War* (New York: Frederick Ungar, 1961), 408–9.
64 John C. L. [Calvin] Smith to the Editor, undated, *DN*, March 16, 1854, 3/2–3.
65 Carvalho, *Incidents*, 188.
66 John C. L. [Calvin] Smith to the Editor, undated, *DN*, March 16, 1854, 3/2–3.
67 Richard E. Bennett, "He is our Friend: Thomas L. Kane and the Mormons in Exodus," *BYU Studies* 48, no. 4 (2009): 41; "Remarks. By President Brigham Young, Tabernacle, p.m., February 17, 1861," *DN,* March 13, 1861, 9/1–3.

68 Fish, *Autobiography*, 43.
69 Fish, *Autobiography*, 43.
70 James H. Martineau, "A Meeting with Fremont: Pioneer Experiences, For The Saturday News by Col. J. H. Martineau," *Deseret Evening News*, February 17, 1917, sec. 2, 14/2–4; reproduced in Martineau, *An Uncommon Common Pioneer,* 743; source identified in James Henry Martineau, *Useful to the Church and Kingdom* (Salt Lake City: Signature Books, 2023), 2:1261–66.
71 Carvalho, *Incidents*, 276; John Steele, journal entry, undated [frame 97], MS D 1847, folder 2, vol. 1, CHL.
72 John Steele, affidavit, box 1, folder 91, CR 100 397, Historian's Office Collected Historical Documents ca. 1851–1869, CHL. This appears to be in James Lewis's handwriting; written on the back is "Affidavit of Oct. 11–58 | John Steele in relation | to Cap. John C. Fremont | carrying off the Surveys of | Center & Coal Creeks in 1854."
73 John C. Frémont, "Col. Fremont's Exploration of the Central Railroad Route to the Pacific to the Editors of The National Intelligencer," *New York Daily Tribune,* June 15, 1854, 5/4–5.
74 Frémont, "Col. Fremont's Exploration," *New York Daily Tribune,* June 15, 1854, 5/4–5; Mary Lee Spence, ed., *The Expeditions of John Charles Frémont Travels from 1848 to 1854* (Chicago: University of Chicago Press, 1984), 3:486. An undated entry in John Steele's journal ([frame 113], MS D 1847, folder 2, vol. 1, CHL) may refer to exploring the country he described to Frémont: "Amongst they many m[i]ssions that I have taken on my own responsibillity exploring the Mountains and the valleys before bothe on the Rio Virgan and the Muddy."
75 Nevins, *Fremont*, 637.
76 Carvalho, *Incidents*, 140.
77 Bean, *Autobiography of George Washington Bean* (Salt Lake City: Utah Printing, 1945), 95.
78 "Brigham Young's Infamy," dateline June 28, 1877, *New York Herald,* July 6, 1877, 2/4–5.
79 "Mormon Rascality!," *New York Herald,* May 10, 1877, 4/1–2.
80 "Brigham Young's Infamy," July 6, 1877, 2/4–5.
81 John Steele to Catherine Campbell Steele, July 30, 1877, box 1, folder 12, Steele Collection, LTPSC.
82 Badger, journal entry, September 26, 1905, MSS 1298, Carlos Ashby Badger Papers, LTPSC.
83 Charles "Chas" Peterson to Dr. Wesley Larsen, May 11, 1998; copy in author's possession. See also "Mormon Rascality!," *Salt Lake Tribune,* May 18, 1877, 3 (reprinted from the *New York Herald*, May 12, 1877); Lee, *Mormonism Unveiled*, 279, 281; Calvin C. Pendleton to George A. Smith, January 16, 1861, box 6, folder 2, G. A. Smith Papers, CHL.
84 Steele, "Extracts from the Journal of John Steele," 26.

85 "Among the Mormons," *New York Herald*, June 13, 1877; quoted in *Salt Lake Tribune*, July 8, 1877, 2/35.

86 S[ingleton] Husted, M.D., to Hon. Mr. [Gen. John G.] Black, Commissioner of Pensions, August 28, 1887, J. Steele pension file [frames 193–94], Utah State Archives, Salt Lake City.

87 Lunt, journal entries, April 6 (6/55) and April 13, 1852 (8/57), "Life of Henry Lunt," BYU typescript, LTPSC; Evelyn K. Jones, *Henry Lunt Biography* (Provo, UT: BYU Family History Copy Library, 1996), 67, quoting James Whittaker Sr.'s journal entry of December 21, 1851.

88 Charles C. Rich to Brigham Young, January 2, May 3, and July 5, 1856, box 41, folder 2, MS 2183, Brigham Young Correspondence, CHL. For Sherwood's trip to California see [untitled], *DN*, December 25, 1852, 2/5. Thomas D. Brown, journal entry, June 25, 1854, *Journal of the Southern Indian Mission: Diary of Thomas D. Brown* (Logan: Utah State University, 1972), 70.

89 Lunt, journal entries, May 23–24, 1851 (17/66, 18/67) and June 6–7, 1852 (25/74–26/75), "Life of Henry Lunt," BYU typescript, LTPSC.

90 J. C. L. [Calvin] Smith to George A. Smith, February 21, 1855, MS 1322, G. A. Smith Papers, CHL.

91 Gary H. Callister called this little pamphlet of poetry "The Blue Book"; it's in box 1, folder 4, Steele Collection, LTPSC; see also Lunt, journal entry, July 24, 1852 (38/87–39/88), "Life of Henry Lunt," LTPSC. Steele wrote, "Or ~~And~~ blast" and "articles than ~~Californe's~~". I have eliminated the crossed-out words.

92 Thomas D. Brown, journal entries, April 29 and May 1, 1854 (14–16), March 18, 1855 (117–19), *Journal of the Southern Indian Mission*.

93 Lunt, journal entries, November 13–14, 1852 (66/115) and November 17, 1852 (67/116–68/117), "Life of Henry Lunt," BYU typescript, LTPSC.

94 John Steele, journal entry, undated [frames 105–6], MS D 1847, folder 2, vol. 1, CHL. "Acts And Resolutions Passed at the Second Session Of The Utah Territorial Legislature," *DN*, January 21, 1853, 2/1–3; Shirts and Shirts, *A Trial Furnace*, 215. For a heavily documented and definitive—as well as interesting—study of Utah iron mining, with a deep look at Iron County, see Evan Y. Jones and York F. Jones, *Iron Mining and Manufacturing in Utah* (Cedar City, UT: Southern Utah University Press, 2019).

95 Lunt, journal entry, November 19, 1852 (68/117), "Life of Henry Lunt," BYU typescript, LTPSC.

96 Martineau, journal entry, February 5, 1854, *Uncommon Common Pioneer*, 28.

97 Martineau, journal entry, December 25, 1852, *Uncommon Common Pioneer*, 20 (the entry is partly reminiscent); John C. L. [Calvin] Smith, January 3, 1853, published as "Iron County," *DN*, February 5, 1853, 2/3–4.

98 *DN*: "Mormon Battalion," January 18, 1855, 3/5; "Mormon Battalion," January 25, 1855, 3/6. John Steele to George A. Smith, February 16, 1855, and John Calvin Lazelle Smith to George A. Smith, February 19, 1855 (both in MS 1322,

G. A. Smith Papers, CHL) included the invitation, and so Steele's letter. A copy of the invitation is in the Dame diaries, 1850–1858, William H. Dame Papers, MIC A 13, Utah Historical Society, Salt Lake City.

99 George A. Smith to J. C. L. [Calvin] Smith, February 28, 1855, Historian's Office letterpress copybooks, 1854–1861, 105, CHL.

100 Lt. Gen. D. H. Wells, [November 29 or December 29], 1854, Nauvoo Legion Records, 1851–1870, letterpress copybook, 1853 October–1870 March, CHL. The March 14, 1855, commission disappeared after it was printed twice in the *Millard County (UT) Chronicle*, in Frank A. Beckwith Sr., "Valuable Relics Found in Old Trunk, July 24, 1930, 1/1, 8/4; and "From the Journal of Elder John Steele (continued)," September 1, 1932, 4/1–4.

Chapter 7

1 B. P. Wulffenstejn [later anglicized to Wulffenstein] to Editor, *Deseret News*, June 28, 1886; published July 21, 1886, p. 431, col. 1.

2 John Steele, journal entry, undated [frames 99–101], folder 2, vol. 1, MS 1847, CHL; "Letter from John D. Lee," dated Parowan, February 20, 1852, *DN*, April 3, 1852, 3/2–3.

3 "Letter from John D. Lee," *DN*, April 3, 1852, 3/2–3; John Steele, journal entry, undated [frames 99–101], MS D 1847, folder 2, vol. 1, CHL.

4 Autobiographical fragment, p. 2, written on the back of a letter dated August 12, 1891, from the Commissioner of Bureau of Pensions to John Steele (box 2, folder 6, Vault MSS 528, John Steele Collection, 1847–1936, L. Tom Perry Special Collections, Harold B. Lee Library, Brigham Young University, Provo, UT (hereafter Steele Collection, LTPSC); John Steele, journal entry, undated [frames 99–101], MS D 1847, folder 2, vol. 1, CHL.

5 John Steele, journal entry, undated [frames 99–101], MS 1847, folder 2, vol. 1, CHL.

6 "Letter from John D. Lee," *DN*, April 3, 1852, 3/2–3. See also the articles in *Utah Historical Quarterly* 39, no. 2 (Spring 1971) by Catherine S. Fowler and Don D. Fowler, "Notes on the History of the Southern Paiutes and Western Shoshonis," 101; and C. Gregory Crampton, "Indian Country," 91.

7 "Letter from John D. Lee," *DN*, April 3, 1852, 3/2–3.

8 John C. L. [Calvin] Smith and John Steele, June 25, 1852, "Letter from Parowan," *DN*, August 7, 1852, 1/5–6.

9 John Steele, journal entry, [frame 113], folder 2, vol. 1, MS D 1847, CHL.

10 Jesse Nathaniel Smith, journal entry, September 10, 1858, *Six Decades in the Early West: The Journal of Jesse Nathaniel Smith* (Provo, UT: Jesse N. Smith Family Assn., 1970), 32.

11 Angus M. Woodbury, "A History of Southern Utah and Its National Parks," *Utah Historical Quarterly* 12, nos. 3–4 (July–October 1944): 142–43; Wayne K. Hinton, *The Dixie National Forest* (Cedar City, UT: U.S. Department of

Agriculture, Forest Service, Intermountain Region, Dixie National Forest, U.S. Government Printing Office, 1987), 22.

12 Phil Robinson, *Sinners and Saints: A Tour Across the States, and Round Them: with Three Months Among the Mormons* (Boston: Roberts Brothers, 1883), 219. Robinson gives an enthusiastic description of Long Valley's Orderville.

13 Meeks, "Journal of Priddy Meeks," typescript by Beth Bringhurst of the Utah Historical Records Survey, WPA, 1937, 111–13.

14 Meeks, "Journal of Priddy Meeks," 111–13.

15 Smith and Steele, June 25, 1852, "Letter from Parowan," *DN,* August 7, 1852, 1/5–6.

16 Smith and Steele, June 25, 1852, "Letter from Parowan."

17 Smith and Steele, June 25, 1852, "Letter from Parowan"; Angus M. Woodbury, *A History of Southern Utah and Its National Parks* (n.p.: self-published, 1950), 124–26, 141–43. Steele also recalled in his journal a trip he took with John L. Smith and Tarlton Lewis to explore the Sevier area in October 1851 and "ware gone about 12 days," visiting the camp Parley P. Pratt called "Smoke Hollow." Steele averred that Heber C. Kimball said it was "Hell & the devil" when he passed over it later (John Steele, journal entries, [frames 101–5], MS 1847, folder 2, vol. 1, CHL). Pratt's company was in this area in December 1849 (William B. Smart and Donna T. Smart, *Over the Rim: The Parley P. Pratt Exploring Expedition to Southern Utah, 1849–50* [Logan: Utah State University, 1999], 39).

18 George Washington Brimhall, *The Workers of Utah* (1889; reprinted, Washington, DC: Lincoln Press, ca. 1960s), 16; undated letter from John C. L. [Calvin] Smith to the Editor, *DN*, March 16, 1854, 3/2–3; Young Elizabeth Steele Stapley, personal history questionnaire, 1936, in Isaac E. Diehl, "Pioneer Personal History Questionnaire," p. 3, WPA Biographies, B-289, box 10, Utah Historical Society, Salt Lake City.

19 See "Robert Campbell's Ute Dictionary" in Smart and Smart, *Over the Rim*, 249–51; John Steele, "Utah Indian Language," box 1, folder 3, Steele Collection, LTPSC. His poetry notebook with the Native American words is in box 3, folder 6.

20 Brimhall, *Workers of Utah*, 16.

21 George A. Smith to Brigham Young, July 2, 1851, box 42, folder 4, MS 2183, Brigham Young Correspondence, CHL.

22 George A. Smith, November 5, 1851, "Mr. Editor," *DN,* November 29, 1851, 3/5–6.

23 John D. Lee to Willard Richards, February 5, 1853, *DN*, March 19, 1853, 2/3–4; Joel H. Johnson to John Lyman Smith, January 22, 1853, G. A. Smith Papers, MS 1322, CHL.

24 James H. Martineau, "Chief Walker's Methods," *Deseret Weekly News,* December 26, 1896, 60/2–3, 61/1; "Santiago" [James H. Martineau] ("Frontier Life in Utah," *Contributor* 10, no. 11 [September 1889]: 405–6) calls the

Native leader "Walker," but this version is as much folklore as history; Luella Dalton Adams, *History of the Iron County Mission: Parowan, Utah* (n.p., n.d.), 76 (Adams's informant was Richard Heber Benson); John D. Lee to Willard Richards, undated, *DN*, March 19, 1853, 2/3–4. A Martineau letter to John Steele dated May 10, 1903, gives Green Jacket the correct name (extract in box 2, folder 10, Steele Collection, LTPSC).

25 John Steele to Brigham Young, April 10, 1853, box 23, folder 7, MS 2183, Brigham Young Correspondence, CHL.

26 Joel H. Johnson to John Lyman Smith, January 22, 1853, MS 1322, G. A. Smith Papers, CHL.

27 Martineau, journal entry, December 2, 1852, and the following entry, dated only "December," *An Uncommon Common Pioneer* (Provo, UT: BYU Religious Study Center, 2008), 20; Johnson to Smith, January 22, 1853, MS 1322, G. A. Smith Papers, CHL.

28 Parowan Conference Minutes, September 10–11, 1853, box 1, folder 24, CR 100 589, CHL (clerk James H. Martineau). According to Lunt, fifty-eight were baptized (journal entries, October 18 [106/57] and October 21, 1852 [107/58], "Life of Henry Lunt," BYU typescript, L. Tom Perry Special Collections, Harold B. Lee Library); "Iron County," *DN*, March 5, 1853, 3/2–3.

29 Adams, *Iron County Mission*, 76.

30 Joel H. Johnson to George A. Smith, January 22, 1853, MS 1322, G. A. Smith Papers, CHL.

31 Adams, *Iron County Mission*, 76.

32 "Young Elizabeth Steele Stapley," copied by Virginia M. Lee, WPA, Utah Section, Biographical Sketches, box 10, Sn–V, Utah Historical Society, Salt Lake City; "Mrs. Young Elizabeth Stapley, First White Child Born in Utah, Dies at Hurricane," *Washington County News*, April 7, 1938, 1/1–2, 6/4–5. If she had only one brother at the time, this visit was before April 6, 1853.

33 "Interesting from Utah," *New York Times*, July 8, 1858, 2/5. Walkara was dead by then so the reporter was relying on the reports of one or more other people.

34 John Steele, "The Late William Laney," *Deseret Weekly News,* January 23, 1892, 159/2. In the body of the story his surname is spelled "Leany."

35 Leany, "William Leany Reminiscences, 1888," 18–19, MS 23134, CHL.

36 Johnson, "Autobiographical Sketch of Nephi Johnson," 8–9, MS 23835, CHL.

37 John Steele to Brigham Young, April 10, 1853, box 23, folder 7, CHL.

38 Steele to Young, April 10, 1853, box 23, folder 7, CHL.

39 Brigham Young to John C. L. [Calvin] Smith and John Steel [*sic*], April 14, 1853, Presidency of Iron County, box 13, folder 11, MS 1234 1, CHL; Martineau, journal entry, April 10, 1853, *Uncommon Common Pioneer,* 21–22.

40 "Territory of Utah: Proclamation by the Governor," *DN*, April 30, 1853, 3/5–6; William Wall, "To the Editor of the Deseret News," May 28, 1853, *DN*, May 31, 1853, 3/3–4.

41 D. B. Huntington to "Mr. Editor," May 1853, *DN*, May 28, 1853, 3/4; Mary

Aikens Smith to John Smith, June 26, 1853, box 1, folder 10, MS 1326, John Smith Papers, CHL.

42 Howard A. Christy, "The Walker War: Defense and Conciliation as Strategy," *Utah Historical Quarterly* 47, no. 4 (Fall 1979): 395–420.

43 Gwinn Harris Heap, *Central Route to the Pacific, from the Valley of the Mississippi to California* (Philadelphia: Lippincott, Grambo, 1854), 90–92.

44 Christy, "Walker War," 405.

45 George A. Smith to Daniel H. Wells, Post Orders of Parowan, September 3, 1853, Utah Territorial Militia Records, series 2210, reel 5, doc. 357, Utah State Archives, Salt Lake City.

46 Lunt, journal entry, November 14, 1852 (66/115), "Life of Henry Lunt," BYU typescript, LTPSC.

47 Mary Aikens Smith to John Smith, June 26, 1853, box 1, folder 10, MS 1326, John Smith Papers, CHL.

48 "Th. Gr. [Anonymous]," "Ein Ritt Nach Californien," in *Das Buch Der Welt*, translated by "TSC," in Michael W. Homer, ed., *On the Way to Somewhere Else: European Sojourners in the Mormon West, 1834-1930* (Spokane, WA: Arthur H. Clark, 2006), 264.

49 "President Young's Visit," *DN*, June 28, 1851, 282/3, 283/1–3, 4/1–3, 284/1; Matthew Carruthers to Editor, *DN*, November 18, 1851, "Local Correspondence," December 13, 1851, 3/1–2; Christy, "Walker War," 407–8.

50 John D. Lee to Brigham Young, September 24, 1853, box 23, folder 4, MS 2183, Brigham Young Correspondence, CHL; Martineau, journal entries, August 7–10, 1853, *Uncommon Common Pioneer*, 24.

51 Brown, journal entry, June 25, 1854, *Journal of the Southern Indian Mission* (Logan: Utah State University, 1972), 70.

52 Martineau, journal entries, August 7–10 and 17, 1853, in *Uncommon Common Pioneer*, 24.

53 George A. Smith to Daniel H. Wells, Post Orders of Parowan, September 3, 1853, Utah Territorial Militia Records, 156–57, 357, Utah State Archives, Salt Lake City.

54 "Fines assessed by the officers at the Court Martial held in Cedar Fort from July the 27th A.D. 1853 to Novr the 15th A.D. 1853," Utah Territorial Militia Records, series 2210, reel 8, folder 50, doc. 3017, Utah State Archives, Salt Lake City.

55 Daniel H. Wells to Lt. Col. James A. Little, August 25, 1853, Utah Territorial Militia Records, series 2210, reel 5 doc. 355, Utah State Archives, Salt Lake City.

56 "Tabernacle, G. S. L. City," *DN*, October 15, 1853, 1/4–6, 2/1–2.

57 "Parowan Conference Minutes Sept. 10–11, 1853," box 1, folder 24, CR 100 589, CHL.

58 "Parowan Conference Minutes Sept. 10–11, 1853," box 1, folder 24, CR 100 589, CHL.

59 Josephine Dart Green, as told to Eleanore Sterns Vener, "Holding Down

the Trail: A Short History of the John Dart Family" (1993), ed. Russell L. McClintick Jr., posted on FamilySearch.org.

60 John Steele to George A. Smith, November 7–8, 1854, MS 1322, G. A. Smith Papers, CHL; partially published—without the reference to the dissenters—in "Parowan, Iron County: Extracts of a letter from Elder John Steele to Elder G. A. Smith," *DN*, November 30, 1854, 3/4–5.

61 "Minutes of a Conference Held at Cedar City, Iron County, November 20th," *DN,* March 2, 1854, 2/6.

62 Thomas D. Brown, journal entry, June 25, 1854, *Journal of the Southern Indian Mission*, 70.

63 J. C. L. [Calvin] Smith to "Editor of the News," *DN,* March 16, 1854, 3/2–3.

64 "The President then nominated Jesse N. Smith. William C. McGregor objected. He was asked his objections, he said, 'We have had some of Jesse's rule while Brother Dame was in prison and it was tyrannical'" (Fish, *Autobiography of Joseph Fish* [n.p.: Lulu, 2009], 154); William Campbell McGregor, "Parowan's Anniversary," January 14, 1896, *Deseret Weekly News*, January 23, 1897, 179/1–2 (the year is misprinted "1896" in the newspaper story); for a transcript see box 3, folder 29, Steele Collection, LTPSC.

65 John Steele, journal entry, [frame 96], MS D 1847, folder 2, vol. 1, CHL.

66 Steele, "Extracts from the Journal of John Steele," *Utah Historical Quarterly* 6, no. 1 (January 1933): 25.

Chapter 8

1 James H. Martineau to George A. Smith, May 30, 1855, box 5, folder 7, MS 1322, G. A. Smith Papers, CHL; portions of this letter were published as "Iron County," *Deseret News* (*DN*), July 11, 1855, p. 144, col. 2; "A Blessing by Georg[e] A Smith upon the head of John Steel being set apart on the Los Vagus Mission May 21/55," box 3, folder 2, Vault MSS 528, John Steele Collection, 1847–1936, L. Tom Perry Special Collections, Harold B. Lee Library, Brigham Young University, Provo (hereafter Steele Collection, LTPSC).

2 Steele, "Extracts from the Journal of John Steele," *Utah Historical Quarterly* 6, no. 1 (January 1933): 27.

3 James H. Martineau to George A. Smith, May 30, 1855, MS 1322, G. A. Smith Papers, CHL; portions of this letter were published in *DN*: "Grasshoppers," June 27, 1855, 125/2–3, and "Iron County," July 11, 1855, 144/2; George A. Smith, May 14, 1855, "Home Correspondence," *DN*, May 30, 1855, 92/3.

4 John Steele, journal entry, May 29, 1855 [frame 114], folder 2, vol. 1, MS 1847, CHL.

5 Will Bagley, *Blood of the Prophets: Brigham Young and the Massacre at Mountain Meadows* (Norman: University of Oklahoma Press, 2002), 47.

6 John Steele, journal entry, June 1, 1855 [frame 115], MS 1847, folder 2, vol. 1, CHL.

7 George W. Bean, journal entry, June 4, 1855, "The Journal of George W. Bean:

Las Vegas Springs, New Mexico Territory, 1856–57," *Nevada Historical Society Quarterly* 15 (Fall 1972): 6.

8 John Steele, journal entry, June 3, 1855 [frame 117], MS 1847, folder 2, vol. 1, CHL.

9 John Steele, "Utah Indian Language," December 4, 1851, box 1, folder 3, Steele Collection, LPTSC.

10 John Steele, journal entry, June 2, 1855 [frame 116], MS 1847, folder 2, vol. 1, CHL.

11 John Steele to George A. Smith, July 25, 1855, MS 1322, G. A. Smith Papers, CHL; partially published in "Elders' Correspondence," *DN*, September 26, 1855, 232/1.

12 John Steele to George A. Smith, October 1, 1855, MS 1322, G. A. Smith Papers, CHL.

13 Richard Francaviglia, *Mapmakers of New Zion: A Cartographic History of Mormonism* (Salt Lake City: University of Utah Press, 2015), 102; Steele, retained copy of a form for "The History of Utah," box 2, folder 6, Steele Collection, LTPSC.

14 Francaviglia, *Mapmakers*, 102–5.

15 John Steele to George A. Smith, July 25, 1855, MS 1322, G. A. Smith Papers, CHL; partially published in "Elders' Correspondence," *DN*, September 26, 1855, 232/1.

16 Lorenzo Brown, journal entry, June 23, 1856, *Journal of Lorenzo Brown, 1823–1900* (n.p.: self-published, n.d.), 69.

17 Frank A. Beckwith Sr., "Moki Bread Made of Mesquite 70 Years Old," *Millard County (UT) Chronicle*, August 18, 1932, 4/2; the typesetter wrote, "to be a of [*sic*]"; I have corrected the word order. Beckwith identifies this as "Moki bread" but the Moki/Hopi made their piki bread of blue cornmeal. Mesquite bread was a Mojave (Paiute) dish, and the time frame Beckwith gives is when Steele was in Las Vegas. For Steele's enthusiasm for mesquite see "Another Shrub for Hedges," *DN*, February 27, 1856, 405/3.

18 Gary Topping, ed., *Gila Monsters and Red-Eyed Rattlesnakes: Don Maguire's Arizona Trading Expeditions, 1876–1879* (Salt Lake City: University of Utah Press, 1997), 118.

19 William Bringhurst to Brigham Young, July 10, 1855, box 23, folder 20, CR 1234 1, MS 2183, Brigham Young Correspondence, CHL.

20 Reddick N. Allred, journal entry, June 24, 1855, https://myallredfamily.com/front-page/what-states/utah/family-histories/redick-newton-allreds-diary.

21 John Steele to George A. Smith, July 25, 1855, MS 1322, G. A. Smith Papers, CHL.

22 Martha C. Knack, *Boundaries Between: The Southern Paiutes, 1775–1995* (Lincoln: University of Nebraska Press, 2004), 21.

23 John Steele, journal entry, June 29, 1855 [frame 122], MS 1847, folder 2, vol. 1, CHL.

24 William Bringhurst to Brigham Young, August 6, 1855, box 23, folder 20, CR 1234 1, MS 2183, Brigham Young Correspondence, CHL.

25 "Los Vegas," *DN*, July 27, 1855, 157/2; Bringhurst's letter was dated July 10, 1855.

26 John Steele, journal entry, June 29, 1855 [frame 122], MS 1847, folder 2, vol. 1, CHL.

27 Lorenzo Brown, journal entry, August 24, 1856, *Journal of Lorenzo Brown, 1823–1900* (n.p.: self-published, n.d.), 72; Thomas D. Brown, journal entry, July 1855, *Journal of the Southern Indian Mission: Diary of Thomas D. Brown* (Logan: Utah State University, 1972), 132.

28 John Steele to George A. Smith, July 25, 1855, MS 1322, G. A. Smith Papers, CHL.

29 John Steele to George A. Smith, October 1, 1855, MS 1322, G. A. Smith Papers, CHL.

30 John Steele to George A. Smith, October 1, 1855, and George W. Bean to George A. Smith, December 11, 1855, MS 1322, G. A. Smith Papers, CHL. An apocryphal story claims Brigham Young told Steele, "Now brother John, we want the friendship of the Lamanites; Ephraim is the ax of the Lord. If you see a good looking girl, take her for a wife from the tribe." "Yes, yes," his wife Catherine is said to have responded, "and Brother Brigham, you set the example; when you take a squaw, John will. Just set the example" (Frank A. Beckwith, "Shameful Friday: A Critical Study of the Mountain Meadow Massacre," 363; copy in author's possession). Beckwith does not give the source of this story, but his major informant about John Steele was John's grandson Mahonri "Hon" Steele. However, he also talked to Hon's brother John Edward Steele as well as their sister, Cathryn Steele Riding. Will Bagley (*The Whites Want Every Thing* [Norman, OK: Arthur H. Clark, 2019], 159) mentions that Mormon men desiring to marry Native women were asked in turn for Mormon women to marry Native men.

31 John Steele, journal entry, on or after September 20, 1855 [frame 131], MS 1847, folder 2, vol. 1, CHL.

32 William Spencer Covert [and John Steele, who wrote the letter] to Brigham Young, October 11, 1855, box 23, folder 21C, MS 2183, Brigham Young Correspondence, CHL.

33 John Steele to George A. Smith, October 1, 1855, MS 1322, G. A. Smith Papers, CHL.

34 Covert [and Steele] to Young, October 11, 1855, box 23, folder 21C, MS 2183, Brigham Young Correspondence, CHL; Knack, *Boundaries*, 22–23.

35 Samuel Thompson to Brigham Young, January 15, 1857, box and folder not given, CR 1234 1, MS 2183, Brigham Young Correspondence, CHL.

36 Covert [and Steele] to Young, October 11, 1855, box 23, folder 21C, MS 2183, Brigham Young Correspondence, CHL.

37 Will Bagley, *Blood of the Prophets: Brigham Young and the Massacre at Mountain Meadows* (Norman: University of Oklahoma Press, 2002), 49.

38 Copied into the Las Vegas mission record book, September 14, 1855 (29), LR 5691 21, CHL; the letter from Young was dated August 23, 1855. George A. Smith to John Steele, August 28, 1855, box 3, folder 2, Steele Collection, LTPSC; the first baptism of a Native, thirty-year-old Chief "Almy" Oantump, is noted on this letter in Steele's hand.

39 Las Vegas mission record book, November 17, 1855, LR 5691 21, CHL, quoting letter from Brigham Young dated October 30.

40 Las Vegas mission record book, May 27, 1856, LR 5691 21, CHL. Steele was then presiding over the mission.

41 John Steele to George A. Smith, October 1, 1855, MS 1322, G. A. Smith Papers, CHL.

42 Las Vegas mission record book, July 4, 1855 (15), LR 5691 21, CHL.

43 John Steele, journal entry, July 21, 1855 [frame 127], MS 1847, folder 2, vol. 1, CHL.

44 John Steele, journal entry, ca. September 14, 1855 [frame 130], MS 1847, folder 2, vol. 1, CHL.

45 John Steele to Catherine Campbell Steele, October 13, 1855, box 2, folder 10, Steele Collection, LTPSC.

46 John Steele to Catherine Campbell Steele, October 13, 1855, box 2, folder 10, Steele Collection, LTPSC.

47 John Steele to George A. Smith, October 1, 1855, MS 1322, G. A. Smith Papers, CHL.

48 John Steele, journal entry, October 21, 1855 [frame 131], MS 1847, folder 2, vol. 1, CHL; John Steele, autobiographical scrap numbered "3," box 3, folder 3, Steele Collection, LTPSC; Las Vegas mission record book, September 19, 1856, LR 5691 21, CHL.

49 Las Vegas mission record book, September 14, 1855 (29); Young's letter was dated August 23, 1855: both in LR 5691 21, CHL. William Bringhurst to Brigham Young, November 7, 1855, box 23, folder 20, CR 1234 1, MS 2183, Brigham Young Correspondence, CHL.

50 John Steele to George A. Smith, October 1, 1855, MS 1322, G. A. Smith Papers, CHL; John Steele, journal entry, November 17, 1855 [frame 132], MS 1847, folder 2, vol. 1, CHL.

51 John Steele to George A. Smith, December 2, 1855, MS 1322, G. A. Smith Papers, CHL.

52 Brigham Young, January 3, 1856, to John "State Esq.," retained draft, box 17, folder 20, CR 1234 1, CHL; a notation on the outside reads "Copy | Fillmore | Jan[y] 3 1856 | From Brigham Young | to John State [Steele] Esq. | wants to be exonerated from his mission." "John State" is an error. The draft is marked up and partly illegible.

53 Joseph Fish, *The Autobiography of Joseph Fish* (n.p.: Lulu, 2009), 65.

54 John Steele, journal entry, uncertain date [frame 133], MS D 1847, folder 2, vol. 1, CHL; William Bringhurst to Brigham Young, February 9, 1856, box 24, folder 15, MS 2183, Brigham Young Correspondence, CHL.

55 Las Vegas mission record book, April 3, 5–6, 10, 12, 1856, LR 5691 21, CHL.
56 Las Vegas mission record book, December 1, 1855; April 13 and May 1 and 4, 1856, LR 5691 21, CHL.
57 John Steele, journal entry, on or after July 21, 1855 [frame 128], MS 1847, folder 2, vol. 1, CHL; Samuel Augustus Mitchell's *A Few Words about Mitchell's New Series of School Geography* (Philadelphia: n.p., n.d.) was in Steele's library when he died, but Mitchell wrote a lot of geography books, beginning as early as 1834, and it's uncertain if Steele's surviving copy is the one he had in Las Vegas. "Peter Parley" was a pseudonym used by Samuel Griswold Goodrich; Steele is referring to Goodrich's *History of All Nations* (1852).
58 Las Vegas mission record book, August 12, 1855 (21), LR 5691 21, CHL.
59 Las Vegas mission record book, June 22, 1855 (13), LR 5691 21, CHL.
60 Lorenzo Brown, journal entry, June 14, 1856, *Journal of Lorenzo Brown, 1823–1900* (n.p.: self-published, n.d.), 68.
61 Las Vegas mission record book, April 20, 1856, LR 5691 21, CHL; Brigham Young to William Bringhurst, March 3, 1856; Young to "Johnathan" C. Wright, June 13, 1856; Young to William B. Lindsay, June 20, 1856; Young to J. C. Wright, June 23, 1856; Young "To All Whom It May Concern," July 7, 1856 (endorsing Nathaniel V. Jones); Young to Isaac Grundy, July 7, 1856; Young to Gilbert Summe, July 7, 1856; Young to Charles C. Rich, July 10, 1856; Young to Nathaniel V. Jones, September 3, 1856 (Young sent Bringhurst a letter the same day); all in the Brigham Young letterpress copybooks, CR 1234 1, box 3, folder 2. John Steele to Catherine Campbell Steele, April 23, 1856, box 1, folder 12, Steele Collection, LTPSC.
62 John Steele to Brigham Young, April 23, 1856, box 25, folder 8, MS 2183, Brigham Young Correspondence, CHL.
63 Brigham Young to John Steele, May 30, 1856, box 3, folder 3, Steele Collection, LTPSC; also in folder 1, MS D 2683, CHL.
64 Quoted in Nelson Winch Green and Mary Ettie V. Smith [Marriette "Mary Etta" Coray Henderson Jones], *Mormonism: It's* [sic] *Rise, Progress and Present Condition* (Hartford, CT: Belknap and Bliss, 1872), 182.
65 Lunt, journal entry, March 4, 1853 (107/156), "Life of Henry Lunt," BYU typescript, LTPSC.
66 Las Vegas mission record book, May 6–7, 1856, LR 5691 21, CHL; John Steele, journal entry, on or after May 6, 1856 [frame 135], MS 1847, folder 2, vol. 1, CHL.
67 John Steele, journal entry, on or after May 6, 1856 [frames 135–36], MS 1847, folder 2, vol. 1, CHL.
68 John Steele, journal entry, on or after June 15, 1856 [frames 136–37], MS 1847, folder 2, vol. 1, CHL; Lorenzo Brown, journal entry, July 7, 1856, *Journal of Lorenzo Brown, 1823–1900* (n.p.: self-published, n.d.), 69.
69 John Steele, journal entry, on or after June 15, 1856 [frame 136], MS 1847, folder 2, vol. 1, CHL.

70 Samuel Thompson to Brigham Young, December 16, 1856, box 25, folder 8, CR 1234 1, MS 2183, Brigham Young Correspondence, CHL.
71 Las Vegas mission record book, July 1, 1855 (14), LR 5691 21, CHL; John Steele, journal entry dated September 14, 1855, but the entry says events happened "yesterday" [frame 130], MS 1847, folder 2, vol. 1, CHL.
72 Las Vegas mission record book, July 30, 1855 (19), LR 5691 21, CHL; John Steele, journal entry, August 6, 1855 [frame 129], MS 1847, folder 2, vol. 1, CHL.
73 Lorenzo Brown, journal entry, August 11, 1856, *Journal*, 71.
74 Brigham Young to William Bringhurst, October 13, 1856, MS 2183, Brigham Young Correspondence, CHL.
75 Las Vegas mission record book, September 19, 1856, LR 5691 21, CHL; this entry is the main source for the details of the showdown described on the following pages.
76 Lorenzo Brown, journal entry, July 20, 1856, *Journal*, 70.
77 Las Vegas mission record book, September 19, 1856, LR 5691 21, CHL.
78 Miles Anderson to Brigham Young, August 23, 1856, box 24, folder 15, CR 1234 1, MS 2183, Brigham Young Correspondence, CHL.
79 Las Vegas mission record book, August 21, 1856, LR 5691 21, CHL.
80 Las Vegas mission record book, September 19, 1856, LR 5691 21, CHL.
81 Las Vegas mission record book, September 19, 1856, LR 5691 21, CHL; Edson Barney to Nathaniel V. Jones, September 21, 1856, box 24, folder 14, CR 1234 1, CHL.
82 Thelma C. Anderson, *Workman Family History* (Salt Lake City: Publishers Press, 1962), 83–84.
83 Las Vegas mission record book, September 19, 1856, LR 5691 21, CHL; there is an ink splotch that, though it has been wiped off, makes reading the following words somewhat difficult: "they wished" and, next line down, what I read as "such miserable." I'm certain of the word "such" and of ". . . rable" but not so sure of "miser"—the word seems longer.
84 Las Vegas mission record book, September 19, 1856, LR 5691 21, CHL.
85 Las Vegas mission record book, September 19, 1856, LR 5691 21, CHL.
86 Las Vegas mission record book, September 19, 1856, LR 5691 21, CHL.
87 Las Vegas mission record book, September 19, 1856, LR 5691 21, CHL.
88 Las Vegas mission record book, July 20, 1856, LR 5691 21, CHL.
89 Gary H. Callister called this little pamphlet of poetry "The Blue Book" (box 1, folder 4, Steele Collection, LTPSC).
90 Las Vegas mission record book, September 19, 1856, LR 5691 21, CHL.
91 Las Vegas mission record book, September 19, 1856, LR 5691 21, CHL.
92 Las Vegas mission record book, September 21, 1856, LR 5691 21, CHL.
93 Brigham Young to William Bringhurst, December 1856, MS 2183, Brigham Young Correspondence, CHL.
94 Lorenzo Brown, journal entry, October 7, 1856, *Journal*, 74.

95 Samuel Thompson to Brigham Young, March 20, 1857, box and folder not given, CR 1234 1, MS 2183, Brigham Young Correspondence, CHL.

96 "A Blessing by Georg[e] A Smith upon the head of John Steel," box 3, folder 2, Steele Collection, LTPSC.

97 John Steele, journal entry, undated [frame 139], MS 1847, folder 2, vol. 1, CHL.

Chapter 9

1 *Deseret News* (*DN*): James H. Martineau to Lt. General Daniel H. Wells, July 14, 1856, published as "Iron County," July 23, 1856, p. 157, col. 3; J. H. Martineau to Editor, September 10, 1856, p. 216, cols. 1–2.

2 John Steele, journal entry, undated [frame 139], folder 2, vol. 1, MS 1847, CHL.

3 Gene A. Sessions, *Mormon Thunder: A Documentary History of Jedediah Morgan Grant* (Urbana: University of Illinois Press, 1982), 207–9, 211–12.

4 "Iron County—Seventies' Conference," *DN*, January 14, 1857, 357/2–3.

5 Brigham Young to John Steele, March 18, 1857, box 4, folder 3, Brigham Young Letterbooks, vol. 3: 1857 April 1–June 10, CHL.

6 John Steele to Catherine Campbell Steele, February 17, 1878, box 1, folder 12, Vault MSS 528, John Steele Collection, 1847–1936, L. Tom Perry Special Collections, Harold B. Lee Library, Brigham Young University, Provo, UT (hereafter Steele Collection, LTPSC).

7 Caroline Keturah Parry Woolley, *"I would to God": A Personal History of Isaac Haight* (Cedar City, UT: Southern Utah University Press, 2009), 92–93; a speech allegedly given by Haight is presented that includes Steele's name, but it is unsourced.

8 James Henry Martineau, journal entries, August 6 and 8–9, 1857, *An Uncommon Common Pioneer* (Provo, UT: BYU Religious Study Center, 2008), 69–70; *DN*: J. V. Long, "Remarks by Elder George A. Smith, Bowery, Sunday Afternoon, September 13, 1857," 226/4, 227/1–3; James H. Martineau, "Correspondence: Trip to Santa Clara," September 23, 1857, 227/3–4.

9 Will Bagley, *Blood of the Prophets: Brigham Young and the Massacre at Mountain Meadows* (Norman: University of Oklahoma Press, 2002), 26.

10 John Doyle Lee, *Mormonism Unveiled* (St. Louis: M. E. Mason, 1891), 223–24; the accuracy of Lee's "confessions" is discussed by Janiece Johnson, *Convicting the Mormons: The Mountain Meadows Massacre in American Culture* (Chapel Hill: University of North Carolina Press, 2023), 125–29. Steele reportedly said it was "a fair account from his standpoint," but it was altered before it was published. Badger, journal entry, September 26, 1905, MSS 1298, Carlos Ashby Badger Papers, LTPSC; Rodney J. Badger, *Liahona and Iron Rod* (Bountiful, UT: Family History Publishers, 1985), 275–76 (September 26, 1905).

11 Joseph Fish, *Autobiography of Joseph Fish* (n.p.: Lulu, 2009), August 26–29, 1857 (53); Richard E. Turley Jr. and Barbara Jones Brown, *Vengeance Is Mine: The Mountain Meadows Massacre and Its Aftermath* (New York: Oxford University Press, 2023), 79, 89, 122–23, 133.
12 Susan E. Martineau to James Henry Martineau, May 30, 1858, folder 5, MS 4786, James Henry Martineau Collection, CHL.
13 Jesse Nathaniel Smith, journal entry, September 3, 1857, *Six Decades in the Early West: The Journal of Jesse Nathaniel Smith* (Provo, UT; Jesse N. Smith Family Assn., 1970), 27.
14 Bagley, *Blood of the Prophets*, 84.
15 *Salt Lake Tribune* (*SLT*): "The Lee Trial," July 30, 1875, 1/2; [untitled], August 5, 1875, 1/2–4.
16 Bagley, *Blood of the Prophets*, 114–15.
17 See the appendix for an annotated transcript of this letter.
18 Jesse Nathaniel Smith, journal entry, September 3, 1857, *Six Decades*, 27; Richard E. Turley Jr. and Ronald W. Walker, eds., *Mountain Meadows Massacre: The Andrew Jenson and Davis H. Morris Collections* (Provo and Salt Lake City: Brigham Young University Press and University of Utah Press, 2009), 274.
19 Jesse Nathaniel Smith to James Henry Martineau, January 2, 1856, folder 1, MS 4786, James Henry Martineau Collection, CHL.
20 Bagley, *Blood of the Prophets*, xv.
21 Turley and Walker, *Collections*. Essential reading for different views of the massacre are Bagley, *Blood of the Prophets;* and Ronald W. Walker, Richard E. Turley Jr., and Glen M. Leonard, *Massacre at Mountain Meadows* (Oxford: Oxford University Press, 2008).
22 Bagley, *Blood of the Prophets*, 116–17; Turley, "John D. Lee, First Trial"; Philip Klingensmith testimony, in Turley and Walker, *Collections,* First Trial, Complete Transcript, sec. 4, p. 582, in "The Mountain Meadows Massacre," https://mountainmeadowsmassacre.com/; Anna Jean Backus, *Mountain Meadows Witness: The Life and Times of Bishop Philip Klingensmith* (Spokane, WA: Arthur H. Clark, 1996), 112–14; Walker, Turley, and Leonard, *Massacre*, 132–33.
23 Turley, "John D. Lee, First Trial"; Elias Morris statement, February 2, 1892, in Turley and Walker, *Collections*, 245, 253; Christopher Jones Arthur, January 26, 1892, 80–83; Turley and Brown, *Vengeance*, 63.
24 "GILBERT MORSE. A Mountain Meadows Witness Whom the Court Needed Not. The Doings at Harmony Before and After the Massacre," *SLT*, September 28, 1876, 4/2.
25 Mary Steele Campbell (unrelated to John or Catherine Campbell Steele), January 24, 1892, statement in Turley and Walker, *Collections*, 43, 47; Turley and Brown, *Vengeance*, 275: anti-Mormon John H. Beadle talked to one Mormon who believed the massacre was committed "only for spoil." Brigham

Young's interpreter, Dimick B. Huntington, wrote in his journal that, as a war measure, Young "gave" permission to Shoshones to take cattle from California immigrants on the northern route to California (Bagley, *Blood of the Prophets*, 112–14).

26 William Fotheringham and Josiah Rogerson to John Steele, November 12, 1876, MS 3995 (not in the Steele Collection, but at LTPSC); M. M. Steele to Josiah Rogerson, July 29, 1877, folder 5, MS 20208, Ann R. Adams Papers, CHL; Fish, *Autobiography*, 64fn2. From the *Utonian* (Beaver): "That Petition," February 15, 1884, 2/2; "District Court," September 19, 1884, 3/3 (Josiah Rogerson indicted for a felony). Josiah Rogerson to John Taylor, February 27, 1884, CR 1 180, CHL; Rogerson copied or wrote a history of the 1850–51 pioneers to Parowan ([untitled], *Parowan Times*, September 27, 1916, 1/6), but I've not been able to locate the manuscript.

27 Josiah Rogerson, "John D. Lee: Miscellaneous Papers pertaining to his trials, guilt, and death," MS 2674, not paginated but actual pages 48–49, CHL.

28 Fish, *Autobiography*, 64.

29 Woolley, "*I would to God,*" is an apologia for Haight by one of his granddaughters.

30 J. V. Long, "Remarks by Elder George A. Smith, Bowery, Sunday Afternoon, September 13, 1857," *DN*, September 23, 1857, 227/2.

31 Martha C. Knack, *Boundaries Between: The Southern Paiutes, 1775–1995* (Lincoln: University of Nebraska Press, 2004), 78–80.

32 Turley and Brown, *Vengeance*, 29, 38.

33 "Minutes of a Conference Held at Cedar City, Iron County, November 20th," *DN,* March 2, 1854, 2/6.

34 Thomas D. Brown, journal entry, *Journal of the Southern Indian Mission* (Logan: Utah State University, 1972), 70–71; Lee, *Mormonism Unveiled*, 380.

35 Juanita Brooks, *The Mountain Meadows Massacre* (Norman: University of Oklahoma Press, 1974), 98. Mormon and federal Indian agent George W. Armstrong claimed the Paiute bands who were part of the massacre were "Quanra's [Kanarra's] band[,] Younggwitch's[, and] Tutsegabbot's" as well as the Moapa (Turley and Brown, *Vengeance*, 34, 187).

36 Bagley, *Blood of the Prophets*, 50–51, 140–155.

37 "Departure," *DN,* June 29, 1859, 132/3, incorrectly reports that fifteen children survived the massacre.

38 Mary S. Campbell statement, January 24, 1892, in Turley and Walker, *Collections*, 44–45, 49–50.

39 John Chatterley, statement, September 18, 1919, in Turley and Walker, *Collections*, 278.

40 Steele was set apart to the High Council on November 27, 1859; however, he was apparently still a major in the militia in 1857. James Henry Martineau, "Parowan Stake History Book," November 27, 1859, William H. Dame Papers, MIC A 13, Utah Historical Society, Salt Lake City; William H. Dame to

George A. Smith, November 29, 1859, box 5, folder 17, MS 1322, G. A. Smith Papers, CHL.

41 Joseph Chatterley to Andrew Jenson, September 18, 1919, in Turley and Walker, *Collections*, 278.

42 Elias Morris, statement to Andrew Jenson, February 2, 1892, in Turley and Walker, *Collections*, 248–49.

43 James H. Martineau, *Useful to the Church and Kingdom: The Journals of James H. Martineau* (Salt Lake City: Signature Books, 2023), 1:148–52.

44 In Turley and Walker, *Collections*: Joseph Chatterley to Andrew Jenson, September 18, 1919 (278); William Barton, January 25, 1892 (62–64).

45 Martineau, journal entry, January 24, 1856, *Uncommon Common Pioneer,* 51.

46 Daniel Sinclair Macfarlane, statement, January 27, 1892, in Turley and Walker, *Collections*, 90, 94, 110–13.

47 Walker et al., *Massacre*, 136.

48 Turley and Brown, *Vengeance*, 34.

49 Turley, "First Trial"; Turley, "John D. Lee, First Trial"; Elias Morris statement, February 2, 1892, in Turley and Walker, *Collections*, 245, 253.

50 Turley and Walker, *Collections*: John Chatterley to Andrew Jenson, September 18, 1919 (278); William Barton, January 25, 1892 (64, 70). Ellott (not Elliot) Willden also referred to the "Tan Bark Council" (January 29, 1892 [91, 221]), and Elias Morris identified himself as being there (January 28, 1892 [248–49]); Morris (February 2, 1892) doesn't mention the private consultation between Haight and Dame (248–49) and says this was the only Council meeting in Parowan he was aware of; Daniel Sinclair Macfarlane, statement, January 27, 1892 (94–119). Will Bagley advised me he had doubts the Tan Bark Council took place.

51 Conversation between Mahonri "Hon" M. Steele Jr. and Frank A. Beckwith reported in Frank A. Beckwith, "Shameful Friday: A Critical Study of the Mountain Meadows Massacre," unfinished partly paginated MS, insert A; copy in author's possession. I'm grateful to the late historian Will Bagley for sharing this document with me.

52 Frank Beckwith asked "Hon" Steele Jr., "Wasn't your grandfather [John Steele] 'disciplined' for talking sass to Haight once?," but that question wasn't directly answered, at least in Beckwith's notes ("Shameful Friday," insert A).

53 Carl A. Badger, journal entry, September 26, 1905, MSS 1298, Carlos Ashby Badger Papers, LTPSC. In analyzing Badger's report in my book *The Women: A Family Story* (Salt Lake City: University of Utah Press, 2016), I incorrectly assumed the Mahonri M. Steele whom Badger referred to was the senior rather than junior M. M. Steele.

54 Beckwith, "Shameful Friday," insert A.

55 "The California Mail," *DN*, December 19, 1857, 317/2.

56 "Brigham's Deposition," *SLT*, August 6, 1875, 2/1.

57 See "Snort's" statement in Brooks, *Mountain Meadows*, app. 2, 226–35.

58 Papers beginning, "1 | then Comes W[m] Strong residing in Salt Lake City in the 10 Ward," box 2, folder 8, Steele Collection, LTPSC; a transcript of this is in the appendix.
59 Walker et al., *Massacre*, 93–94.
60 There is no reference to this in Steele's incomplete English mission journals. He does refer to dispatching questions about Mountain Meadows from his wife Catherine's kin (John Steele to Mrs. Catherine Steele, June 4, 1877 [June 8 addenda], box 1, folder 12, Steele Collection, LTPSC); Mahonri M. Steele, June 1, 1877, Missionary reports: 1878, CHL.
61 Beckwith, "Shameful Friday," 80–81.
62 Turley and Walker, *Collections*, 231 (miscellaneous notes), 245, 253 (Elias Morris, February 2, 1892).
63 Brooks, *Mountain Meadows*, 62–63; Young's letter was dated September 10, 1857, the day before the massacre.
64 "The Lee Trial," *SLT*, Sept 16, 1876, 1/4; Turley and Brown, *Vengeance*, 49.
65 George A. Smith to T. B. H. Stenhouse, April 5, 1858, box 3, folder 12, MS 1322, G. A. Smith Papers, CHL.
66 Charles Lowell Walker, journal entry, March 21, 1858, *Diary of Charles Lowell Walker* (Logan: Utah State University Press, 1980), 25–26.
67 John Steele to John L. Smith, August 10, 1857; John L. Smith to George A. Smith, J. Steele, and Wm. H. Dame, November 2, 1857, box 9, folder 6, MS 1322, G. A. Smith Papers, CHL.
68 John Steele to George A. Smith, June 23, 1858, box 5, folder 16, MS 1322, G. A. Smith Papers, CHL.
69 "Brigham Young's Infamy," *New York Herald,* July 6, 1877, 2/4.
70 Turley and Brown, *Vengeance*, 61.
71 "Brigham Young's Infamy," *New York Herald,* July 6, 1877, 2/4.
72 Anna Jean Backus, *Mountain Meadows Witness: The Life and Times of Bishop Philip Klingensmith* (Spokane: Arthur H. Clark, 1996), 229–35.
73 Turley and Brown, *Vengeance*, 385; Kerry William Bate and JoAnn Bate, "Ebenezer Joseph Hanks Manuscripts and Letters," typescript (1979), 51 (in author's possession).
74 Bagley, *Blood of the Prophets*, 406n104, citing Edna Lee Brimhall, Statement of Benjamin Samuel Johnson and Elvira Martineau Johnson, September 23, 1935 ,"Gleanings of John D. Lee," Arizona Historical Society Library and Archives, Tucson, AZ (copy at CHL).
75 Juanita Brooks, *Quicksand and Cactus* (Salt Lake City: Howe Brothers, 1982), 228–29.
76 Turley and Brown, *Vengeance*, 149–51; Smith, journal entry, August 8–12, 1858, *Six Decades*, 31.
77 Martineau, journal entry, August 10–12, 1858, *Uncommon Common Pioneer,* 93.
78 "Parowan Aug. 8. 1858 of Investigation charges preferred against President W. H. Dame," box 1, folder 22, William H. Dame Papers, Vault MSS 55, BYU; this is a photocopy of the original.

79 "Mormon Rascality!," *Salt Lake Tribune* (*SLT*), May 18, 1877, 3 (reprinted from the *New York Herald*, May 12, 1877); Lee, *Mormonism Unveiled*, 279, 281; Calvin C. Pendleton to George A. Smith, January 16, 1861, box 6, folder 2, MS 1322, G. A. Smith Papers, CHL.

80 Isaac Haight, journal entries, August 10 and 12, 1858, *Journal of Isaac Chauncey Haight* (San Bernardino, CA: Paul Jones, 2010), 123.

81 George A. Smith to [his brother] John Lyman Smith, January 6, 1858; George A. Smith to Brigham Young, August 17, 1859: both in Historian's Office letterpress copybooks, 1854–1879, 1885–1886, vol. 2, 1859–1869, 1854–1861 (CR 100 38); George A. Smith to Mr. St. Clair, November 25, 1869, in David L. Bigler and Will Bagley, eds., *Innocent Blood: Essential Narratives of the Mountain Meadows Massacre* (Norman, OK: Arthur H. Clark, 2008), 271–73.

82 Smith also wrote a cover-up to Brigham Young (August 17, 1859, CR 100 38, Historian's Office letterpress copybooks: 1854–1879, 1885–1886 / vol. 1, 1854–1861, 157, 885–91).

83 Isaac Haight, journal entries, August 10 and 12, 1858, *Journal*, 123.

84 Martineau, journal entries, August 10–12, 1858, *Uncommon Common Pioneer*, 93.

85 Brooks, *Mountain Meadows*, 169. The fact that Jesse N. Smith signed last suggests his lack of enthusiasm for exonerating Dame.

86 "Mormon Rascality!," *New York Herald*, May 10, 1877, 4/1–2.

87 T. S. Kenderdine, *A California Tramp and Later Footprints* (Newtown, PA: self-published, 1888), 137.

88 James Lewis to George A. Smith, March 15, 1859, box 5, folder 18, MS 1322, G. A. Smith Papers, CHL.

89 James Lewis to George A. Smith, May 17, 1859, box 5, folder 18, MS 1322, G. A. Smith Papers, CHL. The petition was dated March 20, 1859.

90 Fish, *Autobiography*, 74, 132–33, 144. James Lewis to George A. Smith, March 15, 1859, box 5, folder 18; Miles Anderson to George A. Smith, September 10, 1860; William Marsden to George A. Smith, December 24, 1873; all in MS 1322, G. A. Smith Papers, CHL.

91 Bagley, *Blood of the Prophets*, 216–18.

92 Turley and Brown, *Vengeance*, 193.

93 Minutes for June 3, 1859, and affidavit from William Carter dated August 22, 1859, Parowan High Priests Quorum Minutes, 1855–1887, LR 6778, series 13, CHL; Martineau, journal entries, May 2–7, 1859, *Uncommon Common Pioneer*, 93.

94 Minutes from March 6, 1860, Parowan Elders Quorum Minutes, 1856–1866, LR 6778, series 13, CHL.

95 Minutes from Elders Quorum, January 24, 1860, Parowan Elders Quorum Minutes, 1856–1866, LR 6778, series 13, CHL; Calvin C. Pendleton to George A. Smith, January 16, 1861, box 6, folder 2, MS 1322, G. A. Smith Papers, CHL; Calvin C. Pendleton to William H. Dame, June 5, 1861, William H. Dame Papers, Utah Historical Society.

96 Minutes from June 3, 1859, and affidavit from William Carter dated August 22, 1859, Parowan High Priests Quorum Minutes, 1855–1887 (Anderson and liquor: January 5, 1860), LR 6778 13, CHL.

97 Minutes 1853–1868 Iron County Probate Court for March 7, 1859 (19) and June 6, 1859 (20, 31–33); "Squatter Sovereign" [James H. Martineau] to Editor, January 23, 1859, *DN*, February 16, 1859, 213/4; Martineau, journal entry, March 10, 1859, *Uncommon Common Pioneer*, 99; "Filed for record," box 2, folder 12, Steele Collection, LTPSC.

98 Minutes from December 1, 1859, Parowan High Priests Quorum Minutes, 1855–1887, LR 6778, series 13, CHL.

99 James Henry Martineau, "Parowan Stake History Book," January 3 and 6, 1860; High Priests Quorum, January 5–6, 1860, and affidavit from William Carter dated August 22, 1859, LR 6778 13, CHL.

100 Ila Bauer, "History of Nelson Stoyle Hollingshead" (1947), 2–3, copy in author's possession. For McGuffie see minutes for March 6 and April 12, 1860, Parowan Elders Quorum Minutes, 1856–1866, March 6, 1860, LR 6778 13, CHL. Calvin C. Pendleton to George A. Smith, January 16, 1861, box 6, folder 2, MS 1322, G. A. Smith Papers, CHL; Calvin C. Pendleton to William H. Dame, June 5, 1861, Dame Papers, Utah Historical Society.

101 For McGuffie see Parowan Elders Quorum Minutes, 1856–1877, LR 6778 (April 12, 1860). Calvin C. Pendleton to George A. Smith, January 16, 1861, box 6, folder 2, MS 1322, G. A. Smith Papers, CHL; Calvin C. Pendleton to William H. Dame, June 5, 1861, Dame Papers, Utah Historical Society.

102 Lee does not give Gregory's first name but a compiled census for Utah for 1856 shows John T. and Jane Gregory in Parowan (*Utah, Compiled Census and Census Substitutes Index, 1850–1890*, accessed through Ancestry.com, 1999). It's my assumption this is candidate Gregory. He may be the John Gregory who left Cedar City during the 1853 cattle rebellion. Woodruff, entry, May 16, 1851, *Wilford Woodruff's Journals*, 2:470.

103 Minutes for June 3, 1859, Parowan High Priests Quorum Minutes, 1855–1887, LR 6778 13, CHL.

104 John D. Lee, entry, February 16, 1861, *A Mormon Chronicle: The Diaries of John D. Lee, 1848–1876* (San Marino, CA: Huntington Library, 1955), 1:298.

105 Bauer, "History of Nelson Stoyle Hollingshead" (1947), 3, copy in author's possession.

106 James Lewis to George A. Smith, March 28, 1861, box 6, folder 2, MS 1322, G. A. Smith Papers, CHL.

107 Calvin C. Pendleton to William H. Dame, June 5, 1861, Dame Papers, Utah Historical Society.

108 "President Brigham Young's Visit South," *DN*, June 12, 1861, 116/1–2.

109 Josiah Rogerson, "John D. Lee: Miscellaneous Papers pertaining to his trials, guilt, and death," CHL, MS 2674, not paginated but actual p. 52.

110 Coombs, journal entry, May 3, 1859, *Isaiah Moses Coombs: Journal 1859 to 1869*, ed. Jim Tagg (n.p.: Amazon, 2017), 5.

111 John D. Lee, diary entry, June 11, 1860, *A Mormon Chronicle,* 1:259; Steele journal, undated [frame 139], folder 2, vol. 1, MS 1847.

112 James Henry Martineau, "Parowan Stake History Book," December 4, 1859, William H. Dame Papers, Utah Historical Society. George A. Smith wrote to one of Martineau's severest critics ("Geo. A. Smith, Letter, 1860 Mar. 7, Great Salt Lake City [Utah] to Bro. James Lewis," Historian's Office letterpress copybooks, 1854–1879, 1885–1886, CR 100 38 / vol. 1, 1854–1861, pp. 915–16).

Chapter 10

1 Todd Compton, "The Big Washout: The 1862 Flood in Santa Clara," *Utah Historical Quarterly* 77, no. 2 (Spring 2009): 108–25; James Godson Bleak, *Annals of the Southern Mission* (Salt Lake City: Greg Kofford Books, 2019), 53; "Mahonri M. Steele (Panguitch Pioneer)," in the Panguitch Daughter of the Utah Pioneers Museum.

2 Richard E. Turley Jr. and Barbara Jones Brown, *Vengeance Is Mine: The Mountain Meadows Massacre and Its Aftermath* (New York: Oxford University Press, 2023), 234.

3 Virginia M. Lee, typist, "Young Elizabeth Steele Stapley," 2, Utah Historical Society, Salt Lake City.

4 Amasa M. Lyman, diary entry, June 6, 1863, *Thirteenth Apostle* (Salt Lake City: Signature Books, 2016), 535; George A. Smith to John L. Smith, September 29, 1862 (CR 100 38), Historian's Office letterpress copybooks, 1854–1879, 1885–1886 / vol. 2, 1859–1869, 163 [frame 379].

5 For a picture of John Steele in front of his house see the frontispiece for Steele, "Extracts from the Journal of John Steele," *Utah Historical Quarterly* 6, no. 1 (January 1933).

6 James A. Little, *Jacob Hamblin, A Narrative of His Personal Experience* (Salt Lake City: Juvenile Instructor, 1881); Todd M. Compton, *A Frontier Life: Jacob Hamblin, Explorer and Indian Missionary* (Salt Lake City: University of Utah Press, 2013), 206–7. I'm heavily reliant on Compton's superb and award-winning biography.

7 Compton, *Frontier Life*, 207. Steele wrote three accounts of this mission. The first, probably penciled and a fragment, December 30, 1862–January 5, 1863, survives in a book of his poetry (box 1, folder 4, Vault MSS 528, Steele Collection, LTPSC, Harold B. Lee Library, BYU hereafter Steele Collection, LTPSC). He rewrote it into his "Mormon Battalion" journal (15 November 1862–5 January 1863 [frames 140–154], MS 1847, folder 2, vol. 1, CHL). The third is in the (self-sanitized) copy of his journal that John Steele sent to George A. Smith (January 8, 1863), Historian's Office collected historical documents, ca. 1851–1869, CR 100 397, CHL. A transcript with better spelling and minor word changes is in "History of Brigham Young," 14-37, and "Journal History," January 8, 1863, 1–13, CHL. My Steele quotes come from these three sources.

8 "Mosiah L. Hancock Journal," filed with Levi Ward Hancock Autobiography, MS 570, folder 5, CHL.
9 "Hancock Journal," 33, MS 570, folder 5, CHL.
10 Compton, *Frontier Life*, 211.
11 "Hancock Journal," 36 [frame 73], MS 570, folder 5, CHL.
12 "Hancock Journal," 34 [frame 69], MS 570, folder 5, CHL.
13 "Hancock Journal," 35–36 [frames 71, 73], MS 570, folder 5, CHL.
14 John Steele, revised diary entry of December 18, 1862, in Steele to George A. Smith, January 8, 1863, Historian's Office collected historical documents, ca. 1851–1869, CR 100 397.
15 Charles S. Peterson, "The Hopis and the Mormons, 1858–1873," *Utah Historical Quarterly* 39, no. 2 (Spring 1971): 182; Charles S. Peterson, *Take Up Your Mission* (Tucson: University of Arizona Press, 1973), 194–250; James H. McClintock, *Mormon Settlement in Arizona: A Record of Peaceful Conquest in the Desert* (Phoenix: self-published, 1921), 67–68; George A. Smith to John L. Smith, March 10, 1863, box 1, folder 3, MSS 1833 (A79-256), Augusta B. Smith [1828–1909] Papers, LTPSC.
16 "Ephesians 5:11" is a website explaining some Masonic rituals (http://www.ephesians5-11.org/handshakes.htm). Mosiah Hancock also saw what he thought were Masonic signs because their aprons had what he interpreted as the square and compass ("Hancock Journal," 40 [frame 81], MS 570, folder 5, CHL).
17 Peterson, *Take Up Your Mission*, 194.
18 "Hancock Journal," 36–38, 44 [frames 73–77, 89], MS 570, folder 5, CHL.
19 James A. Little, "A Narrative of the Traditions, Manners and Customs of the Moqui Indians," *Deseret News* (*DN*), March 23, 1870, p. 71, cols. 1–4, and p. 72, col. 1; "Hancock Journal," 39–40 [frames 79–81], MS 570, folder 5, CHL.
20 John Steele, revised diary entry of December 18, 1862, in Steele to George A. Smith, January 8, 1863, Historian's Office collected historical documents, ca. 1851–1869, CR 100 397, CHL.
21 "Hancock Journal," 40 [frame 81], MS 570, folder 5, CHL.
22 John Steele, revised diary entry of December 17, 1862, in Steele to George A. Smith, January 8, 1863, Historian's Office collected historical documents, ca. 1851–1869, CR 100 397, CHL.
23 John Steele, journal entry, December 21, 1862 [frame 147], MS 1847 folder 2, vol. 2, CHL.
24 J. O. Brew, "Hopi Prehistory and History to 1850," in *Handbook of North American Indians*, vol. 9: *Southwest* (Washington, DC: Smithsonian Institution, 1979), 515–16.
25 J. O. Brew, "Hopi Prehistory and History," 515; "Hancock Journal," 46 [frame 93] , MS 570, folder 5, CHL.
26 John Steele, revised diary entry of December 17, 1862, in Steele to George A. Smith, January 8, 1863, Historian's Office collected historical documents, ca. 1851–1869, CR 100 397, CHL; Peterson, "The Hopis," 184–85.

27 I thank Sondra G. Jones of BYU for explaining this structure was a kiva.
28 John Steele, revised diary entry of December 20, 1862, in Steele to George A. Smith, January 8, 1863, Historian's Office collected historical documents, ca. 1851–1869, CR 100 397, CHL.
29 John Steele, revised diary entry of December 19, 1862, in Steele to George A. Smith, January 8, 1863, Historian's Office collected historical documents, ca. 1851–1869, CR 100 397, CHL.
30 John Steele, revised diary entry of December 17, 1862, in Steele to George A. Smith, January 8, 1863, Historian's Office collected historical documents, 1851–1869, CR 100 397, CHL.
31 Hatch's recollections of this stay can be found in Little, "Moquis Indians," *DN*, March 23, 1870, 71/1–4, 72/1.
32 Compton, *Frontier Life*, 221.
33 See Compton, *Frontier Life*, 223, for a picture of the first three.
34 "Hancock Journal," 46 [frame 93], MS 570, folder 5, CHL.
35 John Steele, revised diary entry of December 25, 1862, in Steele to George A. Smith, January 8, 1863, Historian's Office collected historical documents, 1851–1869, CR 100 397, CHL.
36 John Steele, revised diary entry of December 26, 1862, in Steele to George A. Smith, January 8, 1863, Historian's Office collected historical documents, ca. 1851–1869, CR 100 397, CHL.
37 S[ingleton] Husted, August 28, 1887, J. Steele pension file [frames 193–94], Mexican War pension file, Utah State Archives, Salt Lake City.
38 [Mosiah Lyman Hancock], *The Life Story of Mosiah Lyman Hancock* (published anonymously), 43–44. The published version completes the story of the Hopi visit, which in the manuscript copy ends abruptly. I added the exclamation point in the quote from Steele.
39 Compton, *Frontier Life*, 218–19; McClintock, *Mormon Settlement in Arizona*, 68. McClintock lists Steele as an Arizona pioneer of "Moen Kopi" (37), which must refer to his mission to the Hopi.
40 Hancock, *Life Story*, 44.
41 John Steele, revised diary entry of December 30, 1862, in Steele to George A. Smith, January 8, 1863, Historian's Office collected historical documents, ca. 1851–1869, CR 100 397, CHL.
42 John Steele, revised diary entry of January 4, 1863, in Steele to George A. Smith, January 8, 1863, Historian's Office collected historical documents, ca. 1851–1869, CR 100 397, CHL.
43 Compton quote is from Richard Francaviglia, *Mapmakers of New Zion* (Salt Lake City: University of Utah Press, 2015), 107–9.
44 John Steele, revised diary entry of January 8, 1863, in Steele to George A. Smith, January 9, 1863, Historian's Office collected historical documents, ca. 1851–1869, CR 100 397, CHL.
45 Steele, "Mormon Battalion" journal, [frames 140–154], 15 November 1862–5 January 1863, MS 1847, folder 2, vol. 1, CHL.

46 John Steele to George A. Smith, November 16, 1863, G. A. Smith Papers 1834–1877, MS 1322, CHL.

47 John Alton Peterson, *Utah's Black Hawk War* (Salt Lake City: University of Utah, 1998), 103, 112, 116–17; "Settlements on the Sevier," *DN*, May 18, 1864, 264/3; Nelson S. Hollingshead to George A. Smith, June 8, 1864, and Richard Benson to George A. Smith, June 8, 1864, box 6, folder 11, MS 1322, G. A. Smith Papers, CHL.

48 "Record of the Iron Military District Re-organized by Colonel William H. Dame, May 1864," 1, Utah Territorial Militia Correspondence, 1849–1875 (hereafter UTMC), doc. 1294, Utah State Archives, Salt Lake City.

49 Daniel H. Wells to Col. William H. Dame, April 5, 1864, UTMC, docs. 758, 759. "Battalion Book," [1]; the front page of this booklet says "Battalion Book, [1] doc. 1,288, UTMC, A 385A pt. 2. W. G. Williams Adjutant General." Some pages are unnumbered so I've given actual page numbers in brackets [1]; otherwise, I use the page number on the original document even if it's not technically correct.

50 Angus M. Woodbury, "A History of Southern Utah and its National Parks," *Utah Historical Quarterly* 12, nos. 3–4 (July–October 1944): 167; Col. A. P. Winsor to Major John Steele, December 7, 1866 ("Battalion Book," 38), telling him to draw "3 men from Cannarah." Kanarra was separated from Steele's command by February 1869, when Lorenzo Wesley Roundy of that town was described as a major ("Movements against Indians South," *DN*, March 3, 1869, 42/4).

51 Peterson, *Utah's Black Hawk War*, 76.

52 For more on the Bear River Massacre see Brigham D. Madsen, *The Shoshoni Frontier and the Bear River Massacre* (Salt Lake City: University of Utah Press, 1985). The Bear River death toll was 250-400.

53 "Progress in Utah," *Salt Lake Tribune* (*SLT*), July 9, 1880, 4/2–3; Peterson, *Utah's Black Hawk War*, 3–4, 11–12; Edward Leo Lyman, "Caught in Between: Jacob Hamblin and the Southern Paiutes During the Black Hawk–Navajo Wars of the Late 1860's," *Utah Historical Quarterly* 75, no. 1 (Winter 2007): 23–43 (like all Lyman's work, this is an excellent study). I also benefited from a brief October 26, 2016, conversation with Mr. Lyman about several issues, including John Steele's misidentification of Paiutes as the enemy during the so-called Black Hawk War.

54 "Battalion Book," 17 (September 17 and 19, 1865).

55 Joshua Thomas Willis to Brigham Young, October 31, 1865; Erastus Snow to Brigham Young, November 4, 1865: both in MS 2183, Brigham Young Correspondence, CHL.

56 "Battalion Book," [7–12] (December 26, 1865) (January 15, 1866, lists Steele's and Hutchings' arms).

57 James G. Bleak, January 1866 entry, "Annals of the Southern Utah Mission" (BYU typescript, 1928), 124.

58 "Battalion Book," [17–18]. Bleak, January 1866 entry, *Annals of the Southern Mission*, 124–25.

59 John Steele to George A. Smith, January 22, 1866, MS 1322, G. A. Smith Papers, CHL.

60 John D. Lee to Brigham Young, February 8, 1866, and Robert Gardner to Brigham Young, January 22, 1866, MS 2183, Brigham Young Correspondence, CHL; Compton, *Frontier Life*, 260–68.

61 Lyman, "Caught in Between," 34, quoting Thales Haskell.

62 John Steele to George A. Smith, January 22, 1866, MS 1322, G. A. Smith Papers, CHL.

63 *DN:* "Down South," March 15, 1866, 118/1, and "From the South," March 22, 1866, 125/4; Joseph Fish, *Autobiography of Joseph Fish* (n.p.: Lulu: 2009), 81–83.

64 George A. Smith, journal entries, February 16 and 20, 1866, CHL (this journal is not in his handwriting). Toquerville Social Hall was the new church, now on the Register of Historic Sites. "Battalion Book," [1] doc. 1,288, UTMC, A 385A pt. 2, [27–29], Utah State Archives, Salt Lake City.

65 George A. Smith to Col. W. H. Dame, March 22, 1866, doc. 828, UTMC, A 385A pt. 2, Utah State Archives, Salt Lake City; Smith, journal entries, March 22–27, 1866, George A. Smith journal, CHL; Jesse Nathaniel Smith, journal entry, in *Six Decades in the Early West*, 177–78.

66 Fish, *Autobiography*, 82.

67 Erastus Snow to John Steele, March 16, 1866. The original letter is missing from the Steele Collection at LTPSC, but see "Letter Written by Erastus Snow in 1866 is Found," *Washington County News,* July 2, 1936, 1/6; also see box 2, folder 10, Steele Collection, LTPSC, for a partial transcript.

68 John Steele to Erastus Snow, April 6, 1866, box 2, folder 88, CHL; John M. Higbee to Col. Wm. H. Dame, July 10, 1866, doc. 915, UTMC, A 385A pt. 2.

69 Anson P. Winsor said the Berrys were killed about four miles from Maxwell's (Anson P. Winsor to Brigham Young, April 9, 1866, MS 2183, Brigham Young Correspondence, CHL).

70 John Steele to Erastus Snow, April 9, 1866, box 2, folder 88, CHL.

71 "Battalion Book," 10, shows Mahonri was initially in the second platoon and had half a pound of powder. John R. Young to Mahonri M. Steele, May 12, 1923, and August 28, 1923, transcripts in possession of author; John A. Steele, March 5, 1910, Commissioner of Indian War Service Records, Indian War Service Affidavits, UTAH0004D_02217003-Ind-War-ser-aff-F011_M_00159, Utah State Archives, Salt Lake City; Virgil D. White, transcriber, *Index to Indian Wars Pension Files, 1892–1926* (Waynesboro, TN: National Historical Publishing, 1987), 2:1471.

72 Andrew Karl Larson, *Erastus Snow* (Salt Lake City: University of Utah Press, 1971), 608–9. The quote is from Hebrews 12:6. Erastus Snow to John Steele, June 25, 1866; the original is in the State House Museum in Fillmore, Utah,

of which I have a photocopy. This was published with slight errors, including misdating it 1856, in Frank A. Beckwith Sr., "From the Journal of Elder John Steele (continued)," *Millard County (UT) Chronicle*, September 1, 1932, 4/1–4.

73 Erastus Snow to John Steele, June 25, 1866, State House Museum.

74 John Steele to Erastus Snow, November 26, [1866], doc. 992, UTMC, A 385A pt. 2.

75 Capt. J. D. Pierce [Pearce] to "Maj Steele," December 30, [1866]. This document is filed in the year 1868 but obviously refers to the 1866 action; docs. 944 and 1,150, UTMC, A 385A pt. 2.

76 Fish, *Autobiography*, 91–92. A telegram from Erastus Snow to John Steele dated November 24 (probably 1869) directed Steele to "watch for tracks on Hurricane Hill," near where Gould's was located (box 2, folder 10, Steele Collection, LTPSC).

77 Joshua Thomas Willis to Brigham Young, January 14, 1867, box 32, folder 9, MS 2183, Brigham Young Correspondence, CHL; Jesse W. Crosby to Erastus Snow, January 16, 1867, box 42, folder 19, CHL.

78 *DN,* January 16, 1867: "Deseret State Telegraph," 17/4, and "Home Items," 24/1; Andrew Karl Larson, *I Was Called to Dixie: The Virgin River Basin: Unique Experiences in Mormon Pioneering* (n.p.: self-published, 1979), 526.

79 Col. J. D. L. Pearce to Major Steele, [November?] 2 [1869?], box 2, folder 10, Steele Collection, LTPSC.

80 Clifford Duncan, "The Northern Utes of Utah," in *A History of Utah's American Indians*, ed. Forrest S. Cuch (Salt Lake City: Utah State Division of Indians Affairs and Utah Division of History, 2000), 176, 179–86.

81 Peterson, *Utah's Black Hawk War*, 67, 68–89, 212; William R. Palmer, "Utah Indians Past and Present," *Utah Historical Quarterly* 1, no. 2 (April 1928): 42–43.

82 Sixtus E. Johnson to George A. Smith, March 3, 1869; John Steele to George A. Smith, March 3, 1869: both in MS 1322, G. A. Smith Papers, CHL; *DN,* March 3, 1869: "The Navajoes in the South," 41/2; "Movements Against Indians South," 42/4.

83 Major John Steele to John Wharton Esq., March 21, 1902, retained copy, box 2, folder 1, Steele Collection, LTPSC. Steele wouldn't have had 1864 losses from the Black Hawk War because it didn't start until 1865.

84 John Steele to George A. Smith, February 8, 1867, MS 1322, G. A. Smith Papers, CHL.

85 "Battalion Book," Order No. 2, A. P. Hardy, February 12, 1867, numbered p. 40, otherwise p. 38; John Steele, February 16, 1867, 37, unnumbered 41; "Muster Roll" 43, unnumbered 40 (February 22, 1867); John Steele to Captain A. Minnerly, March 1, 1867, 37, unnumbered 41; Anson P. Winsor, Order No. 2, Headquarters Third Regiment P. M., Rockville, February 12, 1867, 38, unnumbered 40.

86 John Steele to Brigham Young, October 4, 1867, box 45, folder 34, MS 2183, Brigham Young Correspondence, CHL.
87 Anson P. Winsor to Brigham Young, October 6, 1867, box 45, folder 34; Sixtus E. Johnson to Brigham Young, October 11, 1867, box 45, folder 33: both in MS 2183, Brigham Young Correspondence, CHL.
88 Muster Roll, Company G C Battalion 1st Regiment, February 22, 1868, UTMC, series 2210, reel 10, doc. 3369.
89 "From Toker," *DN*, October 14, 1868, 285/1–2.
90 Henry Jennings to E. Snow, November 22, 1868; R. D. Covington to Prest. Snow, November 24, 1868: docs. 1,136, 1,148, UTMC, A 385A pt. 2.
91 L. L. Adams to Major Steele, [November?] 28, [1868], box 2, folder 10, Steele Collection, LTPSC.
92 "Local," *Cactus* (St. George, UT), December 5, 1868, 2/1–2; A. P. Hardy to John Steele and Joshua Thomas Willis, December 5, [1868], box 2, folder 10, Steele Collection, LTPSC.
93 John Steele to George A. Smith, March 3, 1869, MS 1322, G. A. Smith Papers, CHL.
94 Lyman, "Caught in Between," 38–39.
95 John Steele to Erastus Snow, November 8, 1869, doc. 1,193, UTMC, A 385A pt. 2; likely the recipient added, apparently in pencil, "John Steel Maj."
96 Jehiel McConnell to George A. Smith, December 17, 1869, MS 1322, G. A. Smith Papers, CHL; note this letter is indexed with the sender's first name mistakenly given as "Jehu."
97 Orson Welcome Huntsman, diary entry, January 1870, *Diary of Orson Welcome Huntsman Written by Himself*, transcribed by Lila Huntsman (n.p.: n.p., n.d., amended edition, 1995), 20, describes the Hebron incursion.
98 Daniel D. McArthur to John Steele, October 1, 1870, Order No. 7, not paginated but pp. 67–68.
99 Bleak, *Annals*, 197; Lyman, "Caught In Between," 38–41.
100 Compton, *Frontier Life*, 319–23.
101 Lyman, "Caught In Between," 40–41; Larson, *Erastus Snow*, 442–43.
102 *DN*: "From Dixie," January 5, 1871, 595/3; "The Kanab Region," April 26, 1871, 140/3–4; "Indian Troubles in the South," August 23, 1871, 329/4; "Indians Pacific," September 13, 1871, 369/2–3; "Indian Depredations at Kanab," September 20, 1871, 384/1; "Navajoes Exacting," September 27, 1871, 389/3–4; "Dixie Items," October 4, 1871, 401/3; "the Far South," October 11, 1871, 424/4; "Kanab," November 15, 1871, 482/2; "More Telegraphic Extension," December 20, 1871, 539/4. Bleak, *Annals:* for 1871 see 231–54; Erastus Snow to Brigham Young, September 13, 1871, box 42, folder 20, MS 2183, Brigham Young Correspondence, CHL.
103 John Steele, journal entry, undated [frames 155–56], folder 2, vol. 1, MS D 1847, CHL.
104 Steele, "Extracts from the Journal of John Steele," 28.

Chapter 11

1 William T. Barbee, "SOUTHERN UTAH," *Salt Lake Tribune* (hereafter *SLT*), December 19, 1875, col. 4, p. 2; [Wells Spicer], "GOLD: The Auriferous Metal Found in Washington County: Leeds Dull, and Wanting Mills," *Salt Lake Herald* (*SLH;* the newspaper was sometimes called the *Salt Lake Daily Herald*), June 4, 1876, 2/3.

2 John Steele to George A. Smith, August 6, 1870, G. A. Smith Papers, 1834–1877, MS 1322, CHL.

3 John Steele to George A. Smith, March 3, 1869, MS 1322, G. A. Smith Papers, CHL.

4 [John Smith], "Territory of Utah," *Weekly Journal of Commerce* (New York), Thursday, May 3, 1852, vol. 1, no. 20, 3/6.

5 Jay Jones, "How did Zion National Park Become more popular than Yosemite or Yellowstone?," *Los Angeles Times*, September 27, 2019. For the roads see, for instance, from the *Deseret News* (*DN*): J. V. Long, "Remarks by Elder George A. Smith, Bowery, Sunday Afternoon, September 15, 1857," September 23, 1857 (226/4, 227/1–3); J. V. Long, "DISCOURSE: By Elder George A. Smith, Tabernacle, Sunday Afternoon, March 10, 1861," December 25, 1861 (201/1–4, 202/1–3): "I was told at Toquerville that it was impossible to make a road to the valleys up the Rio Virgin." Lorenzo W. Roundy, a southwestern Utah territorial legislator, was jeered at by the (urban) *Salt Lake Tribune* because "he has more cheek than any other member in asking for appropriations," mostly for roads. Roundy was on the Committee on Roads, Bridges, Ferries and Canyons (*SLT*: "Our Legislators," February 1, 1876, 4/3; "Legislative Proceedings," January 12, 1876, 1/1–3). In support of the *Tribune*'s contention, see "Legislative Proceedings," January 20, 1876 (4/5); February 1, 1876 (4/4); February 5, 1876 (4/2).

6 John Steele, "Toquerville, Kane County, Utah, June 26, 1880," p. 9, "Utah Histories," Bancroft Collection, UC Berkeley; Mountain Meadows Massacre Monument Foundation, "Perpetrators of the Massacre," https://mmmf.org/the-story/the-perpetrators; L. W. Macfarlane, *Yours Sincerely, John M. Macfarlane* (Salt Lake City: self-published, 1980), 63–66. See "A Useful Witness," *SLT*, July 20, 1877, 2/1–2, for Wylie. George A. Smith to Jesse Nathaniel Smith, October 6, 1858, Historian's Office letterpress copybooks, 1854–1879, 1885–1886 / vol. 2, 1854–1861 (CR 100 38), 573.

7 "Also thou shalt lie down, and none shall make thee afraid; yea, many shall make suit unto thee" (Job 11:19–20); John Steele, June 26, 1880, "Toquerville, Kane County, Utah, June 26, 1880," "Utah Histories," Bancroft Collection, UC Berkeley; Hubert Howe Bancroft, *History of Utah* (1889; reprint, Salt Lake City: Bookcraft, 1964), 599.

8 John Steele to George A. Smith, March 3, 1869, MS 1322, G. A. Smith Papers, CHL.

9 John Steele to George A. Smith, November 16, 1863, MS 1322, G. A. Smith Papers, CHL.

10 Virginia M. Lee, typist, "Young Elizabeth Steele Stapley," 2, Utah Historical Society; Isaac E. Diehl, "Pioneer Personal History Questionnaire," Young Elizabeth Steele Stapley, 1936, WPA, B-289, box 10, Utah Historical Society.

11 John Steele to George C. Cannon, September 18, 1891, retained copy, box 2, folder 1, Steele Collection, LTPSC.

12 *DN*: "The Dried Peach Business," September 30, 1874, 553/4–5; "Romulus," April 24, 1875; "Dixie Wine at Ten Cents and Laudanum Tea," May 5, 1875, 209/4–5.

13 Joseph Fish, *The Autobiography of Joseph Fish* (n.p.: Lulu, 2009), 77; John Steele, "Toquerville, Kane County, Utah, June 26, 1880." "Utah Histories," Bancroft Collection, UC Berkeley. Steele kept a few postal and other accounts in a bound black book (box 1, folder 6, Steele Collection, LTPSC). Coombs, journal entry, October 5, 1868, *Isaiah Moses Coombs—Journal 1859 to 1869* (n.p.: Amazon, 2017), 335; Coombs journal, "Isaiah Moses Coombs Collection," 1835–1938, vol. 13, 154, MS 1198, CHL.

14 John Steele to Catherine Campbell Steele, June 21 and September 27, 1877, box 2, folder 12, Steele Collection, LTPSC.

15 "Dixie Wine," *Pioche Record* (*PR*), December 10, 1876, 3/3; "Our Dixie Wine," *SLT*, February 2, 1877, 4/3.

16 John Steele to Letisha Connelly Todd, September 12, 1902; copy in author's possession.

17 John Steele to Catherine Campbell Steele, June 1 and October 30, 1877, box 2, folder 12, Steele Collection, LTPSC; Fish, *Autobiography*, 77; John Steele to Susann Adams Steele Bringhurst, February 17, 1878, box 1, folder 12, Steele Collection, LTPSC.

18 John Steele to Latitia Tod [Letisha Todd], August 2, 1897; transcript provided to author by Ileen Judd Johnson.

19 Nell Murbarger, *Sovereigns of the Sage* (Palm Desert, CA: Desert Magazine Press, 1958), 188–89.

20 Notes in book with black binding titled "Abstract Of The Seventh Census," unnumbered but p. 10; October 8 and December [no day given] 1867, box 1, folder 6, Steele Collection, LTPSC; John Steele to Brother G. A. Smith, January 22, 1867, MS 1322, G. A. Smith Papers, CHL.

21 Box 3, folder 10, headed "Figure draws for 20 Mesh | 1872 4 oclock Am," Steele Collection, LTPSC.

22 "Mahonri M. Steele (Panguitch Pioneer)," original in Panguitch Daughters of the Utah Pioneers Museum.

23 Nuttall, diary entry, July 8, 1878, "Diary of L. John Nuttall (1834–1906), Dec. 1876–Mar. 1884" (copied by Brigham Young University, 1948), 185; James Lewis to Friend Steele, July 21 and August 3, 1876, box 1, folder 27, Steele Collection, LTPSC. William Logan, age twenty-nine, is in the 1880 census of Silver Reef and may be the Logan referenced by Steele. He was born in Scotland of Irish parents, which could have been a point of affinity with Steele.

John Steele to Catherine Campbell Steele, October 13, 1877, box 1, folder 12, Steele Collection, LTPSC.

24 James Lewis to Friend Steele, August 25, 1876, box 1, folder 27, Steele Collection, LTPSC.

25 Affidavit notarized by Martin Slack, August 12, 1873, box 2, folder 12, Steele Collection, LTPSC; "Kaysville Survey," *SLT*, June 2, 1878, 1/6.

26 Hanauer, Kohn & Co. Wholesale Clothiers Philadelphia, Spring 1874; unpaginated but the information about Springdale is on actual pages 11–13 [13–33] (box 3, folder 1, Steele Collection, LTPSC); John Steele to Brigham Young, January 22, 1875, box 36, folder 5, MS 2183, Brigham Young Correspondence, CHL.

27 "Kane County Taxes," *DN*, June 26, 1872, 308/2; minutes from March 5, 1874, Kane County Probate Court Minutes, Book A 1865–1883, series 8379, reel 1, p. 75, Utah Historical Society, Salt Lake City; Martin Slack to John Steele, March 9, 1874, box 2, folder 12, Steele Collection, LTPSC.

28 George A. Smith to James Lewis, March 7, 1860, Historian's Office letterpress copybooks, vol. 1, 1854–1861 (CR 100 38), 915–916.

29 Frank A. Beckwith, "Valuable Relics Found in Old Trunk," *Millard County (UT) Chronicle*, June 24, 1930, 1/1, 8/4.

30 Calvin C. Pendleton to George A. Smith, August 11, 1862, G. A. Smith Papers, CHL; Henry Lunt to Brigham Young, August 3, 1862, box 69, folder 5, MS 2183, Brigham Young Correspondence, CHL. Emily's age is uncertain; according to Ancestry.com, she was born August 27, 1849, so she had just turned thirteen, but Ulrich, relying on census records, suggests she was sixteen (Laurel Thatcher Ulrich, "Juanita Brooks's Footnote: History, Memory, and the Murder of Olivia Coombs," *Utah Historical Quarterly* 90, no. 3 [2022]:181–95).

31 Silas S. Smith to George A. Smith, August 11, 1862, MS 1322, G. A. Smith Papers, CHL.

32 George A. Smith to George Wood, August 6, 1862, Historian's Office letterpress copybooks, 1854–1879, 1885–1886 / Vol. 2, 1859–1869, p. 157, [frame 367] (CR 100 38).

33 Silas S. Smith to George A. Smith, August 11, 1862, MS 1322, G. A. Smith Papers, CHL. The petition is numbered 2250 (Utah Historical Society).

34 Photocopy of Steele's 1868 commission (in author's possession); John Steele's retained copy of a biography questionnaire for J. H. E. Webster's "The History of Utah Project," box 2, folder 6, Steele Collection, LTPSC.

35 John Steele, John Batty summons, December 2, 1888, box 2, folder 13, Steele Collection, LTPSC. This folder has Steele's justice of the peace records.

36 Martin Slack, John Steele letter of appointment, Kane County Prosecuting Attorney, March 9, 1873, box 2, folder 12, Steele Collection, LTPSC; *DN*: "Returned from the South," March 5, 1873, 73/1; "Cacti" [J. E. Johnson] to Editor, April 17, 1873, published April 30, 1873, 199/2–3; "Cacti" to *DN*, "Correspondence," May 4, 1873, published May 14, 1873, 240/1.

37 "Complaint is hereby made . . . ," December 25, 1873, box 2, folder 13, Steele Collection, LTPSC; he was appointed again on March 9, 1879. Transcript of the appointment letter from M. Slack, Probate Clerk, made by Iona J. Poling in May 1964 from the original (in author's possession).

38 *Henderson's New Belfast Directory and Northern Repository for 1843–44* (self-published, 1843), 202; Rachel Connelly to John Steele, June 4 and September 22, 1888, box 1, folder 6, Steele Collection, LTPSC; John Steele, journal entry, August 17, 1856 [frame 138], folder 2, vol. 1, MS 1847.

39 *Record of Appointment of Postmasters, 1832–1971,* NARA Microfilm Publication, M841, 145 rolls, Records of the Post Office Department, Record Group 28, roll 128, 30:470, 351, National Archive. Beckwith ("Valuable Relics," 1/1, 8/4) or his typesetter erred in saying the bondsman was "C B Adams"; it would have been O[rson] B. Adams. John Steele's retained copy of a biography questionnaire for J. H. E. Webster's "The History of Utah Project," box 2, folder 6, Steele Collection, LTPSC.

40 James Lewis to John Steele, June 17, 1876, box 1, folder 27, Steele Collection, LTPSC; *Record of Appointment of Postmasters,* NARA Microfilm Publication, M841, Records of the Post Office Department, Record Group 28, roll 128, 30:470, 30:351, 471, National Archive.

41 William Derby Johnson Jr. to John Steele, August 26, 1876, box 1, folder 28, Steele Collection, LTPSC.

42 *Record of Appointment of Postmasters,* NARA Microfilm Publication, M841, Records of the Post Office Department, Record Group 28, roll 128, 30:470, 30:351, 506, National Archive; *Executive Documents of the House of Representatives for the first session of the Fiftieth Congress 1887–'88*, vol. 26 (Washington, DC: Government Printing Office, 1889), Congressional Series of United States Public Documents, vol. 2557, 131.

43 John Steele to Catherine Campbell Steele, September 27, 1877, box 1, folder 12, Steele Collection, LTPSC.

44 Leonard J. Arrington, *Great Basin Kingdom* (Lincoln: University of Nebraska Press, 1968), 245–51.

45 Gertrude Himmelfarb, *The Idea of Poverty* (New York: Vintage Books 1985), 238.

46 *DN:* "Co-Operation and Its Benefits," June 17, 1868, 148/1–2, praising British cooperative movements and criticizing laissez-faire capitalism, which produces riches "entirely at the expense of the laboring classes"; "Mechanics' Meetings," June 17, 1868, 149/2.

47 "Communistic," *Salt Lake Tribune (SLT),* March 25, 1872, 2/1. The *Southern Utonian* (Beaver) unself-consciously headlined a story about a visitor to Orderville with "A Traveler Visits the Communists of Utah" (August 26, 1882, 3/3); this community was based on United Order principles ("Orderville," *DN*, February 28, 1877, 50/2–3).

48 John Steele, "Toquerville, Kane County, Utah, June 26, 1880," "Utah Histories," Bancroft Collection, UC Berkeley. The first dry goods store was

organized April 10, 1869, not May 14 ("Tokerville," *DN*, April 28, 1869, 133/4). According to the *DN*, the Southern Utah Mercantile Co-Operative store opened on April 27 ("Co-operation in 'Dixie,'" May 5, 1869, 151/4; "Co-opervtiae [Co-operative] Sheep Herding," November 30, 1870, 504/4).

49 Erastus Snow telegram to Brigham Young, April 10, 1870, box 42, folder 20, MS 2183, Brigham Young Correspondence, CHL; "Dixie," *DN*, July 6, 1870, 253/3; Iona J. Poling transcript (copy in author's possession). Efforts to set up a dairy cooperative in Toquerville were mentioned in an ad for a dairyman ("Wanted Immediately," *DN*, April 9, 1873, 151/5).

50 Arrington, *Great Basin Kingdom*, 326–27. Leonard J. Arrington, Feramorz Y. Fox, and Dean L. May, *Building the City of God* (Salt Lake City: Deseret Book, 1976), 135–42.

51 Minutes from March 4, 1869, "Toquerville Relief Society Minute Book 1870–1877," CHL.

52 Adelaide Jackson Slack, "Adelaide Jackson Slack," 1, WPA Biographies, B-289, Utah Historical Society; I. C. Haight to Brigham Young, June 30, 1874, box 35, folder 6, MS 2183, Brigham Young Correspondence, CHL.

53 I. C. Haight to Brigham Young, June 30, 1874, box 35, folder 6, MS 2183, Brigham Young Correspondence, CHL.

54 John Steele, J. T. Willis, and William Hill to Brigham Young, September 12, 1874, MS 2183, Brigham Young Correspondence, CHL.

55 Huntsman, diary entry, July 1874, *Diary of Orson Welcome Huntsman Written by Himself*, transcribed by Lila Huntsman (amended edition, 1995), 37.

56 Louise Slack, "Life Sketch of Lorenzo Jefferies Slack", 2; transcript completed September 21, 1937, by Floyd L. Eisenhour, WPA, Ogden, in WPA Biographies, B-289, box 9, Utah Historical Society, Salt Lake City.

57 Harrisburg Mining District Book A, 25, 34, series 23675, reel 1, books 1–3, Utah Historical Society.

58 "A Case of Dixie Wine," *PR*, January 20, 1877, 3/3; Wells Spicer, "Leeds," *SLH*, July 1, 1876, 2/4.

59 Alfred Bleak Stucki, "A Historical Study of Silver Reef: Southern Utah Mining Town" (MA thesis, BYU, August 1966), 11–12; Paul Dean Proctor and Morris A. Shirts, *Silver, Sinners and Saints* (n.p.: Paulmar, 1991), 26–27.

60 Harrisburg Mining District Book A, from the beginning through p. 11 (earlier pages not numbered; dates are February 26 and 28, and March 10, 18, and 21, 1871 [February 26 comes after February 28]); Stucki, "Historical Study of Silver Reef," 13–14.

61 "Biography of Lorenzo Jefferies Slack," Library of Congress Mormon Diaries series, 2.

62 Proctor and Shirts, *Silver*, 37, 44. Barbee's first claim was made on August 23, 1875 (Harrisburg Mining District Book A, 99), and on December 8th the ore he sorted and shipped to Salt Lake assayed at a phenomenal $502 a ton.

63 Harrisburg Mining District Book A, 89; "Silver Reef," *PR*, November 26, 1876, 3/1.

64 Harrisburg Mining District Book A, 119, 126, 169; the damaged book shows that besides the well-known Pride of the West Ledge, there was a Steele-Lamb Ledge. Stucki ("Silver Reef," 22) says twenty-nine claims were filed in 1875, but I've counted and recounted from the original book to be sure; I include sixty-seven that were located and four that were relocated. One of the four was Steele's. It seems probable this is not the same as the Toquerville mine, which shipped several hundred tons of low-grade ore. See also Marietta M. Mariger, *Saga of Three Towns: Harrisburg, Leeds, Silver Reef* (St. George, UT: Washington County News, n.d.), 90.

65 Harrisburg Mining District Book A, 119. This was located December 7, 1875, but the record is badly damaged. John Steele is the locator, and the claim mentions "Steel and Lamb," "south from the Grape . . . [sp]rings."

66 John Steele to Catherine Campbell Steele, August 20 and December 18, 1877, box 1, folder 12, Steele Collection, LTPSC.

67 Proctor and Shirts, *Silver*, 75–77, map, 78, and map on back cover; *SLT*: "Silver Reef City," March 6, 1877, 4/2; "Phoenix" [pseudonym] ("The Leeds Mine," June 3, 1877, 2/3–4) lists the mines in order, north to south, including the Vanderbilt, Steele and Lamb, and Duffin; the Dupaix and Spicer Mill seems to have been south of the Vanderbilt. John Steele, journal entry, by or before May 8, 1877 [frame 159], MS 1847, folder 2, vol. 1, CHL; Wells Spicer, "Leeds," *SLH*, January 24, 1877, 3/2; Erastus Snow to Charles F. Powell, October 2, 1871, in James Godson Bleak, *Annals of the Southern Mission* (Salt Lake City: Greg Kofford Books, 2019), 246–47.

68 Proctor and Shirts, *Silver*, 76.

69 Harrisburg Mining District Book B, 15, 19, 69, 157. Located January 14, 1876.

70 Proctor and Shirts, *Silver*, 75–76; Lorine I. Higbee ("Edwin Ruthven Lamb & his brother, Brigham Young Lamb," copy in author's possession) claims Lamb built the arrastra, but David B. Adams's diary shows that's not correct; perhaps Lamb bult a second one (David B. Adams, diary entries, March 27–28, 1876, 77, MS 1763, CHL).

71 A. W. Nuckols, "Leeds [Harrisburg] District," *SLT*, June 7, 1876, 4/3.

72 Harrisburg Mining District Book C, 63, series 23675, reel 1, books 1–3, Utah Historical Society; *PR*: "Toquerville Items," December 3, 1876, 2/2; "A New Speculation," December 8, 1876, 3/2; Wes Williams to *PR*, January 1, 1877, published as "From Leeds," January 13, 1877, 2/3–4.

73 *SLT*: "Augustus" to editor, March 15, 1876, published as "St. George," March 25, 1876, 4/3; "Moving On," March 26, 1876, 2/2. Stucki ("Silver Reef," 74–75, 104–6) outlines the economic advantages. For Lewis Homan see "Bonanza City," *SLT*, February 13, 1876, 4/4; he was manager of the Grand Gulch Copper Company based in St. George with a mine in Arizona.

74 Erastus Snow to Brigham Young, March 26, 1876, box 42, folder 21, MS 2183, Brigham Young Correspondence, CHL.

75 Mariger, *Saga of Three Towns*, 26.

76 [Wells Spicer], "GOLD: The Auriferous Metal Found in Washington

County: Leeds Dull, and Wanting Mills," *SLH,* June 4, 1876, 2/3 (the article, dated May 29, refers to the Steele arastra starting up "yesterday"); "Harrisburg," *SLH,* July 15, 1876, 3/3–4.

77 "Leeds Mines," *SLT,* January 3, 1878, 4/3; Stucki, "Historical Study of Silver Reef," 23, 23fn42; Proctor and Shirts, *Silver,* 63–66 (*arastra* can also be spelled *arrastra*).

78 "Harrisburg," *SLH,* July 15, 1876, 3/3–4.

79 Wells Spicer, "Leeds," *SLH,* January 24, 1877, 3/2; Higbee, "Edwin Ruthven Lamb & his brother, Brigham Young Lamb" (copy in author's possession)."

80 James Lewis to John Steele, July 21, 1876, box 1, folder 27, Steele Collection, LTPSC.

81 Gary Topping, "Another Look at Silver Reef," *Utah Historical Quarterly* 79, no. 4 (2011): 300–16.

82 Proctor and Shirts, *Silver,* 21; John Steele, journal entry, by or before May 8, 1877 [frames 158–59], MS 1847, folder 2, vol. 1, CHL; "Silver Reef City," *SLT,* March 6, 1877, 4/2; Levi Savage journal, August 9–10, 14, 1877, typescript in John D. Lee Collection, Utah Tech University, St. George; *SLH*: Wells Spicer, "Harrisburg," February 10, 1877, 3/3 (Spicer mentions that "Adjoining these mines are the McKilvy"). J. E. J. [J. E. Johnson] ("Leeds," March 30, 1877, 3/3) refers to "THE MCKELVY MINE," and "Leeds." June 14, 1876, 3/3, mentions "McKelvey." "D McKelvey" is listed as living in Pioche in the 1870 census, and a David McKelvey in Silver Reef in 1880 (Censuses of 1870 and 1880, United States, Utah, Washington County, Silver Reef). The *PR* has several references to him.

83 D. McKenzie for Brigham Young to John Steele, July 30, 1872, retained copy, Brigham Young office files transcriptions, Letterbook vol. 13, 1872 July 29–1873 March 20, CHL (this corresponds to the original letterpress copybook housed in box 9, vol. 13, pp. 159–313, CR 1234 1, CHL); Edyth Romney, Brigham Young Office Files Transcriptions, 1974–1978, box 13, folder 3, MS 3626, CHL. McKenzie's letter indicates Steele had written on July 8, 1872, and refers him to an explanation about the Perpetual Emigration Fund published in the *DN* in response to the request of Steele and others; see "Contributions to Gather the Saints," *Deseret Evening News,* July 29, 1872, 2/1–2.

84 I have written a biography of Young Elizabeth Steele in Bate, *The Women: A Family Story* (Salt Lake City; University of Utah Press, 2016). John Steele to George A. Smith, February 28, 1864, MS 1322, G. A. Smith Papers, CHL; "Married," *DN,* March 30, 1864, 208/4. Elizabeth was trained by Dr. Ane Christendatter Moller Jacobson Christoffersen (1815–1896), who offered midwifery classes, including board, in Cedar City in 1871–72 for eighty dollars—"paid in advance, one half cash and the rest in produce" ("Midwifery," *DN,* November 1, 1871, 456/4, referred to as "A. Christoffersen"; her last husband was John Daniel Thompson McAllister).

85 John Steele to George A. Smith, March 3, 1869, MS 1322, G. A. Smith Papers, CHL.

86 James Jepson Jr., "Memories and Experiences of James Jepson, Jr.," 18, box 16, folder 1, B-103, Juanita Brooks Collection, Utah Historical Society.

87 William Augustus Bringhurst to Brigham Young, June 30 and August 15, 1874, box 35, folder 3, MS 2183, Brigham Young Correspondence, CHL; Louise Slack, "Mary Bringhurst," A 1352, Utah Historical Society, Salt Lake City; "Funeral Held for Aged Resident of Toquerville Nov. 20," *Washington County News*, November 28, 1935, 1/7.

88 "Married," *DN*, February 9, 1876, 19/4.

89 *Iron County (UT) Record*: "Kanarra Letter," December 10, 1909, 1, and "Kanarra Letter," December 24, 1909, 1; "Toquerville," *Washington County News,* February 19, 1914, 54; oral history interview of Edwin Kenneth Slack by author, November 17, 1988, 12–13; Rhea Higbee Wakeling, "History of Rhea Higbee, Wife of Alva T. Wakeling," *Isaac Higbee and Sophia Somers Family Magazine* 3 (1958): 245F (also see 245D)—he is listed as undertaker on George Casper Batty's (May 30, 1900–May 28, 1907) death certificate (Utah State Archives, Salt Lake City); Delphina "Della" Catherine Fish Smith, "Reminiscences and Diary," 19–25, ca. 1928–1933, MS 5197, CHL.

90 *DN:* John Oakley to Editor, May 29, 1869, published June 16, 1869, 217/2; James Lewis to George A. Smith, June 4, 1869, published June 30, 1869, 241/4; "Bellevue, Kane Co.," March 2, 1870, 40/4.

91 Maybelle Harmon Anderson, *Appleton Milo Harmon Goes West* (Berkeley: Gillick Press, 1946), 180.

92 James Henry Martineau, journal entry, June 15, 1869, *An Uncommon Common Pioneer*, 160; John Steel[e] to Brother James A. Little, January 7, 1855, published as "Deseret," *Latter-Day Saints' Millennial Star* 17, no. 21 (May 26, 1855): 334.

93 The Christmas party invitation (1869) and "Duplicate" of agreement to dissolve marriage (September 5, 1870) are in box 1, folder 13, Steele Collection, LTPSC. "Utah Legislature," *SLT*, February 20, 1878, 4/5–6; Brigham Young to John R. Murdock, May 22, 1867, BYU Letterbook Transcriptions, Letterbook vol. 10, 1867 February 26–June 8, 160, CHL. Mary Jane Ould was born February 24, 1851, in Deep River, Cape of Good Hope, South Africa, daughter of Emanuel and Elizabeth (Uren) Ould, of Cornish descent. She married Amos Washington Harmon about 1873 (estimated from the 1900 census of Highland Township, San Bernardino County, CA, in which she reported they had been married twenty-seven years). Mary Jane Ould Steele Harmon died December 10, 1910 ("In the Shadow," *San Bernardino County Sun,* December 11, 1910, 57/3).

94 Anadel Law to Kerry William Bate, August 13, 2019 (in author's possession).

95 Fish, *Autobiography*, 141; "Died," *DN*, December 30, 1874, 763/3.

96 Amasa Mason Lyman, entries for December 12 and 13, 1875, *Thirteenth Apostle* (Salt Lake City: Signature Books, 2016), 848.

97 John Steele to "My Dear Kate" [Sarah Catherine Stapley, later Roundy], February 28, 1878, box 1, folder 31, Steele Collection, LTPSC;

Delphina "Della" Catherine Fish Smith, "Reminiscences and Diary," 19–25, ca. 1928–1933, MS 5197, CHL.

98 "Territorial Dispatches. John D. Lee Arrested," *DN*, November 18, 1874, 672/1; *SLT:* "John D. Lee: The Mountain Meadows Chaplain Captured," November 11, 1874, 4/2; "Vengeance is Mine," November 14, 1874, 4/2–3; "John D. Lee of Mountain Meadows," November 17, 1874, 4/2.

99 Minutes of March 18, 1860, Parowan Elders Quorum Minutes, 353, LR 6775, CHL; Fish, *Autobiography*, 133; Mary Campbell Steele Fish to "Father and Mother," February 7, 1874 (envelope addressed to "Mrs. C. Steele"), MS 24404, CHL; Harrisburg Mining District Book B, 71, 120–21.

100 "Another Scare," *SLT*, June 24, 1875, 4/3.

101 "Indictment," *SLT*, July 28, 1875, 409/4–5.

102 Richard E. Turley Jr. and Barbara Jones Brown, *Vengeance Is Mine: The Mountain Meadows Massacre and Its Aftermath* (New York: Oxford University Press, 2023), 323.

103 "Lee's Trial," *SLT*, July 15, 1875, 4/2–3. I have not found the original letter from Adams and Steele to U.S. Marshal George R. Maxwell, which would include the other signers.

104 John Gary Maxwell, *The Civil War Years in Utah* (Norman: University of Oklahoma Press, 2016), 233–56; "Lee's Trial," *SLT*, July 15, 1875, 4/2–3.

105 *SLT*: "The Lee Trial," July 30, 1875, 1/5; "Obedience to Counsel," July 31, 1875, 2/3.

106 John Chatterley to Andrew Jenson, September 18, 1892, in Richard E. Turley Jr. and Ronald W. Walker, eds., *Mountain Meadows Massacre: The Andrew Jenson and Davis H. Morris Collections* (Provo and Salt Lake City: Brigham Young University Press and University of Utah Press, 2009), 278.

107 Turley and Brown, *Vengeance*, 305.

108 "The Lee Trial," "Our Country Contemporaries," *DN*, August 4, 1875, 431/1; *SLT*: "Penitentiary Notes," January 5, 1876, 4/4; "The Lee Trial," July 13, 1876, 1/2, and succeeding dates; "City Jottings," October 11, 1876, 4/1; "Lee Sentenced," 4/2.

109 John Steele to James Lewis, March 22, 1877. There are two retained copies of letters to Lewis on this date, both in box 2, folder 1, Steele Collection, LTPSC. The text of the letters is different and only one mentions Lee. Their main purpose is discussing Kane County tax collections.

110 Turley and Brown, *Vengeance*, 194.

111 "Funeral of John D. Lee," *SLT*, April 11, 1877, 4/5, quoting from the *Beaver Square Dealer*.

112 John D. Lee's autobiography revealed he was severely physically and emotionally abused as a child. Brigham Young experienced severe corporal punishment, as was also possible for John Steele.

113 Badger, journal entry, September 26, 1905, MSS 1298, Carlos Ashby Badger Papers, LTPSC.

Chapter 12

1 "Miscellaneous," *Salt Lake Tribune* (*SLT*), April 10, 1877, p. 1, col. 1.

2 Mahonri M. Steele to "Ever Affectionate Mother," October 13, 1877, box 1, folder 17, Vault MSS 528, Steele Collection, 1847–1936, 19th Century Western and Mormon Americana, L. Tom Perry Special Collections, Harold B. Lee Library, Brigham Young University.

3 "City Jottings," *SLT*, May 8, 1877, 4/1; [untitled], *Pioche Record,* April 28, 1877, 2/1. James McGuffie named Dan Macfarlane and John Ure as then being in Europe but not that they were sent in 1877. "Brigham Young's Infamy," *New York Daily Herald,* July 6, 1877, 2/4–5; Missionary Department registers, 1860–1959 / Book A, 1860 April 25–1894 April 27, October 27, 1877–January 12, 1878.

4 John Steele, journal entry, August 21, 1877 [frame 175], MS 1847 folder 2, vol. 2, CHL. All quotations from Steele's journal during this mission are from this source and the subsequent journal, MS 1847, folder 2, vol. 3.

5 John Steele to "Dear Catherine," October 13, 1877, box 1, folder 12, Steele Collection, LTPSC; John Steele, journal entry, October 8, 1877 [frame 211], MS D 1847, folder 2, vol. 2, CHL.

6 John Steele to Brother [James] Lewis, March 22, 1877, box 2, folder 1, Steele Collection, LTPSC.

7 John Steele, journal entry, May 8, 1877 [frame 4], MS D 1847, folder 2, vol. 2, CHL; John Steele to "Dear Catherine," May 10, 1877 (dated May 9 but the "9" was crossed out and replaced with "10"), box 1, folder 12, Steele Collection, LTPSC. Steele's first missionary journal (vol. 2) ends May 18, 1877, and his second (vol. 3) begins May 8, 1877, so there is some overlap.

8 John Steele to Mrs. Catherine Steele, May 27, 1877, box 1, folder 12, Steele Collection, LTPSC.

9 *The Annual Directory of the City of Chicago* (Donnelly, Lloyd, 1877), 460: James was not listed; John Steele, journal entry, May 27–28, 1877 [frames 19–21], MS 1847, folder 2, vol. 3, CHL.

10 John Steele to Mrs. Catherine Steele, May 27, 1877, June 4, 7, 1877, box 1, folder 12, Steele Collection, LTPSC.

11 John Steele, journal entry, May 30, 1877 [frame 23], MS 1847, folder 2, vol. 3, CHL; Missionary reports: 1878, Mahonri M. Steele, May 30–31, 1877, CHL; "The Mormon Problem," *Philadelphia Inquirer*, May 30, 1877, 4/2; Mahonri M. Steele, journal entry, May 30–31, 1877, 1, MS 1848, CHL.

12 "Latter Day Saints," *New York Daily Herald*, May 13, 1877, 9/1–2. "A Mormon Autobiography," May 13, 1877, 10/3, includes comments on John D. Lee's *Confessions.*

13 [Jerome B. Stillson], "Among the Mormons," *SLT*, July 8, 1877, 2/3–5, quoted from the *New York Daily Herald;* "Brigham Young's Infamy," *New York Daily Herald,* July 6, 1877, 2/4–5.

14 Missionary reports: 1878, Mahonri M. Steele, June 1, 1877, MS 1848 CHL.
15 M. M. Steele to Josiah Rogerson, Esq., July 29, 1877, folder 5, MS 20208, Ann R. Adams Papers, CHL.
16 Mahonri M. Steele to "Dear Mother," June 2, 1877, box 1, folder 17, Steele Collection, LTPSC.
17 John Steele to Mrs. Catherine Steele, June 4, 1877 (June 6, 8 addenda), box 1, folder 12, Steele Collection, LTPSC.
18 John Steele, journal entry, June 7, 1877 [frame 35], MS 1847, folder 2, vol. 2, CHL.
19 John Steele to "Dear Catherine," June 21, 1877 (June 22 addenda), box 1, folder 12, Steele Collection, LTPSC. Steele spelled Mahonri's name "Mohonri"; I've usually silently corrected it.
20 Stephen C. Taysom, *Like a Fiery Meteor: The Life of Joseph F. Smith* (Salt Lake City: University of Utah Press, 2023), 175.
21 Transcript by Iona J. Poling in author's possession. She described it as "in possession of Kenneth G. Jensen, great-grandson. May, 1964" and "OLD BOOKLET." The original document has not resurfaced.
22 For the journal accounts of the two Steeles about their visit to Ireland see John Steele, journal entries [frames 56–64, 119–137], MS 1847, folder 2, vol. 2, CHL; this is interspersed with genealogical notes of friends and family (July 8–30, 1877). Mahonri M. Steele, journal entries, July 9–30, 1877, MS 1848, 1877 May–December, CHL; Mahonri M. Steele, reports, July 9–30, 1877, Missionary Reports, CHL. Steele wrote "63 Brougham street" in his journal; it is correctly given in *The Belfast and Province of Ulster Directory for 1877* (Belfast: *Belfast News-Letter*, 1877), 94, where Robert Campbell is described as a builder.
23 "Important Sale of Single Dwelling-House in Brougham Street and Two Houses in California Street," *Northern Whig* (Belfast), January 2, 1885, 1/4.
24 John Steele to "Dear Catherine," July 22 and 30, 1877, box 1, folder 12, Steele Collection, LTPSC.
25 "The Mormon Massacre" and "Horrible Case of Infanticide," *Belfast Telegraph*, April 3, 1877, 4/3; "Mountain Meadows Massacre," *BNL*, April 5, 1877, 4/5–6; "The Convict Mormon Bishop and Brigham Young," *Ballymena (Ireland) Observer,* April 21, 1877, 3/3; "Scene at the Execution of a Mormon Bishop," *Kerry (Ireland) Evening Post*, April 7, 1877, 4/4; *New York Herald*: "Retribution in Utah," March 23, 1877, 2/4–5, and "John D. Lee," March 24, 1877, 7/2–3. Though newspapers repeatedly referred to John D. Lee as a bishop, he never held that position.
26 John Steele, journal entry, July 25, 1877 [frame 133], MS 1847, folder 2, vol. 2, CHL.
27 John Steele to Mrs. Letisha Todd, March 21, 1891, transcript supplied by Ileen Judd Johnson to author. He wrote "my my Father"; I have corrected it.
28 Some fraudulent names have been added.

29 John Steele to Wm. Budge, September 9, 1878, two retained non-identical copies, box 3, folder 3, Steele Collection, LTPSC.

30 Mahonri M. Steele, journal entry, July 21, 1877 [frames 22–23], MS 1848, 1877 May–December, CHL. The Barry caricature was published in *Vanity Fair* on December 21, 1889.

31 Joseph F. Smith to Elder John Steel, July 27, 1877, box 30, folder 3, Copybooks, CHL.

32 John Steele to "Dear Catherine," July 30, 1877, box 1, folder 12, Steele Collection, LTPSC.

33 John Steele to Mrs. Catherine Steele, August 20, 1877, box 1, folder 12, Steele Collection, LTPSC; John Steele, journal entries, August 5–7, 1877 [frames 139–42], MS 1847, folder 2, vol. 2, CHL; "Obstructions by Waggons," *Cheshire (England) Observer*, June 22, 1872, 7/2. The 1871 census lists Wallace's occupation as "job labourer." Thomas Lounds, St. John's, Boughton, Chester, Cheshire, England (Ancestry.com and The Church of Jesus Christ of Latter-day Saints); 1881 England Census available online through Ancestry.com. His death was recorded in the fourth quarter of 1881 in Chester.

34 Richard Shannon, *Gladstone 1809–1865* (Chapel Hill: University of North Carolina, 1984), 22–23; William Ewart Gladstone, diary entry, Thursday, August 9, 1877, *Gladstone Diaries* (Oxford: Clarendon, 1986), 9:241.

35 John Steele to Mrs. Catherine Steele, August 20, 1877, box 1, folder 12, Steele Collection, LTPSC.

36 Joseph F. Smith to Henry W. Naisbitt, MS 1325, Joseph F. Smith Papers, 1854–1918, Correspondence, letterpress copybooks 1877 June 6–December 10, box 30, folder 3, p. 376, CHL; Joseph F. Smith to Brigham Young, Brigham Young Correspondence, Letters from Church Leaders and others, 1840–1877; Joseph F. Smith, 1877, CR 1234 1, box 42, folder 12. Thomas Francis Howells and Louis Howell, with slightly different surnames, were church, not biological, brethren and were then in the British mission field (Department missionary registers, 1860–1959 / Book A, 1860 April 25–1894 April 27, October 27, 1877–January 12, 1878, 33, 39).

37 Steele describes David Jones as one "who drives the Carrige, Hearse Etc."; that would match the David Jones, age forty-six, "inndriver/domestic," with wife Harriette, also forty-six, and son William and daughter Sarah Jane, both eleven, all born in Denbigh (Denbigh, Denbighshire, Wales, 1871 Wales Census, available through Ancestry.com). John Steele, journal entry, August 17–18, 1877 [frame 164], MS 1847, folder 2, vol. 2, CHL.

38 John Steele, journal entry, August 18, 1877 [frames 170–71], MS 1847, folder 2, vol. 2, CHL. Steele called Edward Barclay "Edwerd Bartley."

39 John Steele, journal entries, April 28, 1878 [frame 14], June 4, 1878 [frame 38], June 17, 1878 [frame 45], MS 1847, folder 2, vol. 3, CHL.

40 Joseph F. Smith to John Steele, August 15, 1877, box 30, folder 3, Copybooks, CHL (Smith addressed Steele at "Rhullan, Near St. Asaph Flints, N. Wales");

John Steele, journal entry, August 20, 1877 [frame 173], MS 1847, folder 2, vol. 2, CHL.

41 John Steele to Mrs. Catherine Steele, August 20, 1877, box 1, folder 12, Steele Collection, LTPSC; John Steele, journal entry, August 20–21, 1877 [frame 174], MS 1847, folder 2, vol. 2, CHL.

42 John Steele, journal entry, August 23, 1877 [frames 176–77], MS 1847, folder 2, vol. 2, CHL.

43 "Death of Brigham Young," *Liverpool (England) Mercury*, August 31, 1877, 7/5.

44 John Steele, journal entry, July 27, 1877 [frame 134], MS 1847, folder 2, vol. 2, CHL.

45 John Steele, journal entry, September 1, 1877 [frame 184], MS 1847, folder 2, vol. 2, CHL.

46 Joseph F. Smith to John Steel, September 4, 1877, box 30, folder 3, Copybooks, CHL. The letter was in the hand of scribe Henry W. Naisbitt.

47 Mahonri M. Steele to "My Dear Mother," September 25, 1877, box 1, folder 17; John Steele to "Dear Wif[e]," September 27, 1877, box 1, folder 12: both in Steele Collection, LTPSC.

48 John Steele, journal entry, September 6, 1877 [frames 187–91], MS 1847, folder 2, vol. 3, CHL.

49 Elizabeth Connelly to "My Dear brother," May 26, 1877 (photocopy in author's possession).

50 John Steele to "Dear Catherine," probably September 5, 1877, box 1, folder 12, Steele Collection, LTPSC.

51 John Steele to Mrs. Catherine Steele, May 1, 1878 (May 7 addenda), box 1, folder 16, Steele Collection, LTPSC.

52 William McClelland to "Dear Uncle," May 20, 1878 (photocopy in author's possession).

53 D. McKenzie, for Brigham Young, to John Steele, July 30, 1872, box 9, vol. 13, 159–313, Brigham Young Letterbooks, Edyth Romney transcript, CHL.

54 John Steele, journal entries, April 21, 1878 [frames 7–8], May 27, 1878 [frame 33], MS 1847, folder 2, vol. 3, CHL.

55 For John Steele's letters to his wife Catherine see box 1, folder 16, Steele Collection, LTPSC. I have given more details on their relationship in Bate, *The Women: A Family Story* (Salt Lake City: University of Utah Press, 2016).

56 Joseph F. Smith to H. W. Naisbitt, October 15, 1877, 296 [frame 383], box 30, folder 3, Copybooks, CHL; Joseph F. Smith to Prest. Joseph Horne, August 24, 1877, 212, box 30, folder 3, Copybooks, CHL.

57 John Steele to Mrs. Catherine Steele, December 18, 1877, box 1, folder 16, Steele Collection, LTPSC.

58 [Untitled], *Isle of Man Weekly Advertising Circular*, Tuesday, March 27, 1877, 2/2; "The Latest Dime Sensation," *Mona's Herald and Fargher's Isle of Man Advertiser*, Wednesday, March 21, 1877, 3/5.

59 Joseph F. Smith to Francis M. Lyman, August 8, 1877, 161, box 30, folder 3, Copybooks, CHL.

60 "Exile" to Editor, *Deseret News* (*DN*), January 24, 1886; "The Isle of Man," *DN*, March 3, 1886, 98/1–3, reports John Taylor introduced Mormonism on Man, whose people "may be found building up Zion in the tops of the mountains," but emigration depleted the local congregation.

61 The Cronk-y-Voddy fracas is described from Steele's viewpoint in one of the retained drafts of John Steele to "Pres Wm Budge," September 9, 1878, box 3, folder 3, Steele Collection, LTPSC; William Callister to "Sir," January 28, 1878, *Isle of Man Times,* February 2, 1878, 2/7; H. Kaighan to Rev. J. W. Kyte, November 19, 1877, "The Correspondence," *Manx Sun*, January 26, 1878, 4/4–5.

62 Joseph W. Kyte, 1881 English Census, Wood Ditton, Cambridge (Kyte's birth place); *Isle of Man Times*: "Cronk-y-Voddy," October 21, 1876, 5/4 (ministerial patroness and salary); "Extraordinary Charges Against Schoolmaster," January 19, 1878, 4/7; "Letters to the Editor" (subtitled "The Mormons and Cronk-y-Voddy School"); William Callister to "Sir," January 28, 1878, published February 2, 1878, 2/7, and "Truth" to "Sir," January 30, 1878, published February 2, 1878, 2/7; "Cronk-y-Voddy Church," June 8, 1878, 3/5–6.

63 "Truth," to "Sir," January 30, 1878, "Letters to the Editor," *Isle of Man Times,* February 2, 1878, 2/7.

64 "Truth," to "Sir," January 30, 1878, "Letters to the Editor," *Isle of Man Times,* February 2, 1878, 2/7.

65 "The Recent Mormon Invasion of the Cronk-y-Voddy Sun day School" and "The Correspondence," *Manx Sun*, January 26, 1878, 4/4–5.

66 "The Recent Mormon Invasion" and "The Correspondence," *Manx Sun*, January 26, 1878, 4/4–5. This includes a defense of Kyte (probably written by himself); letters by Kyte (January 19, 1878, to "Sir"; January 12, 1878 to A. E. LeMothe, clerk of the German School Committee); a letter of H[ugh] Kaighan (usually spelled "Kaighin") to Rev. J. W. Kyte, November 19, 1878; and A. E. LeMothe to Rev. J. Kyte, January 15, 1878.

67 John Steele to Wm. Budge, September 9, 1878, two retained, non-identical copies, box 3, folder 3; John Steele to "My Dear Wife," December 18, 1877, box 1, folder 12: both in Steele Collection, LTPSC.

68 John Steele to Mrs. Catherine Steele, December 18, 1877, box 1, folder 12, Steele Collection, LTPSC.

69 "Inauguration of the Wigan Miners' Hall," *Wigan (England) Observer*, May 19, 1876, 7/2.

70 "Minutes of a District Meeting Held in the Miners' Hall, Wigan, December 16, 1877," *The Latter-day Saints' Millennial Star* 39, no. 52 (December 24, 1877): 844–45; "The Mormans [Mormons] in Wigan," *Wigan (England) Observer and District Advertiser*, December 22, 1877, 5/3.

71 Parley Parker Pratt, *A Voice of Warning* (Salt Lake City: Deseret Book, 1979), 17; the first half of this book is Pratt's *Key to the Science of Theology*; the second part (with the pagination beginning again at page 1) is *A Voice of Warning*.
72 Pratt, *Voice of Warning*, 28.
73 Mahonri M. Steele to "My dear Mother," October 30 and November 20, 1877, box 1, folder 17, Steele Collection, LTPSC.
74 *DN*: "Legislative Assembly," January 30, 1878, 828/3–4; "Legislative Assembly," February 6, 1878, 841/4–5; "Legislative Assembly," February 27, 1878, 60/3. *SLT*: "Utah Legislature," February 2, 1878, 4/1; "Utah Legislature," February 12, 1878, 4/5.
75 John Steele to Mrs. Catherine Steele, January 30 (addenda February 11) and February 17, 1878, box 1, folder 12, Steele Collection, LTPSC. The latter acknowledged receipt of her letter dated January 17, 1878.
76 John Steele to Jamie [James Steele] Stapley, February 28, 1878; his letter to his granddaughter ("My Dear Kate [Stapley]") is on one side, that to Jamie on the other (copy in author's possession).
77 John Steele to Mrs. Catherine Steele, January 30 (addenda February 11), 1878, box 1, folder 12, Steele Collection, LTPSC.
78 John Steele to "Dear Susan," February 17, 1878, box 1, folder 12, Steele Collection, LTPSC.
79 Mahonri M. Steele to "My dear Mother," October 30, 1877, box 1, folder 17, Steele Collection, LTPSC.
80 John Steele to "Dear Susan," February 17, 1878, box 1, folder 12, Steele Collection, LTPSC.
81 John Steele to "My Dear Wife," April 25, 1878, box 1, folder 12 Steele Collection, LTPSC; Abraham A. Kimball, journal entry, March 10, 1878, transcript, 130, Utah Historical Society, Salt Lake City.
82 John Steele to Catherine Steele, March 11, 1878 (folder 1, MSS 6161), and April 25, 1878, May 1, 1878 (box 1, folder 12), Steele Collection, LTPSC; *SLT*: "City Jottings," August 1, 1876, 4/1; "Quicksilver," April 11, 1877, 4/5.
83 John Steele to Jamie [James Steele] Stapley, February 28, 1878.
84 John Steele to "My Dear Wife," May 1, 1878 (and May 7 addenda), box 1, folder 12, Steele Collection, LTPSC.
85 John Steele to "My Dear Wife," May 1, 1878 (and May 7 addenda), box 1, folder 12, Steele Collection, LTPSC; John Steele, journal entry, May 24[–25], 1878 [frames 31–32], MS 1847, folder 2, vol. 3, CHL; "RELEASES," *Latter-Day Saints' Millennial Star* (*MS*) 40, no. 22 (June 3, 1878): 346.
86 John Steele to "My Dear Wife," May 1, 1878, box 1, folder 12, Steele Collection, LTPSC.
87 John Steele to "My Dear Wife," May 28, 1878, box 1, folder 12, Steele Collection, LTPSC.
88 "Mother C. Steele" to "Dear Daughter Emily," February 20, 1878, copy of original posted on FamilySearch.com; a transcript is included in the appendix.

89 John Steele to "My Dear Wife," March 11, 1878, MSS 6161, folder 1, LTPSC (but not in the Steele Collection).

90 John Steele, journal entry, July 16, 1878 [frame 62], MS 1847, folder 2, vol. 3, CHL; John Steele to "My Dear Wife," May 1, 1878 (with May 7 addenda), box 1, folder 12, Steele Collection, LTPSC.

91 John Steele, journal entry, July 24, 1878 [frames 66–67], MS 1847, folder 2, vol. 3, CHL.

92 Abraham A. Kimball, journal entry, September 9, 1878, 26, Utah Historical Society, Salt Lake City.

93 John Steele to "My Dear Wife," August 15, 1878, box 1, folder 12, Steele Collection, LTPSC.

94 "Mother C. Steele" to "Dear Daughter Emily," February 20, 1878, copy of original posted on FamilySearch.com.

95 John Steele to "My Dear Wife," August 15, 1878, box 1, folder 12, Steele Collection, LTPSC.

96 David Milne to Elder John Steele, August 27, 1878, box 1, folder 29, Steele Collection, LTPSC.

97 John Steele to "My Dear Wife," August 15, 1878, box 1, folder 12, Steele Collection, LTPSC.

98 John Steele, journal entries, August 3–6 and 13, 1878 [frames 69–71 and 74], MS 1847, folder 2, vol. 3, CHL.

99 "Died," *Latter-day Saints' Millennial Star* 40, no. 41 (October 14, 1878): 656.

100 Elizabeth Connelly to "My Dear Brother," August the 21 [1878?], photocopy in author's possession.

101 John Steele to "My Dear Wife," September 1, 1878, box 1, folder 12, Steele Collection, LTPSC.

102 John Steele, journal entry, September 11, 1878 [frame 87], MS D 1847, folder 2, vol. 3, CHL.

103 "General News," *Manx Sun*, Saturday, September 21, 1878, 3/3; John Steele, journal entry, September 13–14, 1878 [frames 88–89], MS 1847, folder 2, vol. 3, CHL; *Manchester (England) Courier and Lancashire General Advertiser,* September 16, 1878: "Departure of Mormons," 5/5; [untitled], 4/5. Also see "Interesting Meeting," *MS* 40, no. 38 (September 23, 1878): 602.

Chapter 13

1 John Steele, journal entry, October 19–20, 1878 [frame 103], MS 1847, folder 2, vol. 3, CHL; Steele, journal entry, January 1933, "Extracts from the Journal of John Steele," *Utah Historical Quarterly* 6, no. 1: 28.

2 John Steele to "My Dear Wife," May 26, 1878, box 1, folder 17, John Steele Papers, Vault MSS 528, Brigham Young University Library, L. Tom Perry Special Collections.

3 Kane County Probate Court Records, Book A 1856–1883 (hereafter KCPCA), 122 (December 30, 1878), 8739, reel 1, Utah Historical Society.

4 KCPCA, 127 (September 1, 1878), 130 (December 1, 1879), 145 (December 6, 1880), 147 (March 7, 1881); *Deseret News* (*DN*): "Utah Legislature," January 18, 1882, p. 812, col. 1–5, and p. 813, col. 3; "Utah Legislature," March 22, 1882, 142/4; "Legislature," January 30, 1884, 30/3–5; "Legislature," March 19 [misprinted on the first page as "March 91, 1884"], 133/4–5.

5 "Abstract of Correspondence," *The Latter-day Saints' Millennial Star* (*MS*) 41, no. 5 (February 3, 1879): 78.

6 "Short Crops in Southern Utah," *Salt Lake Tribune* (*SLT*), July 8, 1879, 2/3; Joseph Fish, *The Autobiography of Joseph Fish* (n.p.: Lulu, 2009), 173. Also see S. K. Gifford to Editors, October 7, 1879, *DN*, October 29, 1879, 611/3.

7 "Amram" to Editors, January 3, 1880, *DN*, January 21, 1880, 803/1–2.

8 *DN*: "Financial," February 11, 1880, 24/4; "Notaries Public," February 25, 1880, 54/1–2.

9 Mahonri M. Steele to "Dear Father & Mother," August 9, 1879, box 1, folder 17, Steele Collection, LTPSC.

10 "Census Enumerators," *DN*, May 19, 1880, 254/5, 255/1–2; "Census Enumerators," *SLT*, May 7, 1880, 4/2 (unlike the *News*, the *Tribune* did not call Steele "Dr."); "Bill Nye, The Laramie City Logician on the Weather. He becomes a victim of the Census Enumerator," *Denver Tribune*, Laramie City, June 4; reprinted in *SLT*, June 9, 1880, 1/6–7.

11 "City Jottings," *SLT*, June 3, 1880, 4/1; "Toquerville, Utah," Wikipedia, population in 1880, US Census, 1880, Utah, Kane County, Toquerville.

12 *Grand Illustrated Catalogue of A. S. Barnes and Company, Publishers. New York Chicago;* Steele wrote his survey notes on the inside front cover and the following four pages of this notebook (box 2, folder 14, Steele Collection, LTPSC); James Godson Bleak, *Annals of the Southern Mission* (Salt Lake City: Greg Kofford Books, 2019), 500; John Steele booklet, February 15, 1881, transcript by Iona J. Poling (copy in author's possession).

13 Oral history interview by author with Reba Roundy LeFevre, July 23, 1987, 3–4 (copy in author's possession).

14 Booklet beginning "Always Bring this Book," February 20, 1881 [2–3], March 2, 1880 [37] (the entries are not in chronological order), box 3, folder 16, Steele Collection, LTPSC.

15 KCPCA, 151 (July 18, 1881), 8739, reel 1, Utah Historical Society; "Kane County Convention," *Salt Lake Herald*, July 19, 1881, 8/2; "Notice of Location of Steele's Spring Dated Nov. 4," 1884, notarized, stamped document (box 2, folder 1) and "Hanauer, Kohn & Co. Wholesale Clothiers Philadelphia, Spring, 1874" notebook, [31–33] (box 3, folder 16): both in Steele Collection, LTPSC; Levi Savage journal, December 4, 1881, typescript in John D. Lee Collection, Utah Tech University, St. George.

16 For instance, "City Jottings," *SLT,* January 17, 1880, 4/1.

17 "Mexican War Badges," *Pioche Record*, February 10, 1877, 3/1. These badges were not issued by the federal government but by South Carolina and a few municipalities.

18 George Q. Cannon to John Steele, January 27, 1877. This partial transcript was made for the Works Progress Administration (WPA) on October 3, 1936, when the original was in the possession of Steele's granddaughter Cathren Steele Riding of Delta. ("Cathren" spelled her first name in various ways during her life; it was probably originally "Catherine," after her grandmother Steele.) Riding's copy of the WPA document is now in box 2, folder 10, Steele Collection, LTPSC. The Utah Historical Society does not know where the WPA originals are.

19 Dr. S[ingleton] Husted, "Surgeon's Certificate," October 5, 1889, in Augustus E. Dodge's Mexican War pension file; Dr. S. G. Higgins, "Surgeon's Certificate," September 8, 1880, and "Proof of Disability," signed by John Steele and Orson B. Adams, August 27, 1880, in Augustus E. Dodge's Mexican War pension file.

20 John Steele, General Affidavit, June 24, 1881, J. Steele Mexican War pension file for Mormon Battalion service, Utah State Archives, Salt Lake City. All the references to Steele's pension records come from this file unless otherwise identified.

21 John Steele, June 24, 1881, Claimant's Affidavit; John Steele, January 10, 1882, General Affidavit (Pendleton, Meeks); Dr. Priddy Meeks, January 10, 1882, Physician's Affidavit; Dr. Israel Ivins, Physician's Affidavit, June 23, 1881; Dr. Israel Ivins, Examining Surgeon's Certificate, March 4, 1882; Dr. C. Mantor, Examining Surgeon's Certificate, June 20, 1882; Lyman Stevens and Orson B. Adams, General Affidavit, June 24, 1881; Wm. W. Dudley to Captain Nelson Higgins, November 28, 1881; Nelson Higgins to Wm. W. Dudley, December 17, 1881; Nelson Higgins, Proof of Disability, March 23, 1882; Augustus E. Dodge and Levi Savage, General Affidavit, January 10, 1882: all in J. Steele Mexican War pension file for Mormon Battalion service, Utah State Archives, Salt Lake City.

22 News of Steele's pension was published in the *United States Pension Bureau, List of Pensioners on the Rolls, January 1, 1883* (Washington, DC: Government Printing Office, 1883), 854, explaining it was for injuries "to back and kidneys"; John Steele to T. H. Kennedy, September 16, 1882, retained copy, box 2, folder 1, Steele Collection, LTPSC.

23 *Catalogue of the Governors, Trustees, and Officers, and of the Alumni and Other Graduates of Columbia College of the City of New York from 1754 to 1882* (New York: Printed for the College, 1882), 144 (Columbia was also known as City College); *Official Register and Directory of Physicians and Surgeons in the States of California 1903* (San Francisco: Medical Society of the State of California, 1903), 132; "Arrested for Threatening," *Deseret Weekly News* (*DWN*), March 5, 1884, 97/2; *DN*: "Arrested for Threatening," February 26, 1884, 3/2 ("belligerent golden-haired little Dr.") and "Hunting Another Bondsman," July 7, 1884, 3/2 ("belligerent little M.D."); "Daubing a Doctor," *Salt Lake Evening* Democrat, June 19, 1885, 4/3.

24 Dr. Singleton Husted, Physician's Affidavit, December 28, 1887, and Dr. Singleton Husted to Hon. Mr. Black, December 28, 1887: both in J. Steele

Mexican War pension file for Mormon Battalion service, Utah State Archives, Salt Lake City.

25 John Steele to Mr. Nathan Bickford, August 27, 1891, J. Steele Mexican War pension file for Mormon Battalion service, Utah State Archives, Salt Lake City. He added a postscript: "PS The last time I was Examined was by Docter Husted of Silver Reef U. T December 24 1887."

26 Olive E. DeMill Stevens to Mr. John Steele, March 26, 1901, box 1, folder 27, Steele Collection, LTPSC.

27 Levi Savage, journal entry, July 3, 1889, typescript in John D. Lee Collection, Utah Tech University, St. George.

28 John Steele to Mrs. Latitie [Letisha] Todd, August 15, 1901 (photograph of original in author's files); original donated to BYU, where it is part of the Steele Collection, LTPSC.

29 John Steele to Mrs. Latities [Letisha] Tod, August 4, 1896, and August 15, 1901 (transcript of the first provided to me by Edith Meredith of Australia, copy of second in author's possession).

30 [John Steele], April 19, 1880, to *DN*, retained copy, box 3, folder 12, Steele Collection, LTPSC; Earthquake Shock," *DWN,* April 21, 1880, 185/4 (from "Monday's Daily," April 19).

31 "Toquerville Unfortunate," *DN,* October 18, 1882, 609/2.

32 "Astrology and the 'Great Tribulation,'" *DN,* May 28, 1879, 264/3–5.

33 "Zadkiel Tao Tze, &c." [Alfred John Pearce], *Zadkiel's Almanac for 1881* (London: Couswas & Co., [1880]), 51–52; "Zadkiel's Predictions," *DN,* June 1, 1881, 281/1–2. One of Steele's basic astrological texts was "Zadkiel," *The Grammar of Astrology Containing all Things Necessary for Calculating a Nativity* (London: Sherwood, Gilbert, and Piper, 1840), which he signed in front, "John Steele Toquerville Utah Territory November 1874," glued on a press-printed "JOHN STEELE" label, and wrote an inscription in the back: "John Steele March 21 1860" (box 3, folder 22). Steele's surviving book collection includes *Zadkiel's* almanacs for 1851, 1855, 1872, 1873, 1874, and 1878 (box 3, folder 18): all in Steele Collection, LTPSC. Alfred John Pearce was "Zadkiel" from 1876 to 1923 ([untitled], "'Zadkiel II'. Dead," *Halifax Evening Courier,* May 4, 1923, 7/4). "Zadkiel," *Zadkiel's 1887* (London: Cousins & Co., 1886), 54; "Zadkiel for the Coming Year," *DN*, November 24, 1886, 713/4.

34 "He Killed the first Gentile," *SLT*, August 4, 1878, 4/4.

35 "City Jottings," *SLT*, June 1, 1876, 4/1.

36 Fish, journal entry, April 19, 1883, *Autobiography*, 208.

37 Sarah Barringer Gordon, *The Mormon Question* (Chapel Hill: University of North Carolina, 2002), 134–35 (this is a very informative book); Gov. Thomas Ford, *A History of Illinois* (Chicago: Lakeside Press, 1945), 2:305.

38 Gustive O. Larson, *The "Americanization" of Utah for Statehood* (San Marino, CA: Huntington Library, 1971), 116.

39 "County Registration Officers," *DN*, September 6, 1882, 1/4; *Ogden Daily Herald*: "The Registrars," August 31, 1882, 3/2, and "Registration

Appointments," September 8, 1882, 3/3; "The Registration Officials," *Southern Utonian* (Beaver), September 9, 1882, 3/3.

40 John Steele to John Stewart, September 9, 1882, retained copy, box 2, folder 1, Steele Collection, LTPSC.

41 "The Test Oath," *DN*, September 13, 1882, 540/3.

42 "County Registration Officers," *DN,* September 6, 1882, 513/4; "Registration Officers," *Deseret Evening News,* August 30, 1882, 2/4, and *Ogden (Utah) Daily Herald*, August 31, 1882, 3/2; "Registration," *Salt Lake Herald*, September 7, 1882, 3/2; "Registration Appointments," *SLH*, September 8, 1882, 3/3; "Registrars," *SLH*, September 10, 1882, 11/4.

43 Amos and Mary J. Harmon, U.S. Census 1880, Washington County, Silver Reef; "Mary Jane Harmon," *San Bernardino Sun*, December 11, 1910, 57/3.

44 Craig L. Foster, "'That Canny Scotsman': John Sharp and the Union Pacific Negotiations, 1869–72," *Journal of Mormon History* 27, no. 2 (Fall 2001): 197–214.

45 John Steele to "Mr John Sharp Chairman of the Peoples party," September 5, 1882, retained copy in a small hand-sewn booklet, box 2, folder 1, Steele Collection, LTPSC.

46 John Steele to John Stewart, September 9, 1882, retained copy, box 2, folder 1, Steele Collection, LTPSC.

47 I haven't been able to find copies of the Montreal newspaper, but Steele identifies the story as "in your paper of September 13 1882 p. 6 third paragraph second Column." He quotes enough from that version for me to find similar ones in other newspapers; I have used the version "The Mormons," *Chicago Tribune*, September 8, 1882, 8/5.

48 John Steele to "Family Herald and weekly Star Publishing Company Montreal Canada," September 23, 1882, retained copy, box 2, folder 1, Steele Collection, LTPSC.

49 "Frisco Notes," *SLT*, August 10, 1880, 1/7.

50 "Iron and Justice Gain the Victory," *DN*, February 2, 1881, "838/1–2.

51 John Gary Maxwell, *Robert Newton Baskin and the Making of Modern Utah* (Norman, OK: Arthur H. Clark, 2013), 170–74; Davis Bitton, *George Q. Cannon: A Biography* (Salt Lake City: Deseret Book, 1999), 249–50.

52 John Steele to "Family Herald and weekly Star Publishing Company Montreal Canada," September 23, 1882, retained copy, box 2, folder 1, Steele Collection, LTPSC.

53 "Territorial Returns," *DN*, December 22, 1880, 737/2–3.

54 John Steele to "Family Herald and weekly Star Publishing Company Montreal Canada," September 23, 1882, retained copy, box 2, folder 1, Steele Collection, LTPSC.

55 Edward Leo Lyman, *Political Deliverance: The Mormon Quest for Utah Statehood* (Urbana: University of Illinois Press, 1986), 80. The proposed bribes included at least $10,000 each for the *New York Times* and the *New York Sun*; the *Philadelphia Times* was worth $5,000 but the *St. Louis Globe Democrat,*

$20,000, while the *San Francisco Call* was to get $500 "to remain quiet." Not all of the newspapers accepted the bribes. Lyman's succeeding book on Utah statehood is as compelling reading as the first: Edward Leo Lyman, *Finally Statehood! Utah's Struggles, 1849–1896* (Salt Lake City: Signature Book, 2019).

56 "Dalton's Death," *DN*, January 12, 1887, 822/1–4, 823/1–3.

57 For example, see Nelle Spilsbury Hatch, *Mother Jane's Story* (Wasco, CA: Shafer, 1964), 47–48; Dan Erickson, *"As a Thief in the Night": The Mormon Quest for Millennial Deliverance* (Salt Lake City: Signature Books, 1998), 192.

58 Larson, *"Americanization,"* 120–21.

59 Mahonri M. Steele to "Dear Father & Mother," September 4, 1887, box 1, folder 17, Steele Collection, LTPSC.

60 Stephen Naegle, *The Life and Times of John Conrad Naegle and Family* (n.p.: self-published, n.d.). Naegle was his birth name but he changed it to Naile and then back to Naegle.

61 "A Proposition and a Reply," *DN*, June 30, 1886, 374/2–3.

62 The following all refer to the Ashton Nebeker debt: J. W. Seaman to John Steele, June 1, 1885, and February 27 and March 22, 1886 (box 3, folder 16); John Steele to J. W. Seaman, March 3, 1886, retained copy on back of preceding letter (box 3, folder 16); Royal J. Cutler to John Steele, March 9, May 24, and August 26, 1886 (box 1, folder 27); J. W. Seaman to John Steele, March 17, 1886 (box 1, folder 28), Steele Collection, LTPSC. The following all refer to the Bocker case: O. S. Bocker to John Steele, October 17, 1886 (box 1, folder 28); as "Rekcob," January 20 and March 15, 1889 (box 1, folder 28), Steele Collection, LTPSC. I am inferring that the Nebeker involved was Ashton, who in early 1887 sent Steele a letter from Globe City, Arizona, indicating he was out of Utah (Ash[ton Nebeker] to John Steele, March 26, 1887, box 1, folder 28, Steele Collection, LTPSC). This is confirmed by a biography of Nebeker, which says he lived in Jerome, Arizona, from 1886 to 1890 (Amy Bell Nebeker Slack, with contributions by Agnes Jane Nebeker Hekking, "Ashton Nebeker," available at FamilySearch.com; also see "Ashton Nebeker Dead," *Washington County News*, September 4, 1911, 2/3; "Ashton Nebeker Dead," *Coconino [AZ] Sun*, September 15, 1911, 1/5 [despite the same title, these are different articles]).

63 Erickson, "*As a Thief*," 192; Larson, *"Americanization,"* 116–17.

64 Larson, *"Americanization,"* 104; W. C. Hall, Certificate of Election, August 1, 1887, box 2, folder 12, Steele Collection, LTPSC; "Completed," *DN*, August 24, 1887, 501/1; *Salt Lake Herald*: "Commissions Issued Yesterday," October 15, 1887, 8/6 (where John is incorrectly given the first name of Joseph); "Commissions Issued," October 16, 1887, 8/6.

65 M[ahonri] M[.] Steele to "Father & Mother," January 9, 1887, box 1, folder 17, Steele Collection, LTPSC.

66 Jane C[.] Jensen to "My Dear Mother," April 18, [1887], box 1, folder 16, Steele Collection, LTPSC.

67 This document also works out the nativity for B. Forsyth's December 30, 1890, 2 p.m. marriage (box 3, folder 10, Steele Collection, LTPSC).

68 Mahonri M. Steele to John Taylor, January 30, 1887, box 20, folder 15, CR 1 180, First Presidency (John Taylor) Correspondence: Letters, 1887 Sm–Su, CHL; Mahonri M. Steele to "Dear Father & Mother," February 17, 1887, box 1, folder 17, Steele Collection, LTPSC.

69 [untitled], *Southern Utonian*, April 29, 1887, 8/1–2; M[ahonri] M. Steele to "Dear Mother," April 29, 1887, box 1, folder 17, Steele Collection, LTPSC.

70 Daniel Tyler to Editor, May 18, 1887, "The Oath in the Second District," *DN*, May 25, 1887, 304/2.

71 Joseph Fish to John Steele, August 9, 1887, box 1, folder 20, Steele Collection, LTPSC. Fish repeated this sentiment in a letter to Steele dated October 13, 1887.

72 Joseph Fish to John and Catherine Steele, March 9, 1888, box 1, folder 20; M[ahonri] M. Steele to "Dear Father and Mother," February 24, 1888, box 1, folder 17: both in Steele Collection, LTPSC; *SLH*: "Panguitch Points," February 24, 1888, 6/4, and "Local Points," September 25, 1888; "Chitchat," *Utonian* (Beaver, UT), March 9, 1888, 8/1. Dr. Wesley P. Larsen, when residing in Toquerville, told me that Bringhurst was turned in by a "spotter." He based this on talking to elderly Edwin Kenneth Slack, who refused to divulge the name of the culprit. Larsen speculated it was Slack's cousin Richard Tait Higbee.

73 John Steele to President Wilford Woodruff, July 30, 1888 (copy in author's possession); published, slightly modified, as John Steele, "Pioneer Reminiscences," *DN*, August 4, 1888, 480/2–3. Woodruff's August 3, 1888, response can be found in MS 2683, folder 2, CHL.

74 "Chit-Chat," *Southern Utonian* (Beaver), March 16, 1888, 8/1; "Served Full Terms" (*Southern Utonian*, September 28, 1888, 3/2–3) reports Bringhurst's release; M[ahonri] M[.] Steele to "Dear Father & Mother," March 19, 1888 (presumably in box 1, folder 20, Steele Collection, LTPSC); Joseph Fish to "Dear Father Steele," March 31, 1888, box 1, folder 20, Steele Collection, LTPSC; "Beaver News," *DWN*, April 4, 1888, 180/5; "Beaver News," *DN*, March 30, 1888, 3/2.

75 Levi Savage, journal entries, October 13–14 and December 8, 1888, typescript in John D. Lee Collection, Utah Tech University, St. George.

76 Mahonri M. Steele to "Dear Father & Mother," August 4, 1887, box 1, folder 17, Steele Collection, LTPSC.

77 Levi Savage, journal entry, May 30, 1888, typescript in John D. Lee Collection, Utah Tech University, St. George.

78 Patrick Q. Mason, *The Mormon Menace: Violence and Anti-Mormonism in the Postbellum South* (Oxford: Oxford University Press, 2011), 161; Erickson, *"As a Thief,"* 149, 181.

79 Erickson, *"As a Thief,"* 200, citing Walker, *Diary of Charles Walker,* 2:704 (December 16–17, 1888).

80 Joseph Fish to "Dear Father John Steele," February 18, 1891, box 1, folder 20, Steele Collection, LTPSC; Dan Erickson, "Joseph Smith's 1891 Millennial Prophecy: The Quest for Apocalyptic Deliverance," *Journal of Mormon History* 22, no. 2 (Fall 1996): 1–34.

81 Erickson, *"As a Thief,"* 135, 136fn57.

82 "It was John W. Young, of Iron County, cousin to John W. Young of this city. It was not Joseph W. Young, the emigration agent" ("'Mormons' and Citizenship," *DWN*, November 23, 1889, 683/2–3, 684/1–3 through 693/1–2).

83 "'Mormons and Citizenship," *DWN*, November 23, 1889, 683/2–3, 684/3.

84 "'Mormons and Citizenship," *DWN*, November 23, 1889, 683/2–3, 684/3. *DWN*: "Killing for Apostasy," December 7, 1889, 746/3, 747/1–2; "'Blood-Atoned' Green," 760/1–2; "Blood Atonement," December 14, 1889, 779/3, 780/1–3, 781/1; "All Manner of Evil Falsely," December 21, 1889, 808/1–2; "Villainous Antagonism—A Scrap of History," 811/2–3, 812/1–3, 813/1–2; "Joseph Cook on 'Mormonism,'" March 22, 1890, 412/1–3, 413/3; "Deliberate and Persistent Villainy," April 5, 1890, 480/1–3.

85 Retained letter fragment, box 3, folder 15, Steele Collection, LTPSC.

86 The Salt Lake City horoscope is written on a retained copy of part of a letter to the *Yankee Blade*, beginning "1890 1891 | 4 then [Lies?] we have been flooded with priests Lawyers Editors . . ." (box 3, folder 15, Steele Collection, LTPSC), and the other part is in box 2, folder 11; Thomas G. Alexander and James B. Allen, *Mormons and Gentiles* (Boulder, CO: Pruett, 1984), 99–100. Larson, *"Americanization,"* 248–49.

87 Mason, *Mormon Menace*, 161.

88 [Abinadi Pratt], "predictions of a Seventy," box 3, folder 7, Steele Collection, LTPSC; Abinadi Pratt, "Notice to the Latter-day Saints," *DN*, January 25, 1888, 26/2. Pratt repudiated his "predictions" in the latter article.

89 Steele's notes on [Abinadi Pratt], "predictions of a Seventy," box 3, folder 7, Steele Collection, LTPSC.

90 Larson, *"Americanization,"* 88–89, especially see 88fn58. The Mormon Church also made a large donation to Anthony's International Council on Women in March 1888, partly to be assured anti-polygamist suffragettes wouldn't attack them (Lyman, *Political Deliverance*, 87–88). In the nineteenth century numerology was called "arithmancy."

91 "A vision Received by an Seventy in Salt Lake Dec. 10 ^1877^" (but also dated 1879, on the bottom of the page), box 3, folder 7, Steele Collection, LTPSC.

92 "A Vision," January 8, 1886, box 3, folder 7, Steele Collection, LTPSC (this is not in Steele's handwriting). Bulkley's prophecy was published in C. C. Anderson, comp., *The Boy Prophet's Wonderful Sermon at the Funeral of King Follett, Nauvoo, Illinois, 1844 also A War Prophecy, or the Story of the White Horse and the Marvelous Visions of George Washington, S.M. Farnsworth, Newman Bulkley, C. D. Evans* (Salt Lake City: self-published, [1906?]), 37–40), but I have used the manuscript copy in the Steele files. The estimated publication year of the Anderson pamphlet is from the Church History Library.

93 Woodruff, entry, presumably written December 31, 1898, *Wilford Woodruff's Journals,* 5:511.

Chapter 14

1 Retained copy of John Steele's biography report for J. H. E. Webster, Historian's Office, 60 E. South Temple, Salt Lake City, box 2, folder 6, Vault MSS 528, John Steele Collection, LTPSC.

2 Woodruff, entry, September 25, 1890, *Wilford Woodruff's Journals,* 5:541–42.

3 Dan Erickson, *"As a Thief in the Night"* (Salt Lake City: Signature Books, 1998), 73–74. Erickson cites Woodruff's journal entry of April 15, 1837 (*Wilford Woodruff's Journal,* 1:142–43).

4 Woodruff, entry, September 25, 1890, *Wilford Woodruff's Journals,* 5:541–42.

5 Thomas G. Alexander, *Things in Heaven and Earth* (Salt Lake City: Signature Books, 1991), 266–67.

6 Mahonri M. Steele to "Dear Father," September 12, 1892, ACCN 0557 Special Collections, J. Willard Marriott Library, University of Utah, Salt Lake City. There is also a closed file about the Bringhurst divorce at the Church History Library.

7 John Steele to Latitia Tod [Letisha Todd], August 2, 1897, transcript by Ileen Judd Johnson in author's possession.

8 Edward Leo Lyman, *Political Deliverance* (Urbana Chicago: University of Illinois Press, 1986), 273–75. Mahonri earned a headline in the *Salt Lake Tribune* for advising congregants at a church meeting to vote Republican ("Church Does Counsel Voters," *Salt Lake Tribune* [*SLT*], November 4, 1904, p. 2, col. 5.

9 See box 3, folder 23, "1894," beginning "To the honorable Gentlemen," and box 2, folder 13: both in Steele Collection, LTPSC; John Steele to David Milne, February 24, 1894, retained copy, transcribed by Iona J. Poling, copy in author's possession.

10 John Steele to "mrs Latisha [Letisha] Todd," November 16, 1890, photograph of this letter in author's possession, original in Steele Collection, box 1, folder 24, LTPSC.

11 M. M. Steele to "Dear Father & Mother," January 11, 1891, MS 24404, CHL.

12 Levi Savage journal, January 11, 1891, typescript in John D. Lee Collection, Utah Tech University, St. George.

13 Levi Savage journal, June 16, 1891, typescript in John D. Lee Collection, Utah Tech University, St. George; William C. McGregor, "Catharine [*sic*] Campbell Steele," *Deseret Weekly News* (*DWN*), June 27, 1891, 24/3, and "The Late Sister Steele," June 25, 1891, 8/6. McGregor's obituary was reprinted in *The Latter-day Saints' Millennial Star:* "Died," August 3, 1891, 496; and "Died," August 17, 1891, 528.

14 Toquerville Relief Society Minute Book, 1889–1890 [*sic:* 1891 included], 99 (July 3, 1891), 148 (undated), CHL.

15 John Steele, June 15, 1891, partial draft, box 1, folder 12, Steele Collection, LTPSC; *Journals of John Steele and Mahonri Moriancumer Steele*, ed. Ileen J. Johnson and Wanda Steele Cox (Cedar City, UT: self-published, 1967), [1:]55–57. This printed source completes the partial draft.

16 William C. McGregor, "Catharine [*sic*] Campbell Steele," *DWN*, June 27, 1891, 24/3; "The Late Sister Steele," *DN*, June 25, 1891, 8/6.

17 John Steele, journal entry, [frame 106] (undated), MS 1847, folder 2, vol. 3, CHL; Levi Savage journal, June 21, 1891, typescript in John D. Lee Collection, Utah Tech University, St. George; John Steele to Latitia [Letisha] Todd, February 2, 1893 (photograph of this letter in author's possession; original in box 1, folder 24, Steele Collection, LTPSC).

18 Joseph Leland Heywood to John Steele, December 10, 1891 (photograph of this letter in author's possession); "Brief Sketch of Wandle Mace," *DWN*, December 20, 1890, 844/2–3.

19 David Milne to John Steele, September 26, 1891, photocopy of this letter in author's possession and in box 1, folder 29, Steele Collection, LTPSC.

20 John Steele, journal entry, [frame 106] (undated), MS 1847, folder 2, vol. 3, CHL.

21 "House of the Lord," *DWN,* April 8, 1893, 499/1–3 through 504/1–3.

22 Paper beginning "Prognostications of the times [1893]," box 3, folder 10, Steele Collection, LTPSC.

23 John Steele, journal entry, July 9, 1878 [frames 58–59], MS 1847, folder 2, vol. 3, CHL.

24 Original photograph in author's possession, a gift of John Steele's great-granddaughter Reba Roundy LeFevre, who got it from her grandmother Young Elizabeth Steele Stapley.

25 "The Immigrants," *Deseret News* (*DN*), June 8, 1887, 336/1; "List of Emigrants," *Salt Lake Herald* (*SLH*), June 5, 1887, 1/6; John Steele, journal entries, July 7–8, 1878 [frames 57–58], MS 1847, folder 2, vol. 3, CHL.

26 1881 Census, England, Staffordshire, Leek, Elijah Booth family; John Drakeford lived in the same house or next door, as did Toquerville's missionary Isaac Duffin ("Minister"); Elijah Booth, Salt Lake City Cemetery Records, 1848–1992, plot 17933 S-32-PAUP-E-10, "Record of the Dead," Utah State Archives, Salt Lake City series 21866.

27 There is a scrap of stationery from the "Department of the Interior, | Pension Office. | Official Business," in box 1, folder 14, Steele Collection, LTPSC.

28 John Steele, journal entries, July 7–8, 1878 [frames 57–58], MS 1847, folder 2, vol. 3, CHL.

29 Matilda Booth to "Dear Son and Daughter," February 14, [1895], box 1, folder 14, Steele Collection, LTPSC.

30 John Steele to President Wilford Woodruff, July 15, 1896, photocopy in possession of the author.

31 Matilda Booth to "Dear Son & daughter," September 8, 1893, box 1, folder 14, Steele Collection, LTPSC.

32 John Steele, journal entry, [frame 107] (undated but retrospective), MS 1847, folder 2, vol. 3, CHL; "Toquerville to the Fore," *DN*, April 18, 1893, 8/2; "Sudden Death of Surveyor-General Blair," *SLH*, February 13, 1901, 5/2–3.
33 John Steele to President Wilford Woodruff, July 15, 1896, photocopy in possession of the author.
34 John Steele, journal entry, undated [frame 108], MS 1847, folder 2, vol. 3, CHL; Charles E. Cheetham draft card, World War I Draft Registration Cards, 1917–1918; certified copy of an Entry of Birth for Albert Henry, son of Elizabeth Booth. Steele called the boy "Albert Townsley Cheatham" in one place, maybe indicating Albert's biological father's surname. The name is spelled both Cheetham and Cheatham.
35 John Steele to President Wilford Woodruff, July 15, 1896 (photocopy in possession of the author); "A Trip Through Southern Utah," *Weekly Kansas Chief* (Troy), December 24, 1896, 2/6–7; John Steele, journal entry, undated [frame 108], MS 1847, folder 2, vol. 3, CHL; Linda King Newell and Vivian Linford Talbot, *A History of Garfield County* (Salt Lake City: Utah State Historical Society, 1998), 206; David Milne to Dear Bro. Steele, October 9, 1893, box 1, folder 29, Steele Collection, LTPSC.
36 T. E. Steele to "My Dear Husband," April 3, 1896, box 1, folder 14, Steele Collection, LTPSC.
37 Photograph in author's possession, a gift from John Steele's great-granddaughter Reba Roundy LeFevre, who got it from her grandmother Young Elizabeth Steele Stapley.
38 Levi Savage, journal entry, April 23, 1893, typescript in John D. Lee Collection, Utah Tech University, St. George.
39 Jane C. Jensen to John Steele, July 9, 1893 (July 10 addenda), box 1, folder 16, Steele Collection, LTPSC.
40 Partial letter beginning "I am directed by the Presidancy," May 10, 1893, box 3, folder 3, Steele Collection, LTPSC; John Steele, journal entry, [frame 112], MS 1847, folder 2, vol. 3, CHL.
41 "Copy of papers Sent to Tamer Elizabeth Steele" (in Steele's hand), August 8, 1895 (papers served in the Third Judicial District Court seeking a divorce), box 1, folder 14, Steele Collection, LTPSC.
42 Matilda Booth to "Dear Son 7 [&] daughter," September 8, 1893, box 1, folder 14, Steele Collection, LTPSC.
43 "Marriages," *Portland (ME) Daily Press*, July 10, 1873, 2/6; marriage of Oliver A. Gould and Lydia S. Peaslee, Boston, Town and Vital Records, 1620–1988. accessed through Ancestry.com; Oliver A. Gould death certificate, Boston, Massachusetts, Vital Records, 1840–1911, New England Historic Genealogical Society, Boston; "List of Patents," *Boston Globe*, August 31, 1882, 1/6; "Chase Will Disallowed," *Boston Globe*, February 21, 1906, 3/4. For astrological advice on marriage, also see Azrael to Mr. John Steele, August 4, 1900, transcript by Iona J. Poling, copy in author's possession. Neither of Azrael's original letters seems to have ended up in the Steele Collection, LTPSC.

44 Oliver Ames Goold to Mr J Steele, September 19, 1893, box 3, folder 10, Steele Collection, LTPSC. This is a copy in Steele's handwriting, misdated 1898, but copyist Iona Jean Poling rightly corrected the date to 1893.
45 Oral history interview by author with Reba Roundy LeFevre, July 29, 1978, 31.
46 John Steele to Mrs. Matilda Booth, October 25, 1893, retained copy; "Mother M. Booth" to John Steele, late October–early November 1894: both in box 1, folder 14, Steele Collection, LTPSC.
47 Matilda Booth to "My Dear Son and Daughter," December 17, 1893, box 1, folder 14 1, Steele Collection, LTPSC.
48 Matilda Booth to "Dear Son and Daughter," January 26, 1894, box 1, folder 14 1, Steele Collection, LTPSC.
49 This is smudged; it could be the number 3.
50 This booklet of medical cures in Steele's handwriting begins with "Cure for Cholera." The pages are unnumbered but the prescription for nervous women is on actual page 14 (box 3, folder 13, Steele Collection, LTPSC).
51 [Matilda Booth] addressed "No 5" to "Dear Lizzie," undated, box 1, folder 14, Steele Collection, LTPSC.
52 Andrew Karl Larson, *"I Was Called to Dixie," The Virgin River Basin: Unique Experiences in Mormon Pioneering* (n.p.: self-published, 1961), 376–80; James Jepson, "Memories and Experiences of James Jepson, Jr.," 25–27, box 16, folder 1, B-103, Juanita Brooks Collection, Utah Historical Society; W. Paul Reeve, *"A Little Oasis in the Desert"* (Salt Lake City: Whirlwind, 1996), 29–30, 39, 50fn46; Dr. Wesley Pratt and Lois Larsen, comps., *Martin Slack's Account Book for the Hurricane Canal 1893* (Hurricane, UT: Hurricane Chapter, Sons of the Utah Pioneers, 2001; the pages are not numbered in this short account book); Albert L. Zobell Jr., "Lest We Forget: Hurricane Ditch," *Improvement Era* 70, no. 10 (October 1967): 60–61. Steele was a speaker at Jepson's wife Lucinda's funeral (David Fiske Stout, diary entry, February 20–21, 1894, *The Diaries of David Fiske Stout*, ed. Byron David Stout and Merle Viola Stout Budd [self-published, n.d.], 146).
53 John Steele to Editor, February 23, 1894, published as "Earliest Native Utonian," *DWN*, March 10, 1894, 370/1.
54 Slip of paper in Steele's *Raphael's Prophetic Almanac* (London: W. Foulsham, 1893), box 3, folder 18, Steele Collection, LTPSC.
55 "Mother M. Booth" to "My Dear Son and Daughter," March 9, 1894, box 1, folder 14, Steele Collection, LTPSC.
56 "Mother M. Booth" to "Dear Son and Daughter," April 13, 1894; Mrs. Matilda Booth to "Dear Son and Daughter," June 29, 1894: both in box 1, folder 14, Steele Collection, LTPSC.
57 John Steele, journal entry, [frames 108–9], MS 1847, folder 2, vol. 3, CHL.
58 This word is uncertain; a letter precedes it, something like an *S* but seems marked out.
59 Tamar to "My Dearest Husband," August 29, 1894, box 1, folder 14, Steele Collection, LTPSC.

60 "Freed of Drug Habit Grip, Former 'Fiend' Pleads for Others Hitting the 'Long Road,' *Salt Lake Telegram*, March 4, 1913, 3/2–4.

61 Tamar to "My Dearest Husband," August 29, 1894, box 1, folder 14, Steele Collection, LTPSC.

62 John Steele, journal entry, [frame 109], MS 1847, folder 2, vol. 3, CHL.

63 "Mother M. Booth" to John Steele, late October–early November 1894, box 1, folder 14, Steele Collection, LTPSC. Top half of pages 1 and 2 were torn off. Mrs. Booth writes, "you will be surprised when I tell you Sadie Browns husband got killed on the railway." Sadie's husband was Rio Grande Western brakeman L. H. Rogers, who was killed in a railroad accident October 28, 1894, which allows us to give a general date for this letter ("Met a Horrible Death," *SLT*, October 29, 1894, 8/4).

64 *SLT*: "Washington County Ticket," October 19, 1894, 3/6, and "Republicans on Top in Utah," November 7, 1894, 1/3; "Obituary, I. C. Macfarlane," *Washington County News*, June 2, 1921, 1/5–6.

65 "Fatal Accident," *DWN*, November 23, 1894, 780/2–3.

66 Steele had sent for Tamar's certificate of marriage to Rennick on May 2, 1892; Matilda Booth to "Dear Son and Daughter," February 14, 1895: both in box 1, folder 14, Steele Collection, LTPSC.

67 Levi Savage, journal entry, July 7, 1895, typescript in John D. Lee Collection, Utah Tech University, St. George.

68 John Steele to President Wilford Woodruff, July 15, 1896, photocopy in author's possession.

69 John Steele, journal entry, undated [frame 109], MS 1847, folder 2, vol. 3, CHL.

70 "Conventions at Richfield," *Daily Enquirer* (Provo), September 23, 1895, 1/2.

71 In the Second Judicial Court, Territory of Utah, County of Beaver, *John Steele, Plaintiff, vs. Tamar E. Steele, Defendant,* August 8, 1985, decree, box 1, folder 14, Steele Collection, LTPSC.

72 Word "one" scratched out after "me" and under "divorce."

73 "Lizzie" to "My Dear Husband," August 27, 1895, box 1, folder 14, Steele Collection, LTPSC.

74 John Howcroft to "Dear John Steele," October: 12 [1895], box 1, folder 14, Steele Collection, LTPSC.

75 Tamara E. Steele, undated Valentine card, box 1, folder 14, Steele Collection, LTPSC.

76 T. E. Steele to "My Dear Husband," April 3, 1896, box 1, folder 14, Steele Collection, LTPSC.

77 He also wrote, "July 4/96 | 2 pm | Lizzi [torn] | Lett[torn]," suggesting a later letter or his response (box 3, folder 10, Steele Collection, LTPSC).

78 Levi Savage, journal entry, May 17, 1896, typescript in John D. Lee Collection, Utah Tech University, St. George.

79 John Steele to President Wilford Woodruff, July 15, 1896, photocopy in possession of the author.

80 George Reynolds to Elder John Steele, July 29, 1896, box 3, folder 3, Steele Collection, LTPSC. For a biography see Bruce A. Van Orden, *Prisoner for Conscience' Sake: The Life of George Reynolds* (Salt Lake City: Deseret Book, 1992).

81 "Town Talk," *SLH*, February 12, 1897, 8/1; "Early Day Events," *SLT*, July 4, 1897, 24/1; "Some 'First' Claims," *Deseret Evening News*, June 26, 1897, 6/1; John Steele to Latitia [Letisha] Tod[d], August 2, 1897, transcript by Ileen Judd Johnson in author's possession.

82 *Pierce's Memorandum Account Book*, box 1, folder 10, Steele Collection, LTPSC. This is the source of information for Steele's life between July 14 and August 31, 1897, unless otherwise noted. *Pierce's* is a journal separate from John Steele's journal, where frames 109–11 discuss this trip (MS 1847, folder 2, vol. 3, CHL).

83 "A Polynesian Reunion," *DN*, July 21, 1897, 6/1–2; "Jubilee Tomorrow," *DN*, July 19, 1879, 5/1–2; "Missionaries Ate Poi," *SLT*, July 20, 1897, 8/4; "Reunion at Lagoon," *SLH*, July 20, 1897, 8/5; "Reunion at Lagoon," *Davis County Clipper*, July 23, 1897, 4/4; John Steele to Latitia [Letisha] Tod[d], August 2, 1897 (transcript by Ileen Judd Johnson in author's possession); *Program of the Utah Pioneer Jubilee. July 20th to 24th 1897* (Salt Lake City: George Q. Cannon and Sons, 1897), unpaginated.

84 John Steele, journal entries, undated [frames 109–11], MS 1847, folder 2, vol. 3, CHL.

85 John Steele, journal entry, July 23, 1897, *Pierce's Memorandum Account Book*, box 1, folder 10, Steele Collection, LTPSC.

86 Elizabeth Schoenfeld, "A Look at Revered Ancestors," *DN*, December 26, 1970, 8T/1–6; Diana Lauritzen and Dr. James Swensen, "Recognizing Faces: Women's Portraits on the Salt Lake City and County Building," *Journal of Academic Research* (April 18, 2013).

87 John Steele, journal entry, July 24, 1897, *Pierce's Memorandum Account Book*, box 1, folder 10, Steele Collection, LTPSC.

88 John Steele to Latitia Tod [Letisha Todd], August 2, 1897, transcript by Ileen Judd Johnson in author's possession.

89 John Steele, journal entry, April 1898 [frame 112], MS D 1847, folder 2, vol. 3, CHL.

90 *SLT*: "City and Neighborhood," July 16, 1898, 16/1; "City and Neighborhood," July 19, 1898, 1/8.

91 "Found His Wife Insane," *SLT*, June 4, 1899, 5/3.

92 "Found His Wife Insane," *SLT*, June 4, 1899, 5/3.

93 "James A. Cheetham" and "Mary H. Cheetham" are listed on the UK and Ireland, Incoming Passenger Lists, 1878–1960, accessed online through Ancestry.com.

94 "Woman Said to Be Insane," *SLT*, October 19, 1899, 6/4; "City and Neighborhood," *SLT*, November 11, 1899, 8/1; death certificate for Elizabeth Renick

Cheatham (with the Cheatham partly erased; she's indexed as "Renick, Elizabeth"), Utah State Archives, Salt Lake City; Mahonri M. Steele to John Steele, September 11, 1903, box 1, folder 17, Steele Collection, LTPSC.

95 "Cheetham Gets Six Months," *SLT*, October 10, 1905, 8/3; "Says Three Boys Robbed the Store," *SLT*, July 19, 1907, 3/2; "Freed of Drug Habit Grip, Former 'Fiend' Pleads for Others Hitting the 'Long Road,'" *SLT*, March 4, 1913, 3/2–4; "Youthful Burglars," *SLH*, February 12, 1898, 8/3; "Boys Happy in Jail," *SLT*, February 13, 1898, 8/3; "In Police Circles," *SLT*, February 16, 1898, 8/4; "Given Another Chance," *SLT*, February 24, 1898, 8/3.

96 *R. L. Polk & Co. Salt Lake City Directory, 1902,* 203; *R. L. Polk & Co. Salt Lake City Directory, 1910*, 265; *R. L. Polk & Co. Salt Lake City Directory, 1913*, 227 (he is in other directories as well); Charles Edwin Cheatham, draft registration, WWI Civilian Draft Registrations. Per the 1920 U.S. Census, Utah, Salt Lake County, Salt Lake City, Cheetham was in the household of Mike Chaves as a lodger, working as a café waiter. "Poisoned Alcohol Kills Man," *SLT*, July 20, 1922, 20/3; "Death Follows Drinking Denatured Alcohol," *SLT*, July 20, 1922, 3/3; Charles Edward Cheetham, death certificate, Utah State Archives, Salt Lake City. (He was Charles Edwin, not Edward, unless he chose to change his middle name.)

Chapter 15

1 The full title of Thomas Oswald Cockayne's book is *Leechdoms, Wortcunning, and Starcraft of Early England. Being a Collection of Documents, for the most part never before printed, illustrating the History of Science in this Country Before the Norman Conquest*, 2 vols. (London: Longman, Green, Longman, Roberts, and Green, 1864). The modern edition of these Anglo-Saxon records is, *Anglo-Saxon Remedies, Charms, and Prayers from British Library MS Harley 585: The Lacnunga*, ed. and trans. Edward Pettit, 2 vols. (Lewiston, NY: Edward Mellen, 2001).

2 "Leechdoms," "wyrt," "cunnan," and "starcraft" from WordSense Online Dictionary: https://www.wordsense.eu; Alaric Hall, *Elves in Anglo-Saxon England: Matters of Belief, Health, Gender and Identity* (Woodbridge, England: Boydell Press, 2007), 6; John Clark Hall, *A Concise Anglo-Saxon Dictionary for the Use of Students* (New York: Macmillan, 1916), 67.

3 "Leeds Brevities," *Salt Lake Tribune* (*SLT*), December 13, 1876, p. 4, col. 2. In 1855, a doctor couldn't even make a living in Salt Lake City according to William Chandless (*A Visit to Salt Lake City; being A Journey Across the Plains and a residence in the Mormon Settlements at Utah* [London: Smith, Elder, 1857], 238–39).

4 John Steele to George A. Smith, January 22, 1867, G. A. Smith Papers 1834–1877, MS 1322, CHL; John Steele to Mrs. Latitie [Letisha] Todd, August 15, 1901, copy in author's possession.

5 Wesley P. Larsen, *Self-Guided Walking Tour of Toquerville, Utah* (n.p.: self-published, n.d.), 23.

6 John Steele to Mrs. Latisha [Letisha] Todd, December 24, 1897, transcription by Ileen Judd Johnson in author's possession.

7 [Willard Richards], "Names of the company and their outfit for Little Salt Lake," *DN*, November 16, 1850, 154/2–3, 155/1, 156/2–3; "Died," *DN*, March 19, 1853, 3/4; John Steele, "Lines writen on the Death of Dr William A Morse Who died at Parowan Iron County, UT. Sunday, 23 January 1853 Aged 66," MS 2054, box 1, folder 18, *Deseret News* editor's files, 1850–1854, Poetry 1850–1854, CHL; Dr. Priddy Meeks, January 10, 1882, Physician's Affidavit, J. Steele Mexican War pension file for Mormon Battalion service, Utah State Archives, Salt Lake City.

8 [George Q. Cannon], "The Germ Theory," *DN*, March 2, 1870, 42/1–2.

9 Robert T. Divett, *Medicine and the Mormons* (Bountiful, UT: Horizon, 1981), 133–34. I found this study very helpful.

10 Katherine Hardy, "Reading Urine in Medieval Medicine," *Public Domain Review* (April 19, 2023); Benjamin Woolley, *Heal Thyself: Nicholas Culpeper and the Seventeenth-Century Struggle to Bring Medicine to the People* (New York: HarperCollins, 2004), 173; Nicholas Culpeper, *Urinalia* (London: Printed For Nath. Brooks at the Golden Angel on Cornhill, neer the Exchange, 1655).

11 John Steele, journal entry, [frame 213], folder 2, vol. 1, MS 1847, CHL.

12 "Local and Other Briefs," *SLH*, December 25, 1889, 8/1; "Almost Drowned," *Ogden Semi-Weekly Standard*, December 28, 1889, 6/7. The Sylvesters are misidentified in the newspapers as the Silvertons. Levi Savage journal, December 24, 1889, typescript in John D. Lee Collection, Utah Tech University, St. George; Gladys Sylvester Olds, "Gladys Sylvester Olds Wife and Mother 1896–1960," in Shirley Olds Bauer, "'As I Remember Mama,' (1976), 7, copy in author's possession; Charles Andrew Olds, July 30, 1984, in author's possession; James Denholm, *The History of the City of Glasgow and Suburbs* (Glasgow: R. Chapman, 1804), 139–41.

13 Oral history interview by author with Charles Andrew Olds, October 11, 1984, 7–9.

14 "Toquerville," *Washington County News*, July 3, 1900, 1/4. The Danish Ranch is in the Pine Valley Mountains northwest of Silver Reef and was owned at the time by Sylvester's father, Joseph.

15 Maureen Smith Bryson and Kerry William Bate, *The Lives and Letters of the Sylvesters and Nicholsons* (Las Vegas, NV: self-published, 1997), 512–21, gives a biographical sketch of Victor Leon Sylvester.

16 Maud Grieve, *A Modern Herbal* (1931; reprint, New York: Dover, 1971), 1:290–93; Pettit, The Lacnunga, 1:211.

17 Steele's list of herbs and their uses begins with "Acconite is monks Hood" (box 3, folder 13, Vault MSS 528, Steele Collection, LTPSC); John Gerard,

Herbal or General History of Plants, revised and enlarged by Thomas Johnson (1633; reprint, New York: Dover, 1975), 353–55; Nicholas Culpeper, *Culpeper's Complete Herbal* (London: Richard Evans, 1814), 91–92.

18 Andrew Jacobs, "Tripping in the Bronze Age," *New York Times,* April 7, 2023.

19 John S. Haller Jr., *The People's Doctor: Samuel Thomson and the American Botanical Movement, 1790–1860* (Carbondale: Southern Illinois University Press, 2000), 257–59.

20 "Journal of Priddy Meeks," typescript by Beth Bringhurst of the Utah Historical Records Survey (WPA, 1937), 111–13.

21 Document beginning with "Cure for Cholera" (box 3, folder 13, Steele Collection, LTPSC); Wesley P. Larsen, *A History of Toquerville* (Cedar City, UT: self-published, 1985), 129.

22 Document beginning with "Cure for Cholera" (box 3, folder 13, Steele Collection, LTPSC).

23 Haller, *The People's Doctor,* 33.

24 Gary Tom and Ronald Holt, "The Paiute Tribe of Utah," in *A History of Utah's American Indians,* ed. Forrest S. Cuch(Salt Lake City: Utah State Division of Indian Affairs / Utah Division of History, 2000), 124; Martha C. Knack, *Boundaries Between: The Southern Paiutes, 1775–1995* (Lincoln: University of Nebraska Press, 2004), 11–12, 19; Wesley P. Larsen, *Folk Histories of Selected Desert Plants as Found at Zion, Arches, Bryce, Great Basin, Capitol Reef, Death Valley, Canyonlands, Grand Canyon* (n.p.: self-published, n.d.); my copy has a note explaining it is "A Work in Progress." It may be a precursor to Dr. Wes Larsen, *A Field Folio of Indian and Pioneer Medicinal Plants* (Toquerville, UT: Third Mesa, 1996). Another version of this work is Larsen, *Indian and Pioneer Medicine* (n.p.: self-published, n.d.). Larsen had a doctorate in biology and was a college professor, making his explorations of this field especially informed. Also see Frank A. Beckwith, *Indian Joe: In Person and In Background* (Delta, UT: DuWil, 1975), 28.

25 Page beginning with "Acconite is monks Hood," box 3, folder 13, Steele Collection, LTPSC.

26 Chandless, *A Visit to Salt Lake City,* 7, 20.

27 Page beginning with "Acconite is monks Hood," box 3, folder 13, Steele Collection, LTPSC.

28 Divett, *Medicine and the Mormons,* 22; Peter Maxwell-Stuart, "Magic in the Ancient World," in *The Oxford Illustrated History of Witchcraft and Magic* (Oxford: Oxford University Press, 2017), 2.

29 Gerard, *The Herbal,* 1582; personal conversation with Dr. Wesley P. Larsen. A letter from Steele's friend David Milne of St. George dated September 21, 1891, hinted Steele felt apologetic about his sexual equipment: "Well Bro. Steele, you could have Knocked me down with a Straw, when I came to that part of your letter, where your courage appears to give out, I concluded you had got the mitten through the interference of Some busy-bodies." Milne

suggested Steele forget about pleasing everyone: "I would try to please mysel[f], then do my best to give satisfaction to the gude-Wife. if I failed, would tell her honestly the spirit was wil[l]ing but the body was weak, no doubt she would find that out her sell [self], but an open confession would be good for the spirit, if not for the flesh." Milne urged Steele not to be "discouraged Keep up your Spunk, no saying what a day may bring forth, maybe a big girl or a buxom Widow there are lots of them wondering 'Wha'a'll be my Man' so if you get the wood, you will very soon get the axe handle—the hole never hunts the mouse, cheer up." Since 1891 was a "Prophetic year," Milne reminded Steele, it may be the time predicted "When seven women will take hold of one man." Steele must have reassured Milne, for Milne's next letter says, "Your ever welcome letter of the 23rd duly rec'd pleased that you feel your courage and muscle tends upwards" (David Milne to John Steele, September 21 and 26, 1891, box 1, folder 29, Steele Collection, LTPSC).

30 John Steele, journal entry, [frames 220–21], folder 2, vol. 1, MS 1847, CHL; "Cure for Ringbone" (March 14, 1872), box 3, folder 13, Steele Collection, LTPSC.

31 For these spells see the document with the first page showing a star and two carefully drawn circles in box 3, folder 10, Steele Collection, LTPSC.

32 Peter Maxwell-Stuart, "Magic in the Ancient World," in *Oxford Illustrated History of Witchcraft and Magic* (Oxford: Oxford University Press, 2017), 2.

33 John Steele papers, "against witchcraft," box 3, folder 10, Steele Collection, LTPSC; Peter Maxwell-Stuart, "Magic in the Ancient World," 8, 15–16; Owen Davies, "The World of Popular Magic," in *Oxford Illustrated History of Witchcraft and Magic* (Oxford: Oxford University Press, 2017), 176–77; Tabitha Stanmore, *Cunning Folk: Life in the Era of Practical Magic* (New York: Bloomsbury, 2024), 82–85.

34 For reproduction of the relevant documents and an extensive discussion see Dan Vogel, *Early Mormon Documents*, 5 vols. (Salt Lake City: Signature Books, 2002), 4:239–71 (for a photograph of the court entry regarding "The Glass Looker" see p. 258); Dan Vogel, *Joseph Smith: The Making of a Prophet* (Salt Lake City, Signature Books, 2004), 81–82; Richard Lyman Bushman with Jed Woodworth, *Joseph Smith: Rough Stone Rolling* (New York: Alfred A. Knopf, 2005), 48–52; D. Michael Quinn, *Early Mormonism and the Magic World View*, rev. ed. (Salt Lake City: Signature Books, 1998), 30ff.

35 *Raphael's Prophetic Almanac . . . 1894* (London: W. Foulsham, 1894), 40.

36 John Steele, journal entry [frame 223], folder 2, vol. 1, MS D 1847, CHL.

37 Samuel R. Wells, *New Physiognomy, or, Signs of Character as Manifested Through Temperament and External Forms* (New York: Samuel R. Wells, 1868), box 3, folder 21, Steele Collection, LTPSC. Imprinted inscription: "JOHN STEELE."

38 Document with the first page showing a star and two carefully drawn circles, box 3, folder 10, Steele Collection, LTPSC.

39 Dov Gera and Wayne Horowitz, "Antiochus IV in Life and Death: Evidence from the Babylonian Astronomical Diaries," *Journal of the American Oriental Society* 117, no. 2 (April–June 1997): 249.

40 John Steele, journal entry, [frame 213], folder 2, vol. 1, MS 1847, CHL.

41 Della Fish Smith, "Reminiscences and diary [ca. 1928–1933]," 22, 24, MS 5197, CHL.

42 Paper beginning "Astronomy What is it[?]," box 3, folder 10, Steele Collection, LTPSC.

43 "The Wicked Tremble but the Righteous are Unmoved," *DN*, August 2, 1865, 348/3–4.

44 A. N. Noon, "Astrology," *DN*, March 6, 1867, 80/1.

45 H. Dharmapala, "Oriental Religious Faiths II: Buddhism," *Improvement Era* 2, no. 2 (December 1898): 85.

46 David J. Whittaker, Paul C. Russell, Chris McClellan, and Bryon D. Dixon, comps., *Register of the John Steele Collection, 1847–1936* (Provo, UT: Brigham Young University, L. Tom Perry Special Collections, 1995).

47 John Steele to "Azrael of the penny magaz[ine]," July 27, 1900, retained copy, box 3, folder 10, Steele Collection, LTPSC. The *Penny Magazine* was published in England from 1832 to 1845. There was the *New Penny Magazine* (1898–1903), then another *Penny Magazine*. Steele must have been referring to the latter in addressing Azrael, but a review of the 1899 and 1900 bound issues (if there were advertisements in the front or back of the issues, they've been removed) doesn't mention Azrael or astrology. They tend to focus on popular issues and cheer on the British Empire.

48 John Steele, journal entry, [frame 213], folder 2, vol. 1, MS 1847, CHL.

49 John Steele, journal entry, [frame 212], folder 2, vol. 1, MS 1847, CHL; James H. Martineau to George A. Smith, December 23, 1855, extract published as "Singular Phenomenon," *DN*, January 16, 1856, 357/4; James Henry Martineau, journal entries, 1852 (15), Friday, March 24, 1854 (29), and March 31, 1855 (37), *Uncommon Common Pioneer* (Provo, UT: BYU Religious Study Center, 2008).

50 Martineau, journal entry, July 10, 1869 (162), *Uncommon Common Pioneer*.

51 Phelps varied the titles of his almanacs. Steele's collection at BYU has them for 1854, 1855, 1859, 1862, 1863, 1864; there may have been others that were dispersed after Steele's death given that Frank A. Beckwith wrote in 1930 that Steele had "Every yearly almanac from 1851 on to his death the calendar of 1853 is the Deseret Almanac published by Richards in Great Salt Lake City" ("Valuable Relics Found in Old Trunk," *Millard County (UT) Chronicle*, July 24, 1930, 1/1, 8/4). His collection of other almanacs does include them up to the year of his death, 1903.

52 *Zadkiel's The Grammar of Astrology, Containing All Things Necessary for Calculating a Nativity*, 2nd ed. (London: Sherwood, Gilbert, and Piper, Paternoster Row, 1840), 4.

53 John Steele to Mrs. Catherine Steele, December 18, 1877, box 1, folder 12, Steele Collection, LTPSC. Box 3, folder 10, has some of Steele's astrological records.

54 M. M. Steele to John Steele Esqr, February 9, 1888, MS 24404, CHL; Olive E. DeMille Stevens to Mr. John Steele, March 26, April 13, 1901 (box 1, folder 27), and David Milne to Dear Bro. Steele, September 16, 1891 (box 1, folder 29): both in Steele Collection, LTPSC.

55 "The New Medical Law," *SLT*, March 30, 1894, 5/4–5; the act took effect March 8, 1894.

56 George Goddard, "Another Honest Man Victimized," *Deseret Weekly*, February 17, 1894, 281/2–3; Samuel E. Newton, M.D., "A Medical Protest," *Salt Lake Herald*, January 19, 1894, 8/4; "Unlicensed Physicians," *SLH*, February 1, 1894, 8 [frame 15]/5; "The Medical Law," *SLH*, February 1, 1894, 4/1–2; "Against the Medical Examiners," *SLH*, August 5, 1894, 10/1 (Dr. Jabez Taylor sues Medical Examiners); "Three Doctors Arrested," *SLT*, May 3, 1895, 8/4.

57 [John Steele] to Honorable James Duffin, January 31, 1897, retained copy, box 2, folder 13, Steele Collection, LTPSC.

58 Haller, *The People's Doctor*, 132.

59 Haller, *The People's Doctor*, 92–93.

60 [John Steele] to Honorable James Duffin, January 31, 1897, retained copy, box 2, folder 13, Steele Collection, LTPSC; for instance, see Haller, *The People's Doctor*, 132.

61 *Utah State Gazetteer and Business Directory, 1903–04* (Salt Lake City: R. L. Polk, 1903), 2:455.

62 John Steele to Latitie [Letisha] Todd, August 15, 1901, copy in author's possession, original donated to Steele Collection, LTPSC.

63 E. Connelly to "My Dear Brother John Steel," December 6, 1877, photocopy in author's possession. The subscription list is in box 2, folder 6, Steele Collection, LTPSC.

64 Prof. H. A. Harraden's *Complete Mail Course of Twenty Illustrated Lessons in Hypnotism*, box 3, folder 9, and box 3, folder 22, Steele Collection, LTPSC; "Three Messages by Mental Vibration," box 3, folder 14, Steele Collection, LTPSC. Also see "Three Messages by Mental Vibration," *Los Angeles Times*, Sunday, July 19, 1903, 1/4–5; "Messages Transmitted by Mental Vibration," *The Times-Democrat* (New Orleans), Sunday, July 19, 1903, 7/6–7.

65 "Original Lectures: Typhoid Fever, by S. M. Bemiss," *The Medical News: A Weekly Journal of Medical Science* (Saturday, December 2, 1882) no. 23: 45 (box 3, folder 25, Steele Collection, LTPSC).

66 "Toquerville," *Washington County News*, January 14, 1899, 1/4, 4/1.

67 "Parowan. Pioneer Day Celebration," *DN*, January 18, 1902, 7/4.

68 [John Steele] to *Family Herald & Weekly Star*, December 8, 1898, and February 8, 1899 (1898 in box 3, folder 16; 1899 in box 3, folder 15, Steele Collection, LTPSC).

69 John Steele to Pres Wilford Woodruff, May 5, 1889, retained copy, box 3, folder 3, Steele Collection, LTPSC.

70 Wilford Woodruff to Elder John Steele, May 9, 1889, MS 2683, folder 3, CHL.

71 Chandless, *A Visit to Salt Lake City*, 193–94; Ronald G. Watt, *The Mormon Passage of George D. Watt, First British Convert, Scribe for Zion* (Logan: Utah State University Press, 2009), 161–62; Woodruff, entry for June 15, 1867, *Wilford Woodruff Journals*, 4:73; William Hepworth Dixon, *New America* (Philadelphia: J. B. Lippincott, 1867), 214–16); this is a one-volume edition. Dixon refers to "a saint named Wall" marrying his half-sister. Most likely this was George D. Watt. Brigham Young said marrying full siblings was prevented by prejudice, not religious scruples. Incestuous marriages among the Mormons were almost unheard of unless one counts marrying stepchildren or stepparents.

72 M. M. Steele to "My Dear Father," December 28, 1891, box 1, folder 17, Steele Collection, LTPSC.

73 "The Law of Adoption," *Deseret Evening News*, April 14, 1894, 9/1–7; John Steele to President George Q. Cannon, April 23, 1894, box 3, folder 3, retained copy, Steele Collection, LTPSC.

74 Uncle John Steele to Latitia [Letisha] Todd, February 2, 1893, copy in author's possession, original donated to Steele Collection, LTPSC.

75 J. Cecil Alter to Frank A. Beckwith, September 23, 1932, copy in author's possession. Alter also wrote: "The manuscript on file in the [Church] Historian's office is in the same handwriting, and many sentences are copied verbatim, but it is a condensation, of the more important facts as shown in greater detail in the journal you sent. Now the fact is, that Church manuscript, which is clearly based entirely on the manuscript you sent, goes on for about one-third its length with material of the same general trend—noteworthy facts of his life—after the termination of the journal you sent. In Other words, both Mr. [A. William] Lund the librarian and I are convinced that there is much more of the journal, at least into the 1880s, and we feel that we ought to locate it by all means, so we could use it in its entirety. We do not want to use a part of it, and then find in later years that there is more of it."

76 John Steele, July 3, 1898, beginning "It was in Eighteen fourty Six," written on the back of a letter from R. G. Dunn & Co. dated July 13, 1894; copy in author's possession. Also see John Steele, verse beginning "Twas in the year of ninety ^nine^," December 17, 1899 (box 3, folder 6, Steele Collection, LTPSC).

77 "Local and General," *Washington County News*, April 14, 1900, 2/2; "Snapshots at Utah," *Salt Lake Telegram*, January 13, 1904, p. 6/3–4 (identical story in "What Is Going On In Utah," *SLT*, January 13, 1904, 3/6).

78 Phil Robinson, *Sinners and Saints* (Boston: Roberts Brothers, 1883), 169.

79 Cowley went through Panguitch, preached in Kanarra with Mahonri Steele,

and went to Toquerville (Kanarraville Ward Record Book B, p. 286 [19 March 1903]); "Journal History of the Church of Jesus Christ of Latter-day Saints," March 26, 1903, p. 6 (CHL), quoting minutes of a meeting of the First Presidency held in the Salt Lake Temple that morning; "Toquerville," *DN,* March 25, 1903, 7/5; Irene M. Bates and E. Gary Smith, *Lost Legacy* (Urbana: University of Illinois Press, 1996), 6–7.

80 H. Michael Marquardt, comp., *Early Patriarchal Blessings of The Church of Jesus Christ of Latter-Day Saints* (Salt Lake City: Smith-Pettit Foundation, 2007) and *Later Patriarchal Blessings of the Church of Jesus Christ of Latter-day Saints* (Salt Lake City: Smith-Pettit Foundation, 2012) give a wide selection of patriarchal blessings.

81 John Steele to Mr James Jepsen [Jepson], July 1, 1893 [1903], retained copy misdated by ten years (box 3, folder 16, Steele Collection, LTPSC).

82 "Raphael," *The Book of Fate Whereby All Questions might be Answered Respecting the Present and Future* (London: W. Foulsham, 1887), preface, [3].

83 "Taylor," *Holbrook (AZ) Argus,* March 28, 1903, 4/2.

84 Josie [Fish Barraclough] to "My dear Grandpa," May 5, 1903, box 1, folder 20, Steele Collection, LTPSC. His illness may have lingered; on July 7 Steele's granddaughter Mary Jensen wrote "so sory your health is so poor" (Mary Jensen to "Dear Grandpa," July 7, 1903, box 1, folder 16, Steele Collection, LTPSC).

85 Mahonri [Steele] to Mr. John Steele, May 28, 1903, box 1, folder 17, Steele Collection, LTPSC.

86 "News from Four States," *Salt Lake Telegram,* June 10, 1903, 2/1; F. E. Eldredge to Brother John Steele, June 20, 1903, box 1, folder 27, Steele Collection, LTPSC.

87 "Kanarra," *Iron County (UT) Record,* July 24, 1903, 1/5.

88 Mahonri M. Steele to Mr. John Steele, September 11, 1903, box 1, folder 17; Josie [Barraclough] to My Dear Grandpa, September 13, 1903, box 1, folder 20: both in Steele Collection, LTPSC.

89 John Steele to "Azrael," [1900], transcript of retained copy by Iona J. Poling in author's possession. Dr. Singleton Husted confirmed Steele had a lower back injury and limped but discerned no scars in the affected area (Dr. S. Husted report, December 24, 1887, in J. Steele pension file for Mormon Battalion service, Utah State Archives, Salt Lake City).

90 "Azrael" to John Steele, [1900], transcript by Iona J. Poling in author's possession.

91 Reba Roundy LeFevre, oral history interview by author January 24, 1987, 21–22; Dr. C[hilds] Mantor, Examining Surgeon's Certificate, Mantor, June 20, 1882, J. Steele pension file for Mormon Battalion service, Utah State Archives, Salt Lake City.

92 Interview by author with Reba Roundy LeFevre, January 24, 1987, 21–22.

93 Copy of the blessing in Mahonri M. Steele's handwriting provided to me by Reba Roundy LeFevre, Elizabeth's granddaughter.

94 "Kanarra," *Iron County (UT) Record*, December 26, 1903, 5/1, with December 17 byline.

95 John Steele, journal entry, [frames 95–96], MS 1847, folder 3, vol. 2; John Steele, journal entry, August 7, 1878 [frame 71], MS D 1847, folder 2, vol. 3, CHL.

96 "Kanarra," *Iron County (UT) Record*, December 26, 1903, 5/1, with December 27 byline.

97 "Another Pioneer Gone: John Steel[e] Goes to His Reward at 83—Holiday Cheers," *Deseret Evening News*, January 5, 1904, 9/1.

98 "What Is Going on In Utah," *SLT*, January 13, 1904, 3/6, reprinting story from missing January 9, 1904, issue of *Iron County (UT) Record*; "Snapshots at Utah," *Salt Lake Telegram*, January 13, 1904, 6/3–4; "Utah State News," *Clipper* (Davis County, UT), January 22, 1904, 2/1; "Utah State News," *Eureka Reporter*, January 22, 1904, 2/1; "Utah State News," *Logan (UT) Republican*, January 23, 1904, 2/1; "Genealogy of Wm C. Mitchell Parowan Utah Aug 20th 1907" (Mitchell's autobiography), filed as a loose page in the Parowan High Priests Quorum Genealogy Record, LR 6778, series 13.

99 "PANGUITCH: DEATH OF JOHN STEEL: Pioneer of Utah and Mormon Battalion: Veteran Closes Brilliant Career," Special Correspondence, *DN*, February 4, 1904, 14/4–5.

100 Howard M. Bahr, *Saints Observed: Studies of Mormon Village Life, 1850–2005* (Salt Lake City: University of Utah Press, 2014), xii.

101 Richard T. Ely, "Economic Aspects of Mormonism," *Harper's Monthly Magazine* 106, no. 635 (April 1903): 667, 669.

102 There are several excellent studies of this subject; see Leonard J. Arrington, Feramorz Y. Fox, and Dean L. May, *Building the City of God* (Salt Lake City: Deseret Book, 1976); Garth L. Mangum and Bruce Blumell, *Mormons' War on Poverty* (Salt Lake City: University of Utah, 1993); and Glen Rudd, *Pure Religion* (Salt Lake City: Church of Jesus Christ of Latter-day Saints, 1995).

103 Janet Burton Seegmiller, *A History of Iron County: Community Above Self* (Salt Lake City: Utah State Historical Society and Iron County Commission, 1998).

Appendix

1 See Wesley P. Larsen, "The 'Letter' or Were the Powell Men Really Killed by Indians?," *Canyon Legacy* 17 (Spring 1993): 12–19; and Don Lago, *The Powell Expedition: New Discoveries about John Wesley Powell's 1869 River Journey* (Reno: University of Nevada Press, 2019), 292–98.

2 "William Leany Reminiscences, 1888," 100–101, 68/69 [double-paged], MS 23134, CHL: "In March of 1857 I dreamed that I [and] Br J Steele stood in a row in the town of parrowan our backs to the North and looking to our left far up the Mountain We saw three large white ship[s] thre[e] deckers and three rows of port holes a[nd] a cannon pointing out at each hole I saw and

remarked they were after a flock of sheep and the sheep we[re?] admiring them at the same time pointing at them with my left fingers and in that time they had passed in front of us to the west and I pointed to th[em] with my right fingers saying [see?] how the [big?] of the things is departed and there they lay the hulks of three canal boats with muddy water and dirty oars in each end Bp. H. Lunt came from the April conf[e]rence the next Month and seemed much afraid of consequences I told him My dream and told him the sheep would beat [bleat?] and the army would not get a good man or a good woman some had ones they might get and We would be better without them and said it would be so and so it was."

3 John Steele, "The Late William Laney" (in the body of the story his surname is spelled "Leany"), *Deseret Weekly News,* January 23, 1892, p. 159, col. 2. Mahonri M. Steele wrote John, "Your old associates are fast gathering to the other side. I am wonderfully well pleased that Elder Laney bore so good a character at his demise. He was one of the Lords Noblemen and I am confident there will be hardly a hairs weight ~~in the scale~~ against him when put into the scales as his surroundings will be taken into consideration. Peace to his ashes" (Mahonri M. Steele to John Steele, January 13, 1892, copy in author's possession).

4 That would place their acquaintance no earlier than 1846, when both were at Council Bluffs. Leany was with John Steele and others in the original Iron County mission ([frames 12–13, 24], "Leany Reminiscences"). Leany's twin brother, Isaac (who spelled his surname "Laney"), lived in the Tenth Ward when John Steele did (as did brothers Jacob and William Hamblin). .

5 This suggests that if there were hard feelings for Leany's part in getting up a successful political opposition to Steele in early 1861, they had dissipated.

6 Presumably the families of Utah pioneer Armela Shanks Berry and Parowan pioneers Priddy Meeks, Orson B. Adams, David Hendricks, and Tarlton Lewis, one-time bishop in Parowan (unrelated to James Lewis).

7 Presumably Bill Smith's "dog" was James Lewis. This was not Leany's first conflict with Apostle Erastus Snow. James Godson Bleak (*Annals of the Southern Mission* [Salt Lake City: Greg Kofford Books, 2019], 190–91) reported in 1869 that "For months past Elder William Leany, of Harrisburg Branch of Washington Ward, has manifested a strong spirit of accusation against the course and policy of President Erastus Snow, of this mission, and against Bishop Robert D. Covington of Washington Ward and as an opposer of Elder James Lewis, of Harrisburg Branch." Pressed to put his charges in writing, Leany made a series of accusations against Lewis but eventually withdrew them and asked for forgiveness.

8 Leany's autobiography reports ("Leany Reminiscences," 19/20, 35/36): "But in the first meeting ever held in a log house in Iron co. pres. G. A. [Smith] told us that he had weltered nine years under pres. youngs displeasure from the falsehoods of a fellow missionary and I have often thought I May have weltered 19 [written over; possibly 18] years under his displeasure by the foul tongue of

judge James Lewis who seems to Me a natural tatler & slanderer for God and some of My neighbors know that I have often said of pres. G A Smith I thought him one of the best of men yes I have often said of him as good as Moses Noah or Abraham though that may be to strong language. But I know the judge done all he could to make strife there and with Presidents J. C. L. Smith and Many others E. snow and Bp. J. T. willis[.] But I write these things not desiring to incite hard feeling[s] again and judge ^Lewis but^ humbly hoping and fervently praying We May all do better and learn to forget and forgive but God and the holy Angels can bear me witness I am and have been clear of all they acused Me of and God and the Angels shall bear me witness I have often in My dreams seen them as dead trees dead logs big A[postles?] and one or More of them as the church dogs and as greedy dogs so often named by Isaiah Ezekiel and the old prophets." Leany's feelings about James Lewis were similar to James Henry Martineau's, as mentioned earlier in this book.

9 From "Names to be Baptized for | Sydney B. Aden | William A. Aden | . . . ," "Leany Reminiscences," [frames 74–75]: "Bp. W. H. Dame sent a [dawd?] of his dogs to kill Me in My own door yard though I never could convict him as two of the worst of his Brs. Inlaw Chas & B[arney]. Carter nor did I ever think him or them as guilty as the tongue of slander I speak of and one pre text was that I had sold the Mountain Meadow Murdered Company onions though I never did it and another was that I had taken in and harbored one of the Company and that was false the facts are that I took in and cared for a young W. A. Aden who came to parrowan with Br [Isaac? or Jas?] Adair who lived and died in Washington and he found Me and knew Me as his Father Dr. S. B. Aden had taken Me in out of a Mob in paris Tennessee some fourteen years befor and cared for me and I could or would not do less for he & his then or to day though I knew I would be shot on the streets like a dog."

10 As Don Lago suggests in *The Powell Expedition* (Reno: University of Nevada Press, 2018, pp. 292–98), this probably refers to a Toquerville tragedy on March 16, 1875: Richard Fryer, in a fit of insanity, killed his wife Teresa and Thomas Batty and shot his own infant son Joseph; Richard was then killed by the sheriff after refusing to surrender. The baby lingered until March 18 (see *DN,* March 31, 1875, which includes the inquests of the deceased). The sheriff was Ashton Nebeker, though one report says his surname was Bringhurst, undoubtedly a confusion with Bishop Bringhurst ("From Toquerville," *DN*, May 26, 1875, 264/4; "From Toquerville," *DN*, August 25, 1875, 473/3; "From Toquerville" and "Beaver City," *Salt Lake Tribune,* March 26, 1875, 4/3).

11 Captain William Henry Hooper was Utah's one-time congressional delegate as well as a merchant and politician who was also engaged in mining. I do not know what Leany was referring to regarding Hooper.

12 It appears the letters *n* and *o* were written here and then dabbed out; perhaps he meant to write "now"; it is at the right end of the page so maybe he ran out of space.

13 George J. Adams, a one-time actor, skilled debater, and effective orator, was excommunicated after Joseph Smith's death and for a time allied himself with fellow excommunicant William B. "Bill" Smith, the disreputable brother of Joseph Smith. James Lewis was in the east with Adams to gather money when he learned the Smith brothers had been killed.

14 LDS Church President John Taylor.

15 Missouri judge—and later governor—Austin A. King; presumably Missouri judge Joel Turnham, justice of the peace Adam Black, and William Mann, who was one of the leaders in the massacre of Mormons at Haun's Mill in Missouri, where William Leany's twin brother, Isaac Laney, was shot seven times but survived.

16 Hosea 4:1: "Hear the word of the Lord, ye children of Israel: for the Lord hath a controversy with the inhabitants of the land, because there is no truth, nor mercy, nor knowledge of God in the land." Hosea 4:2: "By swearing, and lying, and killing, and stealing, and committing adultery, they break out, and blood toucheth blood."

17 Curiously, the meaning of *ward* plays into the interpretation of this letter because if a ward is considered a community, the event Leany describes would presumably have been Parowan. If it happened when Steele lived in Toquerville, *ward* would have referred to a religious congregation, as Leany lived in Harrisburg, which was at one time part of Toquerville Ward.

18 Steele was first ward clerk of the Tenth Ward; William Strong seems to have been the Mormon Battalion member of that name.

19 Lyman Leonard was a Salt Lake City hatter.

20 The transcripts, both handwritten (I suspect by Wesley P. Larsen) and typed, supply these words; however, the document is torn so now these words are missing.

21 This word is supplied by the transcriber, but the original is now illegible.

22 The transcriber interpreted this word as "angry"; the first three letters seem to me to read "Ma" and the rest are illegible. There is no dropped loop as one would expect if the last letter was *y*.

23 The last three letters of this word are a guess.

24 For a transcript of the first, dated May 11, 1884, see Kerry William Bate, *The Women: A Family Story* (Salt Lake City: University of Utah Press, 2016), 69.

25 Emily was apparently staying with her parents near Mesquite Flat, where her father, Edward Bunker, and others established a United Order on January 18, 1877; Mahonri Steele was secretary of this venture (Bleak, *Annals of the Southern Mission*, 496 [1877]). The settlement was named Bunkerville after her father. Mahonri wrote to his mother on February 20, 1878 (the same day she wrote to Emily), "May hap Ill go to the Flatt when I det [get] home."

26 Edward Bunker Jr., who had recently moved from Panguitch back to Mesquite.

27 Arthur Steele, Emily's sickly son, who died in his teens. Mahonri wrote to his

father, "I write to inform you of the death of Arthur who died at 25 min to 12 to day He suffered every thing up to the last minute" (Mahonri M. Steele to John Steele, May 18, 1891, John Steele correspondence, MS 24404, CHL). The elder Steele worked out the horoscope for the time of Arthur's death on the bottom of this letter.

28 Susann Adams Steele, Catherine and John's daughter, married William Augustus Bringhurst and had just given birth to Eleanor Campbell Bringhurst. Selinda Dolby Palmer Bringhurst was his first wife. Johny is presumably Susann's son John Samuel Bringhurst.

29 Emily Abbott Bunker was Emily's mother; her maternal grandmother, who was still living, was Abigail Smith Abbott.

30 Susann Adams Steele Bringhurst, Jane Catherine Steele Jensen, and John Alma Steele, all children of John and Catherine Campbell Steele.

BIBLIOGRAPHY

Adams, Ann R. Papers. MS 20208. Church History Library, Church of Jesus Christ of Latter-day Saints, Salt Lake City.

Alder, Douglas D., and Karl F. Brooks. *A History of Washington County: From Isolation to Destination.* Salt Lake City: Utah State Historical Society and Washington County Commission, 1996.

Alexander, Thomas G., and James B. Allen. *Mormons and Gentiles: A History of Salt Lake City.* Boulder, CO: Pruett, 1984.

Allen, James B. "The Unusual Jurisdiction of County Probate Courts in the Territory of Utah." *Utah Historical Quarterly* 36, no. 2 (Spring 1968): 132–42.

Anderson, Maybelle Harmon. *Appleton Milo Harmon Goes West.* Berkeley, CA: Gillick, 1946.

Anderson, Thelma C. *Workman Family History.* Salt Lake City: Publishers Press, 1962.

Annual Directory of the City of Chicago. Donnelly, Lloyd, 1877.

Arrington, Leonard J. *Great Basin Kingdom: An Economic History of the Latter-day Saints, 1830–1900.* Lincoln: University of Nebraska Press, 1968.

Arrington, Leonard J., Feramorz Y. Fox, and Dean L. May. *Building the City of God: Community and Cooperation Among the Mormons.* Salt Lake City: Deseret Book, 1976.

Backus, Anna Jean. *Mountain Meadows Witness: The Life and Times of Bishop Philip Klingensmith.* Spokane, WA: Arthur H. Clark, 1996.

Badger, Carlos Ashby. Papers. MSS 1298. L. Tom Perry Special Collections, Harold B. Lee Library, Brigham Young University, Provo, UT.

Badger, Rodney J., *Liahona and Iron Rod.* Bountiful, UT: Family History Publishers, 1985.

Bagley, Will. *Blood of the Prophets: Brigham Young and the Massacre at Mountain Meadows.* Norman: University of Oklahoma Press, 2002.

Bagley, Will, ed. *The Whites Want Every Thing.* Norman, OK: Arthur H. Clark, 2019.

Bahr, Howard M. *Saints Observed: Studies of Mormon Village Life, 1850–2005.* Salt Lake City: University of Utah Press, 2014.

Bancroft, Hubert Howe. *History of Utah.* 1889. Reprint, Salt Lake City: Bookcraft, 1964.

Bancroft, Hubert Howe. *Retrospection, Political and Personal.* New York: Bancroft, 1913.

Barney, Ronald O. *The Mormon Vanguard Brigade of 1847: Norton Jacob's Record.* Logan: Utah State University Press, 2005.

Barton, Bea W. *The Mormon Battalion: Mississippi Saints and Pioneers, Douglas*

County, Colorado: Honorable Remembrance to the Latest Generation, 1846–2005. N.p.: Johnson Printing, 2008.

Bate, Kerry William. *The Women: A Family Story.* Salt Lake City: University of Utah Press, 2016.

Bates, Irene M., and E. Gary Smith. *Lost Legacy: The Mormon Office of Presiding Patriarch.* Urbana: University of Illinois Press, 1996.

Bean, George Washington. *Autobiography of George Washington Bean, a Utah Pioneer of 1847, and His Family Records.* Compiled by Flora Diana Bean Horne. Salt Lake City: Utah Printing, 1945.

Bean, George Washington. "The Journal of George W. Bean: Las Vegas Springs, New Mexico Territory, 1856–57." Edited by Harvey C. Dees. *Nevada Historical Society Quarterly* 15 (Fall 1972): 3–29.

Beckwith, Frank A. *Indian Joe: In Person and In Background.* Delta, UT: DuWil, 1975.

Beckwith, Frank A. "Shameful Friday: A Critical Study of the Mountain Meadows Massacre." Typewritten manuscript. Mormon file, c. 1805–1995 (HM 31255), Huntington Library, San Marino, CA.

Belfast Directory for 1831–32. Belfast: Robert Donaldson, ca. 1832.

Belfast and Province of Ulster Directory for 1877. Belfast: Belfast News-Letter, 1877.

Bemiss, S. M. "Original Lectures: Typhoid Fever." *The Medical News: A Weekly Journal of Medical Science* 41, no. 23 (December 2, 1882): 617–21.

Bennett, Richard E. "He is our Friend: Thomas L. Kane and the Mormons in Exodus." *BYU Studies* 48, no. 4 (2009): 37–56.

Bigler, David L., and Will Bagley, eds. *Army of Israel: Mormon Battalion Narratives.* Logan: Utah State University Press, 2000.

Bigler, David L., and Will Bagley, eds. *Innocent Blood: Essential Narratives of the Mountain Meadows Massacre.* Norman, OK: Arthur H. Clark, 2008.

Bitton, Davis. *George Q. Cannon: A Biography.* Salt Lake City: Deseret Book, 1999.

Black, Susan Easton, comp. Membership of The Church of Jesus Christ of Latter-day Saints, 1830–1848. 50 vols. Provo, UT: Brigham Young University Religious Studies Center, 1989.

Blackburn, Abner. *Frontiersman: Abner Blackburn.* Edited by Will Bagley. Salt Lake City: University of Utah Press, 1992.

Bleak, James Godson. *The Annals of the Southern Mission: Record of the History of the Settlement of Southern Utah.* Edited by Aaron McArthur and Reid L. Neilson. Salt Lake City: Greg Kofford Books, 2019.

Brew, J. O. "Hopi Prehistory and History to 1850." In *Handbook of North American Indians,* vol. 9, *Southwest,* edited by Alfonso Ortiz. Washington, DC: Smithsonian Institution, 1979.

Brimhall, George Washington. *The Workers of Utah.* Provo, UT: Enquirer, 1889. Reprint, Washington, DC: Lincoln Press, ca. 1960s.

Brooks, Juanita. *The Mountain Meadows Massacre.* Norman: University of Oklahoma Press, 1974.

Brooks, Juanita. Papers. Juanita Brooks Collection. MIC A 1307. Utah Historical Society, Salt Lake City.

Brooks, Juanita. *Quicksand and Cactus.* Salt Lake City: Howe Brothers, 1982.

Brown, Thomas D. *Journal of the Southern Indian Mission: Diary of Thomas D. Brown.* Edited by Juanita Brooks. Logan: Utah State University, 1972.

Buchanan, Frederick S. "The Ebb and Flow of Mormonism in Scotland." *BYU Studies* 27, no. 2 (1987): 27–52.

Buerger, David John. "The Development of the Mormon Temple Endowment Ceremony." *Dialogue: A Journal of Mormon Thought* 20, no. 4 (Winter 1987): 75–122.

Buerger, David John. "'The Fulness of the Priesthood': The Second Anointing in Latter-day Saint Theology and Practice." *Dialogue: A Journal of Mormon Thought* 16, no. 1 (1983): 10–44.

Bullock, Thomas. Papers. Thomas Bullock Collection. MS 27307. Church History Library, Church of Jesus Christ of Latter-day Saints, Salt Lake City.

Bullock, Thomas. *Thomas Bullock Nauvoo Journal.* Edited by Greg R. Knight. Orem, UT: Grandin Books, 1994.

Bushman, Richard Lyman, with Jed Woodworth. *Joseph Smith, Rough Stone Rolling.* New York: Alfred A. Knopf, 2005.

Campbell, Richardson. *History of the Rechabite Order.* Manchester, England: Board of Directors of the Order, 1911.

Carruth, LaJean Purcell (put under Carruth), and Ronald G. Watt. *Liverpool to Great Salt Lake: The 1851 Journal of Missionary George D. Watt.* Lincoln: University of Nebraska Press, 2022.

Carvalho, Solomon Nunes. *Incidents of Travel and Adventure in the Far West.* Edited by Bertram Wallace Korn. Philadelphia: Jewish Publication Society of America, 1954.

Chandless, William. *A Visit to Salt Lake City; being A Journey Across the Plains and a residence in the Mormon Settlements at Utah.* London: Smith, Elder, 1857.

Christy, Howard A. "The Walker War: Defense and Conciliation as Strategy." *Utah Historical Quarterly* 47, no. 4 (Fall 1979): 395–420.

Clayton, William. *An Intimate Chronicle: The Journals of William Clayton.* Edited by George D. Smith. Salt Lake City: Signature Books, 1995.

Cockayne, Thomas Oswald. *Leechdoms, Wortcunning, and Starcraft of Early England. Being a Collection of Documents, for the most part never before printed, illustrating the History of Science in this Country Before the Norman Conquest.* 2 vols. London: Longman, Green, Longman, Roberts, and Green, 1864.

Colbert, Thomas Burnell. "Poweshiek." *The Biographical Dictionary of Iowa.* Iowa City: University of Iowa Press, 2009.

Compton, Todd. "The Big Washout: The 1862 Flood in Santa Clara." *Utah Historical Quarterly* 77, no. 2 (Spring 2009): 108–25.

Compton, Todd. "Conquering the Black Ridge: The Communitarian Road in Pioneer Utah." *Utah Historical Quarterly* 82, no. 3 (Summer 2014): 222–33.

Compton, Todd. *A Frontier Life: Jacob Hamblin, Explorer and Indian Missionary.* Salt Lake City: University of Utah Press, 2013.

Cooke, Philip St. George. *The Conquest of New Mexico and California, an Historical and Personal Narrative.* Albuquerque: Horn and Wallace, 1964.

Cooke, P[hilip] St. George, Lt. Col. "Report of Lieut. Col. P. St. George Cooke of his March from Santa Fe, New Mexico, to San Diego, Upper California." Edited by Hamilton Gardner. *Utah Historical Quarterly* 22, no. 1 (January 1954): 15–40.

Coombs, Isaiah Moses. *Isaiah Moses Coombs—Journal 1859 to 1869.* Edited by Jim Tagg. N.p: Amazon, 2017.

Crampton, C. Gregory. "Indian Country." *Utah Historical Quarterly* 39, no. 2 (Spring 1971): 90–94.

Culpeper, Nicholas. *Culpeper's Complete Herbal.* London: Richard Evans, 1814.

Dame, William H. Correspondence and Diaries, 1850–1858. William H. Dame Papers. MIC A 13. Utah Historical Society, Salt Lake City.

Dame, William H. Papers. Vault MSS 55. Brigham Young University, Provo, UT.

Denholm, James. *The History of the City of Glasgow and Suburbs.* 3rd ed. Glasgow: R. Chapman, 1804.

Dickson, Charles. *Revolt in the North: Antrim and Down in 1798.* London: Constable, 1997.

Diehl, Isaac E. WPA Biographies, 1936. B-289. Utah Historical Society, Salt Lake City.

Divett, Robert T. *Medicine and the Mormons.* Bountiful, UT: Horizon, 1981.

Dixon, William Hepworth. *New America.* Philadelphia: J. B. Lippincott, 1867.

Driggs, Nevada W. "When Captain Fremont Slept in Grandma McGregor's Bed." *Utah Historical Quarterly* 41, no. 2 (Spring 1973): 178–81.

Duncan, Clifford. "The Northern Utes of Utah." In *A History of Utah's American Indians,* edited by Forrest S. Cuch. Salt Lake City: Utah State Division of Indians Affairs and Utah State Division of History, 2000.

Ely, Richard T. "Economic Aspects of Mormonism." *Harper's Monthly Magazine* 106, no. 635 (April 1903): 667–78.

Erickson, Dan. *"As a Thief in the Night": The Mormon Quest for Millennial Deliverance.* Salt Lake City: Signature Books, 1998.

Erickson, Dan. "Joseph Smith's 1891 Millennial Prophecy: The Quest for Apocalyptic Deliverance." *Journal of Mormon History* 22, no. 2 (Fall 1996): 1–34.

Executive Documents of the House of Representatives for the first session of the Fiftieth Congress 1887–'88 in thirty-two volumes. Vol. 26. Washington, DC: Government Printing Office, 1889. Congressional Series of United States Public Documents, 2557:131.

Ferris, Mrs. [Elizabeth Cornelia] B. G. *The Mormons at Home; With some Incidents of Travel from Missouri to California, 1852–3. In a Series of Letters.* New York: Dix & Edwards, 1856.

Fielding, Robert Kent, comp. and ed. *The Tribune Reports of the Trials of John D.*

Lee for the Massacre at Mountain Meadows. Higganum, CT: Kent's Books, 2006.

Fischer, David Hackett. *Liberty and Freedom.* Oxford: Oxford University Press, 2005.

Fish, Joseph. *The Autobiography of Joseph Fish by Himself with Notes by His Sons Silas and Jesse.* N.p.: Lulu, 2009.

Fish, Seymour P., and Vera P. Fish. *Family of Joseph Fish (1840–1926) Genealogical and Biographical Stories and Sketches.* Provo, UT: J. Grant Stevenson, 1970.

Fleek, Sherman L. *History May Be Searched in Vain: A Military History of the Mormon Battalion.* Spokane, WA: Arthur H. Clark, 2006.

Ford, Thomas. *A History of Illinois from its Commencement as a State in 1818 to 1847.* Edited by Milo Milton Quaife. Chicago: Lakeside Press, 1946.

Foster, Craig L. "'That Canny Scotsman': John Sharp and the Union Pacific Negotiations, 1869–72." *Journal of Mormon History* 27, no. 2 (Fall 2001): 197–214.

Foster, R. F. *Modern Ireland, 1600–1972.* New York: Allen Lane/Penguin, 1988.

Fowler, Catherine S., and Don D. Fowler. "Notes on the History of the Southern Paiutes and Western Shoshonis." *Utah Historical Quarterly* 39, no. 2 (Spring 1971): 95–128.

Francaviglia, Richard. *Mapmakers of New Zion: A Cartographic History of Mormonism.* Salt Lake City: University of Utah Press, 2015.

Gera, Dov, and Wayne Horowitz. "Antiochus IV in Life and Death: Evidence from the Babylonian Astronomical Diaries." *Journal of the American Oriental Society* 117, no. 2 (April–June 1997): 240–52.

Gerard, John. *The Herbal or General History of Plants.* 1633. Revised and enlarged by Thomas Johnson. New York: Dover, 1975.

Gillespie, Raymond, and Stephen A. Royle. *Irish Historic Towns Atlas No. 12, Belfast, Part I, to 1840.* Dublin: Dublin University Press, 2003.

Gladstone, William Ewart. *The Gladstone Diaries.* Edited by H. C. G. Matthew. 14 vols. Oxford: Clarendon, 1986.

Godfrey, Kenneth W. "Crime and Punishment in Mormon Nauvoo, 1839–1846." *BYU Studies* 32, nos. 1–2 (1992): 195–227.

Golder, Frank Alfred, Thomas A. Bailey, and J. Lyman Smith, eds. *The March of the Mormon Battalion from Council Bluffs to California Taken from the Journal of Henry Standage.* New York: Century, 1928.

Gordon, Sarah Barringer. *The Mormon Question: Polygamy and Constitutional Conflict in Nineteenth-Century America.* Chapel Hill: University of North Carolina Press, 2002.

Green, Nelson Winch, and Mary Ettie V. [Marriette "Mary Etta" Coray Henderson Jones] Smith. *Mormonism: It's* [sic] *Rise, Progress and Present Condition.* Hartford, CT: Belknap and Bliss, 1872.

Grieve, Maud. *A Modern Herbal.* 2 vols. 1931. Reprint, New York: Dover, 1971.

Grob-Fitzgibbon, Benjamin. *Turning Points of the Irish Revolution: The British*

Government, Intelligence, and the Cost of Indifference, 1912–1921. New York: Palgrave Macmillan, 2007.

Haight, Isaac Chauncey. *Journal of Isaac Chauncey Haight with Historical Notes.* Edited by Paul Jones. San Bernardino, CA: Paul Jones, 2010.

Hall, Alaric. *Elves in Anglo-Saxon England: Matters of Belief, Health, Gender and Identity.* Woodbridge, England: Boydell, 2007.

Hall, John Clark. *A Concise Anglo-Saxon Dictionary for the Use of Students.* New York: Macmillan, 1916.

Hall, Samuel Carter, and Anna Maria Hall. *Hall's Ireland: Mr and Mrs Hall's Tour of 1840.* Edited by Michael Scott. 1841–43. Reprint, London: Sphere Books, 1984.

Haller, John S., Jr. *The People's Doctor: Samuel Thomson and the American Botanical Movement, 1790–1860.* Carbondale, IL: Southern Illinois University Press, 2000.

Hardy, Katherine. "Reading Urine in Medieval Medicine." *Public Domain Review* (April 19, 2023).

Harrison, J. F. C. *Quest for the New Moral World: Robert Owen and the Owenites in Britain and America.* New York: Charles Scribner's Sons, 1969.

Harwell, William S. *Manuscript History of Brigham Young, 1847–1850.* Salt Lake City: Collier's, 1997.

Hatch, Nelle Spilsbury. *Mother Jane's Story.* Wasco, CA: Shafer, 1964.

Heap, Gwinn Harris. *Central Route to the Pacific, from the Valley of the Mississippi to California: Journal of the Expedition of E. F. Beale, Superintendent of Indians Affairs in California, and Gwinn Harris Heap, from Missouri to California in 1853.* Philadelphia: Lippincott, Grambo, 1854.

Henderson, James Alexander. *The Belfast and Province of Ulster Directory for 1852.* Belfast: James Alexander Henderson, 1852.

Henderson, John. *Henderson's Belfast Directory and Northern Repository for 1846–47.* Belfast: John Henderson, 1846.

Henderson, John. *Henderson's New Belfast Directory, and Northern Repository, for 1843–44.* Belfast: John Henderson, 1843.

Henderson, John. *Henderson's New Belfast Directory, and Northern Repository, for 1846–47.* Belfast: John Henderson, 1846.

Henderson, John. *Henderson's New Belfast Directory, and Northern Repository* [for 1850]. Belfast: John Henderson, 1850.

Henry, Robert Selph. *The Story of the Mexican War.* New York: Da Capo, 1950.

Hess, John W. "John W. Hess, with the Mormon Battalion." *Utah Historical Quarterly* 4, no. 2 (April 1931): 47–55.

Hill, Raymond Lee. "When Mark Twain Worked the Mississippi." *Travel Magazine* 15, no. 7 (April 1910): 334–36.

Himmelfarb, Gertrude. *The Idea of Poverty: England in the Early Industrial Age.* New York: Vintage Books, 1985.

Hinton, Wayne K. *The Dixie National Forest: Managing an Alpine Forest in an Arid*

Setting. Cedar City, UT: USDA, Forest Service, Intermountain Region, Dixie National Forest, U.S. Government Printing Office, 1987.

Holland, Jeffrey R. "'Are We Not all Beggars?'" https://www.churchofjesuschrist.org/study/general-conference/2014/10/are-we-not-all-beggars?lang=eng.

Homer, Michael W. "'Similarity of Priesthood in Masonry': The Relationship between Freemasonry and Mormonism." *Dialogue: A Journal of Mormon Thought* 27, no. 3 (Fall 1994): 1–113.

Hutchison, I. G. C. "Glasgow Working-class Politics." In *The Working Class in Glasgow, 1750–1914*, edited by R. A. Cage. London: Croom Helm, 1987.

Jenson, Andrew. *Latter-day Saints Biographical Encyclopedia*. 1901. Reprint. Salt Lake City: Western Epics, 1971.

Jenson, Andrew. "Manuscript History of Pueblo, 1840–1850." MS 4029. Church History Library, Church of Jesus Christ of Latter-day Saints, Salt Lake City.

Jepson, James, Jr. "Memories and Experiences of James Jepson, Jr." Juanita Brooks Collection. B-103 box 167, folder 1. Utah Historical Society, Salt Lake City.

Johnson, Janiece. *Convicting the Mormons: The Mountain Meadows Massacre in American Culture*. Chapel Hill: University of North Carolina Press, 2023.

Johnson, Joel H. "Autobiographical Sketch of Joel H. Johnson." MS 12931. Church History Library, Church of Jesus Christ of Latter-day Saints, Salt Lake City.

Johnson, Nephi. "Autobiographical Sketch of Nephi Johnson." MS 23835. Church History Library, Church of Jesus Christ of Latter-day Saints, Salt Lake City.

Jones, Evan Y., and York F. Jones. *Iron Mining and Manufacturing in Utah*. Cedar City, UT: Southern Utah University Press, 2019.

Jones, Evelyn K. *Henry Lunt Biography and History of the Development of Southern Utah*. Provo, UT: BYU Family History Copy Center, 1996.

"Journal History of the Church of Jesus Christ of Latter-day Saints." Church History Library, Church of Jesus Christ of Latter-day Saints, Salt Lake City.

Kane, Elizabeth Wood. *Twelve Mormon Homes Visited in Succession on a Journey through Utah to Arizona*. Edited by Everett L. Cooley. Salt Lake City: Tanner Trust, University of Utah Library, 1974.

Kimball, Abraham A. "Abraham A. Kimball Journal." Mss B 34, box 2. Utah Historical Society/Utah State Archives, Millcreek.

Knack, Martha C. *Boundaries Between: The Southern Paiutes, 1775–1995*. Lincoln: University of Nebraska Press, 2004.

Kohl, J. G. *Travels in Scotland*. London: J. & D. A. Darling, 1849.

Lago, Don. *The Powell Expedition: New Discoveries about John Wesley Powell's 1869 River Journey*. Reno: University of Nevada Press, 2019.

Lancaster, Donald R. "Dixie Wine." Master's thesis, Brigham Young University, 1972.

Larsen, Wesley Pratt. *A Field Folio of Indian and Pioneer Medicinal Plants*. Toquerville, UT: Third Mesa, 1996.

Larsen, Wesley Pratt. "The 'Letter' or Were the Powell Men Really Killed by Indians?" *Canyon Legacy* 17 (Spring 1993): 12–19.

Larson, Andrew Karl. *Erastus Snow: The Life of a Missionary and Pioneer for the Early Mormon Church.* Salt Lake City: University of Utah Press, 1971.

Larson, Andrew Karl. *I Was Called to Dixie.* Salt Lake City: Deseret News Press, 1961.

Larson, A[ndrew] Karl. "Zion National Park with Some Reminiscences Fifty Years Later." *Utah Historical Quarterly* 37, no. 4 (Fall 1969): 409–25.

Larson, Gustive O. *The "Americanization" of Utah for Statehood.* San Marino, CA: Huntington Library, 1971.

Lauritzen, Diana, and Dr. James Swensen. "Recognizing Faces: Women's Portraits on the Salt Lake City and County Building." *Journal of Academic Research,* April 18, 2013. http://jur.byu.edu/?p=621.

Leany, William. "William Leany Reminiscences, 1888." Church History Library, Church of Jesus Christ of Latter-day Saints, Salt Lake City.

Lee, John Doyle. "Journal of the Iron County Mission, John D. Lee, Clerk, December 10, 1850–March 1, 1851." Edited by Gustive O. Larson. *Utah Historical Quarterly* 20: (April 1952): 109–34; (July 1952): 253–82; (October 1952): 353–83.

Lee, John Doyle. *Journals of John D. Lee, 1846–47 and 1859.* Edited by Charles Kelly. Salt Lake City: University of Utah Press, 1984.

Lee, John Doyle. *A Mormon Chronicle: The Diaries of John D. Lee, 1848–1876.* Edited by Robert Glass Cleland and Juanita Brooks. San Marino, CA: Huntington Library, 1955.

Lee, John Doyle. *Mormonism Unveiled; Including the Life and Confessions of the Mormon Bishop, John D. Lee (written by himself); and complete life of Brigham Young.* St. Louis, MO: M. E. Mason, 1891.

Little, James A. *Jacob Hamblin, A Narrative of His Personal Experience, as a Frontiersman, Missionary to the Indians and Explorer, Disclosing Interpositions of Providence, Severe Privations, Perilous Situations and Remarkable Escapes.* Salt Lake City: Juvenile Instructor, 1881.

Lunt, Henry. "The Life of Henry Lunt and Family Together with a portion of His Diary." BYU typescript. MSS M270.1 L974, LTPSC. Tom Perry Special Collections, Harold B. Lee Library, Brigham Young University.

Lyman, Amasa Mason. *Thirteenth Apostle: The Diaries of Amasa M. Lyman, 1832–1877.* Edited by Scott H. Partridge. Salt Lake City: Signature Books, 2016.

Lyman, Edward Leo. *Amasa Mason Lyman, Mormon Apostle and Apostate: A Study in Dedication.* Salt Lake City: University of Utah Press, 2009.

Lyman, Edward Leo. "Caught in Between: Jacob Hamblin and the Southern Paiutes During the Black Hawk–Navajo Wars of the Late 1860's." *Utah Historical Quarterly* 75, no. 1 (Winter 2007): 22–43.

Lyman, Edward Leo. *Finally Statehood! Utah's Struggles, 1849–1896.* Salt Lake City: Signature Books, 2019.

Lyman, Edward Leo. *Political Deliverance: The Mormon Quest for Utah Statehood.* Urbana: University of Illinois Press, 1986.

Macfarlane, Lloyd Wayland. *Dr. Mac: The Man, His Land, and His People.* Cedar City, UT: Southern Utah State College Press, 1985.

Madsen, Brigham D. *Gold Rush Sojourners in Great Salt Lake City 1849 and 1850.* Salt Lake City: University of Utah Press, 1983.

Madsen, Brigham D. *The Shoshoni Frontier and the Bear River Massacre.* Salt Lake City: University of Utah Press, 1985.

Madsen, Carol Cornwall. *An Advocate for Women: The Public Life of Emmeline B. Wells, 1870–1920.* Provo, UT: Brigham Young University Press, 2006.

Maguire, W. A. "Arthur McMahon, United Irishman and French Soldier." *Irish Sword* 9, no. 36 (Summer 1970): 207–15.

Mangum, Garth L., and Bruce Blumell. *Mormons' War on Poverty.* Salt Lake City: University of Utah Press, 1993.

Mariger, Marietta M. *Saga of Three Towns: Harrisburg, Leeds, Silver Reef.* St. George, UT: Washington County News, n.d.

Marquardt, H. Michael, comp. *Early Patriarchal Blessings of the Church of Jesus Christ of Latter-day Saints.* Salt Lake City: Smith-Pettit Foundation, 2007.

Marquardt, H. Michael, comp. *Later Patriarchal Blessings of the Church of Jesus Christ of Latter-day Saints.* Salt Lake City: Smith-Pettit Foundation, 2012.

Martineau, James Henry. "Parowan Stake History Book." William H. Dame Papers. MIC A 13. Utah Historical Society, Salt Lake City.

Martineau, James Henry. *An Uncommon Common Pioneer: The Journals of James Henry Martineau, 1828–1918.* Edited by Donald G. Godfrey and Rebecca S. Martineau-McCarty. Provo, UT: Religious Studies Center, Brigham Young University, 2008.

Martineau, James Henry. *Useful to the Church and Kingdom: The Journals of James H. Martineau, Pioneer and Patriarch, 1850–1918, 2 vols.* Edited by Noel A. Carmack and Charles M. Hatch. Salt Lake City: Signature Books, 2023.

Martin's Belfast Directory for 1839. Belfast: M. Martin, 1839.

Martin's Belfast Directory for 1840–41. Belfast: M. Martin, 1840.

Martin's Belfast Directory, for 1842–3. Belfast: Matthew Martin, 1842.

Mason, Patrick Q. *The Mormon Menace: Violence and Anti-Mormonism in the Post-bellum South.* Oxford: Oxford University Press, 2011.

Mason, William Shaw. *Statistical Account, or, Parochial Survey of Ireland.* 1819. Reprint, Dublin: Arkos, 2015.

Maxwell, John Gary. *The Civil War Years in Utah: The Kingdom of God and the Territory that Did Not Fight.* Norman: University of Oklahoma Press, 2016.

Maxwell, John Gary. *Robert Newton Baskin and the Making of Modern Utah.* Norman, OK: Arthur H. Clark, 2013.

Maxwell-Stuart, Peter. "Magic in the Ancient World." In *The Oxford Illustrated History of Witchcraft and Magic.* Edited by Owen Davies. Oxford: Oxford University Press, 2017.

May, Dean L., Lee L. Bean, and Mark H. Skolnick. "The Stability Ratio: An Index of Community Cohesiveness in Nineteenth-Century Mormon Towns." In *Generations and Change: Genealogical Perspectives in Social History*, edited by Robert M. Taylor Jr. and Ralph J. Crandall, 141–58. Macon, GA: Mercer University Press, 1986.

Meeks, Priddy. "Journal of Priddy Meeks." Edited by J. Cecil Alter. *Utah Historical Quarterly* 10 (1942): 143–223.

Murbarger, Nell. *Sovereigns of the Sage.* Palm Desert, CA: Desert Magazine Press, 1958.

Nevins, Allen. *Fremont in the Civil War.* Vol. 2 of *Fremont: Pathmaker of the West.* New York: Frederick Ungar, 1961.

Newell, Linda King, and Vivian Linford Talbot. *A History of Garfield County.* Salt Lake City: Utah State Historical Society, 1998.

Norberg, Peter. Introduction and notes. *Essays and Poems by Ralph Waldo Emerson.* New York: Barnes & Noble Classics, 2004.

Oakley, C. A. *The Second City.* London: Blackie & Sons, 1946.

Official Register and Directory of Physicians and Surgeons in the State of California, 1903. San Francisco: Medical Society of the State of California, 1903.

O'Hanlon, Rev. W. M. *Walks Among the Poor of Belfast.* 1853. Reprint, East Ardsley, England: S. R. Publishers, 1971.

Pakenham, Thomas. *The Year of Liberty: The Great Irish Rebellion of 1798.* London: Abacus, 1969).

Palmer, William R. *Forgotten Chapters of History: A Series of Talks Given over Radio Station KSUB, Cedar City, Utah, 1951*, vol. 1, no. 52 (December 30, 1951). Logan, UT: Merrill Library and Learning Resources Program, October 1978.

Palmer, William R. "George Wood." 1943. William R. Palmer Collection. Southern Utah University.

Palmer, William R. "Indian Names in Utah Geography." *Utah Historical Quarterly* 1, no. 1 (January 1928): 5–26.

Palmer, William R. "Utah Indians Past and Present." *Utah Historical Quarterly* 1, no. 2 (April 1928): 35–52.

Parkin, Louise, and Beulah Gibson, comps. *A Voice from the Mountains: Life and Works of Joel Hills Johnson.* Mesa, AZ: Joel Hills Johnson Arizona Committee, 1982.

Parkman, Francis. *The Oregon Trail.* New York: Library of America, 1991.

Parshall, Ardis E. "'Pursue, Retake, and Punish': The 1857 Santa Clara Ambush." *Utah Historical Quarterly* 73, no. 1 (Winter 2005): 64–86.

[Pearce, Alfred John]. *Zadkiel's Almanac for 1881, containing Predictions of the Weather, Vice of the Stars, Numerous Useful Tables; with a Hieroglyphic: The Great Year.* London: Couswas & Co., 1880.

Peterson, Charles S. "The Hopis and the Mormons, 1858–1873." *Utah Historical Quarterly* 39, no. 2 (Spring 1971): 179–93.

Peterson, Charles S. *Take Up Your Mission: Mormon Colonizing Along the Little Colorado River, 1870–1900*. Tucson: University of Arizona Press, 1973.

Peterson, John Alton. *Utah's Black Hawk War.* Salt Lake City: University of Utah Press, 1998.

Pettit, Edward, editor and translator. Anglo-Saxon Remedies, Charms, and Prayers from British Library MS Harley 585 The Lacnunga, 2 vols. Lewiston, New York: Edward Mellen Press, 2001.

Polk, William R. *Polk's Folly: An American Family History*. New York: Doubleday, 2000.

[Post Office]. *Directory for 1842–43*. Glasgow: John Graham, 1842.

Post Office, Annual Glasgow Directory for 1844–45. Glasgow: Edward H. Khull, 1844.

Post-Office, Belfast Annual Directory for 1843–44. Belfast: J. S. Wilson, 1843.

Post-Office Glasgow Annual Directory 1841–42. Glasgow: John Graham for the Letter-Carriers of the Post Office, 1841.

Post-Office Glasgow Annual Directory for 1843–44. Glasgow: John Graham, 1843.

Post-Office Glasgow Annual Directory for 1844–45. Glasgow: John Graham, 1844.

Proctor, Paul Dean, and Morris A. Shirts. *Silver, Sinners, and Saints: A History of Old Silver Reef, Utah*. N.p.: Paulmar, 1991.

Program of the Utah Pioneer Jubilee, July 20th to 24th, 1897. Salt Lake City: George Q. Cannon and Sons, 1897.

Quinn, D. Michael. *Early Mormonism and the Magic World View*. Rev. ed. Salt Lake City: Signature Books, 1998.

Raphael's Prophetic Almanac; or, the Prophetic Messenger and Weather Guide for 1894 . . . London: W. Foulsham, 1893.

Records of the Post Office Department. Record group no. 28. Roll 128, 30:470, 30:351.National Archives, Washington, DC.

Reeve, W. Paul. "'A Little Oasis in the Desert': Community Building in Hurricane, Utah, 1860–1920." *Utah Historical Quarterly* 62, no. 3 (Summer 1994): 222–45.

Rice, Claton S. *Ambassador to the Saints*. Boston: Christopher Publishing, 1965.

Richards, Willard. Journals and Papers. MS 1490. LDS Church History Library, Church of Jesus Christ of Latter-day Saints, Salt Lake City.

Ricketts, Norma Baldwin. *The Mormon Battalion: U.S. Army of the West, 1846–1848*. Logan: Utah State University Press, 1996.

Roberts, B. H. *History of the Church of Jesus Christ of Latter-day Saints Period II, From the Manuscript History of Brigham Young and Other Original Documents*. Salt Lake City: Deseret Book, 1978.

Robertson, Michael. *The Last Utopians: Four Late Nineteenth-century Visionaries and Their Legacy*. Princeton: Princeton University Press, 2018.

Robinson, Phil. *Sinners and Saints: A Tour Across the States, and Round Them: with Three Months Among the Mormons*. Boston: Roberts Brothers, 1883.

Rodgers, Daniel T. *As a City on a Hill: The Story of America's Most Famous Lay Sermon*. Princeton: Princeton University Press, 2018.

Rudd, Glen. *Pure Religion: Church Welfare Since 1930.* Salt Lake City: Church of Jesus Christ of Latter-day Saints, 1995.

Rugh, Susan Sessions. "Conflict in the Countryside: The Mormon Settlement at Macedonia, Illinois." *BYU Studies* 32, no. 1 (January 1992): 149–74.

Russell, James Burn. *Public Health Administration in Glasgow: A Memorial Volume of the Writings of James Burn Russell.* Edited by A. K. Chalmers. Glasgow: James Maclehose & Sons, 1905.

Savage, Levi. "Journal." John D. Lee Collection. Utah Tech University, St. George.

Schindler, Harold. *Orrin Porter Rockwell: Man of God: Son of Thunder.* Salt Lake City: University of Utah Press, 1966.

Seegmiller, Janet Burton. *A History of Iron County: Community Above Self.* Salt Lake City: Utah State Historical Society and Iron County Commission, 1998.

Sessions, Gene A. *Mormon Thunder: A Documentary History of Jedediah Morgan Grant.* Urbana: University of Illinois Press, 1982.

Shannon, Richard. *Gladstone 1809–1865.* Chapel Hill: University of North Carolina Press, 1984.

Shirts, Morris A., and Kathryn H. Shirts. *A Trial Furnace.* Provo, UT: Brigham Young University, 2001.

Slack, Louise. "Mary J. Bringhurst." Typescript. 1935. Washington County Library, St. George, UT.

Smart, William B., and Donna T. Smart. *Over the Rim: The Parley P. Pratt Exploring Expedition to Southern Utah, 1849–50.* Logan: Utah State University Press, 1999.

Smith, Augusta B. Papers. MS 1833. L. Tom Perry Special Collections, Harold B. Lee Library, Brigham Young University, Provo, UT.

Smith, George A. Papers. MS 1322. Church History Library, Church of Jesus Christ of Latter-day Saints, Salt Lake City, UT.

Smith, Jesse Nathaniel. *Six Decades in the Early West: The Journal of Jesse Nathaniel Smith.* Edited by Oliver R. Smith. 3rd ed. Provo, UT; Jesse N. Smith Family Association, 1970.

Smith, John. Papers. MS 1326. Church History Library, Church of Jesus Christ of Latter-day Saints, Salt Lake City, UT.

Smith, Joseph, et al. *History of the Church of Jesus Christ of Latter-day Saints.* Edited by B. H. Roberts. 7 vols. 2nd rev. ed. Salt Lake City: Deseret Book, 1964.

Sonne, Conway B. *Ships, Saints, and Mariners: A Maritime Encyclopedia of Mormon Migration, 1830–1890.* Salt Lake City: University of Utah Press, 1987.

Spence, Mary, ed. *The Expeditions of John Charles Frémont: Travels from 1848 to 1854.* Urbana: University of Illinois Press, 1984.

Standage, Henry. *The March of the Mormon Battalion from Council Bluffs to California Taken from the Journal of Henry Standage.* Edited by Frank Alfred Golder, Thomas A. Bailey, and J. Lyman Smith. New York: Century, 1928.

Stanmore, Tabitha. *Cunning Folk: Life in the Era of Practical Magic.* New York: Bloomsbury, 2024.

Steele, John. "Extracts from the Journal of John Steele." Edited by J. Cecil Alter. *Utah Historical Quarterly* 6, no. 1 (January 1933): 3–28.

Steele, John. Papers. John Steele Collection. Vault MSS 528. L. Tom Perry Special Collections, Harold B. Lee Library, Brigham Young University, Provo, UT.

Stout, Hosea. *On the Mormon Frontier: The Diary of Hosea Stout.* Edited by Juanita Brooks. 2 vols. Salt Lake City: University of Utah, 1964, 1982.

Stucki, Alfred Bleak. "A Historical Study of Silver Reef: Southern Utah Mining Town." Master's thesis, BYU, August 1966.

Taysom, Stephen C. *Like a Fiery Meteor: The Life of Joseph F. Smith.* Salt Lake City: University of Utah Press, 2023.

Tom, Gary, and Ronald Holt. "The Paiute Tribe of Utah." In *A History of Utah's American Indians*, edited by Forrest S. Cuch, 123–65. Salt Lake City: Utah State Division of Indian Affairs/Utah Division of History, 2000.

Topping, Gary. "Another Look at Silver Reef." *Utah Historical Quarterly* 79, no. 4 (Fall 2011): 300–16.

Topping, Gary. *Leonard J. Arrington: A Historian's Life.* Norman, OK: Arthur H. Clark, 2008.

Topping, Gary, ed. *Gila Monsters and Red-Eyed Rattlesnakes: Don Maguire's Arizona Trading Expeditions, 1876–1879.* Salt Lake City: University of Utah Press, 1997.

Turley, Richard E., Jr., and Barbara Jones Brown. *Vengeance is Mine: The Mountain Meadows Massacre and Its Aftermath.* New York: Oxford University Press, 2023.

Turley, Richard E., Jr., and Ronald W. Walker. *Mountain Meadows Massacre: The Andrew Jenson and David H. Morris Collections.* Provo, UT: Brigham Young University Press, 2009.

Twain, Mark. *Roughing It.* Edited by Harriet Elinor Smith and Edgar Marquess Branch. Berkeley: University of California Press, 1995.

Tyler, Daniel. *A Concise History of the Mormon Battalion in the Mexican War.* Glorieta, NM: Rio Grande Press, 1969.

Ulrich, Laurel Thatcher. "Juanita Brooks's Footnote: History, Memory, and the Murder of Olivia Coombs." *Utah Historical Quarterly* 90, no. 3 (Summer 2022): 180–95.

United States Pension Bureau, List of Pensioners on the Rolls, January 1, 1883. Washington, DC.: Government Printing Office, 1883.

Unwin, Mrs. Cobden [Emma Jane Cobden]. "Introduction." *The Hungry Forties: Life Under the Bread Tax.* London: T. Fisher Unwin, 1904.

Utah State Gazetteer and Business Directory, 1903–04. Salt Lake City: R. L. Polk, 1903.

Van Orden, Bruce A. *Prisoner for Conscience' Sake: The Life of George Reynolds.* Salt Lake City: Deseret Book, 1992.

Vogel, Dan. *Early Mormon Documents.* 5 vols. Salt Lake City: Signature Books, 1996-2003.

Vogel, Dan. *Joseph Smith: The Making of a Prophet.* Salt Lake City, Signature Books, 2004.

Vogel, Dan, ed. *The Wilford Woodruff Journals—Index.* Salt Lake City: Benchmark Books, 2020.

Wakeling, Rhea Higbee. "History of Rhea Higbee, Wife of Alva T. Wakeling." *Isaac Higbee and Sophia Somers Family Magazine* 3 (1958): 245A–245J.

Walker, Charles Lowell. *Diary of Charles Lowell Walker, 2 vols.* Edited by Andrew Karl Larson and Katharine Miles Larson. Logan: Utah State University Press, 1980.

Walker, Ronald W., Richard E. Turley Jr., and Glen M. Leonard. *Massacre at Mountain Meadows.* Oxford: Oxford University Press, 2008.

Wallace, Andrew. *A Popular Sketch of the History of Glasgow From the Earliest to the Present Time.* Glasgow: Thomas D. Morison, 1882.

Watt, Ronald G. *The Mormon Passage of George D. Watt, First British Convert, Scribe for Zion.* Logan: Utah State University Press, 2009.

Wells, Samuel R. *New Physiognomy, or, Signs of Character as Manifested Through Temperament and External Forms, and especially in "The Human Face Divine." With more than One Thousand illustrations.* New York: Samuel R. Wells, 1868. In box 3, folder 21, John Steele Collection, Vault MSS 528, L. Tom Perry Special Collections, Harold B. Lee Library, Brigham Young University, Provo, UT.

White, Virgil D. *Index to Indian Wars Pension Files, 1892–1926.* Waynesboro, TN: National Historical Publishing Company, 1987.

Whittaker, David J., Paul C. Russell, Chris McClellan, and Bryon D. Dixon, comps. *Register of the John Steele Collection, 1847–1936.* Provo, UT: Brigham Young University, L. Tom Perry Special Collections, 1995.

Wilson, Alexander. *The Chartist Movement in Scotland.* New York: Augustus M. Kelley, 1970.

Wood, Wanda. "John W. Hess, with the Mormon Battalion." *Utah Historical Quarterly* 4, no. 2 (April 1931): 46–54.

Woodbury, Angus M. "A History of Southern Utah and Its National Parks." *Utah Historical Quarterly* 12, nos. 3–4 (July–October 1944): 111–209.

Woodruff, Wilford. *The Wilford Woodruff Journals.* Edited by Dan Vogel. 6 vols. plus index. Salt Lake City: Benchmark Books, 2020; published as eBook in 2023.

Woodruff, Wilford. *Wilford Woodruff's Journal, 1833–1898.* Edited by Scott G. Kenney. 9 vols. plus index. Midvale, UT: Signature Books, 1983–1985.

Woolley, Benjamin. *Heal Thyself: Nicholas Culpeper and the Seventeenth-Century Struggle to Bring Medicine to the People.* New York: HarperCollins, 2004.

Woolley, Caroline Keturah Parry. *"I would to God": A Personal History of Isaac Haight.* Edited by Blanche Cox Clegg and Janet Burton Seegmiller. Cedar City: Southern Utah University Press, 2009.

Young, Otis E. *The West of Philip St. George Cooke.* Glendale, CA: Arthur H. Clark, 1955.

Youngberg, Florence C. *Conquerors of the West: Stalwart Mormon Pioneers,* 4 vols. Salt Lake City: National Society for Sons of the Utah Pioneers, 1999.

Yurtinus, John Frank George. "A Ram in the Thicket: The Mormon Battalion in the Mexican War." PhD dissertation, BYU, 1975.

Zabriskie, George A., and Robinson, Dorothy L. "The U. S. Census of Utah, 1851." *Utah Genealogical Magazine* 29, no. 3 (July 1938): 130–42.

Zadkiel's Almanac for 1881, containing Predictions of the Weather, Vice of the Stars, Numerous Useful Tables; with a Hieroglyphic: The Great Year. London: Couswas, 1880.

Zadkiel's Almanac for 1887. London: Cousins, 1886.

Zadkiel's The Grammar of Astrology, Containing All Things Necessary for Calculating a Nativity, By Zadkiel, Author of Several Works on Astrology. 2nd ed. London: Sherwood, Gilbert, and Piper, Paternoster Row, 1840.

INDEX

Page numbers in italics indicate illustrations.